The poverty rate for children in the United States exceeds that of all other Western, industrialized nations except Australia. Moreover, poverty among children has increased substantially since 1970, affecting more than one-fifth of U.S. children. These persistent high rates require new ideas for both research and public policy.

Escape from Poverty presents such ideas. With an eye on welfare reform, the volume examines changing public policies at federal, state, and local levels. Four arenas of possible change are addressed from both policy and research perspectives: mothers' employment, child care, fathers' involvement, and access to health care. Yet much of the policy debate regarding poverty in the United States is not taking children into account. The unique contribution of *Escape from Poverty* is its assessment of the impact on *children* of changing public policies. Regardless of how welfare reform unfolds in the future, the issues facing children are not being heard.

This volume was designed to fill this void. The editors have developed an interdisciplinary perspective, involving demographers, developmental psychologists, economists, historians, health experts, and sociologists – a framework essential for addressing the complexities inherent in the links between the lives of poor adults and children in our society.

Escape from poverty

Escape from poverty

What makes a difference for children?

Edited by

P. LINDSAY CHASE-LANSDALE
University of Chicago

JEANNE BROOKS-GUNN
Teachers College, Columbia University

CAMBRIDGE
UNIVERSITY PRESS

Cambridge

New York   Port Chester   Melbourne   Sydney

Published by the Press Syndicate of the University of Cambridge
The Pitt Building, Trumpington Street, Cambridge CB2 1RP
40 West 20th Street, New York, NY 10011–4211, USA
10 Stamford Road, Oakleigh, Melbourne 3166, Australia

First published 1995

Printed in the United States of America

Library of Congress Cataloging-in-Publication Data
Escape from poverty : what makes a difference for children? / edited
　by P. Lindsay Chase-Lansdale, Jeanne Brooks-Gunn.
　　　　p.　cm.
　　ISBN 0–521–44521–3
　　　1. Poor children—Government policy—United States.　I. Chase-Lansdale,
　P. Lindsay.　II. Brooks-Gunn, Jeanne.
　HV741.E8　1995
　362.7′08′6942–dc20　　　　　　　　　　　　　　　　　　　　　　95–5701
　　　　　　　　　　　　　　　　　　　　　　　　　　　　　　　　　CIP

A catalog record for this book is available from the British Library

ISBN　　0–521–44521–3 Hardback

We dedicate this volume to
Dr. Julius B. Richmond
*who has made an extraordinary difference
in the lives of our nation's children*

Contents

Foreword

The Foundation for Child Development, in its grant making and related work, maintains a strong interest in two broad strategies for improving the lives of children and families in poverty: (1) interventions to promote children's health and development, and (2) efforts to strengthen the employment prospects of parents through education and training. The foundation believes that these strategies, often pursued in isolation from one another, should intersect.

This belief prompted the foundation's decision in 1989 to focus a portion of its grant-making program on the Family Support Act, the 1988 federal legislation that has been an important step in our nation's progress toward welfare reform. Taking an expansive view of the new law, the foundation sought to maximize the potential to link educational and training services provided under the act to other systems of support that could help children grow up healthy and ready to learn.

In the years of start-up and early implementation of the law, the foundation made a number of grants to organizations that share the interest in influencing the Family Support Act of 1988 to benefit children and families. Projects funded under these grants have included policy and program development initiatives focused on such issues as the improvement of the quality of subsidized child care available to children whose mothers were participating in the new training program (JOBS) implemented under the Family Support Act and the assessment of the needs of the entire family when a parent is entering the JOBS program. The Foundation for Child Development is also supporting several key research studies that use observational techniques from the field of child development to enrich survey data on child and family outcomes of welfare-to-work programs. In addition, the foundation has produced several analyses of welfare-to-work issues, including the 1991 monograph, *Pathways to Self-Sufficiency for Two Generations*.

The essays in this volume, written as part of the foundation's program regarding the Family Support Act of 1988, have provided important conceptual guidelines for the foundation's grant-making work. This volume will be a significant resource for those interested in improving the lives of children in poverty, particularly from the perspective of welfare reform.

Barbara B. Blum
President
Foundation for Child Development
New York, NY

Preface

This volume is the result of the work and inspiration of many people. First, we would like to express our deep appreciation to Dr. Julius B. Richmond, who has devoted himself to enhancing the lives of children and families, especially those in poverty. Barbara Blum's leadership and vision regarding the ways in which policy and research can benefit low-income children were invaluable. The support of the Foundation for Child Development is deeply appreciated. We wish to thank the contributors to this volume, each of whom brings considerable expertise to the complex challenge of how to help children escape poverty. We also acknowledge the generous institutional support of the Chapin Hall Center for Children, University of Chicago, and the Educational Testing Service. Cassandra Britton, Tracey Deutsch, and Melissa Lowe provided invaluable help in manuscript preparation. We are also grateful for the insights and guidance from our editor at Cambridge University Press, Julia Hough.

As national and regional policy making focuses increasingly on the challenges of poverty in this nation, we hope that this volume will target attention on children – important members of our society who can be lost in the midst of policies developed for adults. The volume is intended as well for scholars who wish to gain multi-disciplinary perspectives on past and present research and policy for poor children, in addition to knowledge of the scope of work yet to be done.

P. Lindsay Chase-Lansdale
Jeanne Brooks-Gunn

Editors and Contributors

Editors

Dr. P. Lindsay Chase-Lansdale
Assistant Professor
Irving B. Harris Graduate School of
    Public Policy Studies
1155 East 60th Street
Chicago, IL 60637

Dr. Jeanne Brooks-Gunn
Virginia and Leonard Marx Professor
    of Child Development
Teachers College
Columbia University
New York, NY 10027

Contributors

Dr. Janet B. Blumenthal*
Lecturer
Georgia State University
Atlanta, GA

Dr. Andrew J. Cherlin
Griswold Professor of Public Policy
Department of Sociology
The Johns Hopkins University
Charles and 34th Street
Baltimore, MD 21218

Ms. Mary Jo Coiro
Senior Research Analyst
Child Trends, Inc.

*Janet Blumenthal is deceased.

4301 Connecticut Avenue, NW
Suite 100
Washington, DC 20008

Dr. David T. Ellwood
Professor
John F. Kennedy School of
    Government
Harvard University
79 John F. Kennedy Street
Cambridge, MA 02138

Dr. Frank F. Furstenberg, Jr.
Zellerbach Family Professor of
    Sociology
University of Pennsylvania
277 McNeil Building
3718 Locust Walk
Philadelphia, PA 19104

Dr. Irwin Garfinkel
Professor
School of Social Work
Columbia University
622 West 113th Street
New York, NY 10025

Dr. Ron Haskins
Staff Director
Subcommittee on Human Resources
Committee on Ways and Means
U.S. House of Representatives
B-317 Rayburn HOB
Washington, DC 20515

Dr. Katherine S. Lobach
Director
Child Health Clinics of New York
    City
Health and Hospitals Corporation
125 Worth Street
Room 342, Box 23
New York, NY 10013

Dr. Sara McLanahan
Professor
Woodrow Wilson School of Public
    and International Affairs
Department of Sociology
Princeton University
21 Prospect Avenue
Princeton, NJ 08544-2091

Dr. Kristin A. Moore
Executive Director
Child Trends, Inc.
4301 Connecticut Avenue, NW
Suite 100
Washington, DC 20008

Ms. Elizabeth Richards
President
Brown-Richards & Associates
Corporate Child Care
1801 Peachtree Street
Suite 160
Atlanta, GA 30309

Dr. Timothy M. Smeeding
Professor
Maxwell School of Citizenship
Syracuse University
426 Eggers Hall
Syracuse, NY 13244

Ms. Ellen Wolpow Smith
Child Trends, Inc.
4301 Connecticut Avenue, NW
Suite 100
Washington, DC 20008

Dr. Sheila Smith
Director for Research

Foundation for Child Development
345 East 46th Street
New York, NY 10017–3562

Dr. Margaret Beale Spencer
Board of Overseers Professor
Graduate School of Education
University of Pennsylvania
3700 Walnut Street
Philadelphia, PA 19104–6216

Mr. Thomas Stief
Child Trends, Inc.
4301 Connecticut Avenue, NW
Suite 100
Washington, DC 20008

Dr. Maris A. Vinovskis
Professor
Department of History
3636 Haven Hall
University of Michigan
Ann Arbor, MI 48109

Dr. Julie Boatright Wilson
Director, Malcolm Wiener Center for
    Social Policy
John F. Kennedy School of
    Government
Harvard University
79 J.F.K. Street
Cambridge, MA 02138

Dr. Barbara L. Wolfe
Professor
Department of Economics and
    Preventive Medicine
Director, Institute for Research on
    Poverty
University of Wisconsin
7432 Social Science Building
Madison, WI 53706

Dr. Nicholas Zill
Vice President
Westat, Inc.
1650 Research Boulevard
Rockville, MD 20850–3129

Introduction

P. Lindsay Chase-Lansdale and Jeanne Brooks-Gunn

Although childhood poverty has long been a societal concern, the issue has recently entered the spotlight as a top policy priority (e.g., Carnegie Corporation of New York, 1994; National Commission on Children, 1991). The poverty rate for children in the United States exceeds that of all other Western industrialized nations except Australia (Smeeding, Torrey, & Rein, 1988; Smeeding & Rainwater, 1995). In contrast to the declining rates during the 1950s and 1960s, poverty among children has increased substantially since 1970, and high rates prevail (Bane & Ellwood, 1989). In 1991, 21% of all children under 18 years of age were poor, up from 15% in 1970 (U.S. Bureau of the Census, 1992). Although white children comprise the majority of the poor in absolute numbers, children from Hispanic and African-American families are overrepresented: 46% of African-American children and 40% of Hispanic children live below the poverty line, compared to 16% of white children (U.S. Bureau of the Census, 1992). The percentage of young children (under age 3) living in poverty is higher: 24% (U.S. Bureau of the Census, 1992).

When one takes a life-course perspective, asking what is the probability of children being exposed to poverty during childhood, the statistics are even more alarming. Duncan and Rodgers (1988) report that approximately 50% of all children hover near the federal poverty line at some point during their childhood, and that nearly one-third drop below the poverty line by age 15. Again, racial differences are striking. Among African-American children, 24% are likely to spend over 10 to 14 years in poverty on average, compared to less than 1 year for white children (Duncan & Rodgers, 1988). Chronic poverty for African-American children but not for white children is dramatically evident at the neighborhood level as well (Duncan, Brooks-Gunn, & Klebanov, 1994; Sampson, 1992; Wilson, 1991). Persistent poverty poses even greater risks to child development than do short, intermittent spells (Duncan et al., 1994; McLeod & Shanahan, 1993; Parker, Greer, & Zuckerman, 1988).

A number of factors have contributed to the rise in child poverty. Chief among them has been slow growth in earnings (Gould & Palmer, 1988), leaving families less financially equipped to provide for their children. In addition, federal programs

1

to combat poverty have favored the elderly over children, resulting in significant improvements in economic standing for the aged, while children became more concentrated at the lower end of the income distribution (Palmer, Smeeding, & Torrey, 1988). In certain regions of the United States (the Northeast and North Central regions), the concentration of poor families in inner cities has risen (Mc-Geary & Lynn, 1988; Wilson, 1987, 1991, 1994). Other reasons include a decrease in the cash value per family of certain government programs, such as Aid to Families with Dependent Children (AFDC), and changes in the distribution of income across all families. Specifically, families in the middle and top levels of income have experienced increases in economic standing, whereas those at the lowest levels of family income did not improve at the same rates, resulting in greater income inequality in the United States today (Duncan, 1991).

Single motherhood due to divorce and nonmarital childbearing has increased significantly during the past several decades (Cherlin, 1992). Moreover, children in single-mother families are more likely to be poor than those in two-parent house-holds (Bane, 1986; Cherlin, 1992; Garfinkel & McLanahan, 1986; Gould & Palmer, 1988; McLanahan & Sandefur, 1994). For example, among single-mother families, poverty rates for white, African-American, and Hispanic families in 1991 were 40%, 61%, and 60% respectively. The corresponding proportions for children in two-parent families were 8%, 12%, and 24% (U.S. Bureau of the Census, 1992).

These single mothers and their young children – the families most likely to experience long-term welfare dependency, and those whose children are at greatest risk for a lifetime of impoverishment (Bane & Ellwood, 1986) – are the focus of this volume. The overarching goal of this volume is to consider the potential for change in poor children's lives. This is a challenge of utmost importance to our society and requires renewed efforts in both research and policy domains.

A sizable body of research documents the deleterious consequences of growing up poor: impaired cognitive development, problems in socioemotional adjustment, and poor physical health (Danziger & Danziger, 1995; McLeod & Shanahan, 1993; McLoyd, 1990; Huston, 1991a; Huston, Garcia Coll, & McLoyd, 1994; Parker et al., 1988). Such difficulties early in life heighten the risks of problematic development later. Delays in cognitive development in the preschool years increase the likelihood of lower achievement in school, grade retention, and school dropout (Brooks-Gunn, Guo, & Furstenberg, 1993; Campbell & Ramey, 1994; Patterson, Kupersmidt, & Vaden, 1990). Similarly, early behavior problems are associated with subsequent emotional problems, such as poor peer relations, conduct disorder, depression, and delinquency (e.g., Dodge, Pettit, & Bates, 1994; Sampson & Laub, 1994). Poverty also means that children have little access to adequate health care and education services, leading to higher rates of morbidity and a compounding of developmental problems (Egbuonu & Starfield, 1982; McCormick & Brooks-Gunn, 1989). Thus, this probabilistic life-course pattern, with its origins in childhood poverty, portends higher rates of poor health, low productivity, and dysfunction in early adulthood, all of which increase the likelihood that the next generation will be poor (McLanahan, Astone, & Marks, 1991).

As used here so far, *poverty* is defined as a needs-adjusted income line, that is, $13,924 of income for a family of four in 1991 (U.S. Bureau of the Census, 1992). Poverty can also be used as a broad term covering a range of conditions associated with deleterious child outcomes. These conditions, sometimes called "poverty cofactors" (McCormick & Brooks-Gunn, 1989), include poor living situations, crowdedness, few material resources, depleted and often dangerous neighborhoods, inadequate schools, limited access to health care, child care, and other community services and resources, lack of stimulation at home, parental psychological distress, harsh and restrictive parenting, and low levels of social support (e.g., Entwisle & Alexander, 1992; Garrett, Ng'andu, & Ferron, 1994; Hashima & Amato, 1994; Liaw & Brooks-Gunn, 1994; McLoyd, 1990; McLoyd, Jayaratne, Ceballo, & Borquez, 1994). What we do not know is the relative importance of each poverty cofactor vis-à-vis its effects on children. For example, Chase-Lansdale and Gordon (1995) and Duncan et al. (1994) have demonstrated that both family poverty and neighborhood-level poverty are significantly related to developmental problems in children, although family poverty is a more powerful predictor. Smith, in her chapter in this volume, argues that two-generation approaches are needed, whereby children's daily experiences can be enriched in the short term by early childhood education programs, and education and training programs for parents may improve economic standing over the long term. To date, studies that test the relative efficacy of economic versus child-oriented interventions have not been conducted.

Most of the literature involving child outcomes portrays poverty as if it were static (but see Duncan et al., 1994, and Furstenberg, Brooks-Gunn, & Morgan, 1987). What is needed are dynamic models that can conceptualize changes in poverty status and related changes in children's development. This is particularly important, given that so many families move in and out of poverty over time (Duncan & Rodgers, 1988; Duncan, 1991; Duncan & Brooks-Gunn, in press). Even more compelling, however, is the need to design effective interventions that promote and sustain change. Disentangling the distinct influences of individual poverty cofactors on children can provide essential knowledge for designing and targeting interventions (Chase-Lansdale, Brooks-Gunn, & Paikoff, 1991; Huston, 1991b).

What changes in poor families' lives would offset the deleterious developmental outcomes in children? Four arenas of possible change are addressed in this volume: (1) maternal employment; (2) child care; (3) father involvement; and (4) access to health care. These four types of change have all been brought under the umbrella of the Family Support Act, passed in 1988 after several years of debate over welfare reform. The goal of this landmark legislation is to bring about positive changes in the lives of poor families by promoting economic self-sufficiency through education and employment training for single mothers, and by strengthening economic support given by noncustodial fathers to families. Important support services and benefits, such as child care and health care, are provided to mothers as they undergo training, secure a job, and work.

More extensive and far-reaching reforms are being considered by the 104th Congress. Proposed changes include the diminution of the federal role in supporting poor children, which involves block grants to the states. Other proposals focus on the elimination of benefits to teenage mothers and to mothers who bear additional children as well as the specification of time limits for financial assistance. Under the Family Support Act of 1988, over one-half of the states have received waivers from the federal government, allowing states to experiment with the implementation of welfare programs along these lines.

This volume examines the implications for *children* of these new policy-driven changes in adult lives. An interdisciplinary approach, involving demographers, developmental psychologists, economists, historians, and sociologists is essential for addressing the complexities inherent in the links between the lives of poor adults and poor children in our society. Section I of the volume begins with an historical overview by Chase-Lansdale and Vinovskis on the role of families and society in assuming responsibility for poor children, dating back to colonial America. This chapter elucidates the events leading up to the Family Support Act of 1988 and highlights the competing currents in U.S. society vis-à-vis responsibilities of the state versus responsibilities of families for children, and the rights of the state to require mothers and fathers to meet economic as well as psychological standards in child rearing. In chapter 2, Zill, Moore, Smith, Stief, and Coiro present the dimensions of the problem currently facing the United States. Their chapter provides a demographic overview of children in poverty, in particular those in the welfare system.

Section II considers the first arena of potential for change: maternal employment. In chapter 3, Wilson, Ellwood, and Brooks-Gunn examine the changes experienced by mothers on AFDC as they enter and stay in the labor force, as well as the implications of these changes for children's adjustment. Emphasis is placed on a range of psychological dimensions, including mothers' self-esteem, stress, and parenting. In chapter 4, Brooks-Gunn addresses programmatic opportunities for change, for both mothers and children, reviewing the extensive literatures on early intervention, parent education, and programs for adolescent mothers.

Section III is focused on child care for poor children. Cherlin, in chapter 5, analyzes the availability of child care to poor families. He reviews what is known about the supply of child care, the current choices that poor families are making about types and cost of care, and how the demand for and supply of child care may alter as women leave AFDC for employment. In chapter 6, Spencer, Blumenthal, and Richards examine the quality of child care in poor communities and the potential for enhancing poor children's development. Spencer and her colleagues draw attention to the high proportion of minority children among the poor, and the significance of child care settings that acknowledge cultural diversity and incorporate a multicultural approach in their curricula.

Section IV targets the third potential arena for change: access to health care for poor families. In chapter 7, Lobach analyzes the quality of health care services for impoverished children and elucidates barriers to access as well as opportunities for improvement. Wolfe, in chapter 8, examines the links among health insurance (in particular, Medicaid), utilization of health services, and poor children's health status. She reviews the determinants of utilization of health care by poor families, the extent to which the Family Support Act of 1988 expands health care coverage, and alternative strategies for providing health services to poor children.

Section V focuses on fathers. Furstenberg's chapter documents the declining role of fathers in the lives of children, especially those who are poor, and the high rates of failure to provide child support. He also assesses changes in the rates and meaning of marriage, nonmarital childbearing, divorce, and remarriage. He then offers a series of explanations for these developments and considers how public policies such as the Family Support Act of 1988 may elicit new behavior by fathers. In chapter 10, Garfinkel and McLanahan examine the impact of current child support reform on the economic and psychological well-being of children. They explore whether the child support provisions of the Family Support Act result in gains for children in female-headed households in addition to possible increased contact with fathers.

The final section of this volume is oriented toward future policy developments and research initiatives that hold the promise of changing poor children's lives over the next decade. In chapter 11, Haskins discusses important related federal policy decisions before and after the passage of the Family Support Act in 1988. He then provides a political and research analysis of our nation's potential to succeed in welfare reform. From a research perspective, Zill's chapter is highly relevant to current policy changes, as it describes the existing data resources for evaluating the effects of public policies on children. Smeeding follows with a proposal for new interdisciplinary databases that would improve our understanding of the lives of poor children. In keeping with the goal of this volume, Smeeding's proposals argue strongly for the infusion of measures of child development and family functioning into data sets that follow families' economic progress and vulnerability.

The final chapter in this volume, by Smith, highlights the current movement toward two-generation strategies for intervention programs. Until recently, large-scale welfare-to-work programs for adults (e.g., Gueron & Pauly, 1991) and cognitive and social interventions program for children (e.g., Lazar, Darlington, Murray, Royce, & Snipper, 1982) were targeted separately. Smith provides an overview of four new programs that combine these approaches, followed by a review of ongoing research programs that evaluate the effect of these multifaceted interventions on families' economic status and child development.

We believe that our nation is at a crossroads in coming to terms with the tenacity of child poverty and its devastating consequences. Public policies for the poor too often emphasize adults and lose sight of families. The ideas developed here regarding policy and research initiatives offer promising future avenues, especially keeping a spotlight on children. It is our hope that this volume will contribute to our society's renewed efforts to assist children in escaping poverty.

REFERENCES

Bane, M. J. (1986). Household composition and poverty. In S. H. Danziger & D. H. Weinberg (Eds.), *Fighting poverty: What works and what doesn't* (pp. 209–231). Cambridge, MA: Harvard University Press.

Bane, M. J., & Ellwood, D. T. (1986, Winter). Slipping into and out of poverty: The dynamics of spells. *Journal of Human Resources, 21*, 1–23.

Bane, M. J., & Ellwood, D. T. (1989, September 8). One fifth of the nation's children: Why are they poor? *Science*, 1047–1053.

Brooks-Gunn, J., Duncan, G., Klebanov, P., & Sealand, N. (1993). Do neighborhoods influence child and adolescent behavior? *American Journal of Sociology, 99*(2), 353–395.

Brooks-Gunn, J., Guo, G., & Furstenberg, F. F., Jr. (1993). Who drops out of and who continues beyond high school? A 20-year follow-up of black urban youth. *Journal of Research on Adolescence, 3*(3), 271–294.

Campbell, F. A., & Ramey, C. T. (1994). Effects of early intervention on intellectual and academic achievement: A follow-up study of children from low-income families. *Child Development, 65*, 684–698.

Carnegie Corporation of New York. (1994). *Starting points: Meeting the needs of our youngest children.* New York: Carnegie Corporation of New York.

Chase-Lansdale, P. L., Brooks-Gunn, J., & Paikoff, R. (1991). Research and programs for adolescent mothers: Missing links and future promises. *Family Relations, 40*(4), 396–404.

Chase-Lansdale, P. L., & Gordon, R. A. (1995). *Economic hardship and the development of 5- and 6-year-olds: Neighborhood and regional perspectives.* Paper presented at the biennial meeting of the Society for Research in Child Development, March, Indianapolis.

Cherlin, A. J. (1992). *Marriage, divorce, remarriage* (rev. and enlarged ed.). Cambridge, MA: Harvard University Press.

Danziger, S. K., & Danziger, S. (Eds.). (1995). Child poverty and social policies [special issue]. *Children and Youth Services Review.*

Dodge, K. A., Pettit, G. S., & Bates, J. E. (1994). Socialization mediators of the relation between socioeconomic status and child conduct problems. *Child Development, 65*, 649–665.

Duncan, G. J. (1991). The economic environment of childhood. In A. Huston (Ed.), *Children in poverty: Child development and public policy* (pp. 23–50). New York: Cambridge University Press.

Duncan, G. J., & Brooks-Gunn, J. (Eds.). (in press). *Consequences of growing up poor.* New York: Russell Sage Foundation Press.

Duncan, G. J., Brooks-Gunn, J., & Klebanov, P. (1994). Economic deprivation and early-childhood development. *Child Development, 65*, 296–318.

Duncan, G. J., & Rodgers, W. L. (1988). Longitudinal aspects of poverty. *Journal of Marriage and the Family, 50*, 1007–1021.

Egbuonu, B. S., & Starfield, B. (1982). Child health and social status. *Pediatrics, 69*, 550–557.

Entwisle, D. R., & Alexander, J. L. (1992). Summer setback: Race, poverty, school composition, and mathematics achievement in the first two years of school. *American Sociological Review, 57*, 72–84.

Furstenberg, F. F., Jr., Brooks-Gunn, J., & Morgan, P. (1987). *Adolescent mothers in later life.* New York: Cambridge University Press.

Garfinkel, I., & McLanahan, S. S. (1986). *Single mothers and their children: A new American dilemma.* Washington, DC: The Urban Institute Press.

Garrett, P., Ng'andu, N., & Ferron, J. (1994). Poverty experiences of young children and the quality of their home environments. *Child Development, 65*, 331–345.

Gould, S. G., & Palmer, J. I. (1988) Outcomes, interpretations, and policy implications. In J. L. Palmer, T. Smeeding, & B. B. Torrey (Eds.), *The vulnerable* (pp. 413–442). Washington, DC: Urban Institute Press.

Gueron, J. M., & Pauly, E. (1991). *From welfare to work.* New York: Russell Sage Foundation.

Hashima, P. Y., & Amato, P. R. (1994). Poverty, social support, and parental behavior. *Child Development, 65,* 394–403.

Huston, A. (Ed.). (1991a). *Children in poverty: Child development and public policy.* New York: Cambridge University Press.

Huston, A. (1991b). Children in poverty: Developmental and policy issues. In A. Huston (Ed.), *Children in poverty: Child development and public policy* (pp. 1–22). New York: Cambridge University Press.

Huston, A. C., Garcia Coll, C. T., & McLoyd, V. (Eds.). (1994). Special issue on children and poverty. *Child Development, 65,* 275–715.

Lazar, I., Darlington, R. B., Murray, H., Royce, J., & Snipper, A. (1982). Lasting effects of early education: A report from the Consortium for Longitudinal Studies. *Monographs of the Society for Research in Child Development, 47*(2–3, Serial No. 195).

Liaw, F., & Brooks-Gunn, J. (1994). Cumulative familial risks and low-birthweight children's cognitive and behavioral development. *Journal of Clinical Child Psychology, 23*(4), 360–372.

McCormick, M. C., & Brooks-Gunn, J. (1989). The health of children and adolescents. In H. E. Freeman & S. Levine (Eds.), *Handbook of medical sociology* (pp. 347–380). Englewood Cliffs, NJ: Prentice-Hall.

McGeary, M. G. H., & Lynn, L. E., Jr. (Eds.). (1988). *Urban change and poverty.* Washington, DC: National Academy Press.

McLanahan, S. S., Astone, N. M., & Marks, N. F. (1991). The role of mother-only families in reproducing poverty. In A. Huston (Ed.), *Children in poverty: Child development and public policy* (pp. 51–78). New York: Cambridge University Press.

McLanahan, S. S., & Sandefur, G. (1994). *Growing up with a single parent: What hurts, what helps?* Cambridge, MA: Harvard University Press.

McLeod, J. D., & Shanahan, M. J. (1993). Poverty, parenting, and children's mental health. *American Sociological Review, 58,* 351–366.

McLoyd, V. C. (1990). The impact of economic hardships on black families and children: Psychological distress, parenting, and socioemotional development. *Child Development, 61,* 311–346.

McLoyd, V. C., Jayaratne, T. E., Ceballo, R., & Borquez, J. (1994). Unemployment and work interruption among African American single mothers: Effects on parenting and adolescent socioemotional functioning. *Child Development, 65,* 562–589.

National Center for Children in Poverty. (1990). *Five million children: A statistical profile of our poorest young citizens.* New York: Columbia University School of Public Health.

National Commission on Children. (1991). *Beyond rhetoric: A new American agenda for children and families.* Washington, DC: U.S. Government Printing Office.

Palmer, J. L., Smeeding, T., & Torrey, B. B. (Eds.). (1988). *The vulnerable.* Washington, DC: Urban Institute Press.

Parker, S., Greer, S., & Zuckerman, B. (1988). Double jeopardy: The impact of poverty on early child development. *The Pediatric Clinics of North America, 35*(6), 1227–1240.

Patterson, C. J., Kupersmidt, J. B., & Vaden, N. A. (1990). Income level, gender, ethnicity, and household composition as predictors of children's school-based competence. *Child Development, 61,* 485–494.

Sampson, R. J. (1992). Family management and child development: Insights from social disorganization theory. In J. McCord (Ed.), *Advances in criminological theory* (Vol. 3, pp. 63–93). New Brunswick: Transaction Publishers.

Sampson, R. J., & Laub, H. (1994). Urban poverty and the family context of delinquency: A new look at structure and process in a classic study. *Child Development, 65,* 523–540.

Smeeding, T., & Rainwater, L. (1995). Cross-national trends in income poverty and dependence: The evidence for young adults in the eighties. In K. McFate (Ed.), *Poverty, inequality, and the future of social policy.* New York: Russell Sage Foundation.

Smeeding, T., Torrey, B. B., & Rein, M. (1988). Patterns of income and poverty: The economic status of children and the elderly in eight countries. In J. L. Palmer, T. Smeeding, & B. B. Torrey (Eds.), *The vulnerable* (pp. 89–119). Washington, DC: Urban Institute Press.

U.S. Bureau of the Census. (1992). *Poverty in the United States: 1991* (Current Population Reports, Series P 60, No. 181) Washington, DC: U.S. Government Printing Office.

Wilson, W. J. (1987). *The truly disadvantaged: The inner city, the underclass and public policy.* Chicago: University of Chicago Press.

Wilson, W. J. (1991). Studying inner-city social dislocations: The challenge of public agenda research. *American Sociological Review*, *56*, 1–14.

Wilson, W. J. (1994). *Crisis and challenge: Race and the new urban poverty.* The 1994 Ryerson Lecture, University of Chicago.

I. Current and historical overview of children in poverty

1   Whose responsibility? An historical analysis of the changing roles of mothers, fathers, and society

P. Lindsay Chase-Lansdale and Maris A. Vinovskis

Americans have always been concerned about dependent and destitute children, but societal efforts to help these youngsters have varied greatly over time. The purpose of this chapter is to describe the treatment of dependent and poor children in the past, emphasizing the historical analogues to current themes, specifically, the nature and causes of poverty, the responsibility assumed by individuals versus society for its alleviation, the evolving roles of mothers and fathers, and changing perceptions concerning child development. We review how colonial America first dealt with dependent children, consider developments that occurred in the nineteenth century, and then discuss attitudinal and institutional changes in the first half of the twentieth century. Finally, we summarize the recent efforts to reform the Aid to Families with Dependent Children (AFDC) program, discuss events leading to the passage of the Family Support Act of 1988, and outline its implications for the well-being of children. The passage of the Family Support Act in 1988 involved potentially significant changes in the lives of adults in the welfare system. This wave of reform, signaling renewed efforts to move away from a system of income maintenance for poor families, has a long history in the United States. However, historical emphases on income maintenance are being replaced with systems of transitional assistance from economic distress to financial self-sufficiency. Although the system being reformed has the word *children* in its title – Aid to Families with Dependent Children (AFDC) – and indeed represents our society's continued efforts to protect children from the ravages of poverty when their parents cannot, a substantive focus on the lives of children has been lost in the debate over the provisions of the welfare system and its attendant regulations. This is particularly ironic, because the proportion of American children living in poverty was 21% in 1991, reaching a higher level than that of the previous 15 years (Bane & Ellwood, 1989). For minority children, the proportions of poverty are significantly higher: 46% of African-American children and 40% of Hispanic children (U.S. Bureau of the Census, 1992).

Concern over the enormous numbers of poor children in our country (approximately 12.5 million) contributed to the rhetoric of recent welfare reform culminat-

11

ing in the Family Support Act of 1988 (Reischauer, 1989), and the majority of the members of Congress and witnesses participating in congressional hearings over the 2 years of deliberations highlighted without fail the serious plight of our nation's children. Yet parents' lives have been the focus, involving such issues as income eligibility, mandatory employment and education, payment of child support, and transitional health benefits. While these provisions clearly have implications for children, the focus on parental behavior alone has left a conceptual and programmatic void vis-à-vis children's experience and development.

The implementation, evaluation, and reauthorization of Aid to Families with Dependent Children specifically as mandated by the Family Support Act of 1988 provides an opportunity to examine and perhaps reshape future welfare reform involving children's well-being. A useful step in this process is to anchor the current reform in a historical context. Surprisingly, almost no effort has been made to take a historical perspective on the effects of our changing welfare system on children. This limits the ability of decision makers and welfare policy analysts to comprehend the long-term origins of this legislation and to assess the underlying and cultural heritage of the participants in these debates.

Care of dependent children in early America

Role of mothers and fathers. The family in colonial America was the central institution for rearing and educating children and household servants. The father, as the head of the household, was entrusted with overseeing the well-being and obedience of everyone in that home (Coontz, 1988). In the seventeenth-century South, the family occupied a less central place in society as the great imbalance in the gender ratio of the immigrant population and the high death rates made normal family life difficult to attain (Walsh, 1979). In New England, however, more favorable demographic circumstances and the particular emphasis on family life by the Puritans made this institution more important in theory and practice than in either England or the South (Demos, 1970).

While the family was given a central place in early America, families were not left alone if the community felt they had failed to live up to their societal responsibilities. For instance, in New England young children were to be taught to read the Bible in the home and older youths were to be prepared for their adult occupations. If the family failed to educate or train its children properly, the local government authorities often removed the children from their home and placed them in another household (Moran & Vinovskis, 1992). Thus, the popular notion that the colonial American family maintained exclusive control over its children is overstated. The state played an active role in monitoring and regulating family life from the very beginning.

In the mid-seventeenth century, New England men were not only economically responsible for their children, but they were also pressured by the church and local community to legitimate any out-of-wedlock children they had (Vinovskis, 1986).

In the South, on the other hand, while men were held economically responsible for their out-of-wedlock children, they did not face the same moral and social pressures to marry as did their Puritan counterparts in New England (Rutman & Rutman, 1984). Even in New England the intense pressure to marry the pregnant woman diminished somewhat in the late seventeenth and eighteenth centuries, although the obligation to support the unwed mother and child remained (Tracy, 1979). Nevertheless, though the rate of premarital pregnancies in New England by the late eighteenth century reached nearly a third of all first births, few out-of-wedlock children were born (Smith & Hindus, 1974–75).

The Puritan father, rather than the mother, was the primary educator of the children and servants in the household (Demos, 1986). Puritan men were considerably more literate than Puritan women and therefore more capable of teaching children and servants how to read (Lockridge, 1974). When suddenly and unexpectedly New England men stopped joining the church in the mid-seventeenth century, efforts were made to find other means of educating and catechizing children (Axtell, 1974). After several unsuccessful attempts to locate alternative sources for training children, the Puritans reluctantly turned to the mothers, who continued to join the church in large numbers (Moran & Vinovskis, 1992). With the new responsibility of teaching children to read the Bible at home thrust upon women, it became increasingly important that daughters obtain more education than their mothers had received.

Puritans saw and treated children differently than adults, but their view of the child was not the same as contemporary perspectives (Beales, 1975; Moran & Vinovskis, 1992). Puritans perceived children as more precocious intellectually than we do today, and they expected children to learn to read the Bible as soon as they could talk. Though early Americans clearly loved and cared about their children, the society was not as child-centered as it was to become in the nineteenth century (Demos, 1986).

Causes of and remedies for poverty. Children often experienced poverty and hardship in early America – mainly due to the death of one or both of their parents. In seventeenth-century Middlesex County, Virginia, for example, only 46% of 13-year-old children had two living parents, and by age 18, this proportion had decreased to 31% (Rutman & Rutman, 1984). Though most American children never experienced the level and extent of poverty present in England at that time, the sudden death of a parent was a frequent cause of impoverishment and dependency (Vinovskis, 1990). Very few colonial Americans ever divorced, but significant numbers of children found themselves abandoned temporarily or permanently by a father who deserted his family (Cott, 1976).

When parents became too poor to support their families, close relatives were expected to provide assistance. To some degree this occurred, but frequently the impoverished parents or orphaned children found themselves dependent upon community welfare. Though some private charity was available, especially after 1700, most assistance came from the local community, which was viewed as responsible for the children's welfare (Trattner, 1984).

In colonial America, poverty was an expected and accepted part of the social structure though poverty due to an unwillingness to work or an out-of-wedlock birth was strongly condemned (Wisner, 1945). Nevertheless, most of the poor usually did not face the same moral condemnation and personal blame for their situation that became much more characteristic of the nineteenth century. Given the limited resources of local communities, distinctions were made between destitute neighbors and impoverished transients, with the latter receiving little help or sympathy. Even the so-called deserving poor, like widows and their children, received only minimal financial assistance and often in a manner that degraded them (Lee, 1981). Communities often tried to help local poor families stay together in their homes by providing money or goods, but sometimes in the late eighteenth and early nineteenth centuries they broke up the family and auctioned off the members to anyone in the community who promised to care for them at the lowest cost to the taxpayers (Klebaner, 1955).

Because most of the food and articles used in colonial households were either manufactured at home or raised on the farm, married women played an important part in the colonial economy (Cott, 1977). Not surprisingly, although destitute widows with children received some assistance from their relatives, neighbors, or local authorities, they were also expected to work at home as much as possible to provide for their own family (Keyssar, 1974).

The separation of poor children from their destitute families was not uncommon nor viewed as a particularly harsh treatment. Children in colonial America were routinely placed in other homes as apprentices so that the placement of a poor child in another household did not seem too unusual (Demos, 1970). Furthermore, the prevailing belief that children developed rather quickly and were capable of taking care of themselves even as young adolescents made their early separation from their destitute parents seem less problematic than we would view it today.

Dependent children in nineteenth-century America

The family became an even more important and self-contained institution in the nineteenth century than it had been in the colonial period. Nineteenth-century ideology depicted the family as the fundamental unit of society (Ryan, 1982). Whereas servants had been an integral part of family life earlier, they were now regarded as outsiders, and the immediate members of the nuclear family drew closer together (Dudden, 1983). Immediate family members had an increased sense of privacy and a stronger emotional bonding. While government monitoring and regulation of family life were accepted parts of the seventeenth and eighteenth centuries, the nineteenth century saw increasing resistance by middle-class parents to any government interference in familial affairs (Degler, 1980). Indeed, our notion of family life in the past is usually based on the idealized nineteenth-century white Protestant middle-class American family.

The role of schooling. Other developments in the nineteenth century transformed some of the functions and responsibilities of the family. One of the most important was the emergence of private and public schooling and the shift in the responsibility for the education of children from the parents to the state. Sending young children outside the home for their education became commonly accepted and then compulsory after the Civil War, as states began to require school attendance (Vinovskis, 1987). Although education had initially been fostered for religious reasons, the rationale after the American Revolution shifted to the desire for an educated male electorate and trained mothers capable of properly rearing the next generation of voters (Kerber, 1980). As the institution of apprenticeship declined in the 1830s and 1840s, schooling was increasingly seen as the major means of preparing individuals for their future occupations (Rorabaugh, 1986).

At the same time that the state and the public proclaimed the sanctity of the family, there was a growing recognition that the individual rights and needs of family members had to be protected. This was particularly the case if families did not live up to the expectations of the dominant white Protestant middle class, such as indigent or foreign-born families, who were seen as deficient and incapable of properly rearing their children. By the mid-nineteenth century the legal and judicial systems developed the notion of "in the best interests of the child" as a rationale for state intervention whenever the dominant society felt it was desirable to remove children from their "inadequate" families (Grossberg, 1985).

Fathers' roles. In theory, the father remained the head of the household and was responsible for the education and well-being of the children. In practice, the father's direct role in family life diminished even further as his place of work became separated from home (Rotunda, 1985). Fathers continued to be economically responsible for their children, and nineteenth-century mores strongly condemned premarital sexual activity and out-of-wedlock births. With the increasing urbanization of American society and the continued high rate of geographic mobility, some fathers ignored their financial and emotional responsibilities to their children by running away. Rather than pursuing delinquent fathers to other communities or states, neighbors and local authorities usually severely punished the unwed mother and her child by ostracizing them and denying them adequate financial assistance. Even the deserted married woman and her children were often denied aid for fear that this would only encourage other fathers to abandon their families (Rothman, 1971).

Mothers' roles. The role of mothers in the care of young children expanded greatly in the nineteenth century (Ryan, 1981). White women, particularly in the Northeast, began to curtail their fertility and to concentrate more attention on each child as an individual (Vinovskis, 1981). The mother's role in early childhood education was celebrated and seen as essential for the healthy development of the child.

Though an increasingly large proportion of single women taught school, worked in factories, or were domestic servants in the nineteenth century, a very strong norm against any white married woman working outside the home existed. Parents removed their children from school and sent them into the labor force before the mother sought paid outside employment (Mason, Vinovskis, & Hareven, 1978). With the movement of families from the farms to the cities and the collapse of domestic household manufacturing in the early nineteenth century, the role of the white middle-class mother centered almost exclusively on rearing her children and maintaining the home (Dudden, 1983).

While under American slavery the African-American family was tolerated if not encouraged by most antebellum plantation owners, mothers were expected to work in the fields alongside their husbands and children. Following the Civil War, the percentage of employed African-American married women decreased, but remained substantially higher than that of the white population, in large part due to economic necessity (Gutman, 1976).

Important changes were taking place in how children were viewed and treated in the nineteenth century. In the early nineteenth century, children were seen as intellectually capable of beginning to learn to read at ages 3 and 4. The infant school movement in the United States in the 1820s encouraged early learning and was initially intended to help disadvantaged children compensate for their inadequate home life; once middle-class parents saw the benefits of early education, they quickly sent their own children to infant schools. Approximately 40% of 3-year-olds in Massachusetts were enrolled either in a special infant school or in a regular public school during the early 1800s (May & Vinovskis, 1977).

In the 1830s Amariah Brigham (1833), a prominent medical specialist, argued that early intellectual activity among young children stunted the development of their brains and led eventually to insanity. Early childhood education in schools was gradually abandoned so that by the eve of the Civil War, no 3- or 4-year-olds attended school in Massachusetts. When kindergartens were introduced in the United States, they focused on older children and deemphasized any rigorous intellectual activity (Kaestle & Vinovskis, 1980). This momentous and rather sudden change in the medical and popular views of early child development reinforced the idea that young children belonged at home with their mother rather than at school. In addition, young children were believed to be malleable, innocent beings that needed intensive care at home. As a result, when efforts were made in the Civil War era to provide day nursery schools for children of poor working mothers, strong professional and public opposition to sending young children away from home emerged.

Society's responsibility for poor children. The death of a mother or father was still the primary reason for children needing outside assistance. Compared to the high seventeenth-century mortality in the South, living conditions in nineteenth-century America had improved considerably. Still, large numbers of children witnessed the death of one or both parents (Vinovskis, 1990). Divorce, which had been rare in colonial America, became somewhat more commonplace after the Civil War and contributed to the impoverishment of children (Griswold, 1982).

The welfare system for poor parents or dependent children grew in complexity and size in the nineteenth century. Close relatives were still expected to help those in need, but increasingly, indigent families and individuals relied upon private or public charity (Klebaner, 1964). The early nineteenth century saw a proliferation of private, voluntary groups, including those dedicated to alleviating the negative consequences of poverty. As public welfare spending became more restrictive and punitive, private benevolence was seen as an essential and often more humane alternative (Heale, 1968). When women began to staff and control many of these voluntary aid organizations, they often displayed more compassion for the poor and dependent children than when their male counterparts were in charge (Curabler, 1980). Immigrants and workers often formed fraternal organizations that provided modest health and death benefits for its members. Simultaneously, the life insurance industry began to issue more policies in the second half of the nineteenth century, but most of these only covered burial costs (Zelizer, 1979).

Most public assistance continued to be controlled and funded by either local communities or counties. Distinctions between the "deserving" and "undeserving" poor were preserved and local authorities ignored the needs of transients and non-residents. With the great influx of impoverished immigrants starting in the 1840s, states increasingly designated them as state paupers and accepted the responsibility for providing assistance either by reimbursing local authorities for the cost of their care or building state institutions for them (Katz, 1986).

In colonial America, most poor families and dependent children either remained in their own homes or were placed in someone else's home. In the nineteenth century providing cash or supplies to the poor was thought to encourage individuals to be lazy and dependent upon public welfare (Kaplan, 1978). In addition, many reformers and public officials believed that the best help for the destitute was to remove them from their debilitating environment and place them in an asylum. Compared to the poor being auctioned off to the highest bidder, confinement in an institution was viewed as a major improvement both for the state and for the impoverished individual. As a result, the state, county, and local almshouses that housed most of the publicly supported poor adults and dependent children rapidly expanded (Rothman, 1971).

The indiscriminate mixture of the poor, insane, and petty criminals of varying ages in the almshouses led reformers to create specialized institutions for different categories of poor. There was a feeling that children should not be placed in adult facilities, and state training schools and orphanages were set up for boys and girls (Holloran, 1989; Schneider, 1992). Ohio was the first state to pass a law (1861) that mandated the removal of all children from county almshouses and placed them in a separate children's institution (Trattner, 1984).

While most policy makers and professionals in nineteenth-century America favored sending dependent or delinquent children to special institutions, a few ques

tioned the wisdom of this approach and advocated placing them in suitable foster homes. The most famous effort was that by Charles Loring Brace and the Children's Aid Society, which removed more than 50,000 children from New York City and placed them in foster homes in the Midwest (Cordasco, 1972; Holt, 1992).

Nineteenth-century reformers placed great value on the role of the family and the mother in the upbringing of children, but only if they believed that the home environment reflected Protestant, middle-class values. Otherwise, they did not hesitate to remove children from what they considered to be an "unsuitable" family or a "dangerous" urban environment and place them in either a special institution for children or a foster home (Clement, 1979; Langsam, 1964).

The federal government did not play much of a direct role in the nineteenth century in the provision of welfare assistance to children. As a result of the Civil War, however, the federal government did become involved in two areas. One was in trying to help ex-slaves in the South during Reconstruction. Congress established in 1865 the Freedman's Bureau to aid African-Americans in the transition from slavery to freedom. Among its activities were the provision of financial assistance to poor African-American families and the establishment and support of black schools (Jones, 1980). Sometimes the record of the agents of the Freedman's Bureau was mixed in terms of their support for the interests of the African-American parents and their children as opposed to the needs of the white landowners, as in the case of African-American children being apprenticed to their former masters (Scott, 1978). Though the Freedman's Bureau was liquidated in 1872, overall it played a role in assisting poor African-American families and their children in the South (Foner, 1988).

The other major federal intervention was the provision of pensions for disabled Union soldiers or their widows and dependent children. In 1890, of white widows aged 45 to 54, nearly one-fifth had been married to a Civil War soldier or sailor and a large proportion of these widows received state and federal assistance (Vinovskis, 1989). While it is still unclear what impact these federal pensions had on the lives of widows, an interesting case study of rural and urban widows in Kent County, Michigan, in 1880 found that widows receiving pensions were more likely to be working than comparable widows who received no federal assistance (Holmes, 1987). The experience of the federal government with the provision of welfare support for Union widows and dependent children paved the way for state interest in the mothers' pension programs in the early twentieth century and led to the creation of the federal Aid to Dependent Children (ADC) program in 1935 (Orloff, 1988).

Changes in the first half of the twentieth century

Reorientation of welfare policy. Fundamental attitudinal and organizational changes in how private and public assistance was delivered in the first half of the twentieth century profoundly altered the way in which dependent children received assistance. One of the most important changes was in the attitudes of welfare and child care specialists toward the role of the poor family in rearing children. In the early nineteenth century, the removal of children from inadequate families and placement in specialized institutions emphasized the well-being of the impoverished child with less attention paid to the rest of the family. In the late nineteenth century, the growing belief, based more on values than empirical evidence, was that poor and dependent children fared best in homes rather than in orphanages or reform schools (Tiffin, 1982). This sharp reversal in opinion was reinforced by the conclusion of the White House Conference on the Care of Dependent Children in 1909:

> Home life is the highest and finest product of civilization. It is the great molding force of mind and of character. Children should not be deprived of it except for urgent and compelling reasons. Children of parents of worthy character, suffering from temporary misfortune and children of reasonably efficient and deserving mothers who are without the support of the normal breadwinner should, as a rule, be kept with their parents, such aid being given as may be necessary to maintain suitable homes for the rearing of the children. This aid should be given by such methods and from such sources as may be determined by the general relief policy of each community, preferably in the form of private charity rather than of public relief. Except in unusual circumstances the home should not be broken up for reasons for poverty, but only for consideration of inefficiency or immorality. (Breamer, 1971, p. 365)

A major reorientation of welfare policy toward children had occurred in a relatively short period of time. The shift was premised on the belief that the mother–child relationship was fundamental and sacred and that home life should be encouraged and strengthened.

Child assistance in the early twentieth century also became part of the scientific philanthropy. Private foundations like the Commonwealth Fund supported research and demonstration programs to identify and assist "problem children." The child guidance movement began with the idealistic hope of preventing first juvenile delinquency and then mental illness. Over time, the goal of prevention receded but the idea of helping treat emotional problems in children remained. In the early years, the clinics targeted children from immigrant and poor families, but by the 1930s the focus shifted increasingly to helping middle-class children (Horn, 1989).

Origins of child support enforcement. One area that the child savers of the early twentieth century explored in some depth was the problem of fathers who deserted their families and children. The father had always been economically responsible for his children, but in practice most local or state authorities were unwilling or unable to force him to support his family if the delinquent father left the immediate area. Some studies in the early twentieth century claimed that up to one-fifth of women with children seeking relief assistance had been deserted by their husbands (Brandt, 1905; Eubank, 1916).

Many relief agencies, such as the Minneapolis Associated Charities, were reluctant to help deserted wives because they feared that would only encourage more husbands to abandon their families (Mudgett, 1924). The existing laws often made the refusal to maintain minor children only a misdemeanor punishable by a small fine or a short jail sentence. Child welfare reformers wanted to make both nonsupport and desertion criminal offenses. A few even went so far as to call for rendering the delinquent father biologically incapable of having any more children. Because abandoned wives were often afraid or reluctant to undertake legal action, the reformers wanted the legal proceedings to be initiated by a welfare agency (Tiffin, 1982).

In the early twentieth century, statutes were enacted in most states that made the nonsupport or desertion of families with children a criminal offense. Yet confusion persisted as the old statutes with lesser penalties sometimes remained on the books; many states allowed for suspension of the sentence or placing the father on probation. Most states also provided that action against the father could only be taken if the child was destitute and in dire need because the concern of these reformers usually was with the increase in public welfare expenses due to nonsupport or desertion. While there was some increase in the efforts to make delinquent fathers shoulder their responsibilities, the overall rate of compliance was not very high.

Focus on "out-of-wedlock" children. Efforts were also made to improve the situation of "illegitimate" children. English common law had recognized no legal relationship between an out-of-wedlock child and either parent, though both parents were liable for support under the poor laws. Early American laws followed the same basic procedures though some states improved the status of the "illegitimate" child by allowing children to inherit from the mother (Grossberg, 1985). In the second decade of the twentieth century, child welfare reformers tried to expand the rights of "illegitimate" children; a few even advocated encouraging the single mother to keep and rear her child. Though a few states did enact changes in the law, public fear that liberalization of the laws would increase the number of out-of-wedlock births limited achievements in this area. Nevertheless, at least a reconsideration of the rights and needs of children born outside of marriage had been initiated.

Sanctity of the home and the importance of the mother–child relationship. Probably the most far-reaching and important change in the early twentieth century was the effort to provide public assistance for poor mothers or widows so that they could remain at home and care for their children. Poor mothers or widows with young children had often received some private or public relief in the past, but they were also expected to work to support their families. Under these circumstances, many poor mothers or widows found it necessary to send their children temporarily or permanently to relatives or place them in an institution. Now child welfare reformers wanted to help these deserving women rear their children without having to enter the labor force.

Two efforts were aimed at helping poor mothers or widows stay at home and rear their children. One was a program of workman's compensation to provide assistance if the father became injured or disabled at work. A study of institutionalized children in Pittsburgh in 1908 found that 14% of them were there because of an occupational accident or disease of the father (Tiffin, 1982). Though the state workman's compensation legislation was modest, it began to regularize and standardize the obligations of employers and the state for the welfare of injured or disabled workers (Reagan, 1981).

The other major program was to provide pensions for mothers. It was modeled after the Civil War pensions for Union widows and seen as a payment for rearing their children. The pensions were to be state programs funded by both state and local taxpayers and generous enough to allow the impoverished mothers to stay home with their children (Davis, 1930; Pumphrey & Pumphrey, 1983). Illinois passed the first statewide mothers' pension program in 1911 and within a decade, most other states enacted similar legislation (Lubove, 1968). However, before the passage of the Social Security Act in 1935, at least half of the counties in the United States did not provide mothers' pensions (Tiffin, 1982).

Most of the programs were specifically designed for widows. Although some efforts were made initially to provide assistance to deserted or never-married mothers, the subsequent storm of public controversy led to legislative and administrative restrictions so that financial assistance was paid only to widows or wives whose husbands were disabled. While many states had expanded their eligibility criteria somewhat in 1931, 82% of the recipients were widows. Because mothers' pensions were restricted to those living in "suitable homes," (the definition of which was left up to local authorities), poor African-American mothers and out-of-wedlock children were systematically discriminated against (Lopata & Brehm, 1986).

The Great Depression of the 1930s caused major changes in the welfare system. Private charities and state and local welfare providers could not cope with the magnitude and duration of unemployment in the United States. Though Herbert Hoover was unwilling to provide federal assistance for the unemployed or those on welfare, his successor, Franklin Roosevelt, experimented with several large-scale federal programs to assist the unemployed workers and help state and local welfare efforts. The most important program, from the perspective of aiding poor children, was the passage of the Social Security Act of 1935, which initiated on a permanent basis federal aid for old age and welfare assistance. After three centuries of local and state responsibility for welfare, the federal government assumed a new and growing responsibility for the social needs of the aging and dependent populations (Achenbaum, 1986).

The Social Security legislation had as its two major goals the establishment of a contributory social insurance program for old age and the provision of public assistance to help those in need of immediate assistance. Widows of husbands covered under the insurance provisions of the Social Security Act of 1935 were to receive a lump sum based on a percentage of the deceased spouse's benefits. Amendments to the Social Security legislation in 1939 significantly revised and improved the provisions for widows from a modest lump-sum award to annual payments that were seen as substantially more generous than federal support for never-married, separated, or divorced women with children (Lopata & Brehm, 1986).

The Social Security Act of 1935 also provided assistance to indigent children of separated, divorced, and never-married mothers through Aid to Dependent Children (ADC). While considerable attention was paid to unemployment and old age pensions, the ADC provisions were not closely scrutinized. Indeed, Edwin Witte (1962), one of the main drafters of the legislation, observed that "Congress had little interest in children." Though modest levels of support were provided for dependent children, no separate provisions were made for the mothers who took care of them. It was not until 1950 that ADC provided coverage for the caretaker. Given the small amount of assistance provided in most states, many recipients needed to work to provide for their families (Kamerman & Kahn, 1988).

By requiring a state agency to administer the program, mandating statewide assistance, and covering all dependent children rather than just those of widows, Aid to Dependent Children considerably broadened the scope and coverage of assistance for poor single mothers and their children. Before the ADC program was started in 1935, only 285,717 dependent children were receiving assistance under the state mothers' pension programs. In 1938 the number of dependent children receiving assistance rose to 684,282. Furthermore, federal assistance in 1938 for ADC not only totaled $26 million, but it stimulated state and local spending to increase from $42 million in 1935 to $71 million in 1938 (Bucklin, 1939).

Under Aid to Dependent Children, the absent father was financially responsible for supporting his own child, and state agencies were empowered to force him to contribute to the ADC program to offset the benefits paid to the dependent child. In practice, however, most states did not devote much energy or resources to pursuing absent fathers, and only a small proportion of these fathers contributed assistance – a characteristic that would remain part of the welfare system until the 1970s and 1980s (Kamerman & Kahn, 1988).

Although the Aid to Dependent Children program was intended to cover all needy children in single-mother households, states restricted assistance by insisting that children had to live in a "suitable" home. Children of African-American or never-married mothers were particularly singled out unfairly for exclusion from the program. The problem drew national attention when Louisiana implemented a new "suitable home" policy and excluded 6,000 families from its ADC rolls in 1960 (about 25% of its ADC cases). The Kennedy administration moved against this type of discrimination by ruling that states could not deny ADC assistance due to an "unsuitable" home and then leave the child in that home. As long as a needy child remained at home, he or she was entitled to ADC assistance (Bell, 1965). Amendments to the Social Security Act of 1962 raised the federal share of reimbursements to 75%, encouraged the provision of welfare services rather than just cash assistance, and allowed states to provide assistance to families with unemployed fathers. The new direction of the program was symbolized by its being retitled Aid to Families with Dependent Children (AFDC) (Gilbert, 1966).

Thus, by the 1960s the federal government played a large role in providing assistance to single mothers and their children. Because the responsibility for children's welfare was shared among the federal, state, and local authorities as well as among different programs and agencies, the assistance was fragmentary and uncoordinated. No national minimum standards of eligibility or levels of assistance existed. Though in theory absent fathers were financially responsible for the support of their offspring and poor mothers were expected to stay at home with their young children, in practice single mothers other than widows were often forced into the labor force out of economic necessity and were left to rear their children by themselves under difficult circumstances.

Recent efforts to reform the AFDC program

Major changes in the type and amount of federal assistance for the poor in this country have occurred during the past 25 years. Starting with the efforts of the Kennedy and Johnson administrations to help disadvantaged Americans, the federal government has greatly expanded its welfare programs, but most of that assistance has been directed to the elderly rather than to children living in poverty (Burtless, 1986; Cottingham & Ellwood, 1989; Danziger, Haveman, & Plotnick, 1986; Ellwood, 1988).

In the 1950s the public and most policy makers ignored the general issue of poverty and the more specific needs of poor children (Berkowitz & McQuaid, 1980). In the 1960s, however, poverty in America was again "rediscovered" (Berkowitz, 1991; Patterson, 1981). Harrington (1962) and others successfully challenged the notion that America no longer had a serious problem of poverty and called for massive federal intervention.

Coming off his landslide victory in 1964, President Johnson called for a "War on Poverty" and not only expanded the AFDC program, but established the Office of Economic Opportunity (OEO) and enacted a series of education and training programs to assist the poor such as Job Corps, Neighborhood Youth Corps, Head Start, Upward Bound, and the Work Experience Program for AFDC mothers. Important new legislation such as the Food Stamp Act in 1964 and Medicare and Medicaid in 1965 was enacted, and states raised AFDC benefits by 36% between 1965 and 1970 (Garfinkel & McLanahan, 1986).

Though these "Great Society" programs aroused some taxpayer and conservative reactions, most Americans accepted the idea that the federal government should play a large role in helping the "deserving" poor (Brauer, 1982). Federal expenditures for domestic programs increased substantially, but much of the money was directed to improving the coverage and level of benefits for the disabled and the elderly through the Social Security program. For the nonelderly poor, the emphasis was on education and job training or the provision of housing, food, or medical assistance rather than cash assistance (Burtless, 1986).

One of the assumptions of the Great Society programs was that the number of people on welfare rolls would diminish, as programs such as Social Security supported those unable to work and as early education and youth or adult training programs helped others escape from the so-called "cycle of poverty." But the expansion of federal eligibility, the growing client awareness of federal programs, and the reduction in the stigma attached to receiving welfare all contributed to a great increase in the number of people on welfare. The number of families receiving AFDC assistance more than doubled between 1965 and 1970 (Levitan & Taggart, 1976).

Many legislators were upset by the surge in AFDC recipients at a time when the overall unemployment rate was decreasing. They demanded that the Johnson administration reduce or at least curtail the growing number of unmarried or deserted mothers on welfare. Therefore, in 1967 Congress enacted a welfare freeze – no increase in the proportion of children under age 21 could receive AFDC due to desertion or illegitimacy. While this provision was opposed by both Johnson and Nixon and was repealed in 1969, it revealed the extent of frustration and anger in Congress about the seemingly uncontrollable growth of welfare (Wickenden, 1969).

Although single mothers with older children and able-bodied males on welfare were expected to work, destitute mothers with young children were not. But the unanticipated rise in AFDC clients as well as the growth in labor force participation among nonpoor married women led to a fundamental change in the principle that AFDC mothers should not be encouraged or required to work. The Ways and Means Committee of the U.S. House in 1967 signaled this important shift in their report language on the AFDC legislation:

> Your committee intends that a proper evaluation be made of the situation of all mothers to ascertain the extent to which appropriate child care arrangements should be made available so that the mothers can go to work. . . . The committee recognizes that in some instance – where there are several small children, for example – the best plan for a family may be for the mother to stay at home. But even these cases would be reviewed regularly to see if the situation had changed to the point where training or work is appropriate for the mother. (Quoted in Steiner, 1971, p. 43)

The Work Incentive (WIN) program, initiated in 1967, encouraged welfare mothers to work by allowing them to keep a large percentage of their earned income while receiving AFDC payments and by getting states to drop from their AFDC rolls parents or children over 16 not in school who declined "without good cause" to participate in work or training programs (Patterson, 1981). In the 1970s the WIN program was revised and AFDC mothers without children under 6 years of age were now required to participate, but again few actually did (Patterson, 1981). Nevertheless, the idea that AFDC mothers with children either should receive training or enter the labor force had been established, reversing the early-twentieth-century principle that mothers with young children should stay at home.

The growing hostility toward the AFDC program in the late 1960s and 1970s led to a curtailment of any increased benefits, and the average AFDC payment decreased. Benefits like food stamps, energy assistance, Medicaid, and housing assistance, however, meant that federal expenditures (in billions of 1983 dollars) per mother-only families with children rose from $4,113 in 1965 to $6,630 in 1970, $7,402 in 1975, and then fell to $6,404 in 1980 (Garfinkel & McLanahan, 1986).

As criticisms of the AFDC program mounted and the number of different categorical programs for welfare assistance proliferated, many policy makers and academic analysts called for a massive restructuring of the existing system. Surprisingly, President Nixon, often regarded as a traditional conservative, championed the Family Assistance Plan, which would have guaranteed a minimal annual income for all poor families with children and done away with many of the categorical welfare programs. To remain eligible for federal assistance, all able-bodied individuals, including mothers with children over 3 years old, would have been required to enroll in a job-training program or to work (Steiner, 1971).

While many hailed Nixon's Family Assistance Plan as a major innovative attempt to overhaul the existing federal welfare system, others condemned it for failing to provide adequate assistance. After a lengthy and often bitter fight, the Family Assistance Plan was defeated in the Senate by a coalition of conservatives who opposed a guaranteed annual income and of liberals who objected to the inadequate funding levels in the current proposal (Moynihan, 1973). Though Carter tried to resurrect a modified form of the Family Assistance Plan in 1978, his Better Jobs and Income Program failed to attract sufficient public or legislative support to be a viable alternative to the existing set of federal and state welfare programs. Unlike the Family Assistance Plan, Carter's proposal exempted single parents with children under 14 from full-time employment, but expected that mothers would hold a part-time job or receiving training while their children were in school (Lynn & Whitman, 1981).

Events leading to the passage of the family support act of 1988

Given the recent history of repeated failures in reforming the welfare system, one has to ask why momentum developed in the 1980s to try again. Or, as Congressman Levin of Michigan queried during one of the numerous hearings in the reform process, "Why should the 100th Congress expect success where so many have walked unsuccessfully before?" (U.S. Senate, 1987a, p. 141). He and many other federal and state leaders strongly believed that this was an auspicious time for overhauling the welfare system.

A number of factors contributed to this propitious viewpoint. The first was the development of rare common ground between liberals and conservatives regarding the need and rationale for change. Two of the most influential political leaders in this debate – President Reagan and Senator Moynihan – seized the opportunity to push welfare change along similar lines, despite fundamental underlying disagreements. In Reagan's 1986 State of the Union address, he signaled his interest in significant change by announcing that he would request a study of the welfare system. This decision was one in a long line of Reagan's efforts over 20 years to improve the welfare system, both as governor of California and as president. Similarly, 2 decades ago, Moynihan was one of the first to call attention to and prophesy the startling changes in our demographic landscape, specifically the dramatic increase in female-headed families and the implications for poverty and social programs. He then devoted years to bettering AFDC (e.g., as White House aide during the Nixon administration, he worked to forge the Family Assistance Plan). Thus, when Reagan revealed the possibility of an administrative initiative, Congress, too, began to prepare (Haskins, 1991; Szanton, 1991).

Moynihan and other Democrats disagreed with Reagan's conclusion that "in the War on Poverty, poverty has won," and instead countered that the programs launched during the Johnson administration indeed had been successful in reducing poverty in the nation, especially among the elderly. Rather, they added, the problem had become acute regarding children. Yet, despite fundamental disagreements between conservatives and liberals on the importance and effectiveness of social programs, by the mid-1980s most agreed with Moynihan's summary of the flaws in AFDC:

> Over the last 20 years, support for the AFDC program has eroded. . . . Today no one seems to like the program – not those who administer it, not those who contribute their tax dollars to it, and not even those who benefit from it. We are, by now, familiar with the reasons why. The benefit structure is inequitable, payments are too often inadequate, the program discourages work, and it is administratively cumbersome. Worse, the AFDC program does not do a good job of moving mothers off of welfare rolls and onto payrolls. (U.S. Senate, 1987b, p. 7)

It was this latter emphasis on the goal of self-sufficiency that became the second important rallying point for liberals and conservatives interested in reform. As revealed in the previous section, the focus on welfare-to-work was not a new idea in the 1980s. However, two developments contributed to a renewed zeal for creating a program that would successfully help welfare recipients become gainfully employed: (1) a better understanding of the patterns of welfare dependency and (2) innovation at the state level (Haskins, 1991).

New research on welfare spells by Bane and Ellwood (1986) showed that approximately 50% of those on AFDC use the system for short-term assistance in times of crisis, usually brought about by divorce or unemployment. An additional 25% of individuals remain on AFDC for 2 to 7 years. The remaining 25% stay on welfare for over 10 years, and it is this subgroup that accounts for most of the costs of the system. Most important, this subgroup has been identified: Those most likely to have lengthy welfare spells are young unmarried women with children under 3 years of age, exactly the subgroup that has not been targeted for employment training. Thus, this research enabled policy makers to see the AFDC population as diverse, to come to terms with the facts and costs regarding long-term dependency, and to decide to target the latter group (Baum, 1991; Haskins, 1991).

Innovation in welfare reform at the state level occurred in the 1980s due to a series of changes in AFDC legislation during the first year of the Reagan administration. In 1981 Reagan proposed mandatory workfare for all AFDC recipients, called "Community Work Experience" (CWEP). Congress countered by making workfare optional and by initiating the new WIN demonstration programs. Because the original WIN program had been such a failure in its efforts to promote employability (due to severe underfunding and poor administration), the WIN demonstration programs were designed to give states more financial support and equally important, more flexibility in devising methods to help recipients become self-sufficient.

A host of innovative programs developed, including the GAIN (Greater Avenues for Independence) program in California, the E-T (Education and Training) program in Massachusetts, and the Learnfare program in Ohio. By 1985 there were WIN demonstration programs in 38 states (Government Accounting Office, 1987). These programs were comprehensive plans toward independence involving training, education, employment search and experience, child care, transportation, and transitional support services such as health insurance for a period of time after leaving AFDC. Signifying the pioneering efforts of the states, the National Governors' Association made welfare reform its top priority in 1987, and the state innovations served as models for congressional initiatives (U.S. Senate, 1988). Moynihan insisted on referring to the Senate's bill to reform AFDC as the "Governors' bill" (U.S. Senate, 1988). It is noteworthy that then a governor, Clinton was president of the National Governors' Association (NGA), setting the stage for further efforts in welfare reform during his presidential administration (see Haskins, this volume; Lynn, 1993).

Because of the state innovations beginning in the early 1980s, it became possible to evaluate the impact of these employment services on welfare recipients. The Manpower Demonstration Research Corporation (MDRC) was commissioned by eight states to study these programs, using random assignment (Baum, 1991). MDRC did not evaluate the impact of the comprehensive services, but focused strictly on the major employment service, which was job search and work experience. The results indicated modest positive findings: States were successful in requiring AFDC recipients with no children under 6 years to participate. Compared with controls, the experimental group did manage to increase their employment and earnings levels and to reduce their use of welfare. As Gueron, president of MDRC, summarized for the Senate Subcommittee on Social Security and Family Policy, "these results suggest that work/welfare initiatives can make consistent and measurable improvements in people's lives. Multiplied by large numbers of people over a long period of time, these relatively modest improvements take on considerable policy significance" (U.S. Senate, 1987a, p. 165). This evaluation had a strong impact on policy makers' push to forge a welfare system of assistance to self-sufficiency (Wiseman, 1991).

The third factor in promoting reform was the dramatic change in the demographic makeup of U.S. society. As we have discussed, when AFDC was established in 1935, it was designed for widows, who at that time comprised 88% of the caseload.

By 1967 widows were only 6% of the caseload, and by 1982 the proportion was down to 1% (Lima & Harris, 1988). A dramatic transformation has occurred during the past 4 decades such that the majority of AFDC recipients are single mothers due to divorce and nonmarital births.

Additionally, maternal employment had become a majority phenomenon by the mid-1980s; over 72% of women with children aged 6 to 18 years were in the workforce. For mothers of preschoolers, 61% were in the labor force, up from 30% in 1970 and 18% in 1960. Furthermore, 51% of mothers of infants were employed (U.S. Bureau of the Census, 1988). In the words of Senator Moynihan, "It is now the normal experience for women to work, at least part-time. This accounts for the expectation and desire that AFDC mothers should do likewise" (U.S. Senate, 1987a, p. 5).

It is interesting that these demographic changes had such impact on the thinking of those reforming AFDC in the 1980s, because the very same arguments were used forcefully in the reform efforts in the late 1960s and 1970s. It appears that Moynihan's term *normal* is a key change. Although these changes were evident 20 years ago, their impact has been strengthened by the widespread perception that these phenomena now affect the *majority* of children. Yet, ironically throughout our nation's past, poor women have been more likely to seek employment than middle-class women.

The fourth and final element in welfare reform in the 1980s was strong agreement regarding the reiteration and redefinition of parental responsibility to children. The reiteration came in the form of consensus that fathers must be financially responsible for their children from birth to age 18. By the time of the deliberations on the Family Support Act of 1988, federal and state efforts to enforce child support from fathers had improved, but the situation remained appalling (see Garfinkel & McLanahan, this volume). The highlighting of long-term dependency on the part of young unmarried mothers and the fact that such a high proportion of women used AFDC for short periods due to divorce contributed to efforts to improve fathers' participation in their children's economic standing.

The redefinition of parental responsibility refers specifically to mothers. Here, reformers became explicit in stating that the responsibility of mothers to their children is to be employed. This is a dramatic shift from the original intentions of AFDC in 1935, but in reality reflects a changing view of mothers' roles that began in the 1960s.

These events, information, and beliefs led to the passage of the Family Support Act in 1988. Despite the fanfare attendant to the establishment of this new legislation, most policy analysts have concluded that the Family Support Act of 1988 did not represent a radical new program, but rather an incremental change in our welfare system (Reischauer, 1989).

What, then, was new about this act? In brief, the Family Support Act of 1988 has embodied a comprehensive effort to assist AFDC recipients to attainment of self-sufficiency by means of education, training, employment, child support enforcement, and support services, including child care, transportation, and health benefits While all of these pieces have been available in some form to some individuals in previous years, the Family Support Act of 1988 not only has made some provisions more uniformly applicable to all able-bodied recipients, but it also has provided services that are essential to successful employability, and it has highlighted and publicized the importance and necessity of these services.

The major changes include the following:

(1) *JOBS program.* Employment training programs became mandatory for most participants. This was a change from WIN, which although in principle was mandatory, in effect was an optional program. Guidelines as to the content of JOBS are similar to WIN programs, especially to the innovative WIN demonstration programs, where the emphasis is placed on the development of new skills, on-the-job training, job readiness, job search, and job placement. A major new component is the equal emphasis on educational activities to expand participants' qualifications: high school and GED programs, literacy and basic education, and English as a Second Language. Adults under age 20 (without high school degrees) are required to be in school.

The most notable new aspects of the JOBS program are the targeting of specific groups and the focus on mothers with young children. Reflecting new knowledge about the diversity of the AFDC population and the different patterns of dependency, the Family Support Act has targeted long-term participants, those without high school degrees, and those whose children are 16 years of age, thus rendering mothers vulnerable to no assistance within 2 years (when their children turn 18). Unlike the previous legislation, all women with preschool-aged children (3–5 years) have been required to participate half-time in the JOBS program, and states have the option of mandating participation for mothers of children as young as 1 year of age. Those with children age 6 years and over have been required to participate in JOBS full-time. Moreover, the mandatory educational requirement for those under age 20 has applied to mothers with children of any age. Finally, mothers who volunteer receive priority, regardless of the age of their children.

(2) *Child support enforcement.* New provisions have been added to strengthen the existing child support enforcement program. These are: (a) more uniform use within states of guidelines to develop the level of awards; (b) more extensive establishment of paternity among all participant families, especially for children born to single mothers; (c) automatic withdrawal of child support from fathers' wages by employers; and (d) more frequent review of child support awards, for purposes of adjustment with state guidelines. These changes indicate growing consensus that stronger measures are needed to keep fathers from evading their responsibility to their children and to signal that fathers of children born outside of marriage have paternal responsibilities commensurate with those of other fathers.

(3) *Child care and health coverage.* The Family Support Act also recognized the need to assist mothers who leave the welfare system and become employed. Ac-

knowledging the likelihood that first jobs will be low-paying, the Family Support Act has provided child care and health coverage for 12 months after exit from public assistance. States may require fees based on a sliding scale. Although child care and health benefits were available to AFDC participants who became employed in the past, these were offered for much shorter periods, and states often did not promote the use of these services.

These were the only services mandated for children. The child care mandate is oriented simply toward the provision of child care, not its quality. This has been a weak link in the Family Support Act, because the quality of child care available in the United States is variable at best, and most likely to be inadequate for impoverished children (Hayes, Palmer, & Zaslow, 1990). Whether positive effects on children of mothers' successful exit from the welfare system will outweigh negative effects of poor quality child care is a critical question.

Conclusion

This chapter has described the varied patterns in our nation's history of the interplay of responsibility for children among mothers, fathers, and society. The goal of this historical analysis is to inform our understanding of why welfare reform, as exemplified by the Family Support Act of 1988, came about, how it reflects important themes of responsibility from the past, and what its implications may be for the well-being of children. With these goals in mind, the following conclusions can be drawn.

1. Welfare reform must be placed within a larger demographic and economic context in order for expectations about its success to be realistic. In the attempts to improve our nation's welfare system, one should remember that many families remain poor despite the fact that members are gainfully employed. Some have pointed out that the problems of the working poor have been overshadowed by such an intense focus on welfare reform (Ellwood, 1988; Ellwood & Cottingham, 1989; Jencks, 1992; Lynn, 1993; Reischauer, 1989). The Family Support Act should be seen as one part of a larger effort to reduce poverty in the United States, and this point applies particularly to children: Of the 20% of all children who were poor in 1985, only slightly over half were receiving AFDC benefits (Select Committee on Children, Youth, and Families, 1987). An important research question is to compare the development and well-being of children in families on AFDC with children of families whose income is equivalent to those on AFDC. Such an investigation is one way to get at the heart of the debate, which is the belief that welfare *dependency* is more deleterious for children than poverty itself.

2. Our nation's belief that society at large must protect children from poverty dates back to the colonial period. This belief has translated into the practice that minimal daily needs of food and shelter must be provided. This view of protection has remained very stable during our history, but the mechanisms for protecting children from poverty have changed dramatically over time. This change has in-

volved a shift from interventions provided directly to the child to those provided indirectly to the child through his or her family. The direct interventions imply community or state actions that circumvent the family. Many of the early methods of protecting children from poverty involved removal from their homes and severe and permanent separations from family members. During the colonial period, children were removed from their own homes and placed in other homes. Impoverished children were auctioned off to the highest bidder. In the nineteenth century, poor children were put in almshouses with adults and criminals, a situation considered an improvement over auctioning.

The dramatic change in the late nineteenth and early twentieth centuries to assisting poor children in their own homes is the main precursor to our welfare system today. Direct supplementation to children's lives in their own homes came about first with the widow pension program and then with the passage of the Social Security Act of 1935. The specific intent of these programs was to enable impoverished women to rear their children at home. It is noteworthy that the significant shift (i.e., from removing children from their families to making it possible for families to care for their children) is linked to changing views of child development. For example, in the colonial period children were viewed as quite precocious, not requiring the individual attention and emotional responsiveness that were later viewed as essential for healthy development. Despite the widely acknowledged importance of the mother–child relationship and the family setting to children beginning in the nineteenth century, a great deal of discrimination against minorities and out-of-wedlock children persisted within the recent programs, resulting in the removal of children and the denial of assistance.

3. The absence of fathers from children has moved over time from being a private problem to being a public one. The United States has a very strong heritage regarding the importance of fathers to children. In the colonial period, the father was seen as the primary socializer, educator, and caretaker of children. His economic responsibility to his family was unquestioned, and there was strong moral pressure to legitimize children conceived out of marriage. The problem of fathers evading their paternal responsibilities became apparent in the nineteenth century, and increased dramatically in the early twentieth century.

Only in the 1970s and 1980s have there been concerted efforts at the federal level to reinstate societal principles regarding paternal responsibility. Prior to this time, father absence was seen as primarily a family matter. Moreover, the deserted mothers were often ostracized and denied financial assistance by local authorities prior to the mid-1930s.

Not until 1975 did the federal government establish a national child support system as part of the Social Security Act. The system was strengthened and expanded in 1984, but even so, progress was extremely limited. For example, the percent of AFDC payments recovered through child support collections rose from 5.6% in 1979 to 7.3% in 1985 (Lima & Harris, 1988). Only 18.4% of never-married mothers were awarded child support assistance in 1985 (Chase-Lansdale

& Vinovskis, 1988b), and the Family Support Act child support provisions are in part a response to this situation.

The mandates regarding paternal responsibility in general in the Family Support Act of 1988 have come at a period in our history when father absence is a focal point of criticism from many segments of society. Recent research, for example, has revealed that father absence has negative psychological effects on children above and beyond the economic distress that ensues (e.g., Chase-Lansdale & Hetherington, 1990; McLanahan & Sandefur, 1994). The primary motivation behind current welfare reform, however, is the strong belief that fathers must be economically responsible to their children, and that child support payments make a significant difference in a child's economic standing.

4. The changing responsibilities of women epitomize the fundamental challenge to welfare reform: how to reconcile societal beliefs that every adult should be self-sufficient and that mothers have a special nurturing role toward children and the right to rear them. In some respects, our views of the role of women have come full circle. In colonial America women played an important part in the economy and worked at home or on the farm. It was expected that women would continue this labor after their children were born. By the nineteenth century, however, working outside the home became proscribed, as the mother–child relationship was seen as something vital and special that should not be disrupted by employment. During the first half of the twentieth century, the emergence of the child welfare movement and child development as a science also contributed to the growing belief that children needed close emotional ties to their mothers, especially when they were young. Children were considered especially vulnerable at young ages if they were separated from their mothers and from their home settings. This perspective had a dramatic influence on the welfare system, where efforts in the late nineteenth and early twentieth centuries were devoted toward keeping impoverished mothers and children together at home.

By the 1960s this view of mothers came under scrutiny as a number of related developments occurred. Caseloads had expanded enormously and were comprised primarily of divorced or never-married mothers, the women's movement had taken hold, and increasing numbers of mothers of young children were joining the labor force. By this time, women were seen once again as having dual roles – both mother and earner – and thus dual responsibilities – to nurture children and to be economically self-sufficient. This viewpoint was applied to the welfare system in the 1960s and 1970s, but very unsuccessfully. The failure to promote this dual role in the past 2 decades is due to several factors, including insufficient funding for welfare-to-work programs, inadequate research on poor families, little attention to child care, short-term or absent transitional services, and a general economy that reduces incentives to join the working poor, many of whom have less access to benefits and services than those on welfare.

We would emphasize, however, that missing in the debate on welfare reform is a focus on *children*. What happens to children as their mothers are required to obtain a

GED, job training, and transition off welfare? Only a few scholars and policy experts acknowledge the extraordinary difficulties facing impoverished women to combine employment and parenting. Yet among the middle class, mothers' employment, especially during their children's infancy, has been seen as highly controversial, with concerns that healthy child development may be impeded (Chase-Lansdale, 1994; Ellwood, 1988; Skocpol & Wilson, 1994).

As the Family Support Act regulations state, "The Family Support Act of 1988 embodies a new consensus that the well-being of children depends not only on meeting their material needs, but also on the parents' becoming self-sufficient" (p. 15640). What is *not* in the Family Support Act of 1988 is a focus on children's lives during the *process* of their parents becoming economically independent. The challenge before us is to see whether our nation can actually bring about a change in poor children's lives. In other words, is investing in parents' self-sufficiency enough to improve children's well-being, or do the architects of welfare reform need to broaden their adult-oriented perspective to address the developmental needs of children as well? Our history indicates that children have not figured prominently in welfare reform, neither in our distant past nor in recent decades. The extent to which children will be included in reforms at hand remains to be seen.

REFERENCES

Achenbaum, W. A. (1986). *Social Security: Visions and revisions*. Cambridge: Cambridge University Press.

Anderson, M. (1978). *Welfare: The political economy of welfare reform in the United States*. Stanford: Hoover Institution.

Ashby, L. (1984). *Saving the waifs: Reformers and dependent children, 1890–1917*. Philadelphia: Temple University Press.

Axtell, J. (1974). *The school upon a hill: Education and society in colonial New England*. New Haven: Yale University Press.

Bane, M. J., & Ellwood, D. T. (1986, Winter). Slipping into and out of poverty: The dynamics of spells. *Journal of Human Resources, 21*, 1–23.

Bane, M. J., & Ellwood, D. T. (1989, September 8). One fifth of the nation's children: Why are they poor? *Science*, 1047–1053.

Baum, E. B. (1991). When the witch doctors agree: The Family Support Act and social science research. *Journal of Policy Analysis and Management, 10*, 603–615.

Beales, R., Jr. (1975). In search of the historical child: Miniature adulthood and youth in colonial New England. *American Quarterly, 27*, 379–398.

Bell, W. (1965). *Aid to dependent children*. New York: Columbia University Press.

Berkowitz, E. D. (1991). *America's welfare state from Roosevelt to Reagan*. Baltimore: Johns Hopkins University Press.

Berkowitz, E. D., & McQuaid, K. (1980). Welfare reform in the 1950s. *Social Service Reform, 54*, 45–58.

Brandt, L. (1905). *Deserters and their families*. New York: Charity Organization Society.

Brauer, C. M. (1982). Kennedy, Johnson, and the war on poverty. *Journal of American History, 69*, 98–119.

Breamer, R. H. (1971). *Children and youth in America: A documentary history* (Vol. 2). Cambridge, MA: Harvard University Press.

Brigham, A. (1833). *Remarks on the influence of mental cultivation and mental excitement upon health* (2nd ed.). Boston: Marsh, Capen, & Lyon.

Bucklin, D. R. (1939). Public aid for the care of dependent children in their own homes, 1932–38. *Social Security Bulletin, 2*, 24–35.

Burtless, G. (1986) Public spending for the poor: Trends, prospects, and economic limits. In S. H. Danziger & D. H. Weinberg (Eds.), *Fighting poverty: What works and what doesn't* (pp. 18–41). Cambridge, MA: Harvard University Press.

Chase-Lansdale, P. L. (1994). Families and maternal employment during infancy: New linkages. In R. D. Parke & S. M. Kellam (Eds.), *Exploring family relationships with other contexts* (pp. 29–48). Hillsdale, NJ: Erlbaum.

Chase-Lansdale, P. L., & Hetherington, E. M. (1990). The impact of divorce on life-span development: Short and long term effects. In P. B. Baltes, D. L. Featherman, & R. M. Lerner (Eds.), *Life-span development and behavior* (Vol. 10, pp. 107–151). Hillsdale, NJ: Erlbaum.

Clement, P. F. (1979). Families and foster care: Philadelphia in the late nineteenth-century. *Social Service Review, 53*, 406–420.

Coontz, S. (1988). *The social origins of private life: A history of American families, 1600–1900.* London: Verso.

Cordasco, F. (1972). Charles Loring Brace and the dangerous classes: Historical analogues of the urban black poor. *Journal of Human Relations, 20*, 379–386.

Cott, N. F. (1976). Divorce and the changing status of women in eighteenth-century Massachusetts. *William and Mary Quarterly 3*, (Series 33), 586–614.

Cott, N. F. (1977). *The bonds of womanhood: "Woman's Sphere" in New England, 1780–1835.* New Haven: Yale University Press.

Cottingham, P. H., & Ellwood, D. T. (Eds.). (1989). *Welfare Policy for the 1990s.* Cambridge, MA: Harvard University Press.

Curabler, J. T. (1980). The politics of charity: Gender and class in late nineteenth century charity policy. *Journal of Social History, 14*, 99–111.

Danziger, S. A., & Weinberg, D. H. (Eds.). (1986). *Fighting poverty: What works and what doesn't.* Cambridge, MA: Harvard University Press.

Danziger, S. H., Haveman, R. H., & Plotnick, R. D. (1986). Antipoverty policy: Effects on the poor and the non-poor. In S. H. Danziger & D. H. Weinberg (Eds.), *Fighting poverty: What works and what doesn't* (pp. 50–77). Cambridge, MA: Harvard University Press.

Davis, A. J. (1930). The evolution of the institution of mothers' pension in the United States. *American Journal of Sociology, 35*, 573–587.

Degler, C. N. (1980). *At odds: Women and the family in America from the Revolution to the present.* New York: Oxford University Press.

Demos, J. (1970). *A little commonwealth: Family life in Plymouth Colony.* New York: Oxford University Press.

Demos, J. (1986). *Past, present, and personal: The family and the life course in American history.* New York: Oxford University Press.

Dudden, F. E. (1983). *Serving women: Household service in nineteenth-century America.* Middletown, CT: Wesleyan University Press.

Ellwood, D. T. (1988). *Poor support: Poverty in the American family.* New York: Basic Books.

Eubank, E. E. (1916). *A study of family desertion.* Chicago: City of Chicago Department of Public Welfare.

Foner, E. (1988). *Reconstruction: America's unfinished revolution, 1863–1877.* New York: Harper & Row.

Garfinkel, I., & McLanahan, S. S. (1986). *Single mothers and their children.* Washington, DC: Urban Institute Press.

Gilbert, C. E. (1966). Policy-making in public welfare: The 1962 amendments. *Political Science Quarterly, 81*, 196–224.

Government Accounting Office (GAO). (1987). *Work and welfare: Current AFDC work programs and implication for federal policy* (GAO/HRD-87–34). Washington, DC: GAO.

Griswold, R. L. (1982). *Family and divorce in California, 1850–1890. Victorian illusions and everyday realities*. Albany, NY: State University of New York Press.

Grossberg, M. (1985). *Governing the hearth: Law and family in nineteenth-century America*. Chapel Hill: University of North Carolina Press.

Gutman, H. G. (1976). *The black family in slavery and freedom 1750–1925* New York: Pantheon.

Harrington, M. (1962). *The other America: Poverty in the United States*. New York: Penguin Books.

Haskins, R. (1991). Congress writes a law: Research and welfare reform. *Journal of Policy Analysis and Management, 10*, 616–632.

Hayes, C. D., Palmer, J. L., & Zaslow, M. J. (Eds.). (1990). *Who cares for America's children? Child care policy for the 1990s*. Washington, DC: National Academy Press.

Heale, M. J. (1968). Humanitarianism in the early republic: The moral reformers of New York, 1776–1825. *American Studies, 2*, 161–175.

Holloran, P. C. (1989). *Boston's wayward children: Social services for homeless children, 1830–1930*. Rutherford, PA: Fairleigh Dickinson University Press.

Holmes, A. E. (1987). *Remembering the noble ladies: American widows and the Civil War pension system*. Unpublished seminar paper, University of Michigan, Ann Arbor.

Holt, M. I. (1992). *The orphan trains: Placing out in America*. Lincoln: University of Nebraska Press.

Horn, M. (1989). *Before it's too late: The child guidance movement in the United States, 1922–1945*. Philadelphia: Temple University Press.

Jencks, C. (1992, Fall). The poor: Can we limit welfare? *The American Prospect, 11*, 32–40.

Jones, J. (1980). *Soldiers of light and love: Northern teachers and Georgia blacks, 1865–1873*. Chapel Hill: University of North Carolina Press.

Kaestle, C. F., & Vinovskis, M. A. (1980). *Education and social change in nineteenth-century Massachusetts*. Cambridge: Cambridge University Press.

Kamerman, S. B., & Kahn, A. J. (1988). *Mothers alone: Strategies for a time of change*. Dover, MA: Auburn House.

Kaplan, B. J. (1978). Reformers and charity: The abolition of outdoor relief in New York City: 1870–1898. *Social Service Review, 52*, 202–214.

Kaplan, M., & Cuciti, P. (Eds.). (1986). *The Great Society and its legacy*. Durham, NC: Duke University Press.

Katz, M. B. (1986). *In the shadow of the poorhouse: A social history of welfare in America*. New York: Basic Books.

Kerber, L. K. (1980). *Women of the republic: Intellect and ideology in revolutionary America*. Chapel Hill: University of North Carolina Press.

Keyssar, A. (1974). Widowhood in eighteenth-century Massachusetts: A problem in the history of the family. *Perspectives in American History, 8*, 83–119.

Klebaner, B. J. (1955). Pauper auctions: The "New England Method" of public poor relief. *Essex Institute Historical Collection, 91*, 195–210.

Klebaner, B. J. (1964). Poverty and its relief in American thought, 1815–61. *Social Service Review, 38*, 382–399.

Langsam, M. (1964). *Children west: A history of the placing-out of the New York Children's Aid Society*. Madison, WI: State Historical Society.

Lee, C. R. (1981). The poor people: Seventeenth-century Massachusetts and the poor. *Historical Journal of Massachusetts, 9*, 41–50.

Leff, M. H. (1973). Consensus for reform: The mothers' pension movement in the Progressive Era. *Social Service Review, 47*, 397–417.

Levitan, S. A., & Taggart, R. (1976). *The promise of greatness: The social programs of the last decade and their major achievements*. Cambridge, MA: Harvard University Press.

Lima, L. H., & Harris, R. C. (1988). The child support enforcement program of the United States. In A. J. Kahn & S. B. Kamerman (Eds.), *Child support: From debt collection to social policy* (pp. 20–44). Newbury Park, CA: Sage.

Lockridge, K. A. (1974). *Literacy in colonial New England: An enquiry into the social context of literacy in the early modern west*. New York: Norton

Lopata, Z. L., & Brehm, H. P. (1986). *Widows and dependent wives: From social problem to federal program*. New York: Praeger.

Lubove, R. (1968). *The struggle for social security, 1900–1935*. Cambridge, MA: Harvard University Press.

Lynn, L. E., Jr. (1993, Fall). Ending welfare reform as we know it. *The American Prospect, 15*, 83–92

Lynn, L. E., Jr., & Whitman, D. F. (1981). *The president as policymaker: Jimmy Carter and welfare reform*. Philadelphia: Temple University Press.

McLanahan, S. S., & Sandefur, G. (1994). *Growing up with a single parent: What hurts, what helps?* Cambridge, MA: Harvard University Press.

Mason, K. O., Vinovskis, M. A., & Hareven, T. K. (1978). Women's work and the life course in Essex County, Massachusetts, 1880. In T. K. Hareven (Ed.), *Transitions: The family and the life course in historical perspective* (pp. 187–216). New York: Academic Press.

May, D., & Vinovskis, M. A. (1977). "A ray of millennial light": Early education and social reform in the infant school movement in Massachusetts, 1826–1840. In T. K. Hareven (Ed.), *Family and kin in American urban communities, 1800–1940* (pp. 62–99). New York: Watts.

Moran, G. F., & Vinovskis, M. A. (1992). *Religion, family, and the life course: Explorations in the social history of early America*. Ann Arbor: University of Michigan Press.

Moynihan, D. P. (1973). *The politics of a guaranteed income: The Nixon administration and the Family Assistance Plan*. New York: Random House.

Mudgett, M. B. (1924). *Results of the Minnesota's laws for the protection of children born out of wedlock* (U.S. Children's Bureau Publication, No. 28). Washington, DC: U.S. Government Printing Office.

Murray, C. (1984). *Losing ground: American social policy, 1950–1980*. New York: Basic Books.

Orloff, A. H. (1988). The political origins of America's belated welfare state. In M. Weir, A. S. Orloff, & T. Skocpol (Eds.), *The politics of social policy in the United States* (pp. 37–80). Princeton: Princeton University Press.

Patterson, J. T. (1981). *America's struggle against poverty, 1900–1980*. Cambridge, MA: Harvard University Press.

Pumphrey, M. W., & Pumphrey, R. E. (1983). The widows' pension movement, 1900–1930: Preventive child-saving or social control? In W. I. Trattner (Ed.), *Social welfare or social control? Historical reflections on regulating the poor* (pp. 51–66). Knoxville: University of Tennessee Press.

Reagan, P. D. (1981). The ideology of social harmony and efficiency: Workman's compensation in Ohio, 1904–1919. *Ohio History, 90*, 317–333.

Reischauer, R. D. (1989). The welfare reform legislation: Directions for the future. In P. H. Cottingham & D. T. Ellwood (Eds.), *Welfare policy for the 1990s* (pp. 10–40). Cambridge, MA: Harvard University Press.

Rorabaugh, W. J. (1986). *The craft apprentice: From Franklin to the machine age in America*. New York: Oxford University Press.

Rothman, D. J. (1971). *The discovery of the asylum: Social order and disorder in the New Republic*. Boston: Little, Brown.

Rotunda, E. A. (1985). American fatherhood: A historical perspective. *American Behavioral Scientist, 29*, 7–25.

Rutman, D. B., & Rutman, A. H. (1984). *A place in time: Middlesex County, Virginia, 1650–1750*. New York: Norton.

Ryan, M. P. (1981). *Cradle of the middle class: The family in Oneida County, New York, 1790–1865*. Cambridge: Cambridge University Press.

Ryan, M. P. (1982). *The empire of the mother: American writing about domesticity, 1830–1860*. New York: Haworth Press.

Schneider, E. C. (1992). *In the web of class: Delinquents and reformers in Boston, 1810s–1930s*. New York: New York University Press.

Scott, R. (1978). The battle over the child: Child apprenticeship and the Freedman's Bureau in North Carolina. *Prologue, 10*, 101–113.

Select Committee on Children, Youth, and Families. (1987). *U.S. children and their families: Current conditions and recent trends*. Washington, DC: U.S. Government Printing Office.

Skocpol, T., & Wilson, W. J. (1994, February 9). Welfare as we need it. *New York Times*, A16.

Smith, D. S., & Hindus, M. S. (1974–75). Premarital pregnancy in America, 1640–1975: An overview and interpretation. *Journal of Interdisciplinary History, 5*, 537–570.

Steiner, G. Y. (1971). *The state of welfare*. Washington, DC: Brookings Institution.

Szanton, P. L. (1991). The remarkable "Quango": Knowledge, politics, and welfare reform. *Journal of Public Policy and Management, 10*, 590–602.

Tiffin, S. (1982). *In whose best interest? Child welfare reform in the Progressive Era*. Westport, CN: Greenwood.

Tracy, P. J. (1979). *Jonathan Edwards, pastor: Religion and society in eighteenth-century Northampton*. New York: Hill & Wang.

Trattner, W. I. (1984). *From poor law to welfare state: A history of social welfare in America* (3rd ed.). New York: Free Press.

U.S. Bureau of the Census. (1988). *Fertility of American women: June 1987* (Current Population Reports, Series P-20, No. 427). Washington, DC: U.S. Government Printing Office.

U.S. Bureau of the Census. (1992). *Poverty in the United States: 1991* (Current Population Reports, Series P-60, No. 181). Washington, DC: U.S. Government Printing Office.

U.S. Senate. (1987a). *Welfare: Reform or replacement?* (*Work and welfare*) (S. Hrg. 100–320). Hearing before the Subcommittee on Social Security and Family Policy of the Committee on Finance, United States Senate, One Hundredth Congress, February 23. Washington, DC: U.S. Government Printing Office.

U.S. Senate. (1987b). *Welfare: Reform or replacement?* (*Short-term v. long-term dependency*) (S. Hrg. 100–484). Hearing before the Subcommittee on Social Security and Family Policy of the Committee on Finance, United States Senate, One Hundredth Congress, March 2. Washington, DC: U.S. Government Printing Office.

U.S. Senate. (1988). *Welfare reform* (S. Hrg. 100–450. Pt. 3). Hearing before the Committee on Finance, United States Senate, One Hundredth Congress, February 4. Washington, DC: U.S. Government Printing Office.

Van Horn, S. H. (1988). *Women, work, and fertility, 1900–1986*. New York: New York University Press.

Vinovskis, M. A. (1981). *Fertility in Massachusetts from the Revolution to the Civil War*. New York: Academic Press.

Vinovskis, M. A. (1986). Young fathers and their children: Some historical and policy perspectives. In A. B. Elster & M. E. Lamb (Eds.), *Adolescent fatherhood* (pp. 171–192). Hillsdale, NJ: Erlbaum.

Vinovskis, M. A. (1987). Family and schooling in colonial and nineteenth-century America. *Journal of Family History, 12*, 19–37.

Vinovskis, M. A. (1989). Have social historians lost the Civil War? Some preliminary demographic speculations. *Journal of American History, 76*, 34–58.

Vinovskis, M. A. (1990). Death and family life in the past. *Human Nature, 1*, 109–122.

Walsh, L. S. (1979). "Till death us do part": Marriage and family in seventeenth-century Maryland. In T. W. Tate & D. L. Ammerman (Eds.), *The Chesapeake in the seventeenth century: Essays on Anglo-American society and politics* (pp. 126–152). Chapel Hill: University of North Carolina Press.

Wickenden, E. (1969). The '67 Amendments: A giant step backward for child welfare. *Child Welfare, 48*, 388–394.

Wiseman, M. (Ed.). (1991). Research and policy: A symposium on the Family Support Act of 1988. *Journal of Public Policy Analysis and Management, 10*, 588–666.

Wisner, E. (1945). The Puritan background of the New England poor laws. *Social Service Review, 19*, 381–390.

Witte, E. E. (1962). *The development of the Social Security Act*. Madison: University of Wisconsin Press.

Zelizer, V. A. R. (1979). *Moral and markets: The development of life insurance in the United States*. New York: Columbia University Press.

2   The life circumstances and development of children in welfare families: A profile based on national survey data

Nicholas Zill, Kristin A. Moore, Ellen Wolpow Smith, Thomas Stief, and Mary Jo Coiro

One child in seven in the United States is in a family that receives "welfare," or cash income through the Aid to Families with Dependent Children (AFDC) program. As of September 1992 some 9.4 million children under the age of 18 were receiving AFDC (U.S. Department of Health and Human Services, 1993). Because families move on and off welfare, a larger proportion of children receive AFDC for some period between birth and adulthood. Estimates by Martha Hill, Greg Duncan, and their colleagues at the University of Michigan, based on data from the Panel Study of Income Dynamics, are that 22% of U.S. children born in the early 1970s received welfare for at least 1 year before reaching their 15th birthday. For African-American children born during these years, an estimated 55% were dependent for some portion of their childhood (Committee on Ways and Means, 1991, p. 643).

Many people are concerned that large numbers of welfare children are growing up in circumstances that undermine their prospects for developing into healthy, responsible, self-supporting adults. However, being reared in a family that receives AFDC for a period of time does not doom an individual to a life of poverty and dependency. Longitudinal studies have found evidence of substantial social mobility among young people from dependent families (Duncan, Hill, & Hoffman, 1988; Furstenberg, Brooks-Gunn, & Morgan, 1987). Nevertheless, growing up in a welfare family is associated with an elevated risk of adult dependency. In the Panel Study of Income Dynamics, young people who spent time in welfare families while growing up were twice as likely as other individuals to receive AFDC as adults (Hill & Ponza, 1984). Moreover, in the National Survey of Children, youngsters from welfare families had lower educational achievement and occupational attainment levels and higher problem behavior levels as young adults than those who had not grown up in AFDC families (Moore & Stief, 1991). Whether welfare receipt

The preparation of this chapter was made possible by a grant from the Foundation for Child Development. The opinions expressed herein are not necessarily those of the foundation. Special thanks to Margaret L. Daly for editorial assistance in the preparation of this chapter.

38

or some correlated set of factors accounts for these associations has not been established.

Considerable diversity is evident in the welfare population (Zill, Moore, Nord, & Stief, 1991; Weeks et al., 1990) and many families are "on welfare" for short periods of time only (Ellwood, 1986; Duncan et al., 1988). There is little reason to believe that children of short-term welfare recipients are at greater risk of developmental problems than other children whose families have suffered financial hardships. On the other hand, families that are chronically welfare-dependent tend to be those started by unmarried teenage mothers with low skills, limited schooling, and minimal job experience (Moore, 1978; Bane & Ellwood, 1986). These young mothers are apt to suffer from physical health problems and feelings of depression and powerlessness (Zill et al., 1991; Weeks et al., 1990; Hall, Williams, & Greenberg, 1985; Downey & Moen, 1987). They often have histories of drug use or delinquent behavior (Elliot & Morse, 1989; Elster, Ketterlinus, & Lamb, 1990). Welfare grants are low and financial support from the fathers of the children is practically nonexistent (U.S. Department of Health and Human Services, 1990), leading some welfare mothers to engage in subrosa employment or illicit activities in order to make ends meet (Jencks & Edin, 1990). In these "multiple risk" families, prospects for healthy child development seem dim.

Developmental research tells us that youngsters benefit from favorable genetic endowments, nurturing home environments, and access to services such as medical care and preschool education as they strive to grow up physically sound, emotionally secure, and academically successful (Scarr, 1979; Horowitz, 1989). Children in long-term welfare families are apt to be disadvantaged in all these respects (Brooks-Gunn & Furstenberg, 1986, 1989; West & Brick, 1991). Yet even recent welfare reform efforts focus primarily on preparing parents for employment. Despite provisions for subsidized child care and medical insurance during the transition from dependency to what is hoped will be stable employment and economic self-sufficiency, few programs include components that address the developmental obstacles facing welfare children (Rovner, 1988; Smith, Blank, & Bond, 1990; Moynihan, 1990; Smith, this volume). In addition, the experience of a number of welfare-to-work demonstration projects has been that high rates of nonparticipation, especially among the most troubled and chronically dependent recipients, are the norm, not the exception (Quint & Riccio, 1985; Gueron & Pauley, 1991). Hence, programs to serve these families face formidable challenges.

Efforts to steer young people in families that receive AFDC support onto positive developmental pathways could benefit from better information on what the life situations of today's welfare children are like. Policy debates over the kinds of additional resources and services, if any, that AFDC families should be getting have proceeded in the absence of reliable data on the home environments in which welfare children are being reared and the health, learning, and behavior problems of the children themselves. A number of studies of low-income families and children of unmarried adolescent mothers have been conducted (Polit, Kahn, Murray, & Smith, 1982; Angel & Worebey, 1988; Bradley et al., 1989; Brooks-Gunn & Furstenberg, 1989), but the samples have usually been small and not fully representative of the welfare population.

Research objectives

The purpose of the research presented in this chapter is, first, to describe the circumstances of children in families that receive AFDC and compare them with children in other families, using two large and nationally representative samples of U.S. families with children. A second purpose is to determine whether the problems of welfare children are more closely associated with welfare dependency as such or with the low parent education levels, poverty, and family structure of families that receive AFDC. Children whose families have received AFDC payments in the previous 12 months are compared with children in families that are neither poor nor welfare-dependent, and with children in poor families that have not received AFDC in the past year.

A third objective of the research is to ascertain whether the home environments of welfare youngsters are lacking in qualities, such as intellectual stimulation and emotional support, which have previously been found to be associated with higher achievement in children. The final purpose is to determine whether, because of their eligibility for Medicaid and other AFDC-linked programs, welfare children are more likely than other poor children to receive regular medical care and related services.

Data and measures

Representative data on the home environments and development of national samples of welfare children are available through two federally sponsored data collection programs: the National Health Interview Survey on Child Health (NHIS-CH; National Center for Health Statistics, 1989) and the Child Supplement to the National Longitudinal Survey of the Labor Market Experience of Youth (NLSY-CS; Baker & Mott, 1989). The first is a large cross-sectional survey of the child population of the United States, with numerous measures of child health, achievement, and behavior (Zill & Schoenborn, 1990; Dawson, 1991) and questions that make it possible to identify both welfare families and nonwelfare poor families. The second is a study of the children born to a national sample of young women who participated in a 12-year longitudinal study of labor force behavior, begun when the women were still teenagers (Chase-Lansdale, Mott, Brooks-Gunn, & Phillips, 1991; see Zill, this volume). The NLSY-CS sample is not yet a full probability sample of children born to a cohort of women, as some of the women have not yet had their first child. It is, however, a reasonably good sample of children born to teenage and young-adult childbearers.

The sample of 17,110 children ages zero to 1 / studied in the NHIS-CH included 1,752 children (unweighted *n*) whose families reported receiving AFDC sometime in the past 12 months. The sample of 4,971 children studied in the Child Supplement to the NLSY included 1,316 children whose families received AFDC during the previous 12 months.[1]

Measures of child development and well-being in the NHIS-CH were all based on structured questions and scales completed by one of the child's parents, usually the mother, whereas developmental measures in the NLSY were based on direct testing of the child and interviewer observations as well as parent report.

Survey measures of the child's family environment

The NLSY HOME scale. The measures used to assess the quality of the child's family environment in the Child Supplement to the National Longitudinal Survey of the Labor Market Experience of Youth (NLSY) were drawn from the HOME scale. This scale is a well validated and widely used instrument developed by Robert Bradley and Bettye Caldwell. It is designed to appraise whether the child's home is an environment that nurtures the child's intellectual and emotional development and helps prepare him or her for the challenges of school (Bradley & Caldwell, 1981; Caldwell & Bradley, 1984). It assesses the orderliness, cleanliness, and safety of the physical environment, the regularity and structure of the family's daily routine, the amount of intellectual stimulation available to the child, and the degree of emotional support provided by the parents.

Abbreviated versions of the HOME were developed especially for the NLSY-CS, with different forms being used for infants and toddlers, preschoolers, and elementary school-aged children (Baker & Mott, 1989). Although many of the items were coded in a multi-category fashion, the total score developed by the NLSY staff used a binary "yes-no" coding for each item. Thus, the total score for the age 3–5 group could range from zero to 22.

The NLSY HOME proved to have reasonable reliability, with the total score having an alpha reliability of 0.70 for preschool children. However, the subscale measuring "emotional support" (alpha reliability = 0.49 for children aged 3–6) was less reliable than the subscale that measured "intellectual stimulation" (alpha reliability = 0.69) (Baker & Mott, 1989). Using both substantive and distributional criteria, overall scores of 19 or more were labeled "supportive" home environments, scores of 15–18 were dubbed "below average," and scores below 15 were labeled "deficient."

Health-related aspects of the home. The National Health Interview Survey on Child Health contained items relating to health-related aspects of the home environment. These included questions whether the mother or other adults in the household were smokers; the child or adolescent used seatbelts regularly when riding in automobiles; and the child had a regular and reasonable bedtime.

Access to medical care. The NHIS-CH also contained an extensive series of items on the availability and use of medical care for the child. The parent respondent was asked whether the child was covered by private health insurance or Medicaid; whether the child had a regular source of both routine and sick care; what kind of facility provided this care; and whether the child was seen by the same medical professional each time he or she received care. The parent was also asked when the child last received routine medical and dental care.

Findings

Both national survey data sets yielded evidence that the health, well-being, and developmental status of children from families that receive AFDC are less auspicious, on average, than those of children from families that are neither poor nor on welfare. Children in long-term welfare families have more developmental problems than those dependent for short periods. The survey data also showed that welfare parents tend to provide less intellectual stimulation and emotional support to their offspring than do parents in nonpoor families, and that the home environments of the former group tend to be less conducive to child health and safety.

It is important to note, however, that differences between welfare children and poor children whose families did not receive AFDC were found to be relatively small or nonexistent, both with respect to the developmental problems of the children and the non-nurturant qualities of their home environments. One notable difference between welfare and nonwelfare poor children was that children in families receiving AFDC were more likely to have gotten routine medical and dental care.

The health, learning, and behavior of welfare children

Data from the NHIS-CH and the NLSY-CS show that children in families that receive AFDC are significantly less healthy, more than twice as likely to fail in school, and more likely to present serious conduct and discipline problems to their teachers and parents than nonpoor children. By the same token, poor children from families that did not receive welfare had equivalent levels of health and behavior problems, and nearly as severe learning problems, as those from AFDC families. Controlling for parent education, family structure, race, and other background factors substantially reduced, but did not eliminate, developmental differences between welfare and nonpoor children. Nor did it eliminate differences between poor, non-AFDC children and those in nonpoor families.

Welfare children are significantly less healthy than nonpoor children. Due to general improvements in public health in the United States over the past 3 decades, and the accomplishments of programs such as Medicaid and food stamps, the health of most of today's welfare children is reasonably sound, at least as far as their physical condition is concerned. Among children aged 17 and under in the National Health Interview Survey on Child Health, more than 90% of those in AFDC families were said to be in at least "good" health. However, the minority who were not in good health was considerably larger in welfare families than in higher-income families. Three times as many AFDC children as nonpoor children – 7% versus 2% – were said to be in "fair" or "poor" health. Nearly twice as many – 9% versus 5% – had a health condition that limited their mobility, school activities, or play. And 25% of the AFDC children, as opposed to 19% of nonpoor children – nearly a third more – were reported to have had a delay in growth or development, a learning disability, or a significant emotional or behavioral problem.

When general health status, activity limitation, and developmental problems were combined into a joint indicator, it was found that only 32% of children in AFDC families were in excellent health with no activity limitations or developmental problems. By contrast, 48% of children from nonpoor, nonwelfare families had their health described in these positive terms. More than a quarter of AFDC children, as opposed to about a fifth of nonpoor children, had either an activity limitation, a developmental problem, or were rated in fair or poor health (Table 2.1).

Table 2.1. *Health status of U.S. children aged 17 and under by welfare and poverty status of their families, 1988*

Health status indicators	Proportion of children for whom statement applies		n
	Observed proportion	Adjusted proportion[a]	
In excellent health, with no activity limitations or developmental problems			
All children aged 17 and under	45%	45%	16,329
Welfare/poverty status:			
In AFDC family	32%	39%	1,701
In poor, non-AFDC family	32%	39%	1,200
In nonpoor, non-AFDC family	48%[b]	47%[b]	13,428
(eta, beta)	(0.13[c])	(0.06[c])	
In fair or poor health, or has activity limitation or developmental problem			
All children aged 17 and under	21%	21%	16,329
Welfare/poverty status:			
In AFDC family	26%	26%	1,701
In poor, non-AFDC family	25%	25%	1,200
In nonpoor, non-AFDC family	20%[b]	20%[b]	13,428
(eta, beta)	(0.06[c])	(0.05[c])	

Source: Child Trends' analysis of data from the 1988 National Health Interview Survey on Child Health, Washington, DC, 1991.
[a] Adjusted by multiple classification analysis for effects of parent education; family structure; family size; sex, age, and ethnicity of child; region; and metropolitan residence.
[b] Significantly different from mean for AFDC children, $p < 0.001$.
[c] $p < 0.001$.

By adolescence, only about one in four of the welfare youth were found to be in excellent health and free of developmental problems, whereas this was true of 44% of youth from nonpoor families. Furthermore, nearly 40% of welfare youth had a developmental problem, an activity limitation, or were rated in fair or poor health. Because parents with relatively little education have a tendency to understate developmental problems in their children (Zill & Schoenborn, 1990), it is likely that the differences between welfare and nonpoor children were even more pronounced than shown in the survey reports.

Welfare children are twice as likely to fail in school. Among schoolchildren aged 7–17 in the National Health Interview Survey on Child Health, 60% of those from AFDC families were described by their parents as ranking in the bottom halves of their classes. By comparison, 41% of nonpoor schoolchildren were so described. Fully 34% of the AFDC pupils had repeated a grade in school, compared with 15% of nonpoor pupils (Table 2.2).

Table 2.2. *School achievement of U.S. children aged 7–17 by welfare and poverty status of their families, 1988*

	Proportion of children for whom statement applies		
Achievement indicators	Observed proportion	Adjusted proportion[a]	n
In bottom half of class			
All children aged 7–17	44%	44%	9,383
Welfare/poverty status:			
In AFDC family	60%	49%	817
In poor, non-AFDC family	55%[b]	46%	675
In nonpoor, non-AFDC family	41%[c]	43%[c]	7,891
(eta, beta)	(0.13[e])	(0.04[d])	
Repeated a grade			
All children aged 7–17	18%	18%	9,557
Welfare/poverty status:			
In AFDC family	34%	26%	842
In poor, non-AFDC family	28%[b]	22%	692
In nonpoor, non-AFDC family	15%[c]	17%[c]	8,023
(eta, beta)	(0.17[e])	(0.08[e])	

Source: Child Trends' analysis of data from the 1988 National Health Interview Survey on Child Health, Washington, DC, 1991.
[a]Adjusted by multiple classification analysis for effects of parent education; family structure; family size; sex, age, and ethnicity of child; region; and metropolitan residence.
[b]Significantly different from mean for AFDC children, $p < 0.05$.
[c]Significantly different from mean for AFDC children, $p < 0.001$.
[d]$p < 0.01$.
[e]$p < 0.001$.

Slower than average cognitive development was found in younger welfare children as well. Among firstborn children aged 4–7 in the NLSY-CS, 60% of those from AFDC families scored below the 30th percentile on the national norms for the Peabody Picture Vocabulary Test (PPVT). The PPVT is a test of children's word knowledge that correlates well with general intelligence. Only 26% of the AFDC children scored at or above the 50th percentile on the PPVT. By contrast, 54% of the nonpoor, non-AFDC children in the NLSY-CS were at or above the 50th percentile[2] (Table 2.3).

Table 2.3. *Vocabulary test and behavior problems scores of U.S. firstborn children aged 4–7 born to mothers aged 14–25 at birth of child by welfare and poverty status of their families, 1986*

	Proportion of children for whom statement applies		
	Observed proportion	Adjusted proportion[a]	n
Vocabulary score below 30th percentile on PPVT national norms			
All firstborn children aged 4–7 in NLSY-CS	35%	35%	972
Welfare/poverty status:			
In AFDC family	60%	52%	197
In poor, non-AFDC family	47%	42%	116
In nonpoor, non-AFDC family	27%	30%	659
(eta, beta)	(0.27[c])	(0.18[c])	
Vocabulary score at or above 50th percentile			
All firstborn children aged 4–7 in NLSY-CS	46%	46%	972
Welfare/poverty status:			
In AFDC family	26%	33%	197
In poor, non-AFDC family	25%	29%	116
In nonpoor, non-AFDC family	54%	52%	659
(eta, beta)	(0.26[c])	(0.18[c])	
Behavior problems score above 90th percentile on BPI national norms			
All firstborn children aged 4–7 in NLSY-CS	23%	23%	926
Welfare/poverty status:			
In AFDC family	34%	36%	183
In poor, non-AFDC family	32%	30%	110
In nonpoor, non-AFDC family	19%	19%	633
(eta, beta)	(0.16[b])	(0.16[b])	

Source: Child Trends' analysis of data from the 1986 Child Supplement to the National Longitudinal Survey of Labor Market Experience of Youth (NLSY), Washington, DC, 1991.
[a] Adjusted by multiple classification analysis for effects of parent education; family structure; family size; sex, age, and ethnicity of child; region; and metropolitan residence.
[b] $p < 0.01$. PPVT = Peabody Picture Vocabulary Test, Revised
[c] $p < 0.001$. BPI = Behavior Problems Index

Welfare children are more likely to present serious conduct and discipline problems to their teachers and parents. As well as exhibiting a higher rate of learning problems, pupils from families that receive AFDC are more likely than nonpoor pupils to misbehave in class in ways that require disciplinary action by teachers and principals. Of course, achievement and conduct problems are often interrelated.

Among pupils aged 7–17 in the National Health Interview Survey on Child Health, 27% of the parents from AFDC families reported that they had been asked to come in to school for a conference with the teacher or principal, usually due to behavioral problems the child was presenting. The comparable proportion among nonpoor children of the same ages was 17% (Table 2.4). Among adolescents from welfare families, nearly a third had required a school conference, compared with less than one-fifth of nonpoor adolescents.

Pupils from families receiving AFDC were also twice as likely as nonpoor pupils to have been suspended or expelled from school. This had happened to 14% of AFDC children aged 7–17, as opposed to 7% of nonpoor children (Table 2.4, bottom section). By adolescence, nearly one-quarter of welfare youth had been

Table 2.4. *School behavior problems of U.S. children aged 7–17 by welfare and poverty status of their families, 1988*

Behavior problem indicators	Proportion of children for whom statement applies		n
	Observed proportion	Adjusted proportion[a]	
Parent called in for conference			
All children aged 7–17	18%	18%	9,603
Welfare/poverty status:			
In AFDC family	27%	24%	849
In poor, non-AFDC family	22%[b]	20%[b]	700
In nonpoor, non-AFDC family	17%[c]	17%[c]	8,054
(eta, beta)	(0.09[d])	(0.05[d])	
Child suspended or expelled			
All children aged 7–17	8%	8%	9,610
Welfare/poverty status:			
In AFDC family	14%	10%	847
In poor, non-AFDC family	13%	12%	701
In nonpoor, non-AFDC family	7%[c]	7%[c]	8,062
(eta, beta)	(0.10[d])	(0.08[d])	

Source: Child Trends' analysis of data from the 1988 National Health Interview Survey on Child Health, Washington, DC, 1991.
[a] Adjusted by multiple classification analysis for effects of parent education; family structure; family size; sex, age, and ethnicity of child; region; and metropolitan residence.
[b] Significantly different from mean for AFDC children, $p < 0.05$.
[c] Significantly different from mean for AFDC children, $p < 0.001$.
[d] $p < 0.001$.

suspended or expelled, compared with 13% of youth from nonpoor, nonwelfare families.

In addition to reporting misconduct in school, more parents in welfare families report that their children exhibit problem behavior at home. Among firstborn children aged 4–7 in the NLSY-CS, 34% had scores above the 90th percentile on the national norms for the Behavior Problems Index (BPI). This is a short behavior scale that does a good job of identifying children who need psychological help (Zill, 1990). Only about half as many children in nonpoor, non-AFDC families had BPI scores above the 90th percentile (Table 2.3, bottom section).

Poor children from families that do not receive AFDC show similar levels of health and behavior problems, and nearly as many learning problems, as children from AFDC families. Thus far, the national survey findings have demonstrated that children from AFDC families have significantly higher levels of health, learning, and behavior problems than children from families that are not poor and do not receive welfare. But how do the developmental difficulties of welfare children compare with those of young people from poor families that do not receive AFDC? The survey data indicate that the developmental problems of nonwelfare poor children are generally comparable to those of welfare children (see the second row of each display in Tables 2.1–2.4).

In the health area, for example, the NHIS-CH found that just over 32% of children aged 17 and under from non-AFDC poor families were in excellent health with no activity limitations or developmental problems. This was exactly the same proportion as was found for children from AFDC families (Table 2.1).

In the area of academic achievement, pupils from nonwelfare poor families appeared to be doing slightly better than pupils from AFDC families, but still substantially worse than pupils from nonpoor families. Thus, 55% of non-AFDC poor children aged 7–17 were in the bottom halves of their classes, and 28% had had to repeat one or more grades. The comparable figures for welfare children of the same ages were 60% and 34%. In contrast, the figures for nonpoor children were 41% and 15% respectively (Table 2.2).

In the area of school behavior, the parents of poor children who were not receiving welfare were slightly less likely to have been called in for a teacher conference: Twenty-two percent of those with children aged 7–17 had had such a conference, compared with 27% of the parents of AFDC pupils. But as with AFDC pupils, the non-AFDC poor were twice as likely as the nonpoor to have been suspended or expelled from school. Thirteen percent of students from impoverished nonwelfare families had been suspended, compared with 14% of students from AFDC families, but only 7% of students from nonpoor families.

Controls for parent education, family structure, and other background factors reduce developmental differences between welfare and nonwelfare children. There were other indications in the survey results that the problems of welfare children are linked to poverty, low parental education, and family disorganization, rather than to welfare dependency as such. These were found when group differences in the developmental measures were estimated controlling for related variations in parent education, racial and ethnic composition, family structure, region, metropolitan residence, age and sex of child, and family size. Generally, these statistical controls had the effect of reducing the developmental differences among the AFDC, non-AFDC poor, and nonpoor groups. Including these control variables did not totally eliminate differences across the groups, however (see the columns labeled "Adjusted" in Tables 2.1–2.4).

Children in long-term welfare families show lower achievement than the children of short-term recipients. Children in families that were dependent on welfare for long periods of time were found to show significantly lower achievement levels than those in families that received AFDC for relatively short periods of time. Among firstborn children aged 4–7 in the NLSY-CS, 69% of those whose families had received AFDC for 3 years or more scored below the 30th percentile on the PPVT norms, and only 17% scored at or above the 50th percentile. By comparison, among children whose families had received welfare for less than 3 years, 50% scored below the 30th percentile and 31% scored at or above the 50th percentile. (Data not shown in tables.)

The home environments in which welfare children are being reared

Data from the NLSY-CS showed that only about one-third of preschool children from welfare families receive intellectual stimulation and emotional support from their parents comparable to that received by most children in families that are neither poor nor welfare-dependent. Preschoolers in families that are poor but not welfare-dependent also tend to have home environments that are less than optimal in terms of support for emotional health and school achievement. Although minority children in AFDC or poor non-AFDC families are generally more disadvantaged with regard to the supportiveness of their home environments than are their non-minority counterparts, within each ethnic group AFDC families offer less stimulating environments than nonpoor families. Data from the NHIS-CH show that conditions in many AFDC and nonwelfare poor families are less satisfactory than those in nonpoor families as far as injury prevention and health promotion are concerned.

Only one-third of preschoolers in welfare families receive stimulation and support at home comparable to that received by most middle-class children. Based on HOME scale scores in the NLSY-CS, only about one-third of 3- to 5-year-olds whose families received AFDC were being reared in "supportive" home environments (i.e., they were receiving intellectual stimulation and emotional support from their families comparable to that obtained by the vast majority of middle-class children)

Two-thirds were being reared in homes that were at least "below-average" homes, and nearly one-quarter were receiving care that was clearly "deficient" (Table 2.5).

The situation was similar for children whose families were below the poverty line but were not currently receiving AFDC. By contrast, more than two-thirds of the preschoolers whose families were neither poor nor on welfare were receiving "supportive" care. Only 7% of the children in nonpoor, non-AFDC families lived in homes that fell into the "deficient" category.

It is possible that there is bias in the HOME scale. The scale certainly embodies

Table 2.5. *The quality of home environments (HOME scale scores) of U.S. children aged 3–5 born to mothers aged 14–25 at birth of child by welfare and poverty status of their families, 1986*

	Proportion of children whose home environments were			
Quality of home environment (total HOME score)[a]	Deficient (< 15)	Below average (15–18)	Supportive (19+)	Total
All children aged 3–5 in NLSY-CS	11%	30%	59%	100%
Welfare/poverty status:				
In AFDC family	24%	42%	34%	100%
In poor, non-AFDC family	24%	41%	35%	100%
In nonpoor, non-AFDC family	7%	25%	68%	100%
(contingency coefficient)			(0.31[b])	
	Deficient (< 8)	Below average (8–10)	Supportive (11+)	Total
Level of intellectual stimulation				
All children aged 3–5 in NLSY-CS	8%	24%	68%	100%
Welfare/poverty status:				
In AFDC family	17%	34%	49%	100%
In poor, non-AFDC family	13%	39%	48%	100%
In nonpoor, non-AFDC family	6%	20%	74%	100%
(contingency coefficient)			(0.25[b])	
	Deficient (< 6)	Below average (6–7)	Supportive (8+)	Total
Level of emotional support				
All children aged 3–5 in NLSY-CS	12%	26%	62%	100%
Welfare/poverty status:				
In AFDC family	25%	27%	48%	100%
In poor, non-AFDC family	26%	34%	40%	100%
In nonpoor, non-AFDC family	8%	24%	68%	100%
(contingency coefficient)			(0.26[b])	

Source: Child Trends' analysis of data from the 1986 Child Supplement to the National Longitudinal Survey of Labor Market Experience of Youth (NLSY), Washington, DC, 1991.
Note: Unweighted *n*'s: AFDC (365); poor, non-AFDC (210); nonpoor, non-AFDC (969).
[a]Total HOME Scale scores ranged from zero to 22. Intellectual Stimulation subscale ranged from zero to 12. Emotional Support subscale ranged from zero to 10.
[b]$p < 0.001$.

middle-class child-rearing values. At the same time, it has been found to be predictive of school performance among minority as well as nonminority children (Bradley & Caldwell, 1981). The abbreviated HOME has also been found to relate to children's achievement, correlating with vocabulary, reading, and math tests given in the Child Supplement (Parcel & Menaghan, 1989; Menaghan & Parcel, 1991; Dubow & Luster, 1990; Morrison, Myers, & Winglee, 1990). Significant correlations remained even when family social and economic status and mothers' scores on the Armed Forces Qualifying Test (AFQT) were controlled (Moore & Snyder, 1991).

Four in 10 welfare children have mothers who read to them several times a week. Findings with respect to selected items drawn from the HOME scale illustrate the differences between welfare and nonwelfare families in concrete terms. For example, whereas a majority of AFDC children were reported to possess 10 or more books of their own, only about four in 10 had mothers who read to them three times a week or more. Although deprived of parental reading, they were certainly not

Table 2.6. *Reading to child, book ownership, and television watching by ethnicity and welfare and poverty status of family, U.S. children aged 3–5 born to mothers aged 14–25 at birth of child, 1986*

HOME scale items	All ethnic groups	Black	Hispanic	Nonminority
	Proportion of children for whom statement applies, by ethnicity			
Mother read stories to child 3 or more times a week				
Welfare/poverty status:				
In AFDC family	42%	30%	33%	53%
In poor, non-AFDC family	36%	27%	28%	42%
In nonpoor, non-AFDC family	57%	37%	43%	61%
(contingency coefficient)	(0.19[a])	(0.17[a])	(0.18[a])	(0.16[a])
Child has 10 or more books				
Welfare/poverty status:				
In AFDC family	51%	28%	39%	72%
In poor, non-AFDC family	59%	33%	23%	78%
In nonpoor, non-AFDC family	81%	54%	57%	88%
(contingency coefficient)	(0.29[a])	(0.29[a])	(0.27[a])	(0.22[a])
Television is on in home 7 or more hours every day				
Welfare/poverty status:				
In AFDC family	55%	60%	47%	53%
In poor, non-AFDC family	44%	44%	42%	44%
In nonpoor, non-AFDC family	35%	43%	31%	34%
(contingency coefficient)	(0.20[a])	(0.19[a])	(0.18[a])	(0.16[a])

Source: Child Trends' analysis of data from the 1986 Child Supplement to the National Longitudinal Survey of Labor Market Experience of Youth (NLSY), Washington, DC, 1991.
[a]$p < 0.001$.

deprived of television. A majority of AFDC children were in homes where the television was reported to be on 7 or more hours every day. Parents in nonpoor families were more likely to limit their children's exposure to television (Table 2.6).

The lack of intellectual stimulation was more extreme for black and Hispanic children in AFDC families. Within each ethnic group, however, children in AFDC families experienced less reading and more television viewing than those in nonpoor families.

According to interviewer observations, eight out of 10 children in AFDC families had parents whose tone of voice conveyed positive feelings toward the child, had play environments that appeared to be safe, and did not live in homes that were dark or perceptually monotonous. Nonetheless, the minority who failed to pass these items was larger in AFDC families than in nonpoor families. Interviewers were also less likely to observe AFDC children getting a hug or kiss from their parents during the home visit (Table 2.7).

Like the AFDC children, children in poor, non-AFDC families were less likely than those in nonpoor families to own many books or be read to frequently, and more likely to watch a great deal of television. In comparison to the AFDC children, the poor, non-AFDC children were more likely to own books, but less likely to be read to by their mothers. Children in poor, non-AFDC families seemed slightly better off than the AFDC children in material terms, but slightly worse off in terms of emotional support. Thus, the nonwelfare poor were less likely to be living in dark apartments, but also less likely to have been hugged or kissed by their parents during the interview. It is important to note that these environmental differences were relatively small compared to the differences distinguishing the two disadvantaged groups from the children in nonpoor families.

Welfare children are at risk with respect to health-related aspects of the home environment. Families have important roles to play in protecting children from injury and promoting healthful habits. Several indicators from the NHIS-CH pointed to deficiencies in many welfare families with respect to these health promotion functions. For example, welfare children are more likely to reside with a parent or other adult who smokes. Among U.S. children aged 17 and under, nearly 58% of AFDC children lived with an adult smoker, compared with 41% of young people in nonpoor, non-AFDC families (Table 2.8).

Moreover, 45% of children in AFDC families did not use seatbelts regularly while riding in a car. This was true of 27% of children in nonpoor, nonwelfare families. Nonuse of seatbelts increases with age for both welfare and nonwelfare youth (Table 2.8). A 55% majority of adolescents in welfare families failed to use seatbelts, compared with 43% of teens from nonpoor, nonwelfare families.

Welfare youth are also more likely to have irregular or late bedtimes, and to sleep in the same room as one or both parents (Table 2.8, bottom sections). Nearly 26% of AFDC children, versus 15% of nonpoor children, had no regular bedtime or unusually late bedtimes. (Late bedtimes were defined as 10 P.M. or later for children under 12 years of age, and 11:30 P.M. or later for those 12 to 17 years of age.)

Table 2.7. *Parental tone of voice and physical affection toward child, apparent safety and visual
qualities of home, by ethnicity and welfare and poverty status of family, U.S. children
aged 3–5 born to mothers aged 14–25 at birth of child, 1986*

HOME scale items	Proportion of children for whom statement applies, by ethnicity			
	All ethnic groups	Black	Hispanic	Nonminority
Parental tone of voice conveyed positive feeling toward child				
Welfare/poverty status:				
In AFDC family	82%	78%	80%	86%
In poor, non-AFDC family	80%	76%	75%	86%
In nonpoor, non-AFDC family	93%	90%	86%	95%
(contingency coefficient)	(0.17[a])	(0.17[a])	(0.11[a])	(0.15[a])
Parent caressed, kissed, or hugged child at least once				
Welfare/poverty status:				
In AFDC family	30%	19%	27%	38%
In poor, non-AFDC family	23%	14%	29%	27%
In nonpoor, non-AFDC family	45%	36%	42%	47%
(contingency coefficient)	(0.16[a])	(0.20[a])	(0.15[a])	(0.12[a])
Child play environment appears safe				
Welfare/poverty status:				
In AFDC family	83%	84%	80%	75%
In poor, non-AFDC family	82%	81%	77%	83%
In nonpoor, non-AFDC family	93%	89%	90%	94%
(contingency coefficient)	(0.15[a])	(0.12[a])	(0.17[a])	(0.16[a])
Interior of home dark or perceptually monotonous				
Welfare/poverty status:				
In AFDC family	19%	28%	15%	12%
In poor, non-AFDC family	11%	24%	15%	5%
In nonpoor, non-AFDC family	7%	13%	6%	6%
(contingency coefficient)	(0.15[a])	(0.18[a])	(0.21[a])	(0.09[a])

Source: Child Trends' analysis of data from the 1986 Child Supplement to the National Longitudinal
Survey of Labor Market Experience of Youth (NLSY), Washington, DC, 1991.
[a]$p < 0.001$.

Almost 21% of AFDC children, as opposed to less than 8% of nonpoor children,
slept in the same room as the parent. Of course, such arrangements are not necessarily harmful, particularly for young children. In addition, some of these sleeping
arrangements may have been necessitated by meager living accommodations or the
need to double up with other families in order to have any housing at all.

Young people in poverty-level families that are not currently welfare-dependent
also tend to be at risk with respect to these indicators of health promotion and injury
prevention (Table 2.8). Thus, 52% of youth in poor, non-AFDC families had an
adult smoker in the house; 44% did not use seatbelts regularly, 21% had irregular or
late bedtimes; and 17% shared a bedroom with one or both parents. Some of these

Table 2.8. *Health-related aspects of the home environment of U.S. children aged 17 and under by age group and welfare and poverty status of family, 1988*

Home environment indicators	Proportion of children for whom statement applies, by age group					
	Ages 17 and under	Under 1 year	1–2 years	3–4 years	5–11 years	12–17 years
Adult smoker in household						
All children in age group	44%	39%	43%	41%	45%	45%
Welfare/poverty status:						
In AFDC family	58%	59%	59%	50%	61%	56%
In poor, non-AFDC family	52%	43%	51%	47%	52%	56%
In nonpoor, non-AFDC family	41%	34%	39%	39%	41%	43%
Does not use seat belt regularly						
All children in age group	30%	8%	13%	23%	33%	40%
Welfare/poverty status:						
In AFDC family	45%	22%	30%	37%	52%	55%
In poor, non-AFDC family	44%	23%	24%	31%	51%	52%
In nonpoor, non-AFDC family	27%	4%	8%	20%	28%	38%
Irregular or late bedtime[a]						
All children in age group	17%	—	29%	27%	14%	13%
Welfare/poverty status:						
In AFDC family	26%	—	52%	33%	20%	17%
In poor, non-AFDC family	21%	—	27%	43%	19%	14%
In nonpoor, non-AFDC family	15%	—	25%	24%	13%	12%
Sleeps in same room as parent(s)						
All children in age group	10%	43%	23%	15%	6%	2%
Welfare/poverty status:						
In AFDC family	21%	72%	46%	21%	11%	3%
In poor, non-AFDC family	17%	48%	39%	30%	11%	3%
In nonpoor, non-AFDC family	8%	37%	17%	12%	4%	1%

Source: Child Trends' analysis of data from the 1988 National Health Interview Survey on Child Health, Washington, DC, 1991.
[a]Not asked about for children under 1 year of age.

indicators were slightly better than those for AFDC families, but they were all substantially worse than the comparable measures for nonpoor, non-AFDC families with children.

The medical care that children in AFDC families receive

The data just presented demonstrate that welfare and nonwelfare poor children are both at risk with respect to health-related aspects of their home environments. In contrast, other data from the NHIS-CH show that welfare children fare significantly better than nonwelfare poor children on indicators of health insurance coverage and access to preventive care. Indeed, on some of these indicators, the AFDC children do as well as children from families that are neither poor nor welfare-dependent.

Children in poor, non-AFDC families are six times more likely than AFDC children to lack health insurance coverage. Among children aged 17 and under in the NHIS-CH, 43% of those in poor, non-AFDC families were not covered by any form of health insurance. By contrast, only 7% of AFDC children were not covered. In most instances, of course, their coverage was through the Medicaid program. Most children in nonpoor, non-AFDC families had their coverage through private health insurance plans: Twelve percent of these children had no coverage. (Data not shown in tables.)

Children in poor, non-AFDC families are twice as likely as AFDC children to lack routine medical care. Largely because of Medicaid and related health care programs, AFDC children are more likely than other poor children to have a regular source of routine medical care, and to have gotten such care in the recent past. Among children aged 17 and under in the NHIS-CH, nearly 20% of those in poor, non-AFDC families lacked a regular source of routine care. By contrast, 10% of children in AFDC families lacked such a source of care. This was about the same proportion as that for children in nonpoor, non-AFDC families. Nearly 23% of the poor, non-AFDC children had not had routine care in 2 years or more, whereas the same was true of 10% of AFDC children. Also, 35% of children aged 3–17 in poor, non-AFDC families had not seen a dentist in more than 2 years, as opposed to the 20% of AFDC children who had not had dental care. Among children in nonpoor, non-AFDC families, 16% had not had dental care in the same time period.

The medical care that AFDC children receive often lacks continuity. The situation is less favorable for welfare children with respect to having a regular source of sick care and experiencing continuity of care (i.e., seeing the same physician or physician's assistant) at that care facility. In the NHIS-CH, 30% of AFDC children aged 17 and under lacked such regular and continuous care; so did 38% of poor, non-AFDC children. By contrast, 16% of children in nonpoor families were without such a regular care provider.

Discussion

Given the numerous impediments to healthy development faced by children in families receiving welfare assistance, the reader may not find it surprising to learn that these children have substantially more health, learning, and behavior problems than children in families that are not poor. The fact that the results are predictable does not make them any less sobering, however.

Low achievement, grade repetition, and classroom conduct problems are often precursors of school dropout, adolescent parenthood, joblessness, and delinquency. The finding that welfare children exhibit these problems at rates double those shown by nonpoor children means the "cycle of disadvantage" is still very much with us. Unless effective interventions are found and applied, many of these young people will go on to become adult nonworkers and impoverished or dependent parents, possibly producing another generation of high-risk children.

The results of the comparisons between welfare children and children in poor families that are not receiving welfare were less predictable and more instructive. If children in families receiving AFDC had been doing markedly worse than non-welfare poor children, that would lend credence to the argument that there is something especially detrimental about dependency and the single-parent, non-working family configurations that comprise the current welfare population. If, on the other hand, welfare children had been doing markedly better than nonwelfare poor children, that would suggest that it is beneficial for children in low-income families to have their families receiving regular financial support (even if the support is meager), to not have their mothers be required to work, and to be tied into the network of supportive services (Medicaid, food stamps, public housing) to which a family is entitled once they are deemed welfare-eligible.

What was found instead was that both welfare and nonwelfare poor children were faring about equally poorly. Because these are cross-sectional descriptive analyses, we can only speculate regarding causal mechanisms and the promise of interventions. With this caveat, we note several possible conclusions. One is that the varied risk and protective factors in these two groups tended to cancel each other out. A more plausible suggestion is that low parent education, poverty, and family turmoil are detrimental to children's development, no matter what the particular sources of the family's financial support or the predominant family configuration might be. The findings may also mean that if families move from being "welfare poor" to "working poor," the overall life chances of the children in these families will not be enhanced. However, child outcomes may vary for different subgroups.

In particular, there may be a promising note in the finding that children's developmental problems are more closely associated with low parental education than with welfare dependency per se. It may mean that programs that give welfare parents more schooling in order to bolster their employability could also have beneficial effects on their children. This conclusion is merely hinted at, however, not demonstrated. In order to examine this hypothesis rigorously, one would have to show that increases in parental schooling result in positive changes in the learning and behavior of their offspring, not merely that static differences across parents in educational attainment are associated with variations across children in indicators of child development. The national evaluation study of the JOBS program mandated by the Family Support Act of 1988 (Manpower Demonstration Research Corporation, 1991) may shed some light on this issue.

Enriching the home environments of welfare children

The findings from the present study regarding the home environments of children in families that receive AFDC suggest that many mothers in low-income families need more than remedial education or job training. Some need training in effective child-rearing practices, that is, how to give their children the intellectual stimulation, emotional support, and encouragement of healthful habits that youngsters need for optimal development. The national survey data show that many welfare children are not getting the structure, stimulation, support, and encouragement that most middle-class children receive at home. (This is of course true for some proportion of children at all income levels. Our focus here, however, is on children in families that receive AFDC.)

It is *not* the case that welfare mothers do not have high expectations regarding their children's performance in school. Data from the National Survey of Children and other studies (Child Trends, 1991; National Commission on Children, 1991) indicate that virtually all low-income parents want their children to finish high school and, preferably, get some college education. But many low-income mothers do not seem to know precisely what to do at home to get their children ready for school or to support learning once formal education has begun. A lack of parental stimulation may not be the only obstacle, or even the most significant impediment, faced by children in AFDC families or by other poor children. But it is an obstacle that can be addressed through programs such as parenting education, high-quality child care, compensatory preschool, or all three (Powell, 1989).

Survey data also indicate that time pressures are not usually the problem. Most mothers on AFDC do not report feeling rushed. Indeed, many say they have excess time on their hands (Child Trends, 1991). But AFDC mothers do report frequent money worries. Moreover, there is a high incidence of depression among low-income mothers (Zill et al., 1991; Weeks et al., 1990; Hall et al., 1985; Downey & Moen, 1987) and this may interfere with the nurturing of their children (McLoyd, 1990). Thus, parent education programs may need to be expanded in order to address emotional and motivational issues, as well as training low-income mothers in child development principles and child-rearing practices.

The possible decline in child health care as families move from welfare to self-sufficiency

One arena in which children of AFDC mothers were clearly doing better than their counterparts in other low-income families was in their receipt of routine health care. This finding reinforces concerns about the possible negative effects on children of a loss of Medicaid benefits as their parents move from AFDC dependency to precarious self-sufficiency. To some extent, Congress has already moved to reduce this risk by expanding the Medicaid eligibility of low-income families with children and by providing transitional Medicaid coverage for families as they move off AFDC (see Lobach, this volume; Wolfe, this volume). With many states facing severe fiscal problems, however, it is unclear how rapidly and thoroughly these expansions of the Medicaid program will actually be implemented. Obviously, health care is an area where developments will have to be monitored closely to insure that the best possible care can be made available to all children.

NOTES

1. The NLSY appears to have a larger proportion of welfare children than the NHIS-CH because blacks, Hispanics, and low-income whites were oversampled, and women in the sample who had children early tended to be those from low-education and low-income backgrounds. Weights have been developed to adjust for the oversampling of minority and low-income respondents. These weights were used in calculating the statistics reported in this chapter.

2. The current sample of children of NLSY participants is primarily a sample of children born to teenaged and young-adult childbearers. This is an educationally and economically disadvantaged group whose scores on cognitive tests and behavioral scales tend to fall below national norms established on more representative samples of the U.S. population.

REFERENCES

Angel, R., & Worebey, J. L. (1988). Single motherhood and children's health. *Journal of Health and Social Behavior, 29*, 38–52.

Baker, P. C., & Mott, F. L. (1989). *A guide and resource document for the National Longitudinal Survey of Youth 1986 child data.* Columbus: Center for Human Resource Research, Ohio State University.

Bane, M. J., & Ellwood, D. T. (1986). Slipping into and out of poverty: The dynamics of spells. *Journal of Human Resources, 21*(1), 1–23.

Bradley, R. H., & Caldwell, B. M. (1981). The HOME inventory: A validation of the preschool scale for black children. *Child Development, 52*, 708–710.

Bradley, R. H., Caldwell, B. M., Rock, S. L., Ramey, C. T., Barnard, K. E., Gray, C., Hammond, M. A., Mitchell, S., Gottfried, A. W., Siegel, L., & Johnson, D. L. (1989). Home environment and cognitive development in the first 3 years of life: A collaborative study involving six sites and three ethnic groups in North America. *Developmental Psychology, 25*(2), 217–235.

Brooks-Gunn, J., & Furstenberg, F. F., Jr. (1986). The children of adolescent mothers: Physical, academic and psychological outcomes. *Developmental Review, 6*, 224–251.

Brooks-Gunn, J., & Furstenberg, F. F., Jr. (1989). Continuity and change in the context of poverty: Adolescent mothers and their children In J. J. Gallagher & C. T. Ramey (Eds.), *The malleability of children*. Baltimore, MD: Brookes.

Caldwell, B. M., & Bradley, R. (1984). *Home observation for measurement of the environment.* Little Rock: University of Arkansas Press.

Chase-Lansdale, P. L., Mott, F. L., Brooks-Gunn, J., & Phillips, D. A. (1991). Children of the National Longitudinal Survey of Youth: A unique research opportunity. *Developmental Psychology, 27*(6), 918–931.

Child Trends. (1991). Unpublished data from the National Survey of Children. Washington, DC.

Committee on Ways and Means, U.S. House of Representatives. (1991). *Overview of entitlement programs. 1991 green book.* Washington, DC: U.S. Government Printing Office.

Dawson, D. A. (1991). Family structure and children's health and well-being: Data from the 1988 National Health Interview Survey on Child Health. *Journal of Marriage and the Family, 53*, 573–584.

Downey, G., & Moen, P. (1987). Personal efficacy, income, and family transitions: A longitudinal study of women headed households. *Journal of Health and Social Behavior, 28*, 320–333.

Dubow, E. F., & Luster, T. (1990). Adjustment of children born to teenage mothers: The contribution of risk and protective factors. *Journal of Marriage and the Family, 52*, 393–404.

Duncan, G. J., Hill, M. S., & Hoffman, S. D. (1988). Welfare dependence within and across generations. *Science, 239*, 467–471.

Elliott, D. S., & Morse, B. J. (1989). Delinquency and drug use as risk factors in teenage sexual activity. *Youth and Society, 21*, 32–60.

Ellwood, D. (1986, January). *Targeting the would-be long-term recipient of AFDC: Who should be served?* Princeton, NJ: Mathematica Policy Research.

Elster, A. B., Ketterlinus, R., & Lamb, M. E. (1990). Association between parenthood and problem behavior in a national sample of adolescents. *Pediatrics, 85*(6), 1044–1050.

Furstenberg, F. F., Jr., Brooks-Gunn, J., & Morgan, S. P. (1987). *Adolescent mothers in later life.* Cambridge: Cambridge University Press.

Gueron, J., & Pauley, E. (1991). *From welfare to work.* New York: Russell Sage Foundation.

Hall, L. A., Williams, C. A., & Greenberg, R. S. (1985). Supports, stressors and depressive symptoms in low-income mothers of young children. *American Journal of Public Health, 75*, 518–522.

Hill, M. S., & Ponza, M. (1984). *Does welfare dependency beget dependency?* Ann Arbor: Institute for Social Research, University of Michigan.

Horowitz, F. D. (Ed.). (1989). Children and their development: Knowledge base, research agenda, and social policy application [Special issue]. *American Psychologist, 44*(2).

Jencks, C., & Edin, K. (1990). The real welfare problem. *The American Prospect, 1*, 31–50.

Manpower Demonstration Research Corporation. (1991). *JOBS evaluation baseline data collection activities: Supporting justification for OMB clearance.* Prepared for the Office of the Assistant Secretary for Planning and Evaluation and the Office of Family Assistance, Department of Health and Human Services. New York: Author.

McLoyd, V. C. (1990). The impact of economic hardship on black families and children: Psychological distress, parenting, and socioemotional development. *Child Development, 61*(2), 311–346.

Menaghan, E. G., & Parcel, T. L. (1991, May). Determining children's home environments: The impact of maternal characteristics and current occupational and family conditions. *Journal of Marriage and the Family, 53*, 417–431.

Moore, K. A. (1978). Teenage childbirth and welfare dependency. *Family Planning Perspectives, 10*(4), 233–237.

Moore, K. A., & Snyder, N. O. (1991, October). Cognitive attainment among firstborn children of adolescent mothers. *American Sociological Review, 56*, 612–624.

Moore, K. A., & Stief, T. (1991, March). *Attainment among youth from families that received welfare* [paper prepared under ASPE/DHHS Grant No. HD-21537–03, revised]. Washington, DC: Child Trends.

Morrison, D. R., Myers, D. E., & Winglee, M. (1990). *The effects of maternal work and child care during the first three years of life on children's cognitive abilities.* Paper presented at the meeting of the Population Association of America, Toronto, Canada.

Moynihan, D. P. (1990, November 25). The children of the state: Welfare reform, Congress and family responsibility. *Washington Post.*

National Center for Health Statistics. (1989). *Vital statistics of the United States, 1987, Vol. 1, Natality* (DHHS Publication No. [PHS] 89–1100). Washington, DC: U.S. Government Printing Office.

National Commission on Children. (1991). Unpublished data from the National Commission on Children's national survey of children and parents. Washington, DC.

Parcel, T. L., & Menaghan, E. G. (1989). *Child home environment as a mediating construct between SES and child outcomes.* Center for Human Resource Research Report, Ohio State University.

Polit, D. R., Kahn, J. R., Murray, C. A., & Smith, K. W. (1982). *Needs and characteristics of pregnant and parenting teens: The baseline report for Project Redirection* (MDRC Studies of Project Redirection rep.). New York: Manpower Demonstration Research Corporation.

Powell, D. R. (1989). *Families and early childhood programs.* Research Monographs of the National Association for the Education of Young Children, Vol. 3. Washington, DC: Center on Budget and Policy Priorities.

Quint, J. C., & Riccio, J. A. (1985). *The challenge of serving pregnant and parenting teens: Lessons from Project Redirection*. New York: Manpower Demonstration Research Corporation.

Rovner, J. (1988, October 8). Congress approves overhaul of welfare system. *Congressional Quarterly, Human Services*, pp. 2825–2831.

Scarr, S. (Ed.). (1979). Psychology and children: Current research and practice [Special issue] *American Psychologist, 34*(10).

Smith, S. (1991). Two-generation program models: A new intervention strategy. *Social Policy Report, 5*(1), Society for Research in Child Development.

Smith, S., Blank, S., & Bond, J. T. (1990). *One program, two generations: A report of the forum on children and the Family Support Act*. New York: Foundation for Child Development.

U.S. Department of Health and Human Services, Family Support Administration, Office of Family Assistance. (1990). *Characteristics and financial circumstances of AFDC recipients, FY 1988* (1990–722–285/20129). Washington, DC: U.S. Government Printing Office.

U.S. Department of Health and Human Services, Administration for Children and Families. (1993). Unpublished data on AFDC recipients.

Weeks, G. C., Gecas, V., Lidman, R. M., Seff, M., Stromsdorfer, E. W., & Tarnai, J. (1990). *Washington state's family income study: Results from the first year*. Washington State Institute for Public Policy.

West, J., & Brick, J. M. (1991). *The National Household Education Survey: A look at young children at risk*. Paper presented at the annual meeting of the American Statistical Association, Atlanta, GA.

Zill, N. (1990). *Behavior problems index based on parent report*. Washington, DC: Child Trends.

Zill, N., Moore, K., Nord, C. W., & Stief, T. (1991). *Welfare mothers as potential employees: A statistical profile based on national survey data*. Washington, DC: Child Trends.

Zill, N., & Schoenborn, C. A. (1990, November 16). *Health of our nation's children: Developmental, learning, and emotional problems, United States, 1988* (Advance Data from Vital and Health Statistics, 1990).

II. Maternal employment

3 Welfare-to-work through the eyes of children

Julie Boatright Wilson, David T. Ellwood, and Jeanne Brooks-Gunn

In a relatively few years, the nature of public debate regarding work, welfare, and children has undergone a profound shift. There has always been strong sentiment in some quarters that single parents on welfare ought to be encouraged and even required to work. But there was an equally strong belief that it was appropriate and often quite desirable for mothers, particularly mothers of preschoolers, to remain at home with their children, nurturing and protecting them. Women with young children certainly could choose to work, but if these women thought it was better to remain at home, then society was reluctant to interfere with that choice, even if it meant the family remained on welfare for a number of years. Today, both the rhetoric and policies have shifted, with an emphasis on participation in work or training activities for mothers with young children (see Chase-Lansdale & Vinovskis, this volume).

One of the striking features of the current debate, though, is how little attention has really been paid to children. It is often asserted that growing up in a home where no one works and the family is supported by welfare hurts children by distorting their values regarding work, independence, and even marriage. Little research on intergenerational transmission of values, expectations, and behavior exists (Furstenberg, Levine, & Brooks-Gunn, 1990). Policy concerns regarding children have focused instead on day care and child support (see Spencer, Blumenthal, & Richards, this volume; Cherlin, this volume; Furstenberg, this volume).

Inevitably, efforts to move AFDC recipients to economic self-sufficiency have an impact on children. If a woman is encouraged or forced to move into the labor force, the characteristics of her child's life and the nature and quality of parent–child interactions will be affected (Aber, Brooks-Gunn, & Maynard, 1995). Some of the impacts on children will result directly from support provided to them through child care and other social services (Maynard, 1995). But arguably a much larger influence will be the altered home environment as family relationships, level and type of stress, parental concepts of self, and household income all change. What goes on inside the family – how family members respond to changes in their relationships and lifestyles when the mother enters the labor force – has enormous significance for the success of the mother and the long-term well-being of the child.

The basic message of this chapter is a simple one: In our rush to increase the independence of mothers we have ignored some crucial questions about children and family. We lay out some of these questions and examine what we know about them already, and suggest strategies for gathering information to increase our understanding of the likely impacts of welfare reform on children.

Questions about work and welfare

About one in nine children resides in a family that received Aid to Families with Dependent Children (AFDC) in 1990 and 1991 (Zill, Moore, Smith, Stief, & Coiro, this volume). This figure underestimates the numbers of children who will live in a household that is dependent on AFDC for part of their family's income at some point during their childhood or adolescent years. Estimates from the Panel Study of Income Dynamics (PSID) suggest that by the time they are 15, about one in five of children born in the 1970s in the United States will have been in a family receiving welfare. The percentages are over double this rate for African-American children. That so many children at some point reside in families receiving welfare makes the lack of information on the effects on children of parental welfare receipt or parental moving between welfare and work, even more glaring.

Several questions about how parental work and welfare receipt affect children are important. These include: To what extent do a mother's long stays on welfare impede or alter her child's development? What aspects of the welfare system seem to cause the greatest harm to children? Are children from disadvantaged families better off or worse off when their mother works? More generally, what impact will our efforts to move women from welfare to work have on children? This chapter concentrates on the last question.

One strategy to pursue in examining the effects of work programs on children is to concentrate energy on collecting and designing measures of child development and parenting behavior that can be used as additional dependent variables in evaluations that involve parents. Yet a research strategy that only compares childhood outcomes for treatment and control groups would ignore the process by which children are reared and nurtured. When evaluating an employment or training program, if one looks at employment outcomes for mothers, the link between program and outcome is reasonably direct. But when one looks at the developmental outcomes (or, better yet, the outcomes later in life) for children of mothers in a work program, a crucial step is skipped. The effects on children depend on the ways in which the mother, the family, and child rearing are altered by the program. Moreover, many of the outcome variables one might select for young children are likely to relate quite directly to parent–child relationships. Research that addresses such issues is termed the two-generational approach (see Smith, this volume).

If we fail to understand how family functioning changes when mothers move from welfare to work, it is quite possible that vital information about the impact of our programs on children will be lost. Two mothers may react very differently when placed in a program, and their children could have widely divergent outcomes. A mother who feels the work program is legitimate and empowering may do a better job of child rearing. Another woman may feel even more harassed and isolated as a result of the new rules. Her resentment, stress, and reduced sense of personal control may translate into a worsened situation for the child. If we average these effects, we might not notice any change on children overall. If we understand the different intermediate effects on the family, however, we might not only better identify who gained and who lost from the program, but also be able to design programs that reinforce the good outcomes for children and inhibit the undesirable ones.

Another problem with ignoring family issues is that some serious deterrents to work are found within the family, rather than outside it. If children are acting out or doing badly in school, if a family is undergoing intense stress, or if illness has struck a family member, it may be difficult or impossible for a mother to work. Unless we look at families and children, we will never discover these problems and never design sensible and sensitive policies. In brief, not only the impact that welfare-to-work programs would have on children needs to be examined, but so do the ways in which they would affect parenting and family functioning. Because almost nothing is known about how work–welfare programs affect children and families, this chapter focuses on what aspects of family functioning should be examined and on what measures of parental outcomes and family functioning might be collected (see Brooks-Gunn, this volume, for a discussion of child outcomes).

Next, we address the actual process of child rearing and development in the context of transitions from welfare to work. Three questions are addressed: (1) Based on previous theoretical and empirical research, what important aspects of parenting, family life, and children's development are likely to be affected by transitions from welfare to work and by programs to promote this transition? (2) What specific effects might we expect? What (if anything) does existing empirical research tell us about the likely outcomes? (3) What reliable, easy-to-administer, and widely used measures or methods currently exist? Could these measures be incorporated into new or existing work–welfare evaluations to examine the impacts of work–welfare programs on children and families? In the final section we discuss possible research methods and designs that might be used in studying child and family issues.

The chapter itself offers few direct recommendations for policy. But we hope this review and results from new research work along the lines described here will help policy makers understand answers to such key questions as the following: What services do mothers and children need to ensure a productive rather than destructive transition from welfare to work? Do different types of families need different types of support services? How can we most productively distinguish among different types of families in order to target services? For how long do families need support services? Is there a logical sequence to the order in which services are provided and in which public support is removed? What are the child behaviors or other indicators that should be monitored in order to identify children at risk of very negative outcomes? Are there some mothers who should not be encouraged to move into the labor force? If so, which ones? Should some mothers be encouraged to wait until their youngest child is older than 3 before beginning the transition to work? Should mothers start working shortly after their children are born?

Effects of welfare receipt and movement off welfare on child outcome

Welfare receipt is associated with more negative outcomes in the middle childhood and adolescent years. Using the Panel Study of Income Dynamics (PSID), Haveman, Wolfe, and Spaulding (1991) report that welfare receipt increases the likelihood of high school dropout, even after controlling for income. In the Baltimore Study of Teenage Motherhood, welfare receipt during the preschool and childhood years was associated with high school dropout, grade failure, low literacy, early intercourse, and behavior problems (Furstenberg, Brooks-Gunn, & Morgan, 1987; Brooks-Gunn, Guo, & Furstenberg, 1993; Baydar, Brooks-Gunn, & Furstenberg, 1993). More important, going off welfare after the target child's preschool years affected the probability of grade failure by age 16. These findings were still significant after taking into account school readiness scores, which were lower for those children whose mothers were not on welfare then. In an analysis of the predictors of earlier and later grade failure, welfare receipt was associated strongly with later grade failure, suggesting that children who were doing well in early elementary school years (and had relatively positive school readiness scores at age 4 to 6) have difficulty continuing on a positive school course if their families are on welfare (Guo, Brooks-Gunn, & Harris, 1995). Regrettably, the Baltimore study did not have yearly measures of family income, so that direct comparisons with the findings from the PSID are not possible.

The effects of welfare receipt on children also has been examined by Zaslow, Moore, Morrison, and Coiro (1993). Their conceptual framework emphasized not only welfare status, but changes in status over a 2-year period (1986–88). They identify five groups of mothers, based on children who were aged 5 to 10 at the first assessment point: These groups were defined based on mothers' welfare status and family income at two points in time. The groups were (a) continuous welfare receipt, (b) entered welfare at second time point, (c) left welfare at second time point but remained poor, (d) left welfare at second time point but were not poor, and (e) not on welfare at either time point. Those mothers who remained on welfare or left welfare but remained poor had the least adequate home environments, and their children had the lowest achievement test scores and the highest behavior problem scores of the five groups. Regression analyses revealed that some of these differences were due to demographic variation among the groups (i.e., the differences were reduced when adding in maternal education and maternal cognitive ability as well as number of children, ethnicity, child care during the early years, and family income). However, these two groups still had lower child achievement scores than the never welfare group even after entering covariates. Going off welfare but remaining poor does not substantially alter children's well-being.

Two other groups are of interest: the mothers who entered welfare at the second time point and the mothers who had been on welfare but upon leaving, moved out of poverty. Children whose families entered welfare at the second time point also fared less well than children whose families were never poor or on welfare. The differences are not as large as those for the continuous welfare or left welfare but still poor groups. Entering the familial covariates above reduced the group differences, but did not eliminate them entirely. The mothers who left welfare *and* were no longer poor were faring much better than those mothers who left welfare but remained poor. These results suggest that moving out of poverty may have a significant impact on children (see also Smith & Brooks-Gunn, 1995).[1]

Effects on poor families of work and movement from welfare to work

Toby Herr, president of the highly acclaimed Project Match program that seeks to help single parents in the Cabrini-Green Housing Project in Chicago move from welfare to work, reports:

> When a welfare mother starts to work, she is often overwhelmed with the stress of new demands and unfamiliar surroundings. The fact that her natural support system is often not adequate to help her cope with these changes creates additional pressures. Also, it is not unusual for other family members to discourage those who are taking steps to better themselves, adding a psychological dimension to abandonment.

For the children, these changes are often traumatic and potentially harmful. Children of poor families are likely to suffer from inadequate child care arrangements because affordable, quality child care is so difficult to obtain. Also, the children of welfare-dependent mothers must adjust to more than the schedule changes that all children experience when their mothers return to work. Initially, the loss of welfare benefits creates a financial crisis that often means less money for medical care, after-school snacks, and new clothes. Many children complain that their mothers are less available to help with homework. We know that this initial transitional period may be difficult (Herr, Halpern, & Conrad, 1991).

These effects may be quite direct, operating through maternal employment, child care, and increased income. That is, poor children might be affected by separation from the mother and/or substitute child care. Effects also might be more indirect as well; movement from welfare to work affects mothers, who in turn might interact differently with their children, as has been found in two studies (Aber, Brooks-Gunn, & Maynard, 1995; Smith & Brooks-Gunn, 1995). Both direct and indirect effects of maternal employment will be discussed in this chapter (see also Smith, Brooks-Gunn, & Jackson, 1995).

Direct effects of maternal employment

A large literature has examined whether maternal work patterns influence children's achievement and performance. Much of the literature suggests that maternal employment per se does not seem to influence child development very much overall (for reviews, see Gottfried & Gottfried, 1988; Hayes, Palmer, & Zaslow, 1990).

However, maternal employment during a child's infancy may affect child outcomes during the preschool period. Findings from a national data set, the Children of the NLSY (Chase-Lansdale, Mott, Brooks-Gunn, & Phillips, 1991), suggest that children are likely to have somewhat lower scores on vocabulary tests and higher levels of behavior problems at 3 and 4 years if their mothers worked while they were infants (under 1 year of age; Desai et al., 1989; Baydar & Brooks-Gunn, 1991). Additionally, early process-oriented research on small select samples suggests that children whose mothers are employed in the first year of life might exhibit less secure attachments to their mothers than children whose mothers were not employed (Belsky, 1988). These findings have not been replicated across all studies, however (Clarke-Stewart, 1989, 1991).

Most of the observation work has focused on middle-class families with two parents for whom work participation is presumably more or less voluntary. It might be expected that maternal employment effects differ by income level, particularly if lower-income mothers work out of necessity rather than voluntarily and, if they have lower-quality child care or less continuous child care (Hofferth & Wissoker, 1992; Cherlin, this volume; Hofferth & Phillips, 1991). In the Children of the NLSY, though, maternal employment in the child's first 9 months of life was associated with slightly more negative child outcomes at ages 3 and 4 in both poor and nonpoor families alike while maternal employment in the 2nd and 3rd year of life had no effect on children in either poor or nonpoor families (Baydar & Brooks-Gunn, 1991). The examination of maternal employment effects by poverty status of the family is an improvement over previous work that did not consider income. However, the work of Baydar and Brooks-Gunn (1991) does not address directly how income and maternal employment might interact to influence children, nor how income might mediate the maternal employment effect via its influence on other factors such as life stress, social support, maternal mental health, and so forth. Furthermore, research has not considered how welfare receipt, or the move from welfare to work, impacts children and families via child care.

Whether living in a single-parent or two-parent household influences the effects of maternal employment upon children is not known. We know that residence in single-parent and stepparent households, as compared to intact two-parent households, is associated with decrements in child outcomes (Hetherington, 1993; Hetherington & Clingempeel, 1992; Booth & Dunn, 1994). These effects, particularly those for single-parent households, are in part accounted for by income differentials (Brooks-Gunn, this volume; McLanahan, Astone, & Marks, 1991; McLanahan & Sandefur, 1994; Thomson & McLanahan, 1993; Thomson, McLanahan, & Curtin, 1992). At the same time, two-parent households, especially intact two-parent households, may provide more supervision and monitoring of children (Hetherington & Jodl, 1994; Thomson et al., 1992). Maternal employment in single- and two-parent households may influence children differentially, especially because the parental time available to spend with children is restricted in families where the only parent works outside the home (Brooks-Gunn, this volume). Time-use studies are necessary, however, to understand how single parents make trade-offs between income and time (Lazear & Michael, 1988; Hill & Stafford, 1985).

It should be pointed out, however, that none of the maternal employment research has considered potential effects of entering the workplace as part of a JOBS program or other sanctioned programs. It is conceivable that the impact of maternal employment on children differs when mothers are required to work versus choose to work voluntarily (Aber et al., 1995; Smith et al., 1995).

Indirect effects of maternal employment

As Herr suggests, it is inevitable that movement from welfare to work will influence children. Children may suffer or benefit. Several aspects of parenting and family functioning might be influenced negatively or positively by the move from welfare to work. They include parental stress, maternal emotional health, maternal efficacy and self-esteem, parent–child behavior and the home environment, and social networks and social support.

Parental stress

Stress is a commonly used term that may be defined in different ways. In the context of this chapter, we are concerned with stress caused by major life events, day-to-day hassles, and the possible tensions arising from juggling work and family commitments (the latter stressor is often termed *role conflict*).

Stressful life events are more prevalent in families where the mother is a single parent, has little education, or is poor (Brooks-Gunn et al., 1995; Liaw & Brooks-Gunn, 1994; McCormick et al., 1987; McCormick, Brooks-Gunn, Shorter, Holmes, & Heagarty, 1989; Blechman, 1982; Herzog & Sudia, 1974; Weinraub & Wolf, 1983). These life events include being robbed, moving to a new apartment (or being evicted), having a relative or friend die, losing a job, being assaulted, or having a male partner move out. Children are affected by such events, directly as well as indirectly, through the mother's reaction to the event. For example, mothers who experience such stress might spend less time with the child, be more irritable, be less warm, provide less control, or become less organized with respect to the functioning of the household (Hetherington, 1993; Vaughn, Egeland, & Sroufe, 1979; Weinraub & Wolf, 1983).

Whether the move into the workforce would alter the number of stressful life events occurring is not clear. However, a move into the workforce might increase the number of day-to-day hassles the mother experiences, or at least heighten her perception of such hassles (Compas, 1987). We know of no literature that addresses this directly, but find it a plausible assumption.

Evidence suggests that poor mothers with high levels of stress and anxiety make greater demands on their children to take on household responsibilities (doing dishes, caring for siblings, helping with meals, etc.), are less likely to provide help

to their children in these activities, and place greater emphasis on socially appropriate behavior such as obedience. Much of the stress in the lives of poor women
"comes not from the necessity of adjusting to sporadic change, but from steady,
unchanging (or slowly changing) oppressive conditions which must be endured
daily" (Makosky, 1982, p. 36). In addition, mothers under stress may interact with
their children differently. One study reports that poor mothers under more stress
were more inconsistent in their followthrough with threatened punishment than
were poor mothers under less stress (Zelkowitz, 1982, p. 159; see also Brooks-
Gunn, Klebanov, Liaw, & Duncan, 1995). Longfellow, Zelkowitz, and Saunders
(1982) report in a study of poor mothers that "The highly stressed or depressed mother
is likely to behave in a way that is unresponsive, inattentive, and even hostile
toward her children, and her child's sense of security in their relationship is shaken"
(p. 173). The work of McLoyd and her colleagues (1992, 1994) and Conger,
Elder and his colleagues (1990) are paradigmatic of this approach.

Another unanswered question is how a mother's participation in the labor market
might influence her definition of stressful events or her ability to handle stress. If
her income increases faster than her expenses, some stress will be reduced. Likewise, if her sense of self-confidence or self-efficacy increases, some formerly
stress-producing situations may be redefined as no longer stressful and new methods
of coping may be developed. The overall impact may be a reduction in the mother's
perceived level of stress and an increase in her ability to parent effectively in the
long run. Thus, in measuring stress and coping skills, the ideal instrument is one
that can and would be administered longitudinally.

One form of stress that is very likely to increase when a mother moves from
welfare to work is that induced by role conflict. Every AFDC mother has multiple
roles, including those of parent, housekeeper, breadwinner, and client. Women
moving into the labor force are asked to assume a more active role as breadwinner
than that involved in collecting public assistance and to redefine their role as
primary caregiver. When the role of mother as worker is reinforced by family, peer
group, and community norms that value maternal employment and sanction nonmaternal caregiving, movement into the labor force is likely to be the least stressful
and to have the most positive outcomes for both mother and child.

However, many women may experience role conflict (Smith et al., 1995).
Women can simultaneously value both maternal and work roles, constantly feeling
caught in a damned-if-I-do, damned-if-I-don't conflict. Measuring role conflict may
be valuable for a number of reasons. First, it may help indicate where and why
parental stress is greatest when mandatory programs are introduced. Second, attitudes about parental roles might be an important predictor of who will succeed in
employment and training programs. A New York State study found strong variation
in attitudes regarding roles of parenting versus breadwinner among AFDC mothers
(New York State Department of Social Services, March 1991). These differences
may well be related to the likelihood that an employment or training experience was
successful.

The process by which role conflict influences parenting is not clear, but certainly guilt, anxiety, and the resulting stress will have an impact on parenting and a parent's relationship with a child. These responses are likely to be heightened if the work experience is not meaningful to the mother (although conflicts about the appropriateness of her role will undoubtedly influence her response to the job situation as well) or if the child care arrangements are perceived to be unsatisfactory.

Families where the working mother has relatively positive attitudes toward working, less maternal stress, and greater role satisfaction provide "more favorable family environments and children's development" (Gottfried & Gottfried, 1988, p. 278). Owen and Cox report that "one of the major theses since the earliest reviews of research on maternal employment . . . is that a mother's satisfaction with her role, whether employed or not, is more important to her child's outcome than her employment status *per se*" (1988, p. 88). Most research suggests that satisfaction as well as work status contribute to the well-being of children and families (Smith et al., 1995). A number of attempts have been made to measure attitudes toward work, receipt of welfare, and staying home with children (Goodwin, 1972, 1983; New York State Department of Social Services, March 1991), but no studies have measured perceived role conflict among welfare recipients.

Maternal emotional health

Mothers' emotional health is affected by poverty, as mothers who are poor or near poor are more likely to report elevated levels of depression and anxiety (Liaw & Brooks-Gunn, 1994; McLoyd, 1990; Belle, 1991; Brooks-Gunn, Klebanov, & Liaw, 1995).[2] Single mothers also may have poorer emotional health. Little is known about whether receipt of welfare or the move from welfare to work influences emotional health. Work could reduce depression or anxiety, or increase emotional problems if mothers have little time available for managing their households, interacting with their children, and maintaining social support networks. One study reports less depression in mothers who have left welfare than those who stay on or enter welfare (Smith & Brooks-Gunn, 1995).

A mother's emotional health has a significant influence on her interactions with children (Bakeman & Brown, 1980; Field, Dempsey, & Shuman, 1981; Rutter, 1989). Negative child outcomes, especially in the social and emotional domains, are associated with maternal depression across the child's life span. This is true for mothers with high depressive affect as well as for mothers with a clinical affective disorder (Field, 1987; Ferguson, Hons, Norwood, & Shannon, 1984, Downey & Coyne, 1990; Friedlander, Weiss, & Traylor, 1986; Hammen, 1993; Sameroff & Seifer, 1983; Sameroff, Seifer, Barocas, Zax, & Greenspan, 1987; Sameroff, Seifer, Baldwin, & Baldwin, 1993). In the case of mothers with high levels of depressive affect, the links with child behavior problems are not totally accounted for by the fact that mothers who exhibit depressed affect might perceive their children as exhibiting more problems, rather than their children really having more problems. Not only do depressed-affect mothers report that their children have more problems, but so do their teachers (see Richters & Pelligrini, 1989). Consequently, maternal emotional health could be an important determinant in how children of poor mothers fare when their mothers enter the workforce.

Maternal efficacy and self-esteem

One of the most common justifications given for instituting work programs is to increase the sense of efficacy and self-esteem of welfare recipients. Welfare is criticized as isolating and debilitating. It is said to humiliate, stigmatize, and encourage passive or even socially counterproductive behavior. A number of authors have applied expectancy models to welfare dependency, suggesting that repeated failures can lead to a diminished sense of control and even a kind of learned helplessness (see Kane, 1987; Ellwood, 1988). People lose the capacity to see existing opportunities and to regain control of their lives. The links between diminished sense of control and child rearing for women on welfare have not been so fully developed.

An important first question focuses on the association between a mother's sense of confidence and self-esteem and her child's well-being. Some sense of self-worth, ability to control one's environment, and capacity to achieve goals may be passed on directly to children. But indirect effects might exist as well. Women who feel they have little ability to control the world outside their household and who perceive life to be unrewarding and unpredictable may be likely to stress obedience than independence in their children.

Another question is what impact a mother's participation in the labor market actually has on her self-esteem or self-efficacy, and how any changes in self-esteem or self-efficacy will influence the child. Success in the labor market could influence a mother's self-esteem in two ways – directly through her evaluation that she is capable, and indirectly through the feedback she gets from the new set of actors in her life, her co-workers. Changes in a mother's self-esteem will be reflected in her behavior, including interactions with her children, and will influence the well-being of her children both directly through these interactions and indirectly in her ability to structure and in other ways influence their environment. For example, successful participation in the labor force may increase her willingness to deal with school personnel, to insist that they inform her of her child's progress or problems.

Over the long run the self-esteem of women who successfully make the transition to the labor force might become more positive, and this greater self-esteem will have a positive impact on their children. This premise also suggests, however, that failed attempts to enter the labor market will reinforce any negative self-images a woman has, which may in turn have an effect on her children.

Unfortunately both definition and measurement have proven quite difficult. We think of mothers with high self-esteem as having positive images of themselves –

viewing themselves as capable, in control of their lives, and valued by others. Those with diminished self-esteem hold negative views of themselves and their capabilities. Although the process by which a person's sense of self is developed is not completely understood, it seems that a person is both an observer and an object of her own observations, that she continually evaluates herself (the object) based on feedback from other individuals and from other environmental cues regarding her efficacy, and that she (the observer) cares about this evaluation.

Serious difficulties for research are posed by a focus on self-esteem. No consensus exists as to how to measure confidence or self-esteem. Moreover, if positive events improve esteem and negative ones diminish it, cause and effect are almost indistinguishable. More troubling still is the claim that self-esteem is a filter through which situations and feedback are evaluated. Thus, "although the idea of self is open to change and alteration, it appears to be relatively resistant to such changes. Once established, it apparently provides a sense of personal continuity over space and time, and is defended against alteration" (Coopersmith, 1967, p. 21).

Perhaps, unsurprisingly, existing empirical results are ambiguous and unstable (Ellwood, 1988). Evidence suggests that people who have less sense of control are somewhat less successful and at greater risk of poverty. Hill et al. (1985) and Andrisani (1978) report that various measures of personal efficacy and control are correlated with income in a predictable fashion. A greater fear of failure is associated with lower earnings. O'Neill, Douglas, Laurie, and Michael (1984) found a weak association between measures of personal efficacy and welfare durations. Goodwin (1983) also concluded that "high or low expectations to achieve economic independence lead to high or low levels of achieved independence" (p. 129.) Goodban (1985) reports that almost 60% of teenage mothers in New Haven, Connecticut, felt that the reasons they were on welfare were beyond their control.

Unfortunately, as Hill and others have pointed out, it is impossible to infer causality from such results. People who are less successful and who have failed more often probably really *do* have less control over their lives and *are* at greater risk failing. Hill et al. (1985) note that involuntary changes in life like loss of a job or a forced move are associated with a later fall in measures of personal efficacy (see also Schneiderman et al., 1989). Motivation and confidence seem to be more the result than the cause of success or failure (Goodwin, 1983; Schneiderman et al., 1989). In brief, the literature is inconclusive at best. The problem may simply be that self-esteem is difficult to measure.

Parent–child behavior and the home environment

Virtually every theory of child development emphasizes the need for some combination of frequent and ongoing adult–child interaction, a warm emotional climate, provision of stimulating experiences, the satisfaction of basic emotional and physical needs, supervision and monitoring, limit setting, and nonpunitive parenting styles. Family systems theory argues that families are systems and, like other systems, tend toward maintenance of patterns of interaction with one another and with people outside the immediate family. Thus, behavioral change on the part of any family member, even change for the better, alters the system, and family members have a tendency to react in ways that encourage the changed person to return to previous behavior. This model rejects the notion of unidirectional causality in favor of a view that the actions of one household member influence the behavior of others, which in turn affects the first member.

A mother's movement into the labor force, whether or not she is thereby able to leave public assistance completely, is likely to cause major dislocations in family relationships and patterns of interaction. All family members will be affected by this change. The impact of this change on the child may take many forms.

First, movement to employment reduces the amount of time a mother has available to spend with her child and may change the way she uses that available time. Time spent on the job, in training or school, commuting, and studying is time no longer available for being with children. In addition, children compete with the mother herself, relatives, and friends for the small amount of time remaining. For example, a mother who has always supervised her children's homework may now need to do her own homework, do laundry, or prepare meals during that time: Some of the time previously spent on children is now spent on general family matters or on herself.

Second, the distribution of responsibilities within the family will change as a mother increases the number of roles she plays. The extent to which she cedes responsibility for household matters by shifting them to her children, other household members, or other individuals will influence her children directly and indirectly through their relationships and dependence on a new set of individuals. And the child will have additional caretakers with whom to relate or will be more dependent on himself or herself for care (see Spencer et al., this volume). A number of family process instruments have been used in small studies. The most well-known are the Family Environment Scale (Moos, 1974) and the FACES (Olson, 1986).

Developmentalists also study how parents socialize their children and the emotional relationship between mother and child. As in family systems theory, emphasis is placed on multiple influences, bidirectional causality among members of the household, and cultural relativism. However, this field of research focuses greater attention on observing parent–child interaction. Often parents and children are placed in a series of situations where the researchers control the task to be accomplished and then monitor the behaviors of the parent and child. Most tasks that are chosen are ones experienced in the everyday lives of families. For example, when observing preschool children and their parents, the following situations are often constructed: free play, cleanup, problem solving, meal or snack time, story reading (Bornstein, in press; Maccoby & Martin, 1983). Different parental constructs are often coded for each situation (e.g., compliance on the child's part, and strategies for eliciting compliance on the parent's part, are particularly important in cleanup tasks). In addition, constructs often can be coded across situations (e.g., responsivity to the child's cues, harshness, positive affect, and warmth [Berlin et al., in press]).

Home observations of such situations are not often done in evaluations of early childhood or work-to-welfare programs. Several demonstration programs are piloting the feasibility of including such intensive videotaped sessions as part of program evaluations. Examples include the current home observations being conducted in conjunction with the New Chance and the Teenage Parent demonstration programs (Smith, this volume; Smith & Zaslow, in press; Aber et al., 1995).

Most of the research on family systems, parenting styles, parenting behavior, and parent–child interaction uses intensive observational techniques to describe some of the parenting constructs briefly described in this chapter (Darling & Steinberg, 1993; Maccoby & Martin, 1983; Brooks-Gunn & Chase-Lansdale, 1995; Bornstein, 1995). Given that intensive observation, videotaping, and fairly microanalytic coding systems are not possible in all studies of parenting in the context of welfare-to-work programs, several investigators have developed less intensive observation systems that concentrate on global behavior-rating systems, combination rating and interview systems, and developing interview systems for describing a number of parenting behaviors.[3] It is beyond the scope of this chapter to discuss all of these systems.

The measure that has been used in the most studies (virtually hundreds of studies) is the Home Observation for Measurement of the Environment (HOME; Bradley & Caldwell, 1984; Bradley et al., 1989, 1994; Sugland et al., in press; Klebanov, Brooks-Gunn, & Duncan, 1994). Infant, preschool, and elementary school forms are available. The constructs that are assessed include the physical environment, the provision of enriching and stimulating learning experiences, the warmth and engagement of the mother, and the punitiveness of the mother's disciplinary style.[4] The HOME has the advantage of having been used with different ethnic groups, in large nationally representative studies (i.e., Children of the NLSY; Chase-Lansdale, Mott, Brooks-Gunn, & Phillips, 1991), and in welfare-to-work demonstrations (Teenage Parent demonstration; Aber et al., 1995; JOBS evaluation; Moore, personal communication; Project Redirection; Polit, 1989).

The HOME has been criticized on a number of grounds. One of the most important concerns is that the HOME in part depends on income resources for the provision of books and toys (Smith et al., in press). Also, living arrangements may preclude some females from getting high scores (e.g., eating meals with both parents). However, the HOME has been used successfully with welfare samples (Polit, 1989; Aber et al., 1995).

The lack of stimulating materials in the home is associated with lower cognitive and school readiness abilities. The preschoolers' home environment as measured with the HOME is associated with language development, intellectual performance, and academic achievement, in both cross-sectional and longitudinal studies (Bakeman & Brown, 1980; Bee et al., 1982; Bradley & Caldwell, 1976, 1979, 1980; Bradley,

Caldwell, & Elardo, 1979; Ramey & Farran, 1981; Bradley et al., 1989, 1995; Brooks-Gunn, Duncan, Klebanov, & Sealand, 1993; Brooks-Gunn, et al., 1995; Klebanov et al., 1994). Less optimal physical environments and less warm mother–child interactions also are associated with child outcomes.

The HOME score has been shown to be a stronger predictor of children's cognitive development than of socioeconomic status (SES). Or, to put it slightly differently, when HOME has been controlled, some of the observed differences in measured cognitive development (i.e., IQ) between more and less economically disadvantaged children disappear (Brooks-Gunn, Klebanov, & Duncan, in press; Duncan et al., 1994; Goldstein, 1989). The HOME taps variability across social classes and perhaps, more important, within social classes.

Other interview measures are sometimes used to tap the provision of stimulating experiences. An example is the set of scales adopted by Klebanov, Brooks-Gunn, and McCormick (in press). Warmth is sometimes assessed by asking about specific behaviors (hugging, kissing, holding, praising) and punitiveness by asking about disciplinary practices (Giovannoni, 1971, 1989, 1992; Giovannoni & Becerra, 1979; Hetherington & Clingempeel, 1992; Strauss, 1990; Strauss & Gelles, 1986). Because most mothers know which behaviors are socially desirable, it is difficult to assess the validity of results from such interviews. Studies comparing maternal reports of warmth/affection and punitiveness/hostility, and actual observed behavior are needed.

In summary, it is clear that parenting behavior contributes to child outcome, although little is known about the parenting of mothers on welfare or mothers entering the workforce. Instruments are available, however, to assess the parenting behaviors of these women.

Social networks and social support

Social support might be defined as emotional or instrumental support provided to a woman by others. This support can be provided by friends or individuals previously unknown to her, such as child care providers or counselors. Social support can be instrumental in reducing stress and eliminating or redefining stressor situations (Goldberg & Easterbrooks, 1988). Often the amount of social support a woman has is equated with the size of her social network, but the two are not the same.

Members of social networks can provide support, but participation in a social network can be stress-inducing as well (Belle, 1982). Social networks take time to maintain and may entail expectations for certain behavior, including sharing resources. This is particularly true when members of the network demand more from the mother than she receives in return, create stressful situations, or disapprove of her behavior. Stack (1974) provides a now classic ethnography illustrating the complex sharing of economic as well as emotional resources among poor mothers, their kin, their fictive kin, and friends in a poor community. These informal arrangements help keep families afloat. At the same time, they also make it difficult for any individual family to alter its circumstances (see also Belle, 1982). This latter situation is particularly relevant to our discussion in cases where members of her social network do not approve of a mother working.

When a woman enters or prepares to enter the labor market, two changes will occur. First, her relationship with her current social network will change, particularly if she is able to spend less time with members of that network or is less able to provide the reciprocal support that will insure their continued willingness to support her. Second, her social network will be enlarged by the addition of new members from her job or services such as child care. How these changes affect her children will depend on whether or not they provide the support the mother needs to reduce her overall level of stress and whether or not they provide support for specific child-related stressors.

A mother's children also have a social support network of which the mother is a principal member. When a mother enters the labor market, her child's support network will change dramatically, particularly if the child participates in some form of child care arrangement outside the home. Child development theory suggests that regular and stable interaction with a small number of significant adults is essential for normal, healthy development particularly for young children (Clarke-Stewart, 1989). This suggests that shifting support networks (including child care), no matter how supportive, may have a negative impact on child well-being. On the other hand, a strong support network may be instrumental in helping the child adjust to spending less time with mother.

Organizations that seek to help single mothers achieve self-sufficiency often report that social supports are critical to the success of making the transition and to the well-being of the children during the transition period.

Yet, in spite of the generally acknowledged importance of social supports, Cleary (1988) reports that "there is a vigorous debate about what social support is . . . , how its effects are manifest, and how to measure it. As Cohen, Mermelstein, Kamarck, and Hoberman (1985) have observed, '"There are almost as many measures of social support as there are studies'" (p. 198). As a result, we cannot point to any standardized instruments that have been used on large samples by many different researchers. However, the dimensions tapped by the different measures used in smaller-scale studies are similar. Some of the dimensions thought to be important for mental and physical health include social isolation, density of social networks, physical proximity of important members of one's social network, social connectedness to organizations (church groups, clubs, volunteer organizations), and perceived support (Adler & Matthews, 1993; House et al., 1988: Cohen, 1988).

The theoretical and program literature strongly suggests that supports of various sorts can be critical for the well-being and success of both mother and child. For example, the type and amount of social support have been found to influence parenting behavior (Bradley, 1995; Elardo, Bradley, & Caldwell, 1975; Honig & Gardner, 1985). Informal social support and positive parenting are associated (Crnic, Greenberg, Ragozin, Robinson, & Basham, 1983; Crockenberg, 1901, Parke &

Anderson, 1986). Social support also may reduce the impact of stress upon the mother (Crockenberg, 1981).

Social support may be quite low in samples of poor mothers. For example, in the Central Harlem Study of Pregnancy and Postpartum Parental Behavior, prospective mothers were asked a series of questions regarding social support. Situations involving financial and material support, emotional support, and physical support were constructed, following Cohen and Lazarus (1978). One-third of the women had no one to whom they could turn in all six situations (McCormick et al., 1989).

How social support influences parenting behaviors in mothers on welfare has not been the topic of much study (Jackson, 1993). However, evidence from samples of teenage mothers suggests that social support does reduce stress and possibly enhances parenting behavior (Crockenberg, 1981; Brooks-Gunn & Chase Lansdale, 1995). Such findings suggest that poor women may have very limited social support networks. How the move into the workforce might affect such networks needs to be described.

Conclusions

Perhaps the single most valuable and important step in focusing more attention on children and families would be to begin collecting information routinely as part of welfare reform implementation and evaluation. Even if just a few variables were added to existing evaluations, beyond the traditional measures of work and welfare use by the mother, policy makers would have to begin thinking more about children.

If we are ever to understand the full ramifications of welfare policies on children and families, far more detailed and sophisticated methods may need to be employed than are reasonable to contemplate on a large scale. Thus, several are proposed: (1) encourage or require states to collect some information routinely on children as part of their own administration and evaluation of welfare programs; (2) encourage or require planned or existing evaluations of work–welfare programs to include a selected number of variables on children and families in the data collected and analyzed and encourage the inclusion of one or several experts in the planning and analysis; (3) conduct a series of special demonstrations/evaluations that look particularly closely at children and family issues; (4) increase the number of children and family variables available on current longitudinal databases (PSID[s], the Children of the NSLY, and SIPP), and, if possible, conduct new longitudinal studies of families on welfare, and perhaps of children generally (Brooks-Gunn, Brown, Duncan, Moore, 1994).

The careful and rigorous evaluations of some work–welfare programs using randomized control methods are believed to be critical in the adoption of current welfare reform. Yet, as we noted, children and family variables have not been included in such evaluations. In our opinion the issue is important enough and existing measures are good enough to justify the inclusion of additional variables in future and ongoing evaluations.

One feature of the most valuable evaluations was their reliance on relatively easily obtained information, often in machine-readable form. For example, data on earnings could be obtained from state UI files. Information on children cannot be obtained as easily; however information from schools and other programs may be collected, at least in some states, without too much difficulty. Moreover, with additional research money, the more detailed but potentially quite important information on parental stress, role conflicts, and social supports could be collected. And at least for a smaller group of participants, data on home environment with scales such as HOME could be added. We also think including some experts on child development and family functioning on the evaluation teams would be useful.

The advantages of collecting some data include the following. First, we suspect that families facing problems at home, in school, or with health are likely to have a far more difficult time moving off welfare. Parenting and child data would enhance understanding of the impediments to work and of the ways to overcome them. These variables could serve as additional independent explanatory variables, helping researchers predict who leaves and who does not. Second, they can also serve as dependent variables. One could look to see if children of mothers in work–welfare programs did better or worse in school and if those patterns changed over time. With more detailed information on parenting and family functioning, some developmental paths for mothers and families who go from welfare to work, enter a program, or lose a job could be described.

Of course, not all evaluations of these programs will use randomized controls. Yet many of the advantages of collecting parental and child data would accrue to any program with a longitudinal component. Simply tracing the fortunes of families and children over time and exploring the bidirectional links between families/ children and market work would illuminate relevant questions (e.g., what factors interfere with a mother moving from welfare to work? what impacts do such moves seem to have on children over time?; Smith & Brooks-Gunn, in press). Perhaps most important, the inclusion of information like this could expand the focus beyond the mother. Especially if powerful or important findings emerged, the next round of reforms might be informed by high-quality information on both mothers and children.

No one doubts that family is important or that movements on and off welfare are likely to have effects on children. Yet almost no attention has been paid to child and family issues in welfare reform. One might argue that the likely impacts are too small to worry about, or one might conclude that measures of child development or family functioning are too complex, unreliable, expensive, or hard to collect to be of much use in trying to determine these effects. Our admittedly limited review of the literature suggests the contrary. Children whose mothers are on welfare and are entering the workforce with limited job experience may be affected by their mother's decisions. If more effective and humane programs to encourage self-support are to be created, more needs to be known about the effects on children and the family. If we care about the long-term well-being of children, we need to know more about families and the pressures that voluntary or mandatory transitions from welfare to work bring.

NOTES

1. However, comparisons were not made among the initial welfare, move out of poverty, and the other two welfare groups in the regressions (all groups were compared to the never-on-welfare, never-poor group).

2. Excellent measures of emotional health exist. Most focus on depressive affect and, to a lesser extent, anxiety. The most well-known include the Center for Epidemiological Studies Depression Scale (CES-D; Radloff, 1977), which taps depression, somatization, and anxiety. The General Health Questionnaire (GHQ; Goldberg & Hillier, 1979) and the Psychiatric Institute – Depressive Mood Inventory (Kandel & Davies, 1986) are two other scales with good psychometric properties.

3. The Teenage Parent Demonstration Program is examining links between parenting constructs assessed in videotaped situations and parenting constructs assessed by global ratings of the home, interviews with the mother, and survey questioning of the mother. The purpose of this endeavor is to see in what ways the constructs assessed by a variety of techniques converge and diverge in a group of low-income mothers, all of whom are on welfare or are leaving welfare (Aber et al., 1995; Maynard, 1995).

4. The developers of the HOME identify more subscales; however, many of them are highly correlated. The four listed here are those that may be most conceptually distinct (Klebanov et al., 1994; Brooks-Gunn et al., 1995; Chase-Lansdale et al., 1991; Parcel & Menaghan, 1989).

REFERENCES

Aber, L., Brooks-Gunn, J., & Maynard, R. (1995). The effects of welfare reform on teenage parents and their children. *The future of children*.

Adler, N., Boyce, T., Chesney, M. A., Cohen, S., Folkman, S., Kahn, R. L., & Syme, S. L. (1994). Socioeconomic status and health: The challenge of the gradient. *American Psychologist, 49*(1), 15–24.

Andrisani, P. J. (1978). *Work attitudes and labor market experience.* New York: Praeger.

Andrisani, P. J. (1981). Reply to Duncan and Morgan, 1981. *Journal of Human Resources, 16*, 659–666.

Bakeman, R., & Brown, J. (1980). Early intervention: Consequence for social and mental development at three years. *Child Development, 51*, 437–447.

Baydar, N., & Brooks-Gunn, J. (1991). Effects of maternal employment and child-care arrangements in infancy on preschoolers' cognitive and behavioral outcomes: Evidence from the Children of the NLSY. *Developmental Psychology, 27*(6), 932–945.

Baydar, N., Brooks-Gunn, J., & Furstenberg, F. F., Jr. (1993). Early warning signs of functional illiteracy: Predictors in childhood and adolescence. *Child Development, 64*(3), 815, 829.

Bee, H. L., Barnard, K. E., Eyers, S. J., Gray, C. A., Hammond, M. A., Spietz, A. L., Snyder, C., & Clark, B. (1982). Prediction of IQ and language skill from perinatal status, child performance, family characteristics and mother-infant interaction. *Child Development, 53*(5), 1134–1156.

Belle, D. (1982). Social ties and social support. In D. Belle (Ed.), *Lives in stress: Women and depression* (pp. 133–144). Beverly Hills: Sage.

Belle, D. (1991). Poverty and women's mental health. *American Psychologist, 45*(3), 385–389.

Belsky, J. (1988). The "effects" of infant daycare reconsidered. *Early Childhood Research Quarterly, 3*, 235–272.

Benasich, A. A., & Brooks-Gunn, J. (in press). Enhancing maternal knowledge and child-rearing concepts: Results from an early intervention program. *Child Development*.

Berlin, L. J., Brooks-Gunn, J., Spiker, D., & Zaslow, M. J. (in press). Examining observational measures of emotional support and cognitive stimulation in black and white mothers of preschoolers. *Journal of Family Issues*.

Blechman, E. A. (1982). Are children with one parent at psychological risk? A methodological review. *Journal of Marriage and the Family*, 179–191.

Booth, A., & Dunn, J. (1994). *Step-parent families with children: Who benefits and who does not?* Hillsdale, NJ: Erlbaum.

Bornstein, M. (Ed.). (1995). *Handbook of Parenting*. Hillsdale, NJ: Erlbaum.

Bradley, R. H. (1995). Home environment and parenting. In M. Bornstein (Ed.), *Handbook of parenting*. Hillsdale, NJ: Erlbaum.

Bradley, R. H., & Caldwell, B. M. (1976). The relationship of infant's home environment to mental test performance at 54 months: A follow-up study. *Child Development, 47*, 1172–1174.

Bradley, R. H., & Caldwell, B. M. (1979). Home observation for measurement of the environment: A revision of the preschool scale. *American Journal of Mental Deficiency, 84*, 235–244.

Bradley, R. H., & Caldwell, B. M. (1980). The relation of the home environment, cognitive competence, and IQ among males and females. *Child Development, 51*, 1140–1148.

Bradley, R. H., & Caldwell, B. M. (1984). The HOME inventory and family depression. *Developmental Psychology, 38*, 315–320.

Bradley, R. H., Caldwell, B. M., & Elardo, R. (1979). Home environment and cognitive development in the first two years: A cross-lagged panel analysis. *Developmental Psychology, 15*, 246–250.

Bradley, R. H., Caldwell, B. M., Rock, S. L., Ramey, C. T., Barnard, K. E., Gray, C., Hammond, M. A., Mitchell, S., Gottfried, A. W., Sigel, L., & Johnson, D. L. (1989). Home environment and cognitive development in the first three years of life: A collaborative study involving six sites and three ethnic groups in North America. *Developmental Psychology, 25*(2), 217–235.

Bradley, R. H., Mundfrom, D. J., Whiteside, L., Casey, P. H., & Barrett, K. (1994). A factor analytic study of the infant-toddler and early childhood version of the HOME Inventory administered to white, black, and Hispanic American parents of children born preterm. *Child Development, 65*, 880–888.

Brooks-Gunn, J. (1994). Research on step-parenting families: Integrating discipline approaches and informing policy. In A. Booth & J. Dunn (Eds.), *Step-parent families with children: Who benefits and who does not?* (pp. 167–190). Hillsdale, NJ: Erlbaum.

Brooks-Gunn, J., Brown, B., Duncan, G. D., & Moore, K. A. (1994). *Child development in the context of family and community resources: An agenda for national data collections*. Paper for NAS Conference on "Integrating Federal Statistics on Children."

Brooks-Gunn, J., & Chase-Lansdale, P. L. (1995). Adolescent parents. In M. Bornstein (Ed.), *Handbook of Parenting*. Hillsdale, NJ: Erlbaum.

Brooks-Gunn, J., Duncan, G. J., Klebanov, P. K., & Sealand, N. (1993). Do neighborhoods influence child and adolescent behavior? *American Journal of Sociology, 99*(2), 353–395.

Brooks-Gunn, J., Guo, G., & Furstenberg, F. F., Jr. (1993). Who drops out of and who continues beyond high school?: A 20-year study of black youth. *Journal of Research on Adolescence, 3*(3), 271–294.

Brooks-Gunn, J., Klebanov, P. K., & Duncan, G. (in press). Ethnic differences in children's intelligence test scores: Role of economic deprivation, home environment, and maternal characteristics. *Child Development*.

Brooks-Gunn, J., Klebanov, P. K., & Liaw, F. (1995). The learning, physical, and emotional environment of the home in the context of poverty: The Infant Health and Development Program. *Children and Youth Services Review, 17*(2), 231–250.

Brooks-Gunn, J., Klebanov, P., Liaw, F. R., & Duncan, G. (1995). Toward an understanding of the effects of poverty upon children. In H. Fitzgerald, B. M. Lester, & B. Zuckerman (Eds.), *Children of poverty*. New York: Garland.

Brooks-Gunn, J., Phelps, E., & Elder, G. H. (1991). Studying lives through time: Secondary data analyses in developmental psychology. *Developmental Psychology, 27*(6), 899–910.

Chase-Lansdale, P. L., Mott, F. L., Brooks-Gunn, J., & Phillips, D. (1991). Children of the NLSY: A unique research opportunity. *Developmental Psychology, 27*(6), 918–931.

Clarke-Stewart, K. A. (1989). Infant day care: Maligned or malignant? *American Psychologist, 44*, 266–274.

Clarke-Stewart, K. A. (1991). A home is not a school: The effects of child care on children's development. *Journal of Social Issues, 47*(2), 105–123.

Cleary, P. D. (1988). Social support: Conceptualization and measurement. In H. B. Weiss & F. H. Jacobs (Eds.), *Evaluating family programs* (pp. 195–216). New York: Aldine de Gruyter.

Cohen, J. B., & Lazarus, R. S. (1978). *Social support questionnaire.* Berkeley: University of California Press.

Compas, B. E. (1987). Assessment of major and daily stressful events during adolescence: The Adolescent Perceived Events Scale. *Journal of Consulting and Clinical Psychology, 55*(4), 534–541.

Conger, R. D., Conger, K. J., & Elder, G. (in press). Family economic hardship and adolescent academic performance: Mediating and moderating processes. In G. Duncan & J. Brooks-Gunn (Eds.), *Consequences of growing up poor.* New York: Russell Sage Foundation Press.

Conger, R. D., Conger, K. J., Elder, G. H., Jr., Lorenz, F. O., Simons, R. L., & Whitbeck, L. B. (1992). A family process model of economic hardship and adjustment of early adolescent boys. *Child Development, 63*, 526–541.

Conger, R. D., Elder, G. H., Lorenz, F. O., Conger, K. J., Simons, R. L., Whitbeck, L. B., Huck, S., & Melby, J. N. (1990). Linking economic hardship to marital quality and instability. *Journal of Marriage and the Family, 52*, 643–656.

Coopersmith, S. (1967). *The antecedents of self-esteem.* San Francisco: W. H. Freeman.

Corcoran, M., Duncan, G., Gurin, G., & Gurin, P. (1985). Myth and reality: The causes and persistence of poverty. *Journal of Policy Analysis and Management, 4*, 516–536.

Crnic, K. A., Greenberg, M. T., Ragozin, A. S., Robinson, N. M., & Basham, R. B. (1983). Effects of stress and social support on mothers and premature and full-term infants. *Child Development, 54*, 209–217.

Crockenberg, S. G. (1981). Infant irritability, mother responsiveness, and social support influences on the security of infant-mother attachment. *Child Development, 52*, 857–865.

Darling, N., & Steinberg, L. (1993). Parenting style as context: An integrative model. *Psychological Bulletin, 113*, 487–496.

Desai, S., Chase-Lansdale, L., & Michael, R. T. (1989). Mother or market? Effects of maternal employment on cognitive development of 4-year-old children. *Demography, 26*(4), 545–561.

Downey, G., & Coyne, J. (1990). Children of depressed parents: An integrative review. *Psychological Bulletin, 108*, 50–76.

Duncan, G. J. (1991). The economic environment of childhood. In A. C. Huston (Ed.), *Children in poverty* (pp. 23–51). New York: Cambridge University Press.

Duncan, G. J., Klebanov, P. K., & Brooks-Gunn, J. (1994). Economic deprivation and early-childhood development. *Child Development, 65*(2), 296–318.

Duncan, G. J., & Morgan, J. (1981). Sense of efficacy and subsequent change in earnings – A replication. *Journal of Human Resources, 16*, 649–657.

Elardo, R., Bradley, R., & Caldwell, B. M. (1975). The relation of infants' home environments to mental test performance from six to thirty-six months: A longitudinal analysis. *Child Development, 46*, 71–76.

Ellwood, D. (1988). *Understanding dependency: Choices, confidence or culture.* Report prepared for the U.S. Department of Health and Human Services.

Ferguson, D. M., Hons, B. A., Norwood, L. J., & Shannon, F. T. (1984). Relations of family-life events, maternal depression, and child-rearing problems. *Pediatrics, 73*, 773–776.

Field, T. M. (1987). Affective and interactive disturbances in infants. In J. D. Osofsky (Ed.), *Handbook of infant development* (2nd ed.). New York: Wiley.

Field, T. M., Dempsey, J., & Shuman, H. (1981). Developmental follow up of pre and post-term infants. In S. Friedman & M. Sigman (Eds.), *Preterm birth and psychological development.* New York: Academic Press.

Friedlander, S., Weiss, D. S., & Traylor, J. (1986). Assessing the influence of maternal depression on the validity of the child behavior checklist. *Journal of Abnormal Child Psychology, 14*(1), 123–133.

Furstenberg, F. F., Jr., Brooks-Gunn, J., & Morgan, S. P. (1987). Adolescent mothers and their children in later life. *Family Perspectives, 19*(4), 142–151.

Furstenberg, F. F., Jr., Levine, J. A., & Brooks-Gunn, J. (1990). Daughters of teenage mothers: Patterns of early childbearing in two generations. *Family Planning Perspectives, 22*(2), 54–61.

Giovannoni, J. M. (1971). Parental mistreatment: Perpetrators and victims. *Journal of Marriage and the Family, 33*, 637–638.

Giovannoni, J. M. (1989). Definitional issues in child maltreatment. In D. Cicchetti & V. Carlson (Eds.), *Child maltreatment: Theory and research on the causes and consequences of child abuse and neglect.* Cambridge: Cambridge University Press.

Giovannoni, J. M. (1992). *Issues in the definition of child maltreatment.* Background paper prepared for the National Research Council's Panel on Research on Child Abuse and Neglect.

Giovannoni, J. M., & Becerra, R. M. (1979). *Defining child abuse.* New York: Free Press.

Goldberg, W. A., & Easterbrooks, M. A. (1988). Maternal employment when children are toddlers and kindergartners. In A. E. Gottfried & A. W. Gottfried (Eds.), *Maternal employment and children's development: Longitudinal research* (pp. 123–154). New York: Plenum.

Goldstein, N. (1989). *Explaining socioeconomic differences in children's cognitive test scores.* Weiner Center for Social Policy Working Paper, Kennedy School of Government, Harvard University.

Goodban, N. (1985). Psychological impact of being on welfare. *Social Service Review, 59*, 403–422.

Goodnow, J. J. (1984). Parents' ideas about parenting and development: A review of issues and recent work. In M. E. Lamb, A. L. Brown, & B. Rogoff (Eds.), *Advances in developmental psychology* (Vol. 3, pp. 193–242). Hillsdale, NJ: Erlbaum.

Goodwin, L. (1972). *Do the poor want to work?* New York: Vintage Books.

Goodwin, L. (1983). *Causes and cures for welfare.* Lexington, MA: Lexington Books.

Gottfried, A. E., & Gottfried, A. W. (1988). Maternal employment and children's development: An integration of longitudinal findings with implications for social policy. In A. W. Gottfried & A. E. Gottfried (Eds.), *Maternal employment and children's development: Longitudinal research* (pp. 269–287). New York: Plenum.

Guo, G., Brooks-Gun, J., & Harris, K. M. (1995). *Parental labor-force attachment and grade retention among urban black children.* Unpublished manuscript.

Hammen, C. (1993). Parent child relationships and depression. In C. Hammen (Ed.), *Depression runs in families: The social context of risk and resilience in children of depressed women.* New York: Springer-Verlag.

Haveman, R., Wolfe, B., & Spaulding J. (1991). Childhood events and circumstances influencing high school completion. *Demography, 28*(1), 133–157.

Hayes, C. D., Palmer, J. L., & Zaslow, M. J. (1990). *Who cares for America's children? Child care policy for the 1990s.* Washington, DC: National Academy Press.

Herr, T., Halpern, R., & Conrad, A. (1991). *Changing what counts: Re-thinking the journey out of welfare.* Evanston, IL: Center for Urban Affairs and Policy Research, Northwestern University.

Herzog, E., & Sudia, C. (1974). Children in fatherless families. In B. M. Caldwell and H. N. Riccuiti (Eds.), *Review of child development research.* Chicago: University of Chicago Press.

Hetherington, E. M. (1993). An overview of the Virginia longitudinal study of divorce and remarriage: A focus on early adolescence. *Journal of Family Psychology, 7*, 39–56.

Hetherington, E. M., & Clingempeel, W. G. (1992). Coping with marital transitions: A family systems perspective. *Monographs of the Society for Research in Child Development, 57*(2–3, Serial No. 227).

Hetherington, E. M., & Jodl, K. M. (1994). Stepfamilies as settings for child development. In A. Booth & J. Dunn (Eds.), *Step-parent families with children: Who benefits and who does not?* (pp. 55–80). Hillsdale, NJ: Erlbaum.

Hill, C. R., & Stafford, F. P. (1985). Parental care of children: Time diary estimates of quantity, predictability and variety. In F. T. Juster & F. P. Stafford (Eds.), *Time, goods, and well-being* (pp. 415–437). Ann Arbor: Survey Research Center, Institute for Social Research, University of Michigan.

Hill, M., Augustyniak, S., Duncan, G., Gurin, G., Gurin, P., Liker, J., Morgan, J., & Ponza, M. (1985). *Motivation and economic mobility of the poor.* Ann Arbor: Institute for Social Research, University of Michigan.

Hofferth, S., & Phillips, D. (1991). Child care policy research. *Journal of Social Issues, 47,* 1–13.

Hofferth, S., & Wissoker, D. (1992). Price, quality, and income in child care choice. *Journal of Human Resources, Special Issues on Child Care, 27*(1), 70–111.

Honig, A. S., & Gardner, C. G. (1985, April). *Overwhelmed mothers of toddlers in immigrant families: Stress factors.* Paper presented at the biennial meeting of the Society for Research in Child Development, Toronto, Ontario, Canada.

House, J. S., Landis, K. R., & Umberson, D. (1988). Social relationships and health, *Science, 241,* 540–545.

Huston, A. C., Garcia-Coll, C., & McLoyd, V. C. (Eds.). (1994). *Child Development* [special issue on *Children and Poverty*], *65*(2).

Jackson, A. P. (1993). Black single working mothers in poverty: Preferences for employment, well-being, and perceptions of school aged children. *Social Work, 38,* 26–34.

Kane, T. (1987). Giving back control: Long-term poverty and motivation. *Social Service Review, 61,* 405–419.

Klebanov, P. K., Brooks-Gunn, J., & Duncan, G. J. (1994). Does neighborhood and family poverty affect mothers' parenting, mental health, and social support? *Journal of Marriage and the Family, 56*(2), 441–455.

Klebanov, P. K., Brooks-Gunn, J., Hofferth, S., & Duncan, G. J. (1995). *The role of social capital in young children's development.* Paper presented at a symposium on social capital at the biennial meeting of the Society for Research in Child Development, Indianapolis, March 30–April 2, 1995.

Klebanov, P. K., Brooks-Gunn, J., & McCormick, M. C. (1995). Early childhood intervention and maternal social and emotional health: The infant health and development program. Unpublished manuscript.

Klebanov, P. K., Brooks-Gunn, J., & McCormick, M. C. (in press). Early childhood intervention and maternal social and emotional health: The IHDP. *American Journal of Public Health.*

Lazear, E. P., & Michael, R. T. (1988). *Allocation of income within the household.* Chicago: University of Chicago Press.

Liaw, F. R., & Brooks-Gunn, J. (1994). Cumulative familial risk factors and low-birthweight children's cognitive and behavioral development. *Journal of Clinical Child Psychiatry, 23*(4), 360–372.

Longfellow, C., Zelkowitz, P., & Saunders, P. (1982). The quality of mother–child relationships. In D. Belle (Ed.), *Lives in stress: Women and depression* (pp. 163–176). Beverly Hills: Sage.

Maccoby, E. E., & Martin, J. A. (1983). Socialization in the context of the family: Parent–child interaction. In P. H. Mussen & E. M. Hetherington (Eds.), *Handbook of child psychology: Socialization, personality, and social development* (pp. 1–102). New York: Wiley.

Makosky, V. P. (1982). Sources of stress: Events or conditions? In D. Belle (Ed.), *Lives in stress: Women and depression* (pp. 35–53). Beverly Hills: Sage.

Maynard, R. (1995). Teenage childbearing and welfare reform: Lessons from a decade of demonstration and evaluation research. *Children and Youth Services Review* [special issue: Child poverty, public policies, and welfare reform], *17*(1), 309–332.

McCormick, M. C., Brooks-Gunn, J., Shorter, T., Holmes, J. H., & Heagarty, M. C. (1989). Factors associated with maternal rating of infant health in Central Harlem. *Journal of Developmental and Behavioral Pediatrics, 10*(3), 139–144.

McCormick, M. C., Brooks-Gunn, J., Shorter, T., Wallace, C. Y., Holmes, J. H., & Heagarty, M. C. (1987). The planning of pregnancy among low-income women in Central Harlem. *American Journal of Obstetrics and Gynecology, 156*(1), 145–149.

McCormick, M. C., Brooks-Gunn, J., Workman-Daniels, K., Turner, J., & Peckham, G. (1992). The health and developmental status of very low birth weight children at school age. *Journal of the American Medical Association, 267*(16), 2204–2208.

McCormick, M. C., Workman-Daniels, K., Brooks-Gunn, J., & Peckham, G. J. (1993). When you're only a phone call away: A comparison of the information in telephone and face-to face interviews. *Journal of Developmental and Behavioral Pediatrics, 14*(4), 250–255.

McLanahan, S., Astone, N. M., & Marks, N. F. (1991). The role of mother-only families in reducing poverty. In A. C. Huston (Ed.), *Children in poverty: Child development and public policy* (pp. 51–78). New York: Cambridge University Press

McLanahan, S., Astone, N. W., & Marks, N. F. (1991). The role of mother-only families in reducing poverty. In A. C. Huston (Ed.), *Children in poverty: Child development and public policy.* (pp. 57–78). Cambridge, MA: Cambridge University Press.

McLanahan, S., & Sandefur, G. D. (1994). *Growing up with a single parent: What hurts, what helps?* Cambridge, MA: Harvard University Press.

McLoyd, V. C., Jayaratne, T. E., Ceballo, R., & Rorguez, J. (1994). Unemployment and work interruption among African American single mothers: Effects on parenting and adolescent socioemotional functioning. *Child Development, 65*, 562–589.

McLoyd, V. C., & Wilson, L. (1992). Telling them like it is: The role of economic and environmental factors in single mothers' discussions with their children. *American Journal of Community Psychology, 20*(4), 419–442.

McLoyd, V. C. (1990). The impact of economic hardship on black families and development. *Child Development, 61*, 311–346.

Moos, R. H. (1974). *Family environment scale, form R.* Palo Alto: Consulting Psychologists Press.

New York State Department of Social Services. (1987). Unpublished data from a study conducted by the Office of Program Planning, Analysis, and Development, October 1987.

Olson, D. H. (1986). Circumplex model VII: Validation studies and FACES III. *Family Process, 25*, 337–351.

O'Neill, J., Douglas, W., Laurie, B., & Michael, H. (1984). *An analysis of time on welfare.* Report to the U.S. Department of Health and Human Services. Washington, DC: Urban Institute.

Owen, M. T., Cox, M. J. (1988). Maternal employment and the transition to employment. In A. E. Gottfried & A. W. Gottfried (Eds.), *Maternal employment and children's development: Longitudinal research* (pp. 85–118). New York: Plenum.

Parcel, T. L., & Menaghan, E. G. (1990). Maternal working conditions and children's verbal facility: Studying the intergenerational transmission of inequality from mothers to young children. *Social Psychology Quarterly, 53*(2), 132–147.

Parke, R. D., & Anderson, E. (1986). Fathers and their at-risk infants: Conceptual and empirical analyses. In P. Berman & F. Peterson (Eds.), *Men's transition to parenthood: Longitudinal studies of early family experience.* Hillsdale, NJ: Erlbaum.

Polit, D. F. (1989). Effects of a comprehensive program for teenage parents: Five years after Project Redirection. *Family Planning Perspectives, 21*(4), 164–169.

Ramey, C. T., & Farran, D. C. (1981). The functional concern of mothers for their infants. *Infant Mental Health Journal, 2*, 48–55.

Richters, J., & Pellegrini, D. (1989). Depressed mothers' judgments about their children: An examination of the depressed-distortion hypothesis. *Child Development, 60*, 1068–1075.

Rutter, M. (1989). Isle of Wight revisited: Twenty five years of child psychiataric epidemiology. *Journal of the American Academy of Child and Adolescent Psychiatry, 28*(5), 633–653.

Sameroff, A. J., Seifer, R., Baldwin, A., & Baldwin, C. (1993). Stability of intelligence from preschool to adolescence: The influence of social and family risk factors. *Child Development, 64*, 80–97.

Sameroff, A. J., Seifer, R., Barocas, R., Zax, M., & Greenspan, S. (1987). Intelligence quotient scores of 4-year-old children: Social and environmental risk factors. *Pediatrics, 79*, 343–350.

Schneiderman, L., Furman, W. M., & Weber, J. (1989). Self-esteem and chronic welfare dependency. In A. Mecca, N. Smelser, & J. Vasconcellos (Eds.), *The social importance of self-esteem* (pp. 200–244). Berkeley: University of California Press.

Smith, J. R., & Brooks-Gunn, J. (1995). Developmental effects of natural transitions in welfare receipt. Paper presented at the Workshop on Welfare and Child Development, National Academy of Sciences, Washington, DC, December 5–6, 1994.

Smith, J. R., Brooks-Gunn, J., & Jackson, A. (1995). Maternal employment. In R. Hauser (Ed.), *Social indicators of child and family well-being.* New York: Russell Sage Foundation Press.

Smith, J. R., Brooks-Gunn, J., & Klebanov, P. K. (in press). Consequences of growing up poor for young children. In G. Duncan & J. Brooks-Gunn (Eds.), *Consequences of growing up poor*. New York: Russell Sage Foundation Press.

Smith, S., & Zaslow, M. (in press). Two-generation programs research and theory. In S. Smith (Ed.), *Two-generation programs for families in poverty*. Norwood, NJ: Ablex

Smith, S. (Ed.). (in press). *Two-generation programs for families in poverty*. Norwood, NJ: Ablex.

Stack, C. B. (1974). *All our kin: Strategies for survival in a black urban community*. New York: Harper & Row.

Strauss, M. (1990). The Conflict Tactics Scales and its critics: An evaluation and new data on validity and reliability. In M. A. Strauss & R. J. Gelles (Eds.), *Physical violence in American families: Risk factors and adaptations to violence in 8145 families*. New Brunswick, NJ: Transaction Publications.

Strauss, M., & Gelles, R. J. (1986). Societal change in family violence from 1975 to 1985 as revealed by two national surveys. *Journal of Marriage and the Family, 48*, 465–479.

Sugland, B. W., Zaslow, M., Smith, J. R., Brooks-Gunn, J., Coates, D., Blumenthal, C., Moore, K. A., Griffin, T., & Bradley, R. (in press). The Early Childhood HOME inventory and HOME-Short Form in differing racial/ethnic groups: Are there differences in underlying structure, internal consistency of subscales, and patterns of prediction? *Journal of Family Issues*.

Thomson, E., & McLanahan, S. (1993, August). *Family structure and child well-being: Economic resource versus parental behavior*. Paper presented at the annual meeting of the American Sociological Association, Washington, DC.

Thomson, E., McLanahan, S., & Curtin, R. B. (1992). Family structure, gender, and parental socialization. *Journal of Marriage and Family, 54*, 368–378.

Vaughn, B., Egeland, B., & Sroufe, L. A. (1979). Individual differences in infant-mother attachment at twelve and eighteen months: Stability and change in families under stress. *Child Development, 50*, 971–975.

Walker, D. K., & Crocker, R. W. (1988). Measuring family systems outcomes. In H. B. Weiss & F. H. Jacobs (Eds.), *Evaluating family programs* (pp. 153–176). New York: Aldine de Gruyter.

Weinraub, M., & Wolf, B. (1983). Effects of stress and social support on mother-child interaction in single- and two-parent families. *Child Development, 54*, 1297–1311.

Zaslow, M. J., Moore, K. A., Morrison, D. R., & Coiro, M. J. (1993). *The Family Support Act and children: Potential pathways of influence*. Paper presented at the National Health and Policy Forum meeting, Washington, DC.

Zelkowitz, P. (1982). Parenting philosophies and practices. In D. Belle (Ed.), *Lives in stress: Women and depression* (pp. 154–162). Beverly Hills: Sage.

4 Strategies for altering the outcomes of poor children and their families

Jeanne Brooks-Gunn

The plight of poor children, especially those in single-parent families, in America is evident (Baldwin & Cain, 1980; Brooks-Gunn & Furstenberg, 1986; Bumpass, 1984; Ellwood, 1988; McLanahan, 1985; McLanahan & Sandefur, 1994). The well-being of children is drastically reduced by being reared in poverty. Many factors seem to be associated with decreases in social, cognitive, emotional, and physical well-being: economic disadvantage, poor schooling, residence in areas of highly concentrated poverty, young maternal age, single parenthood, low maternal education, and unemployment.

This chapter has three goals: (1) to consider how poverty and child well-being are conceptualized; (2) to examine the ways in which poverty might influence child well-being; and (3) to look at three types of action-oriented research and demonstration programs for poor children and their families. Policy and program designers all want to enhance the likelihood that poor individuals maximize their potential. The ways in which this general good is achieved differ, however. Different disciplines, specifically economic, health, educational, and developmental psychology, have championed various approaches. The three most common approaches have been home-visiting programs, center-based schooling or what is commonly known as early childhood intervention, and parental work and education training programs. Each has had a different goal. However, all three tend to target the mother and child: Other family members, such as the father and other adults involved in the young child's care, are noticeably absent from most program initiatives (Brooks-Gunn & Chase-Lansdale, 1995; Chase-Lansdale, Brooks-Gunn, & Paikoff, 1991; Fursten-berg, this volume; Cherlin, this volume; Garfinkel & McLanahan, this volume).

- The home-visiting programs tend to focus on improving parenting skills, and, in some cases, enhancing health and safety (given strong links with public health

The research reported in this chapter was supported by grants from the National Institutes for Child Health and Development, the Foundation for Child Development, the Robert Wood Johnson Foundation, the NICHD Research Network on Child and Family Well-Being, the Pew Charitable Trust, and the March of Dimes Birth Defects Foundation. I would like to thank the Educational Testing Service and the staff at the Center for Young Children and Families of Teachers College of Columbia University for their support.

nursing). Many provide social service referrals and general social support (given strong links with welfare and social work). Some programs also work directly with the child.

- The center-based education programs tend to focus on providing the child with a variety of experiences to enhance social, emotional, cognitive, and linguistic skills. Additionally, almost all such programs involve the parent, because sustained effects of early education cannot be maintained without family involvement. Involvement, however, varies from parent support groups, to one-on-one work with the parent, to parenting classes, to sporadic parent meetings.
- The work and educational training programs focus on the mother. They provide a variety of experiences to help mothers complete high school, obtain additional vocational or college-level training, acquire skills necessary for entrance into the workforce (or a move up from entry-level jobs), and land jobs.

Please notice what is missing in these thumbnail sketches. These three program types are described as separate entities. Current programs are attempting to integrate aspects of these approaches. One focus is what has been called 2-generation programs, as they target mothers *and* children (Smith, this volume). Another focus is on the integration of services into communities and the alteration of funding streams at the state level (Brooks-Gunn, Duncan, & Aber, in press).

Poverty and children

Measuring poverty

The official poverty level is established by the U.S. government. It is based on the estimated cost of an economy food budget or shopping cart of food, multiplied by 3. The assumption is that food costs comprise one-third of a family's budget. The poverty level is adjusted for family size, the age of the head of the household, and the number of children under age 18. Annual adjustments to the poverty index are made for the cost of living based on the Consumer Price Index (Citro & Michael, 1995).

The official poverty level only includes cash income. It excludes in-kind transfers such as medicial care and food stamps, which may result in an overestimation of poor families. However, the official poverty level may underestimate *severity* of poverty. Variations below the poverty line are extreme. The poverty gap is considered as total dollar amount by which incomes of the poor fall below the poverty level (Duncan, 1991).

Whether poverty is defined at the threshold, at 150% or 185% above the threshold, or as a continuum, most developmental research has not incorporated any measure of economic deprivation. Parental incomes are neither reported reliably by adolescents nor recalled reliably in retrospective studies. With a few notable exceptions (e.g., Children of the National Longitudinal Study of Youth; Chase-Lansdale, Mott, Brooks-Gunn, & Phillips, 1991), developmental studies do not include a measure of family income, or do not obtain more than a single response from parents (Duncan, Brooks-Gunn, & Klebanov, 1994; Hauser, in press). Consequently, research linking poverty with developmental outcomes has assessed socioeconomic status or social class, which is a combination of parental schooling and occupational attainments (Featherman & Hauser, 1987; Parker, Greer, & Zuckerman, 1988). Another approach has been to focus on events such as unemployment (McLoyd, 1990; Elder, 1974), income loss (Conger et al., 1992), and female headship (McLanahan & Sandefur, 1994; Sandefur, McLanahan, & Wojtkiewicz, 1992), which are associated with the onset of economic deprivation.

Income and social class are not the same. Family incomes are quite volatile (Duncan, Hill, & Hoffman, 1988; Duncan, Smeeding, & Rodgers, 1991). Consequently, only modest associations are found between economic deprivation and typical measures of socioeconomic background. The effects on child development of income poverty and those of its correlated events and conditions may be separated statistically (Duncan & Brooks-Gunn, in press; Duncan et al., 1994; Hill & Duncan, 1987; Liaw & Brooks-Gunn, 1994; Sameroff, Seifer, Barocas, Zax, & Greenspan, 1987; Sewell & Hauser, 1975).

Another problem with the literature is that poverty also has a temporal dimension, which is typically not considered. While much poverty is short-term, a surprising amount (especially among black children) lasts for most of childhood (Duncan, 1991; Duncan & Rodgers, 1991). Questions need to be asked about the influence of both the duration and the timing of poverty upon children's well-being (Baydar, Brooks-Gunn, & Furstenberg, 1993; Brooks-Gunn, Guo, & Furstenberg, 1993; Corcoran, Gordon, Laren, & Solon, 1992; Duncan & Brooks-Gunn, in press; Furstenberg, Brooks-Gunn, & Morgan, 1987; Haveman, Wolfe, & Spaulding, 1991).

The number of poor children

Using the U.S. Census Bureau's definition of poverty, in the early 1990s, 21% of American children – over 13 million in all – lived in families in which total income failed to exceed even the spartan thresholds used to define poverty. The percentage of poor is even higher for children under 6 – 23% or 5 million children. Poverty rates are much higher for minority children. Fully one-half of African-American and 40% of Hispanic-American children under 6 were poor in 1990, compared to 14% of white children.

Poverty is associated with single parenthood. Almost 60% of children under age 6 in mother-only single-parent families were poor in 1990. Increases in the divorce rate and in the proportions of mothers having children and not marrying over the past 25 years has resulted in a large number of single-parent households. This is especially true for young mothers – 90% of African-American and 60% of white teenage mothers are not married at the time of their child's birth. Percentages are rising for mothers in their early 20s as well, suggesting that the percentages of single mothers will increase throughout the 1990s. However, single-parent households constitute only 22% of households for children under 6, and two out of five poor children live in married-couple households (Hernandez, 1993; McLanahan & Sandefur, 1994).

While full-time employment of a parent reduces the likelihood of living in poverty, it does not guarantee it. Minimum-wage earnings for a full-time, full-year worker will bring in 50% less than the poverty line for a family of four.

Well-being and children

Measuring child well-being is a central goal for evaluating the impact of poverty on children. We are interested in examining how well children, adolescents, and their parents are doing, and how this changes over time. Many different approaches have been taken, each of which has some value depending on the level of analysis, the age range of interest, the social science discipline undertaking a study, and the context in which individuals are studied. Here, well-being is defined in terms of social, physical, cognitive/academic, and mental/emotional health and development (Brooks-Gunn, 1990).

Cognitive and academic well-being

Cognitive well-being may be conceived of broadly to include intellectual functioning, language skills, academic performance/achievement tests, literacy, and school functioning. Alternatively, each of these may be considered domains in and of themselves (and a great deal of research is done on each separately).

School functioning may be measured by grade failure, placement in remedial classes, placement in gifted classes, school dropout, GPA, high school graduation, GED, or on-time or off-time high school graduation. A problem with all of these measures is that they are influenced by the composition of the school and the neighborhood; teachers, peers, and the administrative structure (and resources provided) differ as a function of race, class, and concentration of poverty (see Alexander & Entwisle [1988] for examples of how first-graders of the same ability are treated differently as a function of race and class; see data on placement in Learning Disabled versus Educable Mentally Retarded as a function of race and class when IQ scores are held constant [Mercer, 1973]).

Achievement tests also provide a window on how well children are doing. They are related to the school functioning factors, and some decisions (e.g., repetition of grade) are in part contingent on such tests (although, at least in inner-city schools, perhaps less than one would think; see recent Baltimore study results on predictors of early and late grade failure; Brooks-Gunn et al., 1993; Guo, Brooks-Gunn, & Harris, submitted).

Literacy tests have become increasingly popular, especially with the movements in some states to require a minimum level of literacy at high school or eighth-grade graduation. Cross-sectional national data are available from Educational Testing Service for the National Assessment of Educational Progress (NAEP); tests have been developed and norms established for nine-, 13-, and 17-year-olds, as well as for young adults. Work is just beginning that looks at ethnic and class differences, predictors of literacy, and consequences of literacy (Miller, 1988). For example, in the Baltimore study, a form of the NAEP Young Adult test was given to 20-year-olds followed from birth; preliminary analyses suggest that many high school graduates are semiliterate (Baydar et al., 1993).

Intelligence tests examine how well individuals do relative to their age-mates on a variety of cognitive tasks. Moderately stable from age 5 and 6 onwards (and even from age 3), they are associated with all sorts of family and environmental variables as well as school achievement indices (Angoff, 1988; Smith et al., in press). However, scores are not as "fixed" as it is often believed (e.g., see size of across-time correlation coefficients and heritability estimates). Thus, change in environment (family, school, neighborhood) may alter them (Liaw & Brooks-Gunn, 1993; Brooks-Gunn, in press). They are not culture-free, and some objections have been raised as to their meaning vis-à-vis later adult success.

Health well-being

Health includes such factors as activities of daily living (limitations due to physical, cognitive, or mental health), perceived health, physical growth (low birth weight, failure to thrive, obesity), and existence of serious or chronic illnesses/conditions (Egbuonu & Starfield, 1982; McCormick, 1989, 1991; McCormick, Shaprio, & Starfield, 1985). Indeed, health is no longer considered the absence of disease or merely physical health, but social and mental health as well (Haggerty, Roghmann, & Pless, 1975; McCormick & Brooks-Gunn, 1989). Thus, pediatricians and epidemiologists define health very broadly, would concur with the multifaceted view of well-being presented here, and would include more than physical measures in their studies of poor children.

The relatively poorer health of disadvantaged children may contribute to the lower cognitive abilities of this group. For example, low birth weight, which is associated with diminished cognitive outcomes broadly defined, is more likely to occur in disadvantaged groups and minority groups (who are more likely to be disadvantaged). These same factors are associated with cognitive dysfunction, putting these children at double jeopardy (Parker et al., 1988; Klerman, 1991; also, see review by McCormick & Brooks-Gunn, 1989). Physical health problems may be more of a burden on the child and the family in poor neighborhoods, given the scarcity of health and educational resources, discrimination, distrust of the medical community, and different informational sources about health and illness (McCormick & Brooks-Gunn, 1989).

Emotional well-being and behavioral competence

Emotional functioning, emotional self-regulation, psychopathology, behavior problems, and self-esteem are all measures of emotional well-being. A large literature exists on behavior problems, their stability over time, and the predictors and consequences of "clinically significant" problems (Benasich, Brooks-Gunn, & McCormick, in press; Earls, 1980; Links, 1983; Robins, 1966). Moderate to severe behavior problems are associated with school difficulties, and it is sometimes difficult to ascertain cause and effect (but see longitudinal studies begun in early or middle childhood). Such problems are exacerbated by the types of environmental conditions seen in poor families. Measures of behavior problems have been derived from clinical psychology and psychiatry traditions and are more likely to sample problem behavior than more positive aspects of mental health. They include such problems as depression, aggression, somatization, obsessions, and anxiety. Often, a distinction is made between externalizing and internalizing behaviors, with aggression/conduct disorders and depression/anxiety respectively characterizing the two. Clearly, both are important to chart in poor children, and the incidence of the former seems to be associated with social class (and some social scientists have used externalizing behaviors in their definition of the underclass). Emotional self-regulation, impulse control, and temperament are three other constructs worth mentioning and ones that need to be studied. All three may be measured in early childhood and are believed to influence later behavior.

Social well-being

Social well-being focuses on relationships with others, the social support received (or perceived to be received) by others, and perceptions of embeddedness in groups. More social cognitive factors such as perceptions of competence, appraisals of the self, and internal motivational factors are sometimes measured (Connell, 1990; Maccoby & Jacklin, 1974). Self-images associated with ethnicity and class are also important domains (Spencer & Dornbusch, 1990). Like the other domains of well-being, but perhaps even more so than the others, social well-being is context dependent. In terms of the developmental literature, most measures have been age-specific, even though underlying constructs are sometimes presumed to be the same.

Effects of poverty on child well-being

To what extent does poverty in the early years affect developmental outcomes and thereby reduce opportunities for success and happiness in adulthood? In contrast with the precision with which poor children are counted, the ways in which economic deprivation influence children are not well understood. Are the effects primarily borne by lack of economic resources, by neighborhood characteristics (i.e., inadequate schools), by maternal behavior (i.e., being less verbally interactive), by maternal aspirations, or by some combination of such factors? Does the mix of factors differ as a function of ethnicity, age of the child, locale (urban versus rural), neighborhood (areas relatively rich and deficient in services, areas of high and low concentrations of poverty)? Which individual characteristics of children render them less able to withstand the onslaught of poverty conditions and all they entail, and which ones promote resilience? Can a change in the mother's situation alter her child's circumstances to any appreciable degree (Bronfenbrenner, 1975; Brooks-Gunn & Furstenberg, 1987; Scarr, 1982)?

Here, I focus primarily on the last question, defining it broadly to include changes in maternal circumstances such as education, marital, work, or welfare status, as well as changes in child circumstances such as movement into nonmaternal child care settings. The implicit assumption underlying the research to be reviewed is that children's development may be altered, within certain ranges, by environmental factors (Brim & Kagan, 1980: Hunt, 1961; Lerner, 1987). Change in maternal circumstances may precipitate a move into the workforce, a change from part-time to full-time work, or a change from sporadic to consistent work. How might such changes affect children, and what child and maternal characteristics might mediate any effects? What economic and psychological resources associated with such changes might account for any changes in child functioning? Changes in child and maternal circumstances, particularly via entrance into nonmaternal child-care situations, may also influence child outcomes, either through direct effects on the child or indirect effects mediated through the mother. Two areas are highlighted:

- Variability in the urban poor and correlates of such variability in mothers and children
- Effects of changes in maternal circumstances on children

Variability in the poor

Even given the bleak prognosis for many poor children and adolescents, striking variability is seen in their lives. For example, looking at a sample of Baltimore teenage mothers 17 years after the birth of their first child, we were surprised by the extent of diversity and the degree of improvement seen over time (Furstenberg et al., 1987). Only about one-quarter of the original teenage mothers were on welfare 17 years after the birth of their first child while one-quarter had family incomes of over $25,000 in 1984. What accounts for such diversity?

Developmentalists look at resilience and vulnerability, specifically in terms of the individual, familial, and institutional factors that render some individuals less vulnerable to the vicissitudes of poverty than others. In the Baltimore study, we found that characteristics of both the teenager's family of origin and of the teenagers themselves were significant predictors of economic success in later life. The important familial factors were educational status of the teenager's parents, family of origin size, and welfare status. Teenagers with parents of higher levels of education, smaller family sizes, and no welfare assistance were more likely to succeed as adults.

Three characteristics of the teenagers themselves predicted economic success in later life: educational attainment and ambition, family size, and marital status. Attendance in a special educational program for teenage mothers was highly predictive of economic success independent of grade-failure rate and aspiration. Both the probability of receiving welfare and of achieving economic security were strongly influenced by the number of additional births that occurred in the 5-year period after the birth of the first child. An important additional pathway away from economic dependency for the teen mothers was stable marriage. Those women who were married at the time of the 5-year follow-up were much more likely to have succeeded economically, presumably because of their husbands' income, than those who had never married. In contrast, women who remained with their families of origin for at least 5 years after their first child was born were less likely to be economically secure and more likely to be on welfare in adulthood. Thus, while living with one's parents for the first year or two promoted school attendance and employment, such an arrangement over the long term posed obstacles to independence and self-sufficiency in adulthood (Brooks-Gunn & Furstenberg, 1987; Furstenberg et al., 1987).

Changes in maternal circumstances

Given such variability, do mothers' efforts to alter their own life-course decisions have any influence on their children? Very few researchers have considered how possible it is to modify a life-course trajectory already in place. Continuity in achievement and behavior problems is found between the preschool and high school years (quite strong for achievement and modest for behavior problems; see Broman, Nicols, & Kennedy, 1975; Kellam, Ensminger, & Turner, 1977; Kagan & Moss, 1962; Werner & Smith, 1982). Once a child embarks upon the path of poor cognitive development or high behavioral problems, in part due to poverty-related circumstances during the first years of life, this trajectory is likely to continue into adolescence and young adulthood. Maternal characteristics and child outcomes are also linked during both the childhood and the adolescent years (Garmezy & Rutter, 1983; Kagan & Moss, 1962; Rutter, 1979). Few studies have attempted to link changes in the mother's life course with changes in children's development over time. Several studies illustrate the importance of looking at change in familial circumstances and child developmental outcomes simultaneously – the Baltimore Study of Adolescent Mothers and the California Study of Children of the Great Depression. (Another example, not presented here, is from the Infant Health and Development Program; Brooks-Gunn et al., 1993, 1994; Duncan et al., 1994.)

Changes in family circumstances: Children of the Great Depression

Perhaps the best example of how economic loss influences children is Elder's study of children of the Great Depression (Elder, 1974). Elder explains how economic loss operates through families to influence children. The working hypothesis is that economic loss is associated with problem behavior. But Elder makes the point that *not all* children are affected by familial economic loss.

Using the Berkeley Guidance Study, Elder examined the problem behavior of parent and child in terms of what each brought to the Great Depression crisis. How did severe income loss influence parent behavior, and was the influence mediated by familial conditions preceding the Great Depression? The 111 families and their children (born 1928–29) that were in the Berkeley Guidance Study experienced a 30% decrease in family income between 1929 and 1933.

Familial economic loss had effects on only two types of problem behavior – temper tantrums (negative self-will, aggression, defiance, control seeking, biting, kicking, striking, throwing things, screaming) and difficult temperament (intense, high-strung, difficult to manage, quarrelsome, irritable). Effects occurred primarily through the harsh, arbitrary, inconsistent dicipline of the father. Fathers who lost jobs were more likely to lash out at their children. As one father said, "Everyone is angry around here. . . . I fly off the handle. . . . My wife can't take it, the kids can't take it. The problems with my son are terrible" (Elder, 1974).

In this sample, mothers did not change their arbitrary, angry behavior as a function of a father's job loss. So no Great Depression effect was seen through their disciplinary pattern. However, their style prior to the Depression *did* relate to child problem behavior.

Reciprocal influences between father and child were seen. The problem behavior (temper tantrums, irritability) of father and child *before* the Great Depression was associated with a rise in arbitrariness of the father during the Great Depression. Basically, income loss was predictive of the father's inconsistent parenting in the Depression only among those fathers who were initially hostile.

Adolescent mothers and their children: The Baltimore study

In the Baltimore study, our question was "What types of maternal changes at what points in time affect the child's outcome?" Child status was assessed during the preschool and middle adolescent years. A change in mother's welfare status (i.e., moving off welfare after the child's preschool years) significantly reduced the likelihood of the child's subsequent grade failure (Brooks-Gunn & Furstenberg, 1987; Brooks-Gunn et al., 1993).

Mothers who entered a stable marriage and advanced their educational standing by the time of their children's adolescence had teens with superior school performance compared to youth whose mothers had not brought about these improvements. In contrast, mothers' early fertility behavior negatively affected preschoolers' performance, but later fertility did not affect adolescents' school achievement. Rapidly increasing family size during the child's early years may have had negative effects because of the intensity of child-rearing demands in the first years of life. Births occurring later seemed not to affect adolescent performance, perhaps because the child-rearing demands were spaced out over time (Furstenberg et al., 1987).

Programs for poor children and their families

Three approaches to enhancing the lives of poor children and families are discussed: home-visiting programs, center-based schooling or early intervention, and welfare–work demonstration programs.

Home-visiting programs

Home-visiting programs for new mothers were popular earlier in this century, and continue in many European countries. In the United States, a resurgence of interest in home visitation occurred in the past decade. Home-visiting programs are more likely to have as an explicit goal the alteration of parenting practices and possibly child abuse and neglect than are center-based programs. Several different models have been employed, including a parent education model (Dunst, Snyder & Mankinen, 1989), a public health model (Olds, Henderson, Chamberlin, & Tatlebaum, 1986; Olds, 1990), a social support model (Barnard, Booth, Mitchell, & Telzrow, 1988), a mental health model (Greenspan et al., 1987), a parenting education and problems solving model (Infant Health and Development Program, 1990; Ramey et al., 1992), and an interactional attachment model (Egeland & Erickson, 1991, 1992). Obviously, overlaps among these models exist (e.g., the public health model includes social support and parenting as program components). The important point is that a variety of approaches have been initiated in the past 10 years. Additionally, all of these approaches have included carefully designed evaluations.

Olds (1990) has reviewed a number of these programs. Generally, home visitation programs start during a woman's pregnancy and continue through the first or second year of life (a few beginning postnatally). Many home visitors see mothers in their homes weekly, others less than once or twice a month. Almost all programs focus on the mother, rather than on other caregivers such as the father or grandmother.

Programs are likely to focus on environmentally at-risk parents, those who are poor, are young, are single, and/or have low education. In a few instances, entire communities are targeted, as in the Hawaii Healthy Start initiative.

The training and experience of home visitors vary across programs. The public health models use public health nurses while other models employ social workers, early childhood educators, and, in some cases, paraprofessionals.

Most home visitors provide families with referrals for social, educational, welfare, and health services. These referrals are often not documented, even though they may make a large impact on families; for example, Olds (1990) reports that mothers who received home visiting completed more education than those in a control group. Brooks-Gunn et al. (1994) report that better-educated mothers who received home visiting were more likely to receive Medicaid-reimbursed health insurance and AFDC than similarly educated mothers who did not receive home-visiting services (presumably these mothers were eligible for this service but were unaware of their eligibility). Often programs not only provide referrals, but are designed to expand the participant's knowledge about available services and the participant's ability to obtain these services (see review from Benasich et al., 1992; Clewell, Brooks-Gunn, & Benasich, 1989).

Programs have reported on a variety of outcomes, primarily for the mothers or for the relationships between mother and child. These include risk factors for poor parenting such as unstable relationships, social isolation, low mental health of parents, lack of knowledge about child development, and harsh or punitive parenting. One program also reports on actual rates of child abuse and neglect (see review by Olds, 1990). Programs have reported success vis-à-vis increasing maternal knowledge, health of the child, safety of the house, and responsive, sensitive parenting. How (and if) these behaviors translate into better child outcomes is not known.

Center-based intervention programs

Nonmaternal care. Nonmaternal care is necessary for mothers to attend school or work; both factors are associated with altering familial poverty status. Type, quality, and availability of child care for poor families are considered in depth in the chapters by Cherlin and by Spencer and her colleagues in this volume. Here, the emphasis is on the possibility of enhanced child, maternal, and family functioning via the provision of high-quality, educationally oriented programs. Such programs represent only a fraction of the centers and family day care homes serving children (both poor and nonpoor alike). However, they represent the "best" that have been implemented and provide a standard of comparison for child-oriented service providers to emulate. They are about the only programs that have, as their express goal, enhancing poor children's cognitive, social, and physical well-being.

Paradoxically, while positive effects of early intervention (often center-based care) were expected and subsequently were demonstrated for disadvantaged children, a separate literature has focused on possible negative effects of day care for middle-class children. This split may be reflective of an insensitivity toward poor families and their children (Ogbu, 1985; Oyemade, 1985; Washington, 1985). Almost no studies have looked at the possible differential effects of early intervention programs on advantaged and disadvantaged children. A major exception is the Infant Health and Development Program, a multisite, randomized control trial to test the efficacy of educational and family support services and high-quality pediatric follow-up on reducing the incidence of developmental delay in low birth weight, premature infants (Brooks-Gunn et al., 1993, 1994; Gross, Brooks-Gunn, & Spiker, 1992; Infant Health and Development Program, 1990). The control group received pediatric follow-up only. About 1,000 children were enrolled in this trial, which provided services through age 3 years. White, African-American, and Hispanic-American families were represented, as well as poor and nonpoor children. The effects of the intervention were significant, vis-à-vis higher IQ scores and less behavior problems at ages 2 and 3 (Brooks-Gunn et al., 1993). The intervention was most effective for the mothers with the lowest education levels (Brooks-Gunn et al., 1992). Sustained effects were seen at age 5 in some subgroups of children, two years after the intervention program ended (Brooks-Gunn et al., 1994).

Early intervention programs

The effects of early intervention programs on poor children and their mothers are reviewed. The major outcomes of interest are cognitive-verbal functioning, school achievement, and socioemotional competence (children), and education, employment, and parenting skills (mothers). The research on middle-class families alluded to earlier will not be reviewed, but see Baydar and Brooks-Gunn (1991) and Desai, Chase-Lansdale, and Michael (1989).

Effects on children

We have learned a great deal about the cost of poverty to children from the ways in which early educational interventions make a difference. Early education for young disadvantaged children has a long history (Brooks-Gunn & Hearn, 1982). The school failures of disadvantaged children became a major concern in the 1960s, when several demonstration programs and ultimately the Head Start program were begun. The Children's Center of Syracuse University was developed by Caldwell and Richmond, who in 1964 laid the groundwork for subsequent programs. At the Children's Center emphasis was placed on the assumption that early group care would not disrupt mother–infant attachment or negatively affect social development. The Children's Center encouraged parental involvement, continuity of care, individualized attention, and exploration of the environment. Children came to the center daily and were separated into groups of 10, usually consisting of infants or toddlers. Following the Syracuse program and a handful of other programs, Head Start was successfully launched in 1965 under the direction of Richmond with over a half-million children being served in the first year. At the same time a number of more targeted intervention programs were initiated. The most well-known are ll programs (about half of which used experimental-control designs) described in the Consortium for Preschool Longitudinal Studies (Lazar, Darlington, Murray, Royce, & Snipper, 1982). These programs focused primarily on black disadvantaged children.

These programs, as well as others, vary in mode of delivery (home, school, or center-based), primary target (mother–child, mother and child or family), and timing of onset (prenatal, infant, preschool period). Programs have worked directly with the child, with the mother to improve mother–child interaction, or with the mother to alter maternal characteristics such as problem-solving abilities, mental health, and self-esteem. An additional strategy in some programs has been influencing other maternal characteristics (e.g., maternal knowledge about child development or maternal perception of child competence that affects the mother's interaction with the child, her aspirations for the child, or her interest in education for both her and her child; Benasich & Brooks-Gunn, in press; Bronfenbrenner, 1975; Woodhead, 1988; Clarke-Stewart & Fein, 1983).

Generally, these programs have proved to be very successful, as almost all of the evaluation reviews report. For brevity's sake, only the consortium results are presented here (see also Benasich et al., 1992; Clarke-Stewart & Fein, 1983; Ramey, Bryant, & Suarez, 1983; Woodhead, 1988). All of the consortium programs demonstrated the efficacy of early education immediately following the treatment (Lazar et al., 1982). The effect sizes using Stanford-Binet IQ scores range from $3\frac{1}{2}$ to $12\frac{1}{2}$ points (standard deviation of 15 to 16 points), controlling for background variables and pretest IQ. To be more concrete, changing IQ scores in the treatment as opposed to the control group (in randomized control trials) by one-half a standard deviation (6 to 8 points) reduces the incidence of children functioning in the mildly retarded range by about *one-half*.

Of importance to policy makers is how the graduates of such programs fare when they enter school. Is their relatively high likelihood of school failure reduced? The answer is a resounding yes. In the consortium, children who attended the preschool program were approximately a half grade ahead in mathematics ability in fourth grade, benefited from the programs regardless of their initial level of functioning (i.e., not just the brighter or less advanced children were helped), were less likely to be assigned to special education classes, were less likely to be classified as underachievers in late elementary school, and were less likely to be held back in grade level.

More recently, several programs have followed children even longer, reporting significant effects persisting into the high school years. Reductions in juvenile delinquency and increases in high school graduation (or a decrease in high school dropout given the ages of the youth in the follow-ups) have been reported. While these studies are small and few and far between, they are nevertheless suggestive in that preschool programs may have long-term effects on the very factors that are associated with educational and job success and, by inference, to the poverty status of the next generation (Berrueta-Clement, Schweinhart, Barnett, Epstein, & Weikart, 1984; Miller & Bizzel, 1984; Schweinhart, Weikart, & Larner, 1986; Seitz, Rosenbaum, & Apfel, 1985; Zigler, Taussig, & Black, 1992).

These remarkable and heartening findings are based on small-scale, single-site studies that were developed and evaluated by early education specialists. All had more or less formal curriculum and teachers were trained in the delivery of it. Additionally, many (but certainly not all) of the center-based programs were full-day, not half-day programs. Such programs serve only a fraction of poor children. Indeed, the largest single program serving disadvantaged preschoolers today (as well as in its first year) is Head Start, a legacy of the War on Poverty that is now 25 years old. As simply yet eloquently stated by President Johnson, "The project is designed to put them [disadvantaged children] on an even footing with their class-mates as they enter school" (Zigler & Valentine, 1979).

The Head Start Evaluation, Synthesis, and Utilization Project (McKey et al., 1985) summarized all of the Head Start evaluations to that date (both published and unpublished). Educationally significant effects were considered as well as statistically significant ones (the former being defined as an effect size of or difference in standard deviation units of 0.25 or more). Along with the studies that have been published subsequent to the McKey report, the general findings on Head Start may be summarized as follows. First, across a variety of study designs, a majority of studies have reported short-term effects (usually statistically significant) on cognitive-verbal functioning. In addition, in the few studies that have focused on competencies other than cognitive or verbal abilities, positive Head Start effects also have been found. For example, in a multisite evaluation of children who attended Head Start, no preschool, or other preschools in the late 1960s, children in Head Start were better able to self-regulate their motoric responses and had higher scores on a competency test designed to assess the skills necessary for early school performance than neighborhood children with no preschool or other preschool experiences (Lee, Brooks-Gunn, & Schnur, 1988; see Shipman, 1972 for a comprehensive description of the Educational Testing Service Head Start Longitudinal Study). Indeed, the effect sizes were greater for these two measures than the verbal ability measure, suggesting that more benefits may accrue than are measured in most studies (given that most studies regrettably focus primarily on verbal ability and intelligence test scores).

Second, a few studies have examined possible long-term effects, even though many have cautioned about expecting too much from 1 year or one summer of half-day preschool educational experience. As Zigler forcefully has stated, "We simply cannot inoculate children in one year against the ravages of a life of deprivation" (1987, p. 258). It may come as little surprise, then, that enhancements tend not be sustained by the end of first grade in most Head Start evaluations. However, this generalization is plagued by methodological problems, given the lack of randomized designs or even quasi-experimental ones in the Head Start evaluations (Hebbeler, 1985; Lee et al., 1988). As we have pointed out, "Many of these studies may have underestimated the efficacy of Head Start, however, given the paucity of statistical controls for initial differences in cognitive *and* demographic characteristics of those who did and did not attend Head Start" (Lee, Brooks-Gunn, Schnur, & Liaw, 1990). Indeed, in the Educational Testing Service Head Start Longitudinal Study where neighborhoods with Head Start centers were canvassed to assess all $3\frac{1}{2}$- to $4\frac{1}{2}$-year-olds in the spring prior to the decision to enter preschool (Head Start or another preschool) or no preschool, differences among those who entered Head Start, no preschool, and other preschools were controlled statistically (keeping in mind that in the absence of a randomized control trial, selection biases are never completely controlled for). In two cities, Head Start attendees had higher scores on the California Preschool Competency Test (effect size, 0.34) at the end of the kindergarten year as well as on the Cooperative Primary Test (effect size, 0.28) at the end of the first grade year (Lee et al., 1990). Third, since the poorest children from any given neighborhood seem to be served by Head Start, based on the embarrassingly small number of studies that have examined this question (keeping in mind that Head Start serves only one-quarter of those eligible), sustained effects might not be expected unless additional help is provided (Hebbeler, 1985; Lee et al., 1990; Schnur, Brooks-Gunn, & Shipman, 1992). The poorest children are likely to come from homes with poorly educated parents and to attend high concentration–low SES schools. Both are risk factors for achievement (Ogbu, 1985, 1986; Spencer, Brookins, & Allen, 1985). Taking seriously the comment about the efficacy of a short-term inoculation like Head Start, a few programs examined Head Start in conjunction with participation in Project Follow Through. While there are problems in evaluating this research (i.e., many Follow Through children did not participate in Head Start and vice versa), it seems that only Head Starters participating in Follow Through exhibited sustained gains 2 years after the preschool program (Abelson, 1974; Kennedy, 1978), thus suggesting the need for longer interventions.

Fourth, given that several of the few long-term studies report decreases in grade failure, high school dropout, and special education placement, McKey and colleagues state that Head Starters may have a long-lasting advantage in social competence that facilitates children's ability to "progress in school, stay in the mainstream, and satisfy teachers' requirements better than their peers who did not attend" (1985, pp. 111–112). However, this premise has not been tested adequately.

In brief, participation in early childhood programs including Head Start results in enhanced functioning in skill domains associated with elementary school success. Additionally, long-term gains have been reported for some programs, again including Head Start. While benefits clearly accrue to poor children, what about their mothers? Do they benefit from such programs as well?

Effects on mothers and families

Interestingly, even though early education programs have been based on the premise that mothers need to participate and to change their behavior, programs for the most part have not examined parenting outcomes as anticipated benefits of these programs (Gray & Wandersman, 1980; Ramey, Bryant, & Suarez, 1983; White & Casto, 1985). The two types of maternal outcomes most likely to have been evaluated are maternal employment and parenting skills.

Child-oriented programs may have an unanticipated benefit of altering maternal education or maternal employment. In a recent review of early childhood interventions (Benasich et al., 1992), of 12 center-based programs, six of seven who looked at the relevant outcome found that mothers whose children participated in early childhood programs were more likely to be in school or employed. Four of 16 primarily home-based programs also reported on maternal employment, with all finding that mothers in the intervention group were more likely to be in school or to be employed than mothers in the control group.

Most programs have enhancing parenting skills as one of their express goals. In our review, five of the 12 center-based and seven of the 16 primarily home-based programs collected information on parent–child interactions via observation. All but one found that parents in the intervention group had better interaction skills (e.g., positive and supportive interactions, less criticism) than mothers in the control group (see also Spiker, Ferguson, & Brooks-Gunn, 1993).

Little research concerning the long-term impact of Head Start on parenting skills or on maternal employment or schooling has been conducted (Slaughter, Oyemade, Washington, & Lindsey, 1988). Two evaluations, one of the Parent–Child Development Centers (not strictly Head Start programs, being more intensive and serving younger children) and one of the Educational Testing Service Head Start Longitudinal Study, suggest that modest positive effects on the mother may be seen in some circumstances (Benasich et al., 1992).

Programs for young parents

Not only do benefits accrue to poor children from the provision of early childhood education, but their development may be accelerated from programs focusing on their mothers. Clearly, evidence of such effects would have implications for the children of mothers enrolled in the JOBS program of the Family Support Act. Many different programs have been initiated for teenage mothers. As has been repeatedly demonstrated, adolescent mothers are less likely to complete high school, find stable employment, be self-supporting, and marry than are older mothers (Brooks-Gunn & Chase-Lansdale, 1995; Furstenberg, Lincoln, & Menken, 1981; Hayes, 1987; Hofferth & Hayes, 1987; Moore & Burt, 1982). And their children also have reduced life chances. Preschool children of teenage childbearers are more likely to have developmental delays and to have behavior problems than are children of older childbearers (Baldwin & Cain, 1980; Brooks-Gunn & Furstenberg, 1986). School failure and juvenile delinquency are more common among youth born to teenage than older mothers (Baldwin, 1993; Moore, Myers, Morrison, Nord, Brown, & Edmonston, 1993).

The teenage mothers' need for child-related services, particularly child care, in order to complete school or work, is now quite evident. Which approaches are most effective for not only young mothers, but also for their children? Unfortunately, few evaluations of the impacts of teenage parenting or child care provision programs (as opposed to teenage educational or employment programs) have been conducted (Klerman, 1979, 1991; Polit, Kahn, & Stevens, 1985; Roosa, 1985). Problems have been found in those that exist. For example, evaluations of service programs for school-age parents often do not use a control or comparison group, have no randomized selection procedures, have poor rates of response, or focus on a limited range of outcomes (Klerman, 1979). These differences are especially evident when focusing on programs offering child-related services.

In a review of teenage parenting programs, Klerman (1981) found that most evaluations up to the 1980s had focused on the mother and her medical and educational status in the prenatal period, at the birth of her infant, and in the months subsequent to delivery. In the few studies looking at child outcomes, the focus is usually on neonatal health, even though research has pointed out long-term effects of teenage parenthood on children's school failure, misbehavior, and early fertility (Baldwin & Cain, 1980; Brooks-Gunn & Furstenberg, 1986; Hofferth & Hayes, 1987; Roosa, Fitzgerald, & Carson, 1982). We have described programs for teenage mothers in which child-related interventions have been evaluated (Clewell et al., 1989). Most of the 14 programs focused primarily on parenting education or offered day care services.

Parenting education programs differ as to whether their services are home-based, part-time center-based, or entirely center-based. However, all have altering parenting skills as a goal. The programs reviewed suggest that home visits can be an effective means of providing parenting education to teenage mothers (Field, Widmayer, Stringer, & Ignatoff, 1980; Gutelius, Kirsch, McDonald, Brooks, & McErlean, 1977). Field (1981) also has demonstrated that low-intensity programs may influence children's development (i.e., the use of neonatal and infancy assessment measures as teaching instruments).

Although home visits can be effective, a few studies suggest that when a center-based approach is compared with a home visit approach, the former is more effective (and may be most effective for teenagers defined as high-risk; Badger, 1981; Field, Widmayer, Greenberg, & Stroller, 1982). Many factors may play a role. Field et al. (1982) surmise that the success of their CETA-supported infant day nursery intervention could have been due to factors such as the pay, the job training, the additional time with infants, or the modeling of parenting skills by the teachers on a daily basis. To date, no program has been designed to see which component (or mix of services) contributes to enhanced parenting behavior or attitudes, or child outcomes.

Although most of the parenting programs we reviewed do not focus directly on maternal schooling or work, several parenting programs, such as the Baltimore program (Hardy, King, Shipp, & Welcher, 1981), report a favorable effect on school completion. The question remains as to what components of *parenting* programs may have the unanticipated benefit of enhancing school completion, besides the obvious strategy of offering such classes in the public schools.

We identified several different models of center-based interventions, including those that are school-based (Clewell et al., 1989). Campbell, Breitmayer, and Ramey (1986), comparing mothers and children who had access to free day care with those who did not, concluded that the easy availability of free day care services resulted in benefits to both mother and child. This supports the contention of other researchers that availability of day care is a crucial factor in the school-age mother's decision to continue her education.

Roosa and Vaughan (1983) suggest that the benefits of parenting classes provided by alternative schools can be enhanced by the offering of child care as well. In their study, the benefits of the day care services accrued to the mother rather than to the child. In general, the offering of day care services in a public school setting is becoming a popular model, even though few have been subject to rigorous evaluation (Sung, 1981; Sung & Rothrock, 1980).

More generally, the day care models we have reviewed all increased the likelihood that mothers stayed in school or entered the workforce. It seems that in those child-oriented programs run by early childhood educators, the children also benefited. One presumes that in these cases a more formal infant development curriculum was implemented, more staff training was done, and/or more highly trained staff were recruited. Any day care program offered to teenage mothers should be implemented using a standard developmental curriculum and be managed or at least overseen by an early childhood specialist who has had experience in setting up and evaluating such programs. The growing awareness of the efficacy of high-quality day care coupled with the increased provision of day care as part of programs for young mothers should lead to more careful evaluation and specification of the content of day care programs (Clewell et al., 1989, p. 208).

Education and work programs for poor mothers

Most of these programs have been developed for young, single-parent mothers – those most likely to be receiving AFDC. These are unlike the home-visiting and center-based interventions, many of which have been developed to serve a larger segment of the poor (i.e., usually do not exclude families with older mothers or with fathers present, if these families are poor). These programs have focused on helping mothers complete education and enter or return to the workforce. Unlike the more child-oriented programs, these are specific to one group of poor families: those with a mother on welfare.

Many states initiated work–welfare programs in the 1980s. Not all were evaluated rigorously (see Haskins, this volume). However, modest effects have been found (Aber, Brooks-Gunn, & Maynard, 1995; Maynard, 1995). In part, the Family Support Act of 1988 was passed with these state-initiated efforts in mind. It takes care of – at least in the short term – the two largest barriers to poor mothers with young children entering the workforce: child care and health insurance.

Welfare–Work Programs

Possible effects of the JOBS programs

Work–welfare programs and the Family Support Act have the potential of influencing the lives of two generations living in poverty. Children as well as mothers may benefit, as the research reviewed demonstrates. Just focusing on single-parent families for the moment, over 3 million receive Aid to Families with Dependent Children (AFDC). Over 80% of these families have at least one preschool child (i.e., under the age of 6; Sonenstein & Wolf, 1991). Several questions are addressed here, with respect to child care, movement in and out of poverty, and birth spacing.

Other questions also come to mind but are not discussed at length. In what circumstances will benefits accrue, and for whom? What characteristics or circumstances may reduce the likelihood of child benefits (e.g., type, quality, quantity, stability, and availability of child care within neighborhoods)? For how many mothers (if any) does the provision of child care support actually result in increased employment, and in what circumstances does this occur? What long-term effects (if any) are seen through the receipt of child care support, and what are the factors associated with enhanced child functioning? How does the provision of child care support influence the residential patterns of mothers and children, particularly with regard to the grandmother?

Child care. Current welfare reforms at the state and federal level require many women on AFDC to enroll in education programs, take job training, or find employment, including those whose youngest child is between 3 and 5 years and, at state discretion, over the age of 1 (Blank, 1989). In addition, young mothers will be required to attend education programs regardless of the age of their youngest child if high school graduation has not occurred. Thus, the availability of child care for children between the ages of 3 and 5 is important to the success of the JOBS program aspect of the Family Support Act (by age 5, most children have entered kindergarten; in 1986, 86% of poor 5-year-olds were enrolled in kindergarten, similar to the percentage of nonpoor children). Currently, in terms of center-based care, including nursery school, about one in four poor 3- and 4-year-olds were receiving such care, in contrast to about two-fifths of their nonpoor age-mates in 1986 (leaving aside the fact that preschoolers also may be taken care of by relatives and nonrelatives; the research reviewed here, and the early childhood evaluations more generally, have focused on center-based programs).

Support of child care for AFDC mothers is critical if they are to make the transition to the workforce. Many of the mothers in the JOBS program are poorly educated, have little work experience, and are likely to earn low wages. Low-income families have to spend a much higher proportion of their income on child care than do more advantaged families (Hofferth & Phillips, 1991). However, it is not known if the provision of cash stipends or vouchers will alter the quality of child care that the child receives, maternal satisfaction with it, or possible enhanced child functioning. In addition, given the discretion given to the states, wide variability will be seen in how child care services will be offered (i.e., stipends, direct services, reimbursement plans). Hopefully, such variation may be seen as a "natural history" opportunity, in that planned variation evaluations may be undertaken. Types of child care available, as well as the child care arrangements actually used by mothers, may influence how many and which mothers complete the JOBS program training and remain in the workforce. Cost, availability, and quality of child care all may influence maternal decision making (Balasubramaniam & Turnbull, 1988; Clarke-Stewart & Fein, 1983; Phillips, 1987; Silverberg, 1988). In addition, perceptions of the adequacy of child care may influence maternal behavior as well.

Again, interstate variations, as well as intrastate variations, will need to be documented and capitalized upon via careful evaluation.

All of these child care factors, and the ones discussed by Cherlin (this volume) and Spencer and her colleagues (this volume), may influence both the mother, vis-à-vis her satisfaction with care arrangements, her motivation to complete training, and even her ability to remain employed or in school. If adequate, convenient, and cost-sensitive child care is not available in a particular locale, the child care vouchers may not have much impact. One important point in designing evaluations is that variations in child care arrangements are most relevant at the neighborhood or district level, not the city, SMSA, or state level. Child care must be convenient to home or work, unless transportation allowances are provided (and these are typically quite costly).

Movement in and out of poverty. How parental movement in and out of the job market (and in and out of poverty) may influence children has not really been systematically studied. The closest we come is looking at receipt of welfare on child outcomes, with both being associated with lowered cognitive and behavioral functioning (Brooks-Gunn & Furstenberg, 1987). Additionally, movement off welfare between the preschool and high school years has positive effects on grade failure, as we have found in the Baltimore study. Finally, duration of welfare does seem to contribute to child outcome decrements, over and above welfare receipt in the early years of life (Baydar et al., 1993). However, we do know that children whose families are near poor have lower IQ and school achievement scores than children whose families are poor, controlling for a host of demographic characteristics (Conger, Conger, & Elder, in press; Smith, Brooks-Gunn, & Klebvanov, in press). Similar, but less strong effects are seen for behavior problems (Hanson, McLanahan, & Thomson, in press; Kurtz, Boulerice, & Tremblay, in press).

Movement in and out of poverty is an important dimension for the Family Support Act. Mothers who move off welfare and into the workforce are probably quite likely to be classified as near poor (between the poverty line and 1.5 times the poverty line). Currently, between 10% and 15% of all preschool children (under age 6) are near poor (an additional 23% are below the poverty line; Hernandez, 1993). We do not know what a change to near poor means in terms of quality of life, nor even purchasing power. Reductions in Medicaid, food stamps, subsidized housing, and school lunch program transfers may be expected (e.g., 47% of near poor children receive at least one of these subsidies, while 77% of poor children do; Zill et al., 1989). These decreases may offset many of the possible economic increases associated with working, especially in terms of how children in these households live (see Sugland et al., in press). Clearly, we need to know more about the economic impact of these transitions, alterations in child resource allocations (if any), and subsequent effects on children (see Lazear & Michael, 1987).

Birth spacing. Will mothers with more children find it difficult to use child care programs as a springboard to employment as compared to mothers with one or two children? Child spacing itself may impact the benefits obtained from a child care program, suggesting important links between benefits and fertility/family planning. For example, the Baltimore study was a hospital-based program that provided comprehensive prenatal and postnatal health services as well as information on parenting and family planning, either in a special clinic for teenagers or in the regular antenatal care clinic. Participation in the special program was associated with enhanced maternal outcomes (i.e., regular contraceptive use, birth spacing, and indirectly, family size) but not to infant/child outcomes (i.e., percentage of low birth weight infants, preschool verbal ability). However, limitation of family size produced an indirect effect on child outcomes by enhancing preschool verbal scores (Furstenberg et al., 1987). In addition, in four early childhood intervention evaluations, intervention mothers had fewer children and had increased the birth spacing between their children as compared to mothers in the control group (reviewed in Benasich et al., 1992).

Two-generation programs

A new set of demonstrations are taking a more explicitly 2-generational approach to helping poor families. These demonstrations all are providing comprehensive, integrated services for poor families. Many blend work and education training, high quality child care, service referrals, and parenting classes. Obviously, these programs are borrowing from the three major approaches reviewed here. Two of the more innovative are the Comprehensive Child Development Program (CCDP), and the New Chance Demonstration (see Smith, this volume, and in press, for a review of these and other programs). Another approach involves intensive case management and sanctioning of mothers who do not participate in education and training (Maynard, 1995). Additionally, over one-half of the states have received waivers from the U.S. Department of Health and Human Services to alter their welfare programs. Changes include sanctions for nonparticipation, family development plans, family caps (no additional AFDC payments for additional children), residential requirements for teenage mothers, and contracts for performance. None of these innovations take a 2-generational approach. Additionally, 1995 House and Senate proposals to alter the welfare system do not look at children specifically.

Conclusion

The goal of most programs for young poor children is not one of eradicating poverty. Instead, services are provided in order to ameliorate the effects of poverty on families (e.g., the WIC program, AFDC, food stamps, school lunch programs) or to lessen the likelihood of poverty reappearing across generations (e.g., Head

Start, Title IX). The JOBS program more directly targets poverty in helping mothers enter the workforce. Generally, programs for poor families and their children have focused either on a specific group of parents, often teenage mothers, or on a group of children, most typically disadvantaged preschool children. Regrettably, little coordination has occurred between programs for poor, young mothers and for poor, young children, even though the two populations overlap to a considerable degree. And each literature does not acknowledge the other with any frequency.

Child-focused programs typically focus on the cognitive functioning of the child: The long-term goal is to enhance the probability of high school graduation and postgraduate work or schooling. In the short term, programs aspire to reduce developmental delays associated with later school failure and to prevent behavior problems associated with later juvenile delinquency and misbehavior. Early childhood interventions are targeted toward the parent, the child, the interaction between the two, or all three. As we have seen, many have been extremely successful, in terms of enhancing both child and maternal outcomes (Clewell et al., 1989).

Programs directed toward young parents usually focus more on the parents than do most early childhood programs reviewed in this chapter. The goals are to enhance maternal employment, education, and/or parenting skills. As more comprehensive services are provided to pregnant and parenting teenagers, child-focused services (child care or parenting classes, or both) are more likely to be offered (McGee, 1982; Schinke, 1978).

Child-focused services to teenage parents are most often provided in the context of a more comprehensive program; they may be offered as day care provision, home visits, and/or center-based parenting classes. Child-related services vary tremendously in terms of focus, intensity, and length. Although day care has been repeatedly cited as one of the services most needed by teenage mothers (Guttmacher, 1981; Hayes, 1987; Klerman, 1975; Maynard, 1995; McGee, 1982; Moore & Burt, 1982), it is also one that is least likely to be available. Of the possible child-focused services, parenting classes are most frequent. Programs may attempt to alter maternal internal resources for coping with a poverty existence (i.e., programs focusing on decision-making strategies, maternal self-esteem, efficacy), to urge the mother to move toward self-sufficiency (via schooling, job training, or entrance into the workforce), or to operate in an advocacy role to obtain more services for the family (or, in ideal circumstances, to help the mother be a better consumer of the myriad of social service programs for her child). This focus on the parent is hoped to reap benefits for the child. Child care provides additional experiences for the child, typically in terms of interactions akin to those in school, adequate nutrition, and so on. Strategies for influencing the mother's child-directed behaviors include programs to teach her how to interact with her child in more effective ways, to alter her expectancies for child achievement, to provide knowledge about child-rearing practices, and/or to encourage maternal participation in child care programs (Brooks-Gunn & Furstenberg, 1987). Our review suggests that these endeavors may be very successful, again for both mothers and children (Clewell et al., 1989, p. 202).

In conclusion, 2-generation programs may influence children in several ways, with some of these pathways summarized as follows:

- *Effects of Maternal Education or Employment.* As a mother moves from welfare into a job, her actions may influence her child's well-being. Benefits may accrue to the mother that potentially impact the child via economic pathways (i.e., moving to a better neighborhood, school, or apartment; residing in less crowded conditions; purchasing more educational materials), psychological pathways (i.e., the mother may become less depressed, become more able to cope with daily stresses, and have more self-confidence as a function of a job-training program, any of which could result in more maternal responsivity), or educational pathways (i.e., given increases in maternal education and/or literacy, mothers may learn more about child development, may provide more educational materials, may spend more time reading to the child, or work with the child's school more directly).
- *Effects of Nonmaternal Care.* Nonmaternal child care may influence child outcomes. As reviewed here, high-quality educational day care has been shown to enhance disadvantaged children's cognitive competence (Clewell et al., 1989; Lazar et al., 1982; Ramey & Suarez, 1984; Zigler & Gordon, 1982). Thus, adequate child care may influence the well-being of future generations, not just the current welfare recipient.
- *Effects of an Alteration in Maternal Aspirations.* Mothers who have the opportunity to enter the workforce or to complete their education may alter their beliefs about the importance of education, armed with the evidence that education results in paid employment. In the Baltimore study, high educational aspirations and being on grade level at the time of pregnancy were the strongest predictors of occupational success 17 years later. This in turn could influence how the mother treats her child vis-à-vis educationally stimulating activities, how she speaks of education, and what she expects her child to achieve educationally. Indeed, in the Baltimore study, educational aspirations for one's child, as measured before the child had entered school, were associated with a high likelihood of high school completion and of being literate when the children were 20 years of age (Baydar et al., 1993). This effect was found after controlling for welfare receipt, home environment, number of siblings, being a single parent, and preschool cognitive abilities.
- *Effects of Changes in Maternal Parenting Skills.* Effects on maternal attitudes and behavior also may accrue because of participation in quality child care programs. Many early childhood intervention specialists suspect that enhanced child functioning in part is due to maternal changes in educational domains (i.e., higher educational aspirations, more time spent on homework, more interaction with the elementary school, better skills at negotiating for educational services for the child) or in enhanced parenting skills (e.g., more verbally responsive, less critical, more focused teaching skills). As our review suggests, early education programs do influence actual parent–child interaction (Benasich et al., 1989), as well as maternal aspirations (Lazar et al., 1982; Shipman, 1976).

REFERENCES

Abelson, W. (1974). Head Start graduates in school: Studies in New Haven, Connecticut. In S. Ryan (Ed.), *A report on longitudinal evaluations of preschool programs. Volume 1: Longitudinal evaluations.* Washington, DC: U.S. Department of Health, Education, and Welfare.

Aber, J. L., Brooks-Gunn, J., & Maynard, R. (1995). The effects of welfare reform on teenage parents and their children. *The future of children.*

Alexander, L. K., & Entwisle, D. R. (1988). Achievement in the first 2 years of school: Patterns and processes. *Monographs of the Society for Research in Child Development, 53* (2, Serial No. 218)

Angoff, W. H. (1988). The nature-nurture debate, aptitudes, and group differences. *American Psychologist, 43*(9), 713–720.

Badger, E. (1981). Effects of parent education program on teenage mothers and their offspring. In K. Scott, T. Field, & E. Robertson (Eds.), *Teenage parents and their offspring.* New York: Grune & Stratton.

Balasubramaniam, M., & Turnbull, B. (1988). *Exemplary preschool programs for at-risk children: A review of recent literature.* Washington, DC: Policy Studies Associates.

Baldwin, W. (1993). The consequences of early childbearing: A perspective. *Journal of Research on Adolescence, 3*(4), 349–352.

Baldwin, W., & Cain, V. S. (1980). The children of teenage parents. *Family Planning Perspectives, 12*(1), 34–43.

Barnard, K. E., Booth, C. L., Mitchell, S. K., & Telzrow, R. (1988). Newborn nursing models: A test of early intervention to high-risk infants and families. In E. Hibbs (Ed.), *Children and families: Studies in prevention and intervention* (pp. 63–81). Madison, CT: International Universities Press.

Baydar, N., & Brooks-Gunn, J. (1991). Effects of maternal employment and child-care arrangements in infancy on preschoolers' cognitive and behavioral outcomes: Evidence from the Children of the NLSY. *Developmental Psychology, 27*(6), 932–945.

Baydar, N., Brooks-Gunn, J., & Furstenberg, F. F., Jr. (1993). Early warning signs of functional illiteracy: Predictors in childhood and adolescence. *Child Development, 64*(3), 815–829.

Benasich, A. A., & Brooks-Gunn, J. (in press). Enhancing maternal knowledge and child-rearing concepts: Results from an early intervention program. *Child Development.*

Benasich, A. A., Brooks-Gunn, J., & Clewell, B. C. (1992). How do mothers benefit from early intervention programs? *Journal of Applied Developmental Psychology, 13*, 311–362.

Benasich, A. A., Brooks-Gunn, J., & McCormick, M. C. (in press). Behavioral problems in the two-to-five-year-old: Measurement and prognostic ability. *Journal of Developmental and Behavioral Pediatrics.*

Berreuta-Clement, J. R., Schweinhart, L. J., Barnett, S., Epstein, A., & Weikart, D. P. (1984). *Changed lives: The effects of the Perry Preschool Program on youths through age 19.* Monographs of the High/Scope Educational Research Foundation, 8. Ypsilanti, MI: High/Scope Press.

Branch, A., & Quint, J. (1981, September). *Project Redirection: Interim report on program implementation.* New York: Manpower Demonstration Research Corporation.

Brim, O. G., Jr., & Kagan, J. (1980). *Constancy and change in human development.* Cambridge, MA: Harvard University Press.

Broman, S. H., Nicols, P. L., & Kennedy, W. A. (Eds.). (1975). *Preschool IQ: Prenatal and early developmental correlates.* Hillsdale, NJ: Erlbaum.

Bronfenbrenner, U. (1975). Is early intervention effective? In M. Guttentag & E. L. Struening (Eds.), *Handbook of evaluation research, 2.* Beverly Hills: Sage.

Bronfenbrenner, U. (1979). Contexts of child rearing: Problems and prospects. *American Psychologist, 34*(10), 844–850.

Bronfenbrenner, U. (1986). Ecology of the family as context for human development: Research perspectives. *Developmental Psychology, 22*(6), 723–742.

Bronfenbrenner, U. (1988). Interacting systems in human development research paradigms: Present and future. In N. Bolger, A. Caspi, G. Downey, & M. Moorehouse (Eds.), *Persons in context: Developmental processes* (pp. 25–49). New York: Cambridge University Press.

Brooks-Gunn, J. (1990). Overcoming barriers to adolescent research on pubertal and reproductive development. *Journal of Youth and Adolescence, 19*(5), 425–440.

Brooks-Gunn, J. (1994). Research on step-parenting families: Integrating discipline approaches and informing policy. In A. Booth & J. Dunn, *Step-parent families with children: Who benefits and who does not?* (pp. 167–190). Hillsdale, NJ: Erlbaum.

Brooks-Gunn, J., & Chase-Lansdale, P. I. (1991) Children having children. Effects on the family system. *Pediatric Annals, 20*(9), 467–481.

Brooks-Gunn, J., & Chase-Lansdale, P. L. (1995). Adolescent parenthood. In M. Bornstein (Ed.), *Handbook of parenting*. Hillsdale, NJ: Erlbaum.

Brooks-Gunn, J., Duncan, G., & Aber, J. L. (Eds.). (in press), *Neighborhood poverty: Context and consequences for development*. New York: Russell Sage Foundation Press.

Brooks-Gunn, J., & Furstenberg, F. F., Jr. (1986). The children of adolescent mothers: Physical, academic and psychological outcomes. *Developmental Review, 6*, 224–251.

Brooks-Gunn, J., & Furstenberg, F. F., Jr. (1987). Continuity and change in the context of poverty: Adolescent mothers and their children. In J. J. Gallagher & C. T. Ramey (Eds.), *The malleability of children* (pp. 171–188). Baltimore, MD: Brookes.

Brooks-Gunn, J., Guo, G., & Furstenberg, F. F., Jr. (1993). Who drops out of and who continues beyond high school? A 20-year follow-up of black urban youth. *Journal of Research on Adolescence, 3*(3), 271–294.

Brooks-Gunn, J., & Hearn, R. (1982). Early intervention and developmental dysfunction: Implications for pediatrics. *Advances in Pediatrics* (pp. 497–527). New York: Yearbook Publishers.

Brooks-Gunn, J., Klebanov, P. K., Liaw, F., & Spiker, D. (1993). Enhancing the development of low birth weight, premature infants: Changes in cognition and behavior over the first three years. *Child Development, 64*(3), 736–753.

Brooks-Gunn, J., Klebanov, P. K., & Liaw, F. (1995). The learning, physical, and emotional environment of the home in the context of poverty: The Infant Health and Development Program. *Children and Youth Services Review, 17*(2), 231–250.

Brooks-Gunn, J., McCarton, C., et al. (1994). Early intervention in low birth-weight, premature infants: Results through age 5 years from the Infant Health and Development Program. *Journal of the American Medical Association, 272*(16), 1257–1262.

Brooks-Gunn, J., McCormick, M., Shapiro, S., Benasich, A. A., & Black, G. (1994). The effects of early education intervention on maternal employment, public assistance, and health insurance: The Infant Health and Development Program. *American Journal of Public Health, 84*(6), 924–931.

Brooks-Gunn, J., Phelps, E., & Elder, G. H. (1991). Studying lives through time: Secondary data analyses in developmental psychology. *Developmental Psychology, 27*(6), 899–910.

Brayfield, A., Diech, S., & Hofferth, S. (1993). *Caring for children in low-income families: A substudy of the National Child Care Survey 1990*. Washington, DC: The Urban Institute Press.

Bumpass, L. L. (1984). Children and marital disruption: A replication and update. *Demography, 21*(1), 71–82.

Burt, M. R., Kimmich, M. H., Goldmuntz, J., & Sonenstein, F. L. (1984, February). *Helping pregnant adolescents: Outcomes and costs of service delivery*. Final report on the Evaluation of Adolescent Pregnancy Programs. Washington, DC: Urban Institute.

Campbell, F. A., Breitmayer, B., & Ramey, C. T. (1986). Disadvantaged single teenage mothers and their children: Consequences of free educational day care. *Family Relations, 35*, 63–68.

Chase-Lansdale, P. L., Brooks-Gunn, J., & Paikoff, R. (1991). Research and programs for adolescent mothers: Missing links and future promises. *Family Relations* [special issue, "Adolescent Pregnancy and Parenting: Interventions, Evaluations, and Needs"], *40*, 396–404.

Chase-Lansdale, P. L., Brooks-Gunn, J., & Zamsky, E. S. (1994). Young African-American multi-generational families in poverty: Quality of mothering and grandmothering. *Child Development, 65*(2), 373–393.

Chase-Lansdale, P. L., Mott, F. L., Brooks-Gunn, J., & Phillips, D. (1991). Children of the NLSY: A unique research opportunity. *Developmental Psychology, 27*(6), 918–931.

Citro, C., & Michael, R. (1995). *Measuring poverty: A new approach*. Washington, DC: National Academy of Sciences Press.

Clarke-Stewart, K. A., & Fein, G. G. (1983). Early childhood programs. In P. H. Mussen (Ed.), *Handbook of child psychology* (pp. 918–999). New York: Wiley.

Clewell, B. C., Brooks-Gunn, J., & Benasich, A. A. (1989). Evaluating child-related outcomes of teenage parenting programs. *Family Relations*, 201–209.

Conger, R. D., Conger, K. J., & Elder, G. (in press). Family economic hardship and adolescent academic performance: Mediating and moderating processes. In G. Duncan & J. Brooks-Gunn (Eds.), *Consequences of growing up poor*. New York: Russell Sage Foundation Press.

Conger, R. D., Conger, K. J., Elder, G. H., Jr., Lorenz, F. O., Simons, R. L., & Whitbeck, L. B. (1992). A family process model of economic hardship and adjustment of early adolescent boys. *Child Development*, *63*, 526–541.

Connell, J. P. (1990). Context, self, and action. A motivational analysis of self-system processes across the life-span. In D. Cicchetti (Ed.), *The self in transition: Infancy to childhood*. Chicago: University of Chicago Press.

Corcoran, M., Gordon, R., Laren, D., & Solon, G. (1992). The association between men's economic status and their family and community origins. *Journal of Human Resources*, *27*(4), 575–601.

Desai, S., Chase-Lansdale, L., & Michael, R. T. (1989). Mother or market? Effects of maternal employment on cognitive development of 4-year-old children. *Demography*, *26*(4), 545–561.

Duncan, G. J. (1991). The economic environment of childhood. In A. C. Huston (Ed.), *Children in poverty* (pp. 23–50). New York: Cambridge University Press.

Duncan, G., & Brooks-Gunn, J. (Eds.). (in press). *Consequences of growing up poor*. New York: Russell Sage Foundation Press.

Duncan, G. J., Brooks-Gunn, J., & Klebanov, P. K. (1994). Economic deprivation and early-childhood development. *Child Development*, *65*(2) 296–318.

Duncan, G. J., Hill, M. S., & Hoffman, S. D. (1988). Welfare dependence within and across generations. *Science*, *1*, 467–471.

Duncan, G. J. & Rodgers, W. (1991). Has children's poverty become more persistent? *American Sociological Review*, *56*, 538–550.

Duncan, G. J., Smeeding, T. M., & Rodgers, W. (1991, December). W(h)ither the middle class? A dynamic view. Paper presented at the Levy Institute Conference on Income Inequality, Bard College, New York.

Dunst, C. J., Snyder, S. W., & Mankinen, M. (1989). Efficacy of early intervention. In M. C. Wang, M. C. Reynolds, & H. J. Walberg (Eds.), *Handbook of special education: Research and practice: Vol. 3. Low incidence conditions. Advances in education* (pp. 259–294). Oxford, England: Pergamon Press.

Earls, F. (1980). The prevalence of behavior problems in 3-year-old children. *Journal of the American Academy of Child Psychiatry*, *19*, 439–452.

Egbuonu, L., & Starfield, B. (1982). Child health and social status. *Pediatrics*, *69*, 550–557.

Egeland, B., & Erickson, M. F. (1991). Rising above the past: Strategies for helping new mothers break the cycle of abuse and neglect. *Zero to Three*, *11*(2), 29–35.

Egeland, B., & Erickson, M. (1992). Attachment theory and findings: Implications for prevention and intervention. In S. Kramer & H. Parens (Eds.), *Prevention in mental health: Now, tomorrow, ever?* Northvale, NJ: Jason Aronson.

Elder, G. H., Jr. (1974). *Children of the Great Depression: Social change in life experience*. Chicago: University of Chicago Press.

Ellwood, D. T. (1988). *Poor support: Poverty in the American family*. New York: Basic Books.

Featherman, D. L., & Hauser, R. M. (1987). *Opportunity and change*. New York: Academic Press.

Field, T. M. (1981). Early development of the preterm offspring of teenage mothers. In K. Scott, T. Field, & E. Robertson (Eds.), *Teenage parents and their offspring* (pp. 145–175). New York: Grune & Stratton.

Field, T. M., Widmayer, S., Greenberg, R., & Stroller, S. (1982). Effects of parent training on teenage mothers and their infants. *Pediatrics*, *69*(6), 703–707.

Field, T. M., Widmayer, S. M., Stringer, S., & Ignatoff, E. (1980). Teenage, lower-class, black mothers and their preterm infants: An intervention and developmental follow-up. *Child Development*, *51*(2), 426–436.

Furstenberg, F. F., Jr., Brooks-Gunn, J., & Morgan, S. P. (1987). *Adolescent mothers in later life*. New York: Cambridge University Press.

Furstenberg, F. F., Jr., Lincoln, R., & Menken, J. (Eds.). (1981). *Teenage sexuality, pregnancy and childbearing*. Philadelphia: University of Pennsylvania Press.

Garmezy, N., & Rutter, M. (1983). *Stress, coping and development in children*. New York: McGraw-Hill.

Gray, S. W., & Wandersman, L. P. (1980). The methodology of home-based intervention studies: Problems and promising strategies. *Child Development, 51*, 993–1009.

Greenspan, S. I., Weider, S., Lieberman, A., Nover, R., Louile, R., & Robinson, M. (Eds.). (1987). *Clinical infant reports: No. 3. Infants in multirisk families: Case studies in preventive intervention*. New York: International Universities Press.

Gross, R. T., Brooks-Gunn, J., & Spiker, D. (1992). Efficacy of comprehensive early interventions for low birth weight, premature infants and their families: The Infant Health and Development Program. In S. L. Friedman & M. D. Sigman (Eds.), *The psychological development of low birth weight children: Advances in applied developmental psychology* (pp. 411–433). Norwood, NJ: Ablex.

Guo, G., Brooks-Gunn, J. & Harris, K. M. (submitted). *Parental labor-force attachment and grade retention among urban black children*.

Gutelius, M. F., Kirsch, A. D., MacDonald, S., Brooks, M. R., & McErlean, T. (1977). Controlled study of child health supervision: Behavioral results. *Pediatrics, 60*(3), 294–304.

Guttmacher, A. (1981). *Teenage pregnancy: The problem that won't go away*. New York: Alan Guttmacher Institute.

Haggerty, R. J., Roghmann, K. H., & Pless, I. B. (1975). *Child health and the community*. New York: Wiley.

Hanson, T., McLanahan, S., & Thomson, E. (in press). Economic resources, parental practices and child well-being. In G. Duncan & J. Brooks-Gunn (Eds.), *Consequences of growing up poor*. New York: Russell Sage Foundation Press.

Hardy, J. B., King, T. M., Shipp, D. A., & Welcher, D. W. (1981). A comprehensive approach to adolescent pregnancy. In K. G. Scott, T. Field, & E. G. Robertson (Eds.), *Teenage parents and their offspring* (pp. 265–282). New York: Grune & Stratton.

Hauser, R. M. (in press). Does poverty in adolescence affect the life chances of high school graduates? In G. Duncan & J. Brooks-Gunn (Eds.), *Consequences of growing up poor*. New York: Russell Sage Foundation Press.

Haveman, R., Wolfe, B., & Spalding, J. (1991). Childhood events and circumstances influencing high school completion. *Demography, 28*, 133–157.

Hayes, C. D. (Ed.). (1987). *Risking the future: Adolescent sexuality, pregnancy, and childbearing* (Vol. 1). Washington, DC: National Academy of Sciences Press.

Hebbeler, K. (1985). An old and a new question on the effects of early education for children from low income families. *Educational Evaluation and Policy Analysis, 7*(3), 207–216.

Hernandez, D. J. (1993). *America's children: Resources from family, government, and the economy*. New York: Russell Sage Foundation Press.

Hernandez, D. J. (in press). Poverty trends. In G. Duncan & J. Brooks-Gunn (Eds.), *Consequences of growing up poor*. New York: Russell Sage Foundation Press.

Hill, C. R., & Duncan, G. (1987). Parental family income and the socioeconomic attainment of children. *Social Science Research, 16*, 39–73.

Hofferth, S. L. (1995). Caring for children at the poverty line. *Children and Youth Services Review, 17*(2), 1–31.

Hofferth, S. L., & Hayes, C. D. (Eds.). (1987). *Risking the future: Adolescent sexuality, pregnancy, and childbearing* (Vol. 2). Washington, DC: National Academy of Sciences Press.

Hofferth, S. L., & Phillips, D. A. (1991). Child care policy research. *Journal of Social Issues, 47*, 1–13.

Hunt, J. M. (1961). *Intelligence and experience*. New York: Ronald Press Company.

Infant Health and Development Program (1990). Enhancing the outcomes of low-birth-weight, premature infants. *Journal of American Medical Association, 263*, 3035–3042.

Kagan, J., & Moss, H. A. (1962). *Birth to maturity*. New York: Wiley.

Kellam, S. G., Ensminger, M. E., & Turner, R. J. (1977). Family structure and the mental health of children. *Archives of General Psychiatry, 34*, 1012–1022.

Kennedy, M. M. (1978). Findings from the Follow Through Planned Variation study. *Educational Researcher, 7,* 3–11.

Klerman, L. V. (1975). Adolescent pregnancy: The need for new policies and new programs. *Journal of School Health, 45,* 263–267.

Klerman, L. V (1979). Evaluating service programs for school-age parents; Design problems. *Evaluation and Health Professions, 21*(1), 55–70.

Klerman, L. V. (1981). Programs for pregnant adolescents and young parents: Their development and assessment. In K. G. Scott, T. Field, & E. Robertson (Eds.), *Teenage parents and their offspring* (pp. 227–248). New York: Grune & Stratton.

Klerman, L. V. (1991). The health of poor children: Problems and programs. In A. C. Huston (Ed.), *Children and poverty: Child development and public policy* (pp. 136–157). New York: Cambridge University Press.

Kurtz, L., Boulerice, B., & Treemblay, R. (in press). The influence of poverty upon elementary school children's classroom placement and behavior problems. In G. Duncan & J. Brooks-Gunn (Eds.), *Consequences of growing up poor.* New York: Russell Sage Foundation Press.

Lazar, I., Darlington, R. B., Murray, H., Royce, J. & Snipper, A. (1982). Lasting effects of early education: A report from the Consortium for Longitudinal Studies. *Monographs of the Society for Research in Child Development, 47* (2–3, Serial No. 195).

Lazear, E. P., & Michael, R. T. (1987). *Allocation of income within the household.* Chicago: University of Chicago Press.

Lee, V. E., Brooks-Gunn, J., & Schnur, E. (1988). Does Head Start work? A one-year follow-up comparison of disadvantaged children attending Head Start, no preschool, and other preschool programs. *Developmental Psychology, 24,* 210–222.

Lee, V. E., Brooks-Gunn, J., Schnur, E., & Liaw, T. (1990). Are Head Start effects sustained? A longitudinal comparison of disadvantaged children attending Head Start, no preschool, and other preschool programs. *Child Development, 61,* 495–507.

Lerner, R. M. (1987, February). *Early adolescent transitions: The lore and the laws of adolescence* (Report No. 15). Philadelphia, PA: Scholarly Report Series, Center for the Study of Child and Adolescent Development.

Liaw, F. R., & Brooks-Gunn, J. (1993). Patterns of low birth weight children's cognitive development and their determinants. *Developmental Psychology, 29*(6), 1024–1035.

Liaw, F., & Brooks-Gunn, J. (1994). Cumulative familial risks and low-birthweight children's cognitive and behavioral development. *Journal of Clinical Child Psychology, 23*(4), 360–372.

Links, P. S. (1983). Community surveys of the prevalence of childhood psychiatric disorders: A review. *Child Development, 54,* 531–548.

Maccoby, E. E., & Jacklin, C. N. (1974). *The psychology of sex differences.* Stanford: Stanford University Press.

Massey, D. F., & Eggers, M. L. (1990). The ecology of inequality: Minorities and the concentration of poverty 1970–1980. *American Journal of Sociology, 95*(5), 1153–1188.

Maynard, R. (1995). Teenage childbearing and welfare reform: Lessons from a decade of demonstration and evaluation research. *Children and Youth Services Review* [special issue: Child poverty, public policies, and welfare reform], *17*(1), 309–332.

McCormick, M. C. (1989). Long-term follow-up of infants discharged from neonatal intensive care units. *Journal of the American Medical Association, 261*(12), 1767–1772.

McCormick, M. C., & Brooks-Gunn, J. (1989). The health of children and adolescents. In H. E. Freeman & S. Levine (Eds.), *Handbook of medical sociology* (pp. 347–380). Englewood Cliffs, NJ: Prentice-Hall.

McCormick, M. C., Shapiro, S., & Starfield, B. H. (1985). The regionalization of perinatal services: Summary of the evaluation of a national demonstration program. *Journal of the American Medical Association, 253*(6), 799–804.

McGee, E. (1982). *Too little, too late: Services for teenage parents.* New York: Ford Foundation.

McKey, R. H., Condelli, L., Granson, H., Barrett, B., McConkey, C., & Plantz, M. (1985). *The impact of Head Start on children, families and communities.* Final report ot the Head Start Evaluation, Synthesis, and Utilization Project. Washington, DC: CSR.

McLanahan, S. S. (1985). Family structure and the reproduction of poverty. *American Journal of Sociology, 90*(4), 873–901.

McLanahan, S., & Sandefur, G, D, (1994) *Growing up with a single parent. What hurts, what helps?* Cambridge, MA: Harvard University Press.

McLoyd, V. C. (1990). The impact of economic hardship on black families and development. *Child Development, 61,* 311–346.

Mercer, J. (1973). *Labeling the mentally retarded.* Berkeley, CA: University of California Press.

Miller, L. B., & Bizzel, R. P. (1984). Long-term effects of four preschool programs: Ninth- and tenth-grade results. *Child Development, 55,* 1570–1587.

Miller, S. A. (1988). Parents' beliefs about children's cognitive development. *Child Development, 59,* 259–285.

Moore, K. A., & Burt, M. R. (1982). *Private crisis, public cost: Policy perspectives on teenage childbearing.* Washington, DC: Urban Institute Press.

Moore, K. A., Myers, D. E., Morrison, D. R., Nord, C. W., Brown, B., & Edmonston, B. (1993). Age at first childbirth and later poverty. *Journal of Research in Adolescence, 3*(4), 393–422.

Ogbu, J. U. (1985). A cultural ecology of competence among inner-city blacks. In M. B. Spencer, G. K. Brookins, & W. R. Allen (Eds.), *Beginnings: The social and affective development of black children* (pp. 45–66). Hillsdale, NJ: Erlbaum.

Ogbu, J. U. (1986). The consequences of the American caste system. In U. Neisser (Ed.), *The school achievement of minority children.* Hillsdale, NJ: Erlbaum.

Olds, D. L. (1990). Can home visitation improve the health of women and children at risk? In D. L. Rogers & E. Ginzberg (Eds.), *Improving the life chances of children at risk* (pp. 79–103). Boulder, CO: Westview Press.

Olds, D. L., Henderson, C. R., Chamberlin, R., & Tatlebaum, R. (1986). Preventing child abuse and neglect: A randomized trial of nurse home visitation. *Pediatrics, 78,* 65–78.

Oyemade, U. J. (1985). The rationale for Head Start as a vehicle for the upward mobility of minority families: A minority perspective. *American Journal of Orthopsychiatry, 55*(4), 591–602.

Parker, S., Greer, S., & Zuckerman, B. (1988). Double jeopardy: The impact of poverty on early child development. *The Pediatric Clinics of North America, 35*(6), 1227–1240.

Phillips, D. A. (Ed.). (1987). *Quality in child care: What does research tell us?* Washington, DC: National Association for the Education of Young Children.

Polit, D. F. (1989). Effects of comprehensive program for teenage parents: Five years after Project Redirection. *Family Planning Perspectives, 21*(4), 164–169.

Polit, D. F., Kahn, J., & Stevens, D. (1985, April). *Final impacts from Project Redirection: A program for pregnant and parenting teens.* New York: Manpower Demonstration Research Corporation.

Polit, D. F., Tannen, M., & Kahn, J. (1983). *School, work and family planning: Interim impacts in Project Redirection.* New York: Manpower Demonstration Research Corporation.

Ramey, C. T., Bryant, D. M., & Suarez, T, M. (1983). Preschool compensatory education and the modifiability of intelligence: A critical review. In D. Detterman (Ed.), *Current topics in human intelligence* (pp. 247–296). Norwood, NJ: Ablex.

Ramey, C. T., Bryant, D. M., Wasik, B. H., Sparling, J. J., Fendt, K. H., & LaVange, L. M. (1992). The Infant Health and Development Program: Program elements, family participation, and child intelligence. *Pediatrics, 3,* 454–465.

Ramey, C. T., & Suarez, T. (1984). Early intervention and the early experience paradigm: Toward a better framework for social policy. *Journal of Children in Contemporary Society, 17*(1), 3–13.

Robins, L. N. (1966). *Deviant children grown up: A sociological and psychiatric study of sociopathic personality.* Baltimore: Williams & Wilkins. Reprinted and published by Robert E. Krieger Publishing Co., Huntington, NY, 1974.

Roosa, M. W. (1985). *Adolescent mothers, school dropouts and school based intervention programs.*

Paper presented at the biennial meeting of the Society for Research on Child Development, Toronto, Ontario, Canada.

Roosa, M. W., Fitzgerald, H. E., & Carson, N. A. (1982). Teenage and older mothers and their infants: A descriptive comparison. *Adolescence, 17*, 1–15.

Roosa, M. W., & Vaughn, L., (1983). Teen mothers enrolled in an alternative parenting program: A comparison of their peers. *Urban Education, 18*, 348–360.

Rutter, M. (1979). *Changing youth in a changing society*. London: Nuffield Provincial Hospitals Trust; Cambridge, MA: Harvard University Press.

Sameroff, A. J., Seifer, R., Barocas, R., Zax, M., & Greenspan, S. (1987). Intelligence quotient scores of 4-year-old children: Social-environmental risk factors. *Pediatrics, 79*(3), 343–350.

Sandefur, G. D., McLanahan, S., & Wojtkiewicz, R. A. (1992). The effects of parental marital status during adolescence on high school graduation. *Social Forces, 71*(1), 103–121.

Scarr, S. (1982). Development is internally guided, not determined. *Contemporary Psychology, 46*, 932–946.

Schinke, S. P. (1978). Teenage pregnancy: The need for multiple casework services. *Social Casework, 59*, 406–410.

Schnur, E. S., Brooks-Gunn, J., & Shipman, V. (1992). Who attends programs serving poor children? The case of Head Start attendees and nonattendees. *Journal of Applied Developmental Psychology, 13*(3), 405–421.

Schweinhart, L., Weikart, D., & Larner, M. (1986). Consequences of three preschool curriculum models through age 15. *Early Childhood Research Quarterly, 1*, 15–45.

Seitz, V., Rosenbaum, L. K., & Apfel, N. H. (1985). Effects of family support intervention: A ten-year follow-up. *Child Development, 56*(2), 376–391.

Sewell, W., & Hauser, R. (1975). *Education, occupation, and earnings: Achievement in the early career*. New York: Academic Press.

Shipman, V. C. (Ed.). (1972, December). *Disadvantaged children and their first school experiences: ETS Head Start Longitudinal Study* (ETS Technical Report Series PR-72-27). Princeton, NJ: Educational Testing Service, ERIC Document Reproduction Service.

Silverberg, M. (1988). Nonmaternal care: Implications for children and parents. Report for the Rockefeller Foundation by Mathematica Policy Research, Princeton, NJ.

Slaughter, D. T., Oyemade, U. J., Washington, V., & Lindsey, R. (1988). Head Start: A backward and forward look. Chicago: Northwestern University.

Smith, S. (1995). *Two-generation programs for families in poverty: A new intervention strategy*. Norwood, NJ: Ablex.

Smith, J. R., Brooks-Gunn, J., & Klebanov, P. K. (in press). In G. Duncan & J. Brooks-Gunn (Eds.), *Consequences of growing up poor*. New York: Russell Sage Foundation Press.

Sonenstein, F. L., & Wolf, D. A. (1991). Satisfaction with child care: Perspectives of welfare mothers. *Journal of Social Issues, 47*(2), 15–31.

Spencer, M. B., Brookins, G. K., & Allen, W. R. (Eds.). (1985). *Beginnings: The social and affective development of black children*. Hillsdale, NJ: Erlbaum.

Spencer, M. B., & Dornbusch, S. (1990). Challenges in studying minority youth. In S. Feldman & G. R. Elliott (Eds.), *At the threshold: The developing adolescent*. Cambridge, MA: Harvard University Press.

Spiker, D., Ferguson, J., & Brooks-Gunn, J. (1993). Enhancing maternal interactive behavior and child social competence in low-birth-weight, premature infants. *Child Development, 64*(3), 754–768.

Sugland, B. W., Zaslow, M., Smith, J. R., Brooks-Gunn, J., Coates, D., Blumenthal, C., Moore, K. A., Griffin, T., & Bradley, R. (1995, in press). The Early Childhood HOME inventory and HOME-Short Form in differing racial/ethnic groups: Are there differences in underlying structure, internal consistency of subscales, and patterns of prediction? *Journal of Family Issues*.

Sung, K. (1981). The role of day care for teenage mothers in a public school. *Child Care Quarterly, 10*(2), 113–124.

Sung, K., & Rothrock, D. (1980). An alternate school for pregnant teen-agers and teen-age mothers. *Child Welfare, 59*, 427–436.

Wachs, T. D., & Gruen, G. E. (1982). *Early experience and human development.* New York: Plenum.

Washington, V. (1985a). Head Start: How appropriate for minority families in the 1980s? *American Journal of Orthopsychiatry, 55*(4), 577–590.

Washington, V. (1985b). Social policy, cultural diversity, and the obscurity of black children. *Journal of Educational Equity and Leadership, 5*(4), 320–335.

Werner, E. E., & Smith, R. S. (1982). *Vulnerable but invincible: A longitudinal study of resilient children and youth.* New York: McGraw-Hill.

White, K., & Casto, G. (1985). An integrative review of early intervention efficacy studies with at-risk children: Implications for the handicapped. *Analysis and Intervention in Developmental Disabilities, 5*, 7–31.

Woodhead, M. (1988). When psychology informs public policy: The case of early childhood intervention. *American Psychologist, 43*(6), 443–454.

Zigler, E. F. (1987). Formal schooling for four-year-olds? No. *American Psychologist, 42*(3), 254–260.

Zigler, E. F., & Gordon, E. W. (Eds.). (1982). *Day care: Scientific and social policy issues.* Boston: Auburn House.

Zigler, E., Taussig, C., & Black, K. (1992). Early childhood intervention: A promising preventative for juvenile delinquency. *American Psychologist, 47*(8), 997–1006.

Zigler, E. F., & Valentine J. (Eds.). (1979). *Project Head Start: A legacy of the war on poverty.* New York: Macmillan.

Zill, N., Krysan, M., Stief, T., & Peterson, J. L. (1989). *Young children in poverty in the United States: A statistical profile.* Paper prepared for the National Center for Children in Poverty, Columbia University, New York.

III. Child care

5   Policy issues of child care

Andrew J. Cherlin

Current efforts to reform the U.S. welfare system have been driven by the growing sentiment that the best way to assist the persistently poor is to encourage economic self-sufficiency. The opinion is now common that long-term dependence on public assistance – and long-term withdrawal from the labor market – are harmful for reasons that extend beyond a lack of income. Both are said to reinforce attitudes and behavior that make it hard for the poor to ever get and hold a job. More generally, there is a sense among some observers that widespread, long-term dependence on welfare in inner-city ghetto neighborhoods fosters a social climate characterized by a lack of initiative and personal responsibility – a climate that discourages people from taking the steps necessary to escape from poverty.

And so, during the late 1980s and early 1990s, a broad-based policy consensus emerged that took reducing dependence on public assistance to be the central goal of welfare reform. The new consensus was celebrated in summit meetings of conservative and liberal academics, intellectuals, and activists (American Enterprise Institute, 1987). It became the basic principle of the Family Support Act of 1988, which attempted to turn a heretofore income assistance program into a job-training program (Haskins, this volume). And it lived on in President Clinton's 1992 pledge to "end welfare as we know it" by limiting cash assistance without employment to 2 years. When Richard Nixon proposed "workfare" as a solution to the welfare problem, Democrats and liberal Republicans were outraged; now most liberal members of Congress appear either to support a similar principle or to remain silent.

Whether accurate or not, this new consensus on welfare is based on a model of the behavior of *adults*. It considers the reasons why men and women do or do not develop an attachment to the labor force. Sometimes these reasons are thought to be rational, economic responses to the costs and benefits of becoming part of the world of work; sometimes they are thought to be the result of attitudes and behaviors antithetical to those needed in the work world. In either case, little attention has been paid to the implications of work-oriented welfare reform on the children of the adults. This chapter addresses the effects of child care policies associated with welfare reform, in particular the Family Support Act of 1988, on children. The basic

121

question is whether changes on the part of mothers – from receiving public assistance to participating in the labor force with transitional child care assistance – will be beneficial, on balance, to their children.

The costs and benefits
of welfare reform to children

From the children's perspective, the fundamental day-to-day effect of welfare reform, if successful, is to remove more of them from the full-time care of their mothers so that the mothers can become economically self-sufficient. Stating the effect this starkly makes clear what some of the trade-offs may be for children whose mothers will participate in new employment, training, or education programs. There are two types of benefit, indirect and direct, which might accrue to children. The indirect benefits are that if their mothers are able to enter and stay in the labor market, the family environment of children may become more favorable to their social, emotional, and cognitive development. It is these indirect benefits – acting through the effects of maternal employment – that have received the most attention in public discussions and are emphasized in Haskins' chapter in this volume. The mechanisms are that, first, family income may improve, at least in the long run, as work for wages replaces public assistance. Second, if mothers learn how to read better or improve other skills, the cognitive environment in the home – the presence of books and newspapers, and parental involvement in the children's schooling – may improve (Bradley & Caldwell, 1976). And third, the climate in the family, it is hoped, will emphasize personal initiative and responsibility in a fashion that may increase the likelihood that children will stay in school, postpone becoming parents, and begin successful work careers.

This is the theory, at least. Few would dispute that a higher family income is better for children. Yet in the short run, it is not clear how much improvement in income low-wage work will provide over public assistance, especially if medical coverage is problematic. In some high-benefit states, the combination of AFDC benefits, food stamps, and Medicaid coverage may be nearly as beneficial financially as a minimum-wage job (Ellwood, 1988). As for increased education, there is, in fact, evidence that children do better when their parents have more education. Indeed, the great increase in the average education of parents, black and white, is one of the major positive trends of the past few decades that has affected the well-being of children (Zill & Rogers, 1988).

It is not known whether a climate of initiative would occur in the home if mothers get jobs nor to what extent this would alter the lives of children. Common sense seems to suggest that in a home in which the mother is at work, better-educated, and economically self-sufficient, children's chances of successful work and personal lives will be increased. This belief is part of the consensus that led to the passage of the Family Support Act of 1988 (see Chase-Lansdale & Vinovskis, this volume). Yet studies that purport to show a relationship between maternal employment and positive child outcomes may be misleading, as Haskins (this volume) argues, because a mother who is currently employed may be different in unmeasured ways from a mother who might become employed at a result of a training program. To be sure, studies do show that children who grow up in single-parent families complete fewer years of schooling, are more likely to become teenage parents, and suffer related difficulties. But studies do not clearly show that being in a single-parent family that receives AFDC is much worse for children than being in a single-parent family that does not receive AFDC. For example, McLanahan (1985) found inconsistent evidence in the Panel Study of Income Dynamics. Being in a family that received AFDC benefits reduced the chance that white 17-year-olds were in school and that they would graduate by their early 20s – controlling for family structure and other relevant variables. But for blacks, the effects of AFDC receipt on being in school at 17 were smaller; and 17-year-old black young adults whose families received AFDC were *more* likely to graduate from high school than those whose families did not – controlling again for family structure. These inconsistent findings show no clear effect of welfare receipt, over and above its association with poverty and with being in a single-parent family, on the educational attainment of black young adults (McLanahan, 1985).

In addition to these sometimes elusive indirect benefits of welfare reform on children, there is a potential direct benefit that has received less attention. The mandatory provision of child care assistance to mothers participating in the JOBS (Jobs, Opportunities, and Basic Skills) program or working in the year afterward provides an opportunity to affect children's daily environments directly. There is evidence that children can benefit from child care settings that provide enriched curricula, although experts differ sharply in their evaluation of it – even in this volume (see Brooks-Gunn, this volume; Haskins, this volume; Spencer, Blumenthal, & Richards, this volume). Head Start, for example, benefits poor children more than attendance at conventional preschool programs or than not attending any preschool program (Lee, Brooks-Gunn, & Schnur, 1988), although it is not known how long these benefits last.

Against the potential for these direct and indirect benefits for children, however, one must balance the potential costs to children of welfare reform. Substantial numbers of children may be placed in custodial child care arrangements that are inferior to the care they are now receiving from mothers, grandmothers, and other relatives. There is no guarantee – nor even a likelihood – that the out-of-home care to be arranged for the children of welfare-to-work participants will consist largely of the kind of enriched programs that can provide compensatory gains. Nor is it even to be expected that most care will be provided in "high-quality" settings, as defined by experts in child development (Hayes, Palmer, & Zaslow, 1990).

High-quality care, not to mention an educationally enriched program, is very expensive. As states utilize their limited child care funds, and as participants use their income disregards or child care vouchers, concerns about cost will conflict with concerns about quality. One's assessment of how to make this trade-off depends in part on an assessment of the importance of the indirect versus direct benefits to children. If one believes that children are helped in the long run primarily by encouraging their mothers to be self-sufficient, then one might opt for spreading the child care funds widely to maximize the number of mothers who can participate in the JOBS program – even at the cost of providing less-than-optimal care for the children. If one believes that compensatory programs offer a more direct and effective means of helping poor children, then one might choose to concentrate the funds on enriched child care, even at the cost of limiting the number of mothers who can be enrolled in employment training and schooling (Phillips, 1991).

Unfortunately, at current and foreseen levels of funding, difficult trade-offs such as this one are facing administrators of AFDC. Given the pressure to achieve legally mandated participation rates, and given the focus of attention on the mothers, it is very likely that the quality of the care received by the children of participants will not receive high priority. States may be more likely to use child care funds to create the maximum number of subsidized places versus using the funds to create high-quality, compensatory places. As of early 1993, however, it still was not possible to determine how many families in the JOBS program were receiving child care assistance, and state-to-state variation appeared to be substantial (Greenberg, 1992).

Child care supply and demand

It is important to review what is known about patterns of child care and children's well-being. Let me begin with a brief overview of what is known about the supply of and demand for paid child care services. Then I will turn to questions about the usage of care by low-income families: What kinds of care are low-income children of employed mothers receiving now? What are the cost and quality of that care? What kinds of care are likely to be demanded and supplied as a result of welfare reform? Although some news reports and commentaries still maintain that there is a serious shortage of child care spaces for children, it is the consensus among social scientists that no general, overall shortage of child care spaces exists (Hayes et al., 1990). That is to say, the sheer number of spaces available for the care of children is, in general, comparable to the number of children whose parents wish to purchase child care services. There are two main reasons for this conclusion. First, there has been a great expansion in the supply of care offered for preschool children; for example, there were about three times as many child care centers in 1990 as in the mid-1970s, and about four times as many children were enrolled in these centers (Hofferth, 1992). The growth in spaces seems to roughly match the growth in the number of children whose parents want care (Hofferth, 1992). Second, if there were a general shortage of spaces, one would expect to see the price of care rise. But there have been only modest increases in the price of center-based care and care in family day care homes – the two most widely used forms of paid care – since the mid-1970s. In 1990 dollars corrected for inflation, the average cost of care at a center in 1975 was $1.40 an hour; in 1990 it was $1.67 an hour. Care in a family day care home rose only from $1.29 an hour to $1.35 an hour over the same period (Hofferth, Brayfield, Deich, & Holcomb, 1991).

This does not mean there are no problems in the child care market. For one thing, the increase in the supply of care has been greatest for children age 2 and over because many child care centers will not take children younger than 2. So it is possible that spaces for infant care have not kept up with the demand. (During the 1980s the percentage of mothers of infants who were working outside the home rose sharply [Cherlin, 1992].) It is also possible that care for children with special needs, such as handicapped children, has not expanded as greatly. In addition, the vast majority of centers and family day care homes offer care during standard, daytime work hours. It may be much more difficult for parents who work nonstandard hours – evenings, nights, or weekends – to find spaces for their children. This problem may be particularly acute for participants in the JOBS program. An advocacy group in West Virginia that is monitoring that state's implementation of the JOBS program reported that, of persons who left Aid to Families with Dependent Children (AFDC) to take jobs, 61% said that they worked weekends, 38% said that they worked nights, and 16% said that they had a child with a handicap or special needs (Angel & Perroncel, 1992). These parents may have a much tougher time finding adequate paid care.

Parents who need daytime, Monday-through-Friday care for a healthy 2-, 3-, or 4-year-old – and possibly for younger children as well – generally will find places available. I realize that this conclusion seems inconsistent with media reports of long waiting lists at many centers. But parents appear to put their names on many lists at once and do not always remove their names from a center's list when they find a space somewhere else. In any case, two important problems remain in the child care market: Parents, especially those with low incomes, may not be able to afford the price of the care that is available; and the quality of the care may not be as high as they would like. Studies of the child care market, then, suggest that if there is a problem with supply and demand, it is a problem of cost and quality rather than of availability. The dilemma is that increasing the quality of care may also raise its cost. In the following pages, I will discuss the implications of these two potential problems for low-income families.

Child care for low-income children:
What is known

Little is known specifically about the child care choices of mothers receiving AFDC, but there is information on the child care arrangements of mothers with low incomes. The best recent information comes from the 1990 National Child Care Survey, for which a random sample of 4,392 households with one or more children under 13 were interviewed by telephone (Hofferth et al., 1991). Table 5.1 shows the primary child care arrangement used by the parents for the youngest child under age 5 in households with a mother who worked outside the home. Five kinds of care

Table 5.1. *Primary child care arrangement used by parents for the youngest child under age 5 in households in which the mother worked outside the home, United States, 1990*

	Parent (%)	Relative (%)	In-home provider (%)	Family day care (%)	Center (%)	Other (%)	Total %	Population estimate (thousands)	Sample size
All	28	19	3	20	28	2	100	7,436	1,180
< 1 year	38	22	4	20	14	2	100	1,495	237
1–2 years	29	21	3	23	22	2	100	3,061	486
3–4 years	21	16	2	16	43	2	100	2,659	422
< high school	31	33	1	12	22	2	100	456	72
High school	27	24	2	19	25	3	100	2,847	452
Some college	32	16	1	25	25	1	100	1,787	284
College	28	14	4	20	32	2	100	1,419	225
Graduate school	19	11	8	18	44	0	100	707	112
< $15,000	31	24	0	16	25	4	100	1,074	170
$15,000–$24,999	30	23	2	16	27	2	100	1,226	195
$25,000–$34,999	29	24	1	20	23	3	100	1,222	194
$35,000–$49,999	31	15	4	20	29	1	100	1,713	272
$50,000+	21	14	5	26	34	0	100	1,712	272
Above poverty	28	18	3	20	29	2	100	6,022	956
Below poverty	29	26	0	16	22	7	100	644	105
Mother only	11	26	3	19	38	3	100	1,208	192
Mother and father	31	18	3	20	26	2	100	6,007	954
White	31	17	3	22	26	1	100	5,436	863
Black	14	27	0	11	45	3	100	989	157
Hispanic	25	30	4	15	23	3	100	664	105

Source: Reprinted with permission from The Urban Institute (Hofferth, S. L., Brayfield, A., Deich, S., & Holcomb, P. [1991]. *National Child Care Survey, 1990* [Urban Institute Report 91–5] Washington, DC: Urban Institute Press)

arrangement are distinguished: care by a parent (either the mother or her husband), by a relative (either in the parents' household or elsewhere), by a nonrelative in the home, in a family day care home, or in a child care center. The first row of the table shows that nearly half of these children were cared for by parents (28%) or other relatives (19%). The usage of care by parents and relatives varied greatly by the characteristics of the mother and the child. Mothers of children under 3 – and especially under 1 – relied on fathers and relatives heavily and relied secondarily on family day care homes. This pattern reflects a mix of preference and constraint. Parents prefer to leave small children with relatives or in homelike settings. In addition, many day care centers will not take very young children.

More directly relevant for this chapter are the rows in the table that present type of care by mother's education, income, and family structure. It can be seen, first of all, that the lower the education of the mother, the more likely she is to use care by relatives. The pattern for low-income families differs greatly by whether a father is present in the home. Data from the National Child Care Survey are not available on this point, but relevant tabulations have been published from the winter 1984–85 supplement to the Current Population Survey conducted by the U.S. Bureau of the Census (U.S. House of Representatives, 1989). These data demonstrate that married mothers with low incomes relied heavily on their husbands, who provided 42% of the primary child care among married couples below the poverty level. Among mother-only families, not surprisingly, father care was minimal; still, single mothers in low-income families were more likely to rely on relative care in the home than were better-off single mothers. Relatives in the home provided 45% of the primary child care for employed, single mothers living below the poverty level. In contrast, center-based care accounted for just 20% of the primary child care for single mothers living in poverty, a lower percentage than for better-off single mothers.

Grandmother care

Most of the relatives providing care for children of single mothers are grandmothers. More detailed information was obtained by Parish, Hao, and Hogan (1991) from a nationally representative sample of young mothers aged 19 to 26 in 1984. High levels of coresidence among grandmothers, their unmarried daughters, and their grandchildren were prevalent, particularly among blacks. Forty-five percent of the black single mothers in the sample were living in the same household with their mothers, as were 23% of the white single mothers. Employed single mothers, both black and white, relied heavily on their mothers for child care. The survey ascertained who was providing care for the youngest child of the mothers who were employed. Forty-eight percent of the black single mothers reported that grandmothers were providing the care, as did 45% of the white single mothers (Parish et al., 1991).

What are we to make of all of this care by grandmothers? By objective standards, it is generally of good quality. That is to say, if we compare it to out-of-home care on such conventional indicators as number of caregivers per child and stability of caretakers, grandmother care fares well. It is mostly unpaid care, although a minority of relatives providing care are paid. It allows young children to be cared for in their homes or the homes of relatives and to have sustained contact with family members. Given these positive characteristics, there is a tendency to regard a further expansion of grandmother care as an easy and preferable solution to the child care needs of employed single mothers. Indeed, a recent study finds positive effects of grandmother care on poor children's cognitive and social development (Baydar & Brooks-Gunn, 1991).

However, it would be a mistake to conclude that grandmothers can supply most of the additional care that the young mothers would need if the Family Support Act of 1988 is successful in encouraging labor market participation. Not every single mother has a nearby, willing mother who can provide care. It is reasonable to assume that those who have not yet used grandmother care are less likely to have a grandmother they can ever use. Despite the presence of grandmothers, surveys show that single mothers are much more likely to report that the lack of satisfactory child care is a constraint on their labor force participation than are married mothers. In the 1984 National Longitudinal Survey of Youth (NLSY), 72% of the black single mothers aged 19 to 26, and 53% of comparable whites, responded that they would work more hours (if they were already working), look for work (if they were unemployed), or seek more schooling or job training if "satisfactory child care were available" (Hogan, Hao, & Parish, 1990).

Furthermore, data from the Current Population Survey (CPS) show that employed mothers whose children received unpaid care by relatives report higher levels of constraints on work effort. In the June 1977 current population survey, employed mothers were asked, "If you could find additional satisfactory child care at reasonable cost, would you work more hours?" Among part-time workers, those whose children were receiving unpaid care by relatives were most likely to respond positively – 27% when the care was occurring in the child's home and 36% when the care was occurring in the relative's home. Among full-time workers, the only higher level of constraint was reported by those whose children were cared for in their homes by nonrelatives. Among all employed women, those who were purchasing care from family day care homes or child care centers reported the lowest levels of constraint on work effort (Presser & Baldwin, 1980). To be sure, these questions are vague and hypothetical; it is impossible to know what the respondents think the phrase "satisfactory care at reasonable cost" means. Yet the CPS and NLSY data do suggest strongly that unpaid care by relatives is not an easily expandable, available source of additional child care for single mothers.

In addition, many of the grandmothers who might be potential caretakers are working or rearing children – or both – themselves. According to an estimate by Presser, one-third of grandmothers who provide child care to their preschool grandchildren are themselves employed outside the home. It appears that, in most cases, the grandmothers work different shifts from their daughters (Presser, 1989). Presser writes: "If the children are sleeping while the grandmother is sleeping, and the mother works nights in this way, then this child-care mode may be satisfactory, but how is the mother caring for the child when she gets home and has had no sleep? To what extent are these children actually alone or being cared for by somewhat older siblings?" (1992, pp. 30–31).

The Family Support Act of 1988 legislation identifies parents under 24 without high school diplomas and with limited work experience as a high-priority population. These young mothers will in turn have a disproportionate number of young mothers, many still in their 30s. Burton and Bengtson (1985) have found that these young grandmothers often experience grandmotherhood as a distressing "off-time" event. They love their grandchildren, of course, and want to help their daughters; but they are not ready to think of themselves as grandparents and they are busy leading lives as parents and workers. One 27-year-old grandmother, who herself had a new baby, told Burton: "Everyone is pissed off at each other. No one wants to take responsibility for raising this baby [the 12-month-old grandchild]. Not even my mother [the great-grandmother]; she's too busy doing her own thing. . . . I'm so mad. . . . But who do I have to talk to about the way *I* feel?" (Burton & Bengtson, 1985, p. 62).

These tensions may be responsible, in part, for the higher proportions of employed mothers who report unpaid care by relatives to be unsatisfactory. Grandmothers provide care when they can, but they often do so at considerable personal cost. They squeeze the additional care in with their other work and family responsibilities. As a temporary measure, care by relatives, when available at all, provides necessary assistance to young mothers. But such arrangements may break down in the longer term. Parish et al. (1991) report that the amount of kin support to young mothers declines sharply with age. Extended family households break up, they suggest, and grandmothers, uncles, and aunts tire of providing assistance.

Moreover, a recent observational study of multigenerational African-American families in Baltimore found that coresidence among the grandmothers (all of whom had been teenage mothers), their daughters, and their daughters' young children was associated with a lower quality of parenting by both the grandmothers and the daughters than occurred when the grandmother and daughter lived in separate households – except when the daughters had given birth in their early teens (Chase-Lansdale, Brooks-Gunn, & Zamsky, 1994). And in a study of psychological distress among children ages 10 to 17 in a Michigan county, McLoyd and Wilson (1991) asked the children to list all of the persons they had received support from during the previous 2 months and the type of support each person had given. The authors found that children who had received more diverse types of support or who had received support from nonrelatives showed more psychological distress than did other children. These findings are similar to results that Furstenberg and I found among a national sample of children whose grandparents were interviewed in 1983: Children whose grandparents reported that they were closer to and had more contact with their grandchildren were doing no better, and sometimes worse, in their behavior

and school performance achievement than were children whose grandparents reported less involvement (Cherlin & Furstenberg, 1992). These studies suggest that
coresidence and close involvement between grandparents and their grandchildren
tends to occur when there are family difficulties. Grandparents, as Furstenberg and I
wrote, are like the "family national guard"; they are called and willingly serve when
their children and grandchildren need them. But, like the national guard, they often
have jobs and personal lives that they must return turn to.

According to Polit and O'Hara (1989), the provision in the Family Support Act
that limits exemptions to mothers with children under 3, rather than the current
exemption in state programs for mothers with children under 6, will nearly double
the number of mothers eligible for mandatory program participation to enhance
employability. If the exemption were lowered to all mothers with children under 1,
as states have the option to do, the number of mothers eligible would nearly
quadruple. Grandmothers cannot absorb this increase. Many of those who are living
with or near their daughters already have been pressed into service. They selflessly
provide help, but not without overload and distress in their own lives. Furthermore,
the help they provide is usually temporary. Those looking for a solution to the
expanded child care needs that welfare reform requires must look elsewhere.

Paid care

Let us then examine the paid care used by low-income mothers. The most striking
fact is how high the cost of paid care is for low-income mothers relative to their
earnings. Hofferth et al. (1991) examined the cost of care as a percentage of income
in the National Child Care Survey. The data show, first, that employed mothers in
higher-income families were more likely to pay for care than were employed mothers in lower-income families. Among employed mothers with a child under age 5,
70% of those with a family income of $50,000 or more paid for care, compared to
42% of those with a family income less than $15,000. And Figure 5.1 shows that,
among all employed mothers with a child under 5 who did pay for care, mothers
with family incomes of less than $15,000 paid 23% of their family income on child
care, whereas mothers in families with higher incomes paid far less of their family
incomes for care. If we consider just poverty/nonpoverty status, poor, employed
white mothers with children under 5 paid 24% of the family income for care,
compared to 8% of nonpoor, employed mothers. For blacks, the comparable figures
were 17% for the poor mothers and 10% for the nonpoor mothers (Hofferth et al.,
1991).

Tabulations from the 1985 National Longitudinal Survey of Youth concerning the
difference in expenditures by receipt of AFDC show a similar story. Among all
mothers receiving AFDC, child care expenditures averaged 22% of family income
and an even higher proportion – 32% – of the mother's earnings. In contrast, child
care expenditures averaged 9% of family income – and 23% of mother's earnings –
for those not receiving AFDC (Hofferth, 1987). As Hofferth notes, the proportion of

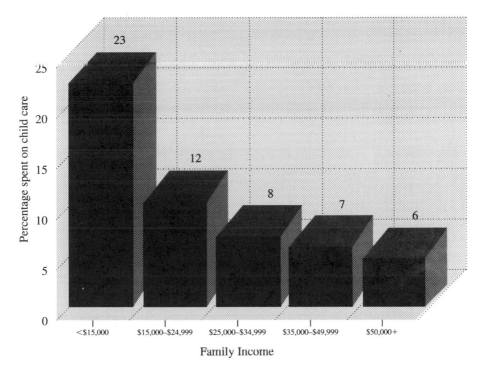

Figure 5.1 Mean percentage of family income spent on child care by family income, for employed mothers who are paying for care and whose youngest child is under age five, 1990. *Source*: Reprinted with permission from Lawrence Erlbaum Associates Inc. (Hofferth, S. D. [1992]. The demand for and supply of child care in the 1990s. In A. Booth [Ed.], *Child care in the 1990s: Trends and consequences* [pp. 3–25]. Hillsdale, NJ: Lawrence Earlbaum).

income spent on child care represents an enormous burden for the poor and those on AFDC; at 22% it is comparable to the share of income spent on housing. It clearly is a much greater financial burden than is the case for middle-class young mothers.

Table 5.1 showed that 20% of employed mothers with children under 5 use family day care homes. Most of the family day care in this country is provided in a vast gray market of about 1 million providers, perhaps 60% to 90% of them unlicensed and unregistered (Hayes et al., 1990). Observers agree that many of the unlicensed providers do not pay taxes on their incomes, although some of their clients claim the dependent care tax credit on their income tax returns. This informal arrangement helps keep the price of care down, although it has been discouraged by a recent IRS rule that requires parents claiming the tax credit to list the tax identification numbers of their care providers. In fact, the number of taxpayers claiming the dependent care tax credit for 1989, the first year that the new rule applied, dropped by 2.6 million, or 30%, from 1988 levels (Lewin, 1991).

Observers also suspect that the costs of family day care may be held down by keeping the quality of the care limited. The only constraints on the number and age composition of children that an unlicensed provider may care for in her home are self-imposed; there are no standards of size, safety, and cleanliness. The lack of regulation allows parents to pay less but it may also place their children at a higher risk of receiving poor-quality care. Nevertheless, there is little direct evidence of lower quality in unregulated family day care homes, as Haskins (this volume) argues. The difficult nature of the trade-off between quality and cost is made clear when one tries to calculate what it would cost to provide objectively high-quality day care to children. Experts in child development point to several factors that make a difference in the quality of out-of-home care that children receive, with evidence that the benefits are more pronounced for children from low-income families (Spencer et al., this volume). Among the characteristics that appear to make a difference are the number of children per caregiver, the size of the groups of children, the amount of staff turnover, and the level of staff training (Hayes et al., 1990). All of these factors are directly connected to the wages of the caregivers. In fact, wages account for the bulk of the costs of out-of-home care. By these criteria, the higher the wages, the better the care.

Clifford and Russell (1989) have attempted to estimate the costs of providing relatively higher or lower levels of quality in center-based care. They calculated the costs of several alternative models of care. Their highest-quality model met the accreditation standards of the National Association for the Education of Young Children. It included staff salaries that were high compared to actual rates paid in most centers, although still surprisingly low: about $20,000 per year for teachers and $10,000 to $14,000 for assistant teachers. It also included relatively low child-to-staff ratios (4:1 for infants, 8:1 for 3-year-olds, and 12:1 for school-age children), as well as modest funds for staff development and parent involvement.

Clifford and Russell's lowest-quality model decreased salaries for teachers to $12,000 per year and for assistant teachers to $8,000 to $10,000. It increased child-to-staff ratios to 6:1 for infants, 12:1 for 3-year-olds, and 20:1 for school-age children and reduced funds for staff development and parent involvement. This may seem like a very low-level program, but in fact Clifford and Russell maintain that it is most similar to the typical existing program in the United States. The estimated annual cost per child of this lower-quality program is $2,937, an amount similar to the average costs reported by parents in surveys.

The estimated annual cost of the higher-quality model is $5,267 per child per year. This is a 79% increase over the lower-quality model. It still leaves average staff salaries well below the level of elementary school teachers. Clearly, it would be very costly to raise the level of care in out-of-home settings to match the still modest standards of NAEYC and other early childhood associations. Low-income parents, who already are burdened by child care costs, would not be able to absorb the increase. And yet, it is not clear that programs similar to Clifford and Russell's lower-quality model will have a beneficial effect on children's development. To produce direct benefits for children's development, child care is expensive.

Overall, then, the evidence on child care usage by low-income, single-parent families suggests the following conclusions. Poor single parents are more likely to make use of unpaid care by relatives, primarily grandmothers, than are other mothers. But it is unlikely that the supply of grandmothers can be expanded – or even that it should be expanded – enough to meet the need that may be created by welfare reform. That leaves paid care, which is provided disproportionately by family day care providers, rather than centers, for low-income families. Most of the care is provided in unregulated, unlicensed settings of unknown quality. Moreover, the costs of paid care impose a great financial hardship on many poor families. Yet it is clear that increasing the quality of that care, as through greater efforts at licensing and regulation, also will increase the cost. Difficult trade-offs will exist for policy makers and program administrators among availability, quality, and cost of the care to be used by participants in welfare-to-work programs such as JOBS.

Unresolved issues

The child care cliff

There are other problems that need further exploration as well. One is what might be called the *child care cliff*. For example, the Family Support Act of 1988 requires that child care assistance be provided, on a sliding fee scale, for 12 months after mothers enter employment as a result of the program. This provision is one of the great advances over most existing state welfare programs, because studies have shown that the costs of child care are a continuing barrier to employment for low-income mothers. Yet the mothers who are fortunate enough to obtain employment through the JOBS program will mostly be working for low or moderate wages, and their need for child care subsidies will not go away 12 months after they start to work. It is possible, then, that some of the mothers who obtain employment through JOBS may be forced to leave work after the transitional benefits expire. Others may be forced to place their children in less than satisfactory care settings.

States need to address what they might do to prevent newly employed mothers from falling off this child care cliff a year after starting work. Continuing subsidies would seem to be of obvious value. But total funds for child care subsidies for low-income parents, whether on public assistance or not, are limited. If women who obtain employment through JOBS become eligible for extended subsidies that greatly exceed the subsidies available to other low-income women, an incentive might be created unwittingly for women to apply for public assistance, thus raising the welfare rolls. Consequently, costs and benefits need to be thought through.

Supply

Current welfare reform has greatly increased the number of child care slots that are needed. How to expand the supply of slots and match openings with children in need of care is another unresolved issue. Mathematica Policy Research recently conducted a survey of the child care market in three low-income areas: the south side of Chicago; Camden, New Jersey; and Newark, New Jersey. The results showed that center care was running at near capacity. Family day care, on the other hand, was reported to be "plentiful" (Maynard, 1989).

But even with the surprising capacity in family day care, problems existed in these low-income areas. Only 5% of the excess capacity in family day care was available for infant care. Yet the new policy requiring that young AFDC mothers without a high school degree participate in educational activities will increase the need for infant care. Second, the quality of the family day care (over 90% of which was unregulated) may have been lower than that of center care. Forty percent of the family day care providers had less than a high school degree, whereas nearly all center staff had a high school degree and a certificate of advanced training, or a college degree.

Perhaps most important, there appeared to be a lack of fit between the perceived needs of the parents and the supply of care available – what Maynard (1989) calls "some form of market failure." Nearly 60% of the low-income mothers in the study who were not working responded that they would work if "adequate and affordable child care were available to them." Yet they defined affordable cost as $50 to $60 per week, which is comparable to the average cost in their local markets. Some of these women had infants, for whom the supply of care clearly was tight. Others seemed to prefer better-quality care; the most common reason for low-income mothers in the study to report unhappiness with their current child care arrangements was the wish that their children could learn more. Others might not have known of openings, or may have worked nonday shifts when little care was offered, or have had other reservations about available care.

It would be valuable to learn more about the child care market in low-income areas. It does not seem that the problem is simply that all types of care are in short supply. Rather the difficulties may involve the type of care offered, the ages of the children, the hours parents work, the difficulty of finding information about potential caregivers, parental reservations about the quality of care, and probably other unknown factors as well. Increasing child care supply and matching it with parents' needs is a complex task, one that could benefit from research and intervention studies. For example, research projects that investigate the effectiveness of various strategies to encourage providers to enter the market, to encourage them to meet state standards, or to increase the efficiency of referral services would all be valuable.

There are many existing resource and referral agencies that have accumulated a great deal of expertise in finding slots, recruiting providers, encouraging them to become licensed, providing them with resources, and matching this information with parents' needs. But most of these agencies are not directly tied to public assistance programs, or even to any social service agency. It would be valuable to establish demonstration projects that would seek to apply this existing expertise to the particular problems of expanding the supply of child care for AFDC children whose mothers are attempting to leave welfare for training or employment.

The benefits of enriched care

Still, the major unknown in welfare reform policy decisions about child care is the relative benefit to children of the indirect effects of having a mother who is employed versus the direct effects of enriched, high-quality, out-of-home care. One might object that there is no need to pose these benefits as exclusive. To be sure, one would hope that as many children as possible could enjoy both sets of benefits (see Smith, this volume). But the cost of enriched care makes it unlikely that the Family Support Act of 1988, for example, will foster both, unless states interpret the regulations broadly and supplement the federal funds with funds of their own.

Therefore, perhaps the most important role for further research and demonstration projects would be to increase our knowledge about whether enriched care provides benefits to children that policy makers might see as worth the extra investment. In this regard, it is particularly unfortunate that a demonstration project, Expanded Child Care Options, begun by Mathematica Policy Research in three urban counties in New Jersey, was abandoned due to lack of financial support. The project was intended to investigate the effects over time of enrollment in educationally enriched care settings versus standard settings for children whose mothers were on public assistance and were enrolled in job-training programs. It involved creating educationally enriched settings, convincing a randomly selected subset of mothers to enroll their children in enriched care, and following the children's progress for 15 years. The project also included a second treatment, designed to test what occurs when child care assistance is continued past the 12-month cutoff point. It would have provided a random sample of mothers in the program with a guarantee of subsidized care, on a sliding fee scale, until the mother's youngest existing child reached school age. The effects of providing this extended subsidy were to be assessed by comparing outcomes for mothers and children with a control group.

Research projects such as this one are sorely needed. They would provide the best way of increasing our knowledge about enriched care and experimenting with innovative approaches to saving mothers from falling off the child care cliff. There are related questions that similar projects might examine. For example, it would be of interest to examine the needs of children of young mothers and their responsiveness to enriched care. The children of teenage parents are particularly at risk for not receiving adequate opportunities for cognitive growth and social and emotional development (Chase-Lansdale, Brooks-Gunn, & Paikoff, 1991). Current welfare reform includes strong new requirements that young mothers without a high school degree return to school or otherwise continue their education. A logical question, then, is whether targeting enriched care on the children of young mothers, rather than on all children, would be good compromise between the goals of providing high-quality care and of subsidizing a large number of slots.

More generally, it might be argued that young mothers would benefit particularly from a more integrated, case management approach to delivering services for their children. There is interest in providing more mothers with a comprehensive approach to services that would include not only child care but also nutrition, health care, parenting skills, and so forth. The services would be coordinated by a central case manager who would be able to commit a diverse set of resources if necessary. As promising as these approaches may sound, there is little solid information at the moment to support arguments for targeting young mothers or other special subpopulations with enriched care or case-managed services. But important information will be available by mid-decade from the New Chance research and demonstration program that is being coordinated by the Manpower Demonstration Research Corporation (Quint, Fink, & Rowser, 1991). It is providing comprehensive services to mothers in 16 locations who are high school dropouts and are receiving welfare.

There is much more, then, that we need to know about the trade-offs and dilemmas of how to treat the children of the mothers who will be participating in the employment and skills training programs. The costs of providing services that attempt to directly improve children's environments – such as educationally enriched child care – are so high that policy makers will need more evidence that the benefits would be as substantial as many advocates think. The bureaucratic difficulties of coordinating comprehensive service delivery to children are substantial enough that bureaucracies must be convinced of the value of doing so. There is an important role for research and demonstration projects in providing this evidence so that welfare reform can be implemented in ways that maximize its benefits for children.

REFERENCES

American Enterprise Institute. (1987). *A community of self-reliance: The new consensus on American welfare policy.* Washington, DC: American Enterprise Institute.

Angel, F., & Perroncel, C. (1992). A study of West Virginia recipients of transitional child care and Medicaid benefits under the Family Support Act. Children's Policy Institute of West Virginia.

Baydar, N., & Brooks-Gunn, J. (1991). Effects of maternal employment and child-care arrangements on preschoolers' cognitive and behavioral outcomes: Evidence from the Children of the National Longitudinal Survey of Youth. *Developmental Psychology, 27,* 932–945.

Bradley, R. H., & Caldwell, B. M. (1976). Early home environment and changes in mental test performance in children from 6 to 36 months. *Developmental Psychology, 2,* 93–97.

Burton, L. M., & Bengtson, V. L. (1985). Black grandmothers: Issues of timing and continuity of roles. In V. L. Bengtson & J. F. Robertson (Eds.), *Grandparenthood* (pp. 61–77). Beverly Hills: Sage.

Chase-Lansdale, P. L., Brooks-Gunn, J. & Paikoff, R. (1991). Research and programs for adolescent mothers: Missing links and future promises. *Family Relations, 40,* 396–404.

Chase-Lansdale, P. L., Brooks-Gunn, J., & Zamsky, E. S. (1994). Young African-American multigenerational families in poverty: Quality of mothering and grandmothering. *Child Development, 65,* 373–393.

Cherlin, A. J. (1992). *Marriage, divorce, remarriage* (rev. and expanded ed.). Cambridge, MA: Harvard University Press.

Cherlin, A. J., & Furstenberg, F. F., Jr. (1992). *The new American grandparent: A place in the family, a life apart*. Cambridge, MA: Harvard University Press.

Clifford, R. M., & Russell, S. D. (1989). Financing programs for preschool-aged children. *Theory into Practice, 28*, 19–27.

Ellwood, D. T. (1988). *Poor support: Poverty and the American family*. New York: Basic Books.

Golden, O., & Skinner, M. with Baker, R., and with the assistance of Clark, W. (1989, November). *Welfare reform and poor children: An interim report*. Background paper for the Foundation for Child Development Research Forum on Children and the Family Support Act, Washington, DC.

Greenberg, M. (1992). *Welfare reform on a budget: What's happening in JOBS*. Washington, DC: Center for Law and Social Policy.

Hayes, C. D., Palmer, J. L., & Zaslow, M. J. (Eds.). (1990). *Who cares for America's children: Child care policy for the 1990s*. Washington, DC: National Academy Press.

Hofferth, S. L. (1987, August). *The current child care debate in context*. Revised version of a paper presented at the annual meeting of the American Sociological Association.

Hofferth, S. L. (1992). The demand for and supply of child care in the 1990s. In A. Booth (Ed.), *Child care in the 1990s: Trends and consequences* (pp. 3–25). Hillsdale, NJ: Erlbaum.

Hofferth, S. L., Brayfield, A., Deich, S., & Holcomb, P. (1991). *National child care survey, 1990* (Urban Institute Report 91–5). Washington DC: Urban Institute Press.

Hogan, D. P., Hao, L., & Parish, W. L. (1990). Race, kin networks, and assistance to mother-headed families. *Social Forces, 68*, 797–812.

Lee, V. E., Brooks-Gunn, J., & Schnur, E. (1988). Does Head Start work? A 1-year follow-up comparison of disadvantaged children attending Head Start, no preschool, and other preschool programs. *Developmental Psychology, 24*, 210–222.

Lewin, T. (1991, January 6). Data show wide tax cheating on child care, I.R.S. says. *New York Times*, A14.

Maynard, R. A. (1989, June). *Child care, welfare programs and federal policy*. Unpublished manuscript. Princeton, NJ: Mathematica Policy Research.

McLanahan, S. S. (1985). Family structure and the reproduction of poverty. *American Journal of Sociology, 90*, 873–901.

McLoyd, V. C., & Wilson, L. (1991). The strain of living poor: Parenting, social support, and child mental health. In A. C. Huston (Ed.), *Children in poverty: Child development and public policy*. Cambridge: Cambridge University Press.

Parish, W. L., Hao, L., & Hogan, D. P. (1991). Family networks, welfare, and work of young mothers. *Journal of Marriage and the Family, 53*, 203–215.

Phillips, D. A. (1991). With a little help: Children in poverty and child care. In A. C. Huston (Ed.), *Children in poverty: Child development and public policy* (pp. 158–189). Cambridge: Cambridge University Press.

Polit, D. F., & O'Hara, J. J. (1989). Support services. In P. H. Cottingham & D. T. Ellwood (Eds.), *Welfare policy for the 1990s* (pp. 165–198). Cambridge, MA: Harvard University Press.

Presser, H. B. (1989). Some economic complexities of child care provided by grandmothers. *Journal of Marriage and the Family, 51*, 581–591.

Presser, H. B. (1992). Child-care supply and demand: What do we really know? In A. Booth (Ed.), *Child care in the 1990s: Trends and consequences* (pp. 26–32). Hillsdale, NJ: Erlbaum.

Presser, H. B., & Baldwin, W. (1980). Child care as a constraint on employment: Prevalence, bearing, and correlates on the work and fertility nexus. *American Journal of Sociology, 85*, 1202–1213.

Quint, J. C., Fink, B. L., & Rowser, S. L. (1991). *New Chance: Implementing a comprehensive program for disadvantaged young mothers and their children*. New York: Manpower Demonstration Research Corporation.

U.S. House of Representatives, Select Committee on Children, Youth, and Families. (1989). U.S. children and their families: Current conditions and recent trends, October, Table 38. Washington, DC.

Zill, N., & Rogers, C. C. (1988). Recent trends in the well-being of children in the United States and their implications for public policy. In A. Cherlin (Ed.), *The changing American family and public policy* (pp. 31–115). Washington, DC: Urban Institute Press.

6   Child care and children of color

Margaret Beale Spencer, Janet B. Blumenthal, and
Elizabeth Richards

Many mothers – all of them poor – have entered the workforce as required under the
Family Support Act of 1988 (FSA). The act provides for child care if it is needed to
enable welfare-dependent mothers to work or to finish high school. While it is aimed
at getting adults off welfare rolls and onto payrolls, children will be profoundly
affected as well. In pledging to provide child care, the federal government is giving
states wide latitude in how much or what kind of support will be given. Implicit in
recent welfare reform under the Family Support Act of 1988 is the opportunity to give
thousands of low-income youngsters supportive, enriching childhood experiences
while helping their mothers become economically self-sustaining. However, it is also
possible that children will encounter care that meets minimum standards – or even
worse, poor quality care – and fails to address the needs of poor children.

One result of a work requirement is an influx of poor children into an already
inadequate patchwork of child care arrangements – leaving young children in the
care of relatives, family day care homes, corporate day care centers, and commer-
cial day care. For mothers who are currently working, problems of availability,
affordability, and quality of care exist (Hayes, Palmer, & Zaslow, 1990). Realistically, lower-income mothers may have fewer child care choices than higher-
income mothers. And poor children, who are most in need of the best day care we
can devise, may not receive high-quality care. In this chapter we consider the effects
of poverty on children and the effects of quality of child care on poor children. We
emphasize the importance of providing community-based, culturally appropriate
child care. We stress the desirability of involving many community organizations in
the provision of child care, with an emphasis on public–private collaborations.

Poor children in the United States

According to recent census data (U.S. Bureau of the Census, 1991) on poverty, 40%
of the nation's poor are children under 18 years. More than any other age group,

The authors gratefully acknowledge the assistance of Beverly O'Shea and LaShun Simpson in the
preparation of this chapter, which was supported in part by the Ford and Spencer Foundations.

138

children continue to be overrepresented among the poor. Minority children still constitute well over half of those considered chronically poor (i.e., chronic versus situational poverty), with many living in economically improverished environments (see Slaughter, 1988). Over 7 million children in this country live in households receiving Aid to Families with Dependent Children (AFDC), substantially less than the number of minority children considered chronically poor. Nearly 3 million of these are children under 5 (Stipek & McCroskey, 1989). Over half (60%) of children dependent on AFDC are of minority status. African-American children, who make up only 13% of the U.S. population (Farley & Allen, 1987), comprise nearly half (41%) of all welfare children; Hispanic children comprise 16%; and American Indian and Asian-American children each comprise 1.5% of the total (Family Support Administration, 1989). Half of all AFDC recipients are teenage mothers, and one in three has only a ninth-grade education.

In addition to poverty and minority status, many AFDC children have problems including homelessness (Bassuk, Rubin, & Lauriat, 1986) and drug exposure in utero. By almost every known indicator (i.e., family income, parental education, parental occupation, parental welfare status, age of mother, family intactness, housing, neighborhood, etc.) poor children are at risk for delayed or diminished intellectual and socioemotional development and, as a consequence, lack the skills necessary to become productive members of society (Goelman & Pence, 1987). Compared to more advantaged children, poor children are at risk for low school test scores, grade retention, placement in special education classes, and dropping out. They are also likely to make less money as adults, to become unmarried teenage parents, to commit crimes, and to become welfare-dependent as adults (see Furstenberg, Brooks-Gunn, & Chase-Lansdale, 1989; Lazar, Darlington, Murray, Royce, & Snipper, 1982; Levine, 1989; Ramey, Bryant, & Suarez, 1985; Washington & LaPoint, 1988; Weikart, 1989). We acknowledge that some poor families are strong and healthy, and that some low-income minority children grow up to be productive members of society. However, in the 1990s, the odds are increasingly against this for welfare-dependent children and families (Bane & Ellwood, 1989; Levin, 1989; Weikart, 1989; Wilson, 1987).

In the early 1960s political and social scientists "discovered" that poor – especially poor minority – children did not do as well in school as middle-income children (Zigler & Valentine, 1979). This finding sparked research that continues today on the effects of poverty on child development. The earliest descriptions of the risks of poor children for academic problems focused on their early home environments. More recently, complex formulations have conceptualized links between poverty and child development that reflect interactions of the child, the family, the family's socioeconomic status and resources, and larger issues of economic and social organization and values (for examples, see Bronfenbrenner, 1979; Levine, 1977; Ogbu, 1981; Slaughter, 1983; Wilson, 1987). Additionally, increased emphasis has been placed on poor families' resourcefulness in developing adaptive responses to their environments (Ogbu, 1981; Spencer, 1990). Finally, the fact that minority group status per se profoundly affects family and child development, beyond poverty status, has been recognized (Spencer, 1988).

One conceptual framework for understanding children's at-risk status considers the roles of risk, resilience, and vulnerability (Garmezy, 1988; Rutter, 1979, 1981, 1988; Spencer, Kim, & Marshall, 1987). White (1959) suggested that human development is undergirded with an intrinsic motivation toward competence or effective interaction with the environment. Most theorists share the basic assumption that context-linked feedback offers individuals information concerning how their actions influence environmental consequences (Foote & Cottrell, 1955; DeCharms, 1968). Many impoverished African-American youth reside in resource-weak neighborhoods that are often infused with chronic, economic-linked problems. Garbarino (1983) defines risk as being impoverished of the basic social and psychological necessities of life. Therefore, the ability to effectively interact with the environment is undoubtedly compromised. In this view, poverty creates contextual risk (Spencer, 1989) – extreme economic hardship. Contextual risk, however, represents a situational condition; it does not directly describe a psychological characteristic.

Vulnerability refers to a psychological characteristic (Anthony, 1974). Low-income children (who are situationally at-risk) may be very resilient, extremely vulnerable, or somewhere in-between. Resiliency is exemplified among highly vulnerable youth residing in high-risk environments who do not manifest or exhibit adverse behavioral outcomes even in the context of psychological risk. Adverse behavioral outcomes may be expected from children demonstrating both psychological vulnerability and situational (e.g., economic) risk. Highly vulnerable youth in low-risk environments (e.g., middle-income suburbs) may be less likely to manifest adverse behavioral outcomes than vulnerable youth in high-risk environments. Furthermore, research suggests that specific aspects of socioemotional functioning (e.g., group [cultural] identity and cultural socialization) may decrease vulnerability (Spencer, Dobbs, & Swanson, 1988; Spencer et al., 1987).

Characterized by chronic frustration, societal inconsistency (Chestang, 1972) is reflective of minority status that represents the experience of personal injustice from which there is no legal protection. This phenomenon is particularly important for minorities because it is the rejection of one's group that is experienced on an individualized basis. These experiences and the confounding effects of poverty make the intersubjective processes described potentially damaging psychologically as individuals attempt to offset feelings of powerlessness. It is, however, critical to remember that individuals may be affected by conditions of society, but not necessarily shaped by them as is seen among resilient youth. As such, minority status alone does not guarantee adverse outcomes (Spencer, 1988), contrary to early theorizing (e.g., Kardiner & Ovesey, 1951; Pettigrew, 1964).

Individual family members vary widely as to their life-course trajectories; many minority families are strong, healthy, and successful (see Hill, 1972). Outcomes may be linked to individual characteristics such as resilience and vulnerability and to the availability, perceptions, and uses of resources (Spencer, 1990).

Certain contexts are enormously potent in that they are likely to be translated into certain psychological responses. For example, adequate economic resources are associated with family stability, nurturing relationships, and social supports that undergird safe and predictable environments and usually result in adequate intellectual and socioemotional development (McLoyd, 1990).

As they develop, low-income children, especially low-income minority children, face many other serious and cumulative contextual risks. For example, when they enter school, they may be judged by the color of their skin or by the way they speak (foreign or tribal languages or black English), and they may face the cultural insensitivity of teachers or otherwise inadequate school settings. As risk factors accumulate, the probability of school performance problems for these children increases. Too often, policy remedies focus on "fixing" children or blaming the parents rather than on reducing situational risk factors.

While not a panacea for poverty, carefully designed, culturally responsive, high-quality day care offers the potential to provide a setting that reduces or eliminates some of the contextual risks and increases children's resiliency. An important aspect of welfare reform is that it affirms and forges a tripartite relationship among schools or child care settings, homes, and workplaces.

Child care for poor children: Reducing the risk through quality child care

Three research lines address the links between child care and child development in poor children: evaluation of early intervention programs, effects of day care on children, and effects of after-school care on children. In this chapter we will address the first two.

Intervention programs. Early intervention programs developed in the United States during the 1960s and 1970s had the goal of improving the school performance of economically disadvantaged children by enhancing early intellectual and social development. These model interventions were often conducted under university sponsorship, guided by skilled researchers and educators, staffed by highly trained personnel, and equipped with well-planned curricula and ample budgets (Andrews et al., 1982; Haskins, 1989; Lally, Mangine, & Honig, 1987; Lazar et al., 1982; Ramey & Campbell, 1987; Ramey, Farran, & Campbell, 1979; Ramey, Yeats, & Short, 1984).

The "model" interventions generally served children from ages 2 to 5 years, but sometimes served infants as well; programs commonly included a center-based care preschool format but also sometimes included visiting or parent education as well (Andrews et al., 1982; Lazar et al., 1982). In addition, two model interventions took the form of day care models serving the same group continuously from early infancy through age 5 (Lally et al., 1987; Ramey et al., 1979). The vast majority of children in all of these intervention programs were low-income African-Americans.

The model programs were evaluated in two ways. First, at the end of the programs (generally when children were between 3 and 5 years old) program children were compared to control children on a variety of measures, primarily intelligence tests. These programs had a significant positive effect on the intellectual development of participating children (Andrews et al., 1982; Haskins, 1989; Lally et al., 1987; Lazar et al., 1982; Ramey et al., 1979, 1984).

Because the model programs were intended to improve school performance, long-term follow-up of participants has been carried out (Berrueta-Clement, Schweinhart, Barnett, Epstein, & Weikart, 1984; Lally et al., 1987; Lazar et al., 1982; Ramey & Campbell, 1987). In a recent review of follow-up studies, Haskins (1989) concluded that while strong evidence exists that these model programs reduce the likelihood of special education placement and grade retention, only modest evidence exists that they alter teenage pregnancy, delinquency, welfare status, and employment outcomes.

The "model" intervention programs are often cited as exemplars of the beneficial effects of early intervention for disadvantaged children, and indeed would suggest that if child care for poor children whose mothers are venturing to work were to incorporate similar procedures, benefits would accrue to the children. However, the unusual nature of the early interventions must be taken into account: They were well-funded, small, highly controlled, high-quality curriculum models, and may not represent what happens when a program is administered on a larger scale. Additionally, these programs were effective in what they set out to do – to increase early intellectual development. But we also know enough about the context of development of low-income children to realize that most of these programs only addressed a portion of their needs; problematic social conditions, such as racism, which compromise social and emotional functioning, were largely ignored. Additionally, benefits to the mother and the families were not evaluated in many programs (Benasich, Brooks-Gunn, & Clewell, 1992).

Effects of child care on poor children. Child care research is largely based on community programs whose major function is daily child care; by contrast, intervention research is based on programs designed to foster child development. Thus, child care studies might appear to be more useful in predicting children's developmental outcomes in poor families in which the mother is entering the workforce. However, studies of child care typically focus on economically advantaged families (see Baydar & Brooks-Gunn, 1991, as an exception). Additionally, child care research usually contrasts the effects of varying day care environments (e.g., caretaker:child ratios) on child outcomes (e.g., language development). This kind of comparison is similar to the kinds of decisions encountered by poor mothers returning to work: Mothers' choices are not whether to put their children in care, but what kind and quality of care their children will receive.

Child care quality varies widely, but high quality is generally the most expensive form of day care. Phillips (1987) coined the term "iron triangle" to represent group size, caregiver:child ratio, and caregiver qualifications as the primary definition of quality of child care. These variables are almost always associated with developmental outcomes for children in centers (Clarke-Stewart & Fein, 1983; Hayes, Palmer, & Zaslow, 1990; Phillips, 1987; Ruopp, Travers, Glantz, & Colen, 1979), and are often the basis of state regulations, as they are easily measured. Other variables (e.g., caregiver–child interactions), though less easily measured, are more closely related to developmental outcome. These include caregiver–child interactions, promotion of ethnic pride, spontaneity, and curiosity (Washington & Oyemade, 1987).

Reviews of the effects of day care on child development (Clarke-Stewart & Fein, 1983; Hayes et al., 1990; Phillips, 1987) have primarily focused on the links between child care and intellectual development. High-quality child care is linked to positive cognitive and language development, although given the few long-term studies available in day care, it is difficult to assess long-term effects.

A study examining day care in Bermuda vividly demonstrates the association between high-quality day care and intellectual development of low-income children. Of nine centers studied, eight were private and had paying clients, and one was government-subsidized and enrolled low-income children (McCartney, Scarr, Phillips, & Grajek, 1985; Phillips, Scarr, & McCartney, 1987). The center for low-income children was found to be of the highest quality on the basis of improved scores on cognitive measures; the poor children in this center had higher scores on the measures than did the more economically advantaged children in the other day care centers.

High-quality child care influences socioemotional development as well (Hayes et al., 1990). Such care is associated outcomes that include increased cooperation with adults and lower behavior problems (Haskins, 1989). However, two child care intervention studies have previously suggested that for low-income children, the transition from early high-quality programs to a more formal school setting (e.g., age 6 years and beyond) may create difficulty in complying with adult authority (Lally et al., 1987; Ramey & Campbell, 1987).

Two issues bear consideration here. Though it is risky to compare findings involving child care and intervention, those findings tell us that it will be critical to design programs to help low-income children become familiar with and practiced in the behavior that will be expected of them in school (Lee, Brooks-Gunn, & Schwin, 1988).

Child care researchers have also found that high-quality care fosters positive peer group relations (Hayes et al., 1990). Lower-quality care is particularly distressing when low income is factored in, because poor children (particularly boys) are already at risk for developing antisocial (e.g., criminal) behavior that may be linked to cognitive awareness of their risk status along with expectations for male provider roles. It could therefore be inferred that low-quality child care may actually increase the likelihood of antisocial behavior. Although lacking in empirical evidence, it is certainly an area worth investigation.

Another aspect of socioemotional competence involves the development of a view of oneself as a competent individual with goals for school and life achievement. Extreme poverty increases children's exposure to nonproductive social role models and produces negative effects on family dynamics. Thus, low-income children may be less likely to have positive role models and supportive, available parents than high-income children (Brooks-Gunn, Duncan, Kato, & Sealand, 1991). These issues are especially critical to the socioemotional development of minority children.

Risks facing minority children in child care

Developing child care services for minority children has been hampered by a lack of research (Cross, Bazror, Denis, & Isaacs, 1989). This trend is reflective of research concerning minority children more generally. The finite studies that incorporate issues of culture or minority status often fail to account for the sociocognitive developmental processes that are influenced by ethnicity. The research that does exist has typically fueled misconceptions and misinterpretations of minority children (Washington, 1988; Spencer, 1984). Race-comparative studies resulted in deficit interpretations of language, behavior, and abilities. Even among studies with racially homogeneous samples, there has been the assumption of homogeneity among group members and/or interpretations based on implicit comparisons with the majority group. Thus, many studies appear either atheoretical or pathology-driven.

However, basic research by Alejandro-Wright (1985), Semaj (1985), and Spencer (1985, 1987) suggests that African-American and other minority youth have special needs and require certain considerations as a function of structural features of the larger environment. Nearly 50 years of empirical research, from Clark and Clark (1939, 1940) to more recent findings (Spencer, 1988), indicate that even preschool children are aware of biases and assumptions at the broad, abstract level of the environment. Decades of empirical research indicate that African-American preschool children show white- or Eurocentric-preferred attitudes and beliefs. Without delineating the relationship between self-concept and racial attitudes, the Eurocentric preferences led some theorists to suggest that African-American children suffered from lowered self-esteem or more general personality disorganization. The studies inferred self-concept from racial attitude data (see Spencer, 1984).

In twentieth-century America, for white children (Spencer & Horowitz, 1973), African-American children (McAdoo, 1973; Spencer, 1970, 1982, 1984), and Hispanic children (Rotheram & Phinney, 1987), societal inconsistencies remain evident in white- or Eurocentric-preferred attitudes and beliefs. However, Afrocentricity or own-group preferences appear to function independently of self-esteem for African-American children. Importantly, competence-related performance during the primary school years is linked to early group consciousness, as found in examining the role of cognitive maturation in shaping racial attitudes and preferences

(Spencer, 1988). As African-American youngsters reach middle childhood, empirical findings suggest that an Afrocentric cultural orientation is linked to better stress-coping resources and better school performance (Spencer, 1987). The association is crucial for low-income children, who must cope with both racial and economic discrimination. Sadly, their families are likely to have difficulty promoting cultural attitudes and beliefs since African-American parents report little specific cultural socialization (Bowman & Howard, 1985; Spencer, 1983). Many African-American parents report their perceived task as that of rearing "human beings" as opposed to a task that includes preparing children to deal with discrimination. Thus, children risk encountering situations for which they are unprepared. They do not experience the buffer that frank conversations about race and racial discrimination could offer. Given that children are unlikely to receive the Afrocentric cultural orientation associated with better academic performance and improved coping at home, educators and other service providers may provide such socialization.

Multiculturalism and quality child care

In a model developed by Cross et al. (1989), racial attitudes and beliefs are conceptualized as a continuum, going from most to least damaging. Various positions described by this model provide a useful framework for examining child care policy.

The first position on Cross's continuum is policies and practices destructive to cultures. Relative to day care, it is clear that policies and practices destructive to cultures also harm individuals within the cultures. To illustrate: Services that were set up to "help" American Indians, such as the placement of children in boarding schools that ignored and even actively repressed their culture, represent policies that did not promote cultural competence, as shown by the deleterious effects on the intended recipients of the "service."

Cultural incapacity, the next position on the continuum, is not maliciously intended, but the policies practiced fail to help minorities. An example would be when teachers lower their expectations of minority children (Irvine, 1990). The underlying premise is that children are motivated if they experience successes, which in turn will build self-confidence. As such, teachers lower their expectations under the guise of motivation, but it does not truly challenge the student to perform and is therefore intellectually undermining.

Cultural blindness, next on the continuum, is the belief that color or culture makes no difference. This is the perspective of many liberal-minded care providers and, as mentioned earlier, parents of some minority children. Beginning with the preschool years, a "color-blind" policy that assumes sameness for all children places minority children at great risk. Implicit in the perspective is the belief that services or helping approaches traditionally used by the dominant culture are all the same or are universally applicable (Cross et al., 1989). Although well-intended, this belief may render most services useless except to highly assimilated people of color, a group that does not typically include poor minority children. Child care adherents to this philosophy ignore cultural strengths and traditions, encourage assimilation, and generally blame the children or their families for their problems (Fillmore & Britsch, 1988). The assumption is that color-blind treatment affords equal opportunities. However, this perspective fails to consider institutionalized practices and biases that are informally communicated and have a significant impact on children's socioemotional development.

Precompetence, the next level on the Cross et al. continuum, is characterized by the desire to deliver quality services and a commitment to civil rights. The approach's potential for failure lies in the practice of tokenism. For example, the hiring of one or more (often assimilated) staff members may be viewed as acquiring the cultural sensitivity required for promoting healthy socioemotional development in minority youngsters. However, it must be remembered that minority professional staff are often schooled or credentialed in the majority culture's frame of reference and therefore may be no more competent or sensitive in practice than their non-minority co-workers (Slaughter & McWorter, 1985).

At the most positive end of the cultural competence spectrum is cultural proficiency. Such a position represents a posture that holds culture in high esteem, increases cultural knowledge, and continually recycles new cultural information and insights back into the curriculum to encourage culturally competent staff practices and children's healthy socioemotional functioning. Thus, the range of educational practices expected in a true "multicultural" program should represent the diversity of lifestyles, beliefs, and cultural traditions (James, 1981).

At the same time, better-trained and more culturally sensitive teachers are needed to promote socioemotional competence in addition to traditional school-based skills (Irvine, 1990; Washington & LaPoint, 1988). For all children, the awareness of differences in people aids the development of favorable attitudes toward those different from themselves (James, 1981). The multicultural ideology suggests that teachers are likely to operate from a framework of economic, political, social, and cultural realities of which the education system is only a part. In other words, teachers may have ideologies based on their own social, economic, and cultural perspective that are different from the implied "celebration of differences" that characterizes a true multicultural perspective.

Irvine (1989) has suggested that culturally different teachers and students may be culturally "out of sync" with one another. As an example (Byers & Byers, 1972, cited in Irvine, 1989), a white child was found to be far more successful in engaging a white nursery-school teacher than was an African-American child who made far more attempts to catch the teacher's eye. Irvine attributed the differences to a lack of cultural correspondence: The teacher and the white child had an implicit understanding of rules of communication and this led to productive and enjoyable learning and interaction. But for the African-American child, the experience was one of failure and frustration. Irvine presented several other examples of studies that concluded that African-American students have less favorable interactions with white teachers than white children do. Irvine (1989) suggested that African-American teachers, as a group, are more effective with African-American students than Caucasian teachers are. We would add that it seems logical from Irvine's work to infer that other minorities (American Indians, Hispanics, and Asian-Americans) might also benefit from having more ethnically and culturally similar teachers in their classrooms.

Balancing work and child care requirements

All mothers who are employed must cope with the difficulties inherent in balancing work and child care responsibilities. These effects might be more difficult for poor mothers, given the likelihood of low-paying jobs, lower job flexibility, longer transportation times between work and child care, residence in neighborhoods with fewer or poorer quality child care options, and lack of other adults with whom to share child rearing.

Additionally, low-income mothers lack resources, including knowledge about how to support their children's development (Andrews et al., 1982; Spencer, 1990; Weikart, 1989). Clarke-Stewart (1989) suggested that mothers of infants in day care may be especially stressed by their dual role of working and having a very young child, and that this stress might result in the mother's being unresponsive and psychologically unavailable to the infant when they are together. She concluded that these mothers may need extra parenting support.

This need for extra support and education is even greater for poor women who will be affected by the FSA, and it extends beyond infancy (Andrews et al., 1982; Weikart, 1989). Institutional responses to reducing the difficulties that these poor mothers will have in balancing work and child care requirements include corporate child care partnerships, state responses to the provision of child care, and local initiatives to increase child care availability. Since other chapters in this volume examine federal and state issues (Cherlin; Haskins; Smith), individual responses (Brooks-Gunn; Wilson et al.), and other initiatives (Smith), we focus primarily on corporate partnerships here.

Corporate child care partnerships

The workplace represents the third member of the tripartite partnership that can potentially change American society through its involvement with and commitment to employees. In the past few years, corporations have joined with parents in trying to locate, or in some cases, in providing high-quality care for children of their employees. American companies now lose $3 billion a year as a result of employees who miss work to take care of their children (Belluck, 1988). Among the child care services currently offered are after-school care, summer programs for school-age children, sick child care initiatives, referrals, financial assistance, parenting seminars, contributions to community programs and centers, and benefits such as job sharing, flexible hours, and flexible workplace. Corporate involvement was sparked by the loss of many middle- and upper-income parents (whose departures meant companies lost their investment in employee training); low-income parents have heretofore not been the main beneficiaries of such programs. More recently, the business community has turned its attention to meeting the needs of the working poor, responding to a report (Johnston, 1987) that makes a strong case for taking the following steps:

1. Reconciling the conflicting needs of women, work, and families. Sixty percent of all women over age 16 will work in the year 2000, yet most policies covering pay, benefits, time off, pensions, and welfare were designed for a society in which men were breadwinners and women stayed home.
2. Integrating African-American and Hispanic workers fully into the economy. The shrinking number of young people, the rapidly changing technologies, and the increasing skill requirements of the emerging economy make the task of effectively training minority workers particularly urgent. Both cultural changes and education and training investments will be needed to create true equity in employment opportunities. Too often, programs tend to keep middle-class people in the helping professions busy without making jobs available to those who need them.
3. Improving the educational preparation of all workers. As the economy grows more complex and more dependent on human capital, the standards set by the American educational system must by raised (Johnston, 1987, p. 4).

The report was timely, and it gave definition to a situation that employers were already experiencing. Human resources managers were feeling the effects of increasing numbers of women in the workforce, and employers had begun to respond by sponsoring child care programs. Fel-Pro, a Chicago-based manufacturing company, has continued to demonstrate leadership and advocate for corporate responsiveness to concerns of child care for employees for at least a decade. The success of child care programs at the worksite has been a factor in the dramatic increase in the number of child care benefits offered.

Two Atlanta child care centers serve as examples of the potential for corporate-sponsored care to serve a more diverse population and thus surpass its original goal of retaining middle- and high-level employees. The Clifton Child Care Center, a consortium sponsored by Emory University, the Centers for Disease Control, and Henrietta Egleston Hospital for Children, offers high-quality care – reflected in weekly tuition rates of $85 to $89. Recognizing that such fees are prohibitive for low-income workers, the consortium subsidizes tuition on a sliding scale. While this center is unusual for the commitment given by employers to the whole workforce, it serves as a model for other employers in the area, state, and nation.

Atlanta's Downtown Child Development Center provides a model for child care employment of former welfare mothers, who are benefiting from corporate partnership involvement through provision of jobs, training, and above-market wages. Mothers receive not only employment, but on-the-job training under the supervision of lead teachers and the center director. Often they enroll their own children in the center at reduced fees, thus enabling them to work and know that their children are receiving high-quality care.

States' response

The Family Support Act of 1988 gives states wide latitude in determining what kind of child care can be provided for thousands of at-risk children. Each state is required to establish its own standards for care and will have to meet increasing participation quotas in order to receive federal funds. In providing child care, states must pay at least the lesser of either the actual cost of child care, or the dollar amount of the child care income disregard for which the family would be eligible otherwise (i.e., $200 a month for children younger than 2; $175 a month for older children). States are allowed to use "no-cost" child care. Importantly, states may also choose to reimburse up to the market rate, thus making low-income children eligible to attend high-quality centers. We do not yet know how states are responding to their child care responsibilities. For example, we do not know if states will ultimately offer only enough child care to meet the quotas for working parents, thus denying care to other welfare-dependent mothers who want to work but cannot afford child care. We also do not know what reimbursement levels or mechanisms states will choose, nor if they will choose to tighten or loosen child care regulations. We believe it is imperative to closely monitor how state decisions affect the quality, availability, and choices of child care for AFDC mothers.

Child care regulations are most often aimed at structural features, which are easily defined and measured. However, standards based on specifying the daily experiences of children are also becoming available (e.g., accreditation criteria of the National Association for the Education of Young Children, the National Black Child Development Institute, the Early Childhood Environment Rating Scale, etc.). All of these go beyond structural features to include criteria for both staff–child and staff–parent interactions. While child care centers may voluntarily adopt any of these criteria, they are rarely obliged to do so. States, which generally use only structural regulations, are responsible for establishing their own standards. Ratio, for example, is regulated in almost every state for center and family day care, but it varies widely among states. (For infants state regulations range from a low of 3:1 to a high of 7:1; for 3-year-olds, ratios vary from 6:1 to 15:1; and for 5-year-olds, ratios range from 12:1 to 25:1.) Group size is regulated in family day care in all but three states, but varies from a maximum of four to 16 children. Finally, regulations for caregiver training are extremely variable among the states: Only 27 states require preservice training for child care center teachers and only 12 require it for family day care workers. It should be restated here that low-income mothers tend to use lower-quality arrangements; middle-class mothers are more likely to be aware of quality indicators such as adult:child ratio and to be able to identify high-quality care, regardless of state regulations. In addition, poor mothers and/or poor minority mothers may look at other variables (e.g., language, culture). Thus, if states continue to determine what constitutes acceptable care, poor mothers in the states with the weakest regulations are at risk of getting substandard or unacceptable care for their children

Local community responses. The difficulties low-income single mothers face in finding affordable child care have already been discussed and will not be repeated here. However, we are concerned that some of the (few) high-quality child care options currently available to working low-income mothers will be lost to FSA participants. There must be provisions for expanding the high-quality child care programs in this country; displacing children (and creating child care headaches for women already stressed by poverty and sole parental responsibility) is not acceptable. There have already been public charges that low-income working women are being locked out of subsidized care in order to save places for FSA participants (White, 1989). The partnership of workplace, home, and school/child care must work to develop more high-quality child care and to see that it is made available to workers of every income.

Familial responses. Married couples frequently share child care responsibilities in an arrangement that has come to be known as "sequential parenting" (Presser, 1989). Nonstandard hours, common in the expanding service industries, and different schedules have combined to leave children in the care of one parent at a time. Though welfare-dependent families have typically been headed by a single parent, the FSA will make Aid to Families with Dependent Children available to families with two unemployed parents (with the work requirement). Moreover, some welfare-dependent families may have marital arrangements that are not legally recognized (Asante, 1981; Gary, 1981; Staples, 1978), but will be affected by sequential parenting. While children might benefit from such an arrangement, which affords more private time with adults, its effect on marital or parental care arrangements has to be examined.

How current knowledge can be used to create demonstrations

Just as there is now wide variability among states in day care regulations and funding, there is every reason to believe that this variability will continue as the states individually implement their FSA day care regulations. The result is likely to be child care of varying quality. "Passive" experiments could track state regulations, then choose states with regulations that would seem to point to higher-quality or lower-quality care, and carry out new research both on the development of a subset of children in those states and on parental employment. Tracking the implementation of regulations by state with special emphases on minorities should be sought since caste status further exacerbates the effects of poverty.

"Passive" or naturalistic observational research involving relations between variations of quality in FSA day care and child development will be valuable and should be carried out; however, there are clear methodological problems such as possible preselection biases regarding child or maternal characteristics and type of care selected. Research with random assignment – for example, to model programs versus parent selected care – would probably tell us more. Relying on passive research of naturally occurring variations also leads to a substantive error. We might have difficulty locating ideal day care models specifically designed to address the needs of children who will be in FSA-mandated child care. While some high-quality programs for children would probably be available, many critical areas of poor children's (and especially poor minority children's) development are rarely addressed in day care or in intervention research. We should develop models that would offer the opportunity to see the results of the best day care interventions we know how to design, and they could serve as the yardsticks by which other programs are measured. It will be important to keep in mind that family day care is especially prevalent in low-income neighborhoods, and that model programs should be developed for all arrangements, including family day care, which are provided to children under the Family Support Act of 1988.

Without specialized training, teachers and child care workers are unlikely to be sensitive to culturally linked learning styles, such as American Indians' learning through demonstration and imitation rather than by verbal explanation; without cultural sensitivity, children's behavior will be subject to misinterpretation. The Family Support Act's implementation lacks the long-range planning time needed to recruit and train minority teachers. For the short term, we would suggest making every teacher of minority children aware of subtle cultural differences; bridging the cultural communication gap is the first step toward breaking stereotypes that can do a lifetime of harm. We would also suggest, that for language-different minorities, child care be combined with a program to teach children standard English, though care should be taken to make sure they retain their first language, particularly if it is spoken in their homes (Fillmore & Britsch, 1988). Curricula must be designed with the diversity of FSA-affected children in mind; the effectiveness of those curricula in teaching children to celebrate their own culture and to appreciate diversity must be measured. This is a task not only for the educational system, but for families and the business community.

Corporations were originally motivated to become involved in finding high-quality child care because the lack of it affected their bottom line: profit/cost. It is likely that corporations will continue to seek ways to provide top-quality care without losing sight of costs to the company and to employees. Corporations may be justly proud of the role some already serve in low-income communities by training and hiring former welfare recipients to reenter the workforce in child care centers and by making child care affordable even to low-wage workers. Moreover, corporations are making increased commitments to their entry-level workforce; they are aware that by the year 2000, their new employees are likely to be people now labeled as "unemployable." The effects of the child care benefits offered by the corporate world need to be measured: We would like to know which forms of assistance are associated with various developmental outcomes for children as well as how the programs affect former AFDC employee recruitment, retention, and absenteeism. Corporations are moving to the forefront in recognizing the cost-effectiveness of making sure that high quality care is available. As child care assistance explodes in the workplace, we look forward to seeing the next calculation of the bottom line for the work, child care, and home tripartite.

REFERENCES

Alejandro-Wright, M. N. (1985). The child's conception of racial classification: A socio-cognitive developmental model. In M. B. Spencer, G. K. Brookins, & W. R. Allen (Eds.), *Beginnings: The social and affective development of black children* (pp. 185–200). Hillsdale, NJ: Erlbaum.

Andrews, S., Blumenthal, J., Johnson, D., Kahn, A., Ferguson, C., Lasater, T., Malone, P., & Wallace, D. (1982). The skills of mothering: A study of parent-child development centers. *Monographs of the Society for Research in Child Development, 47* (6, Serial No. 198).

Anthony, E. J. (1974). Introduction: The syndrome of the psychologically vulnerable child. In E. J. Anthony & C. Kourpernik (Eds.), *The child in his family: Children at psychological risk* (Vol. 3). New York: Wiley.

Asante, M. K. (1981). Black male and female relationships: An Afrocentric context. In L. E. Gary (Ed.), *Black men* (pp. 75–82). Beverly Hills: Sage.

Bane, M., & Ellwood, D. (1989). One fifth of the nation's children: Why are they poor? *Science, 245,* 1047–1053.

Bassuk, E., Rubin, L., & Lauriat, A. (1986). Characteristics of sheltered homeless families. *American Journal of Public Health, 76,* 1097–1108.

Baydar, H., & Brooks-Gunn, J. (1991). Effects of maternal employment and child care arrangements in infancy on preschoolers' cognitive and behavioral outcomes: Evidence from the Children of the NLSY. *Developmental Psychology, 27*(6), 932–945.

Belluck, P. (1988, October 5). Agency says lack of child care costs businesses billions. *The Atlanta Constitution,* p. C-9.

Benasich, A., Brooks-Gunn, J., & Clewell, B. (1992). How do mothers benefit from early intervention programs? *Journal of Applied Developmental Psychology, 13*(3), 311–362.

Berrueta-Clement, J., Schweinhart, L., Barnett, W., Epstein, A., & Weikart, D. (1984). *Changed lives: The effects of the Perry Preschool Program on youth through age 19.* Ypsilanti, MI: High/Scope.

Blakeslee, S. (1989, September 17). Crack's toll among babies: A joyless view of even toys. *New York Times,* pp. 1, 12.

Bowman, P., & Howard, C. (1985). Race-related socialization, motivation, and academic achievement: A study of black youth in three-generation families. *Journal of the American Academy of Child Psychiatry, 24,* 134–141.

Bronfenbrenner, U. (1979). *The ecology of human development.* Cambridge, MA: Harvard University Press.

Brooks-Gunn, J., Duncan, G., Klebanor, P. K., & Sealand, N. (1993). Do neighborhoods influence child and adolescent development? *American Journal of Sociology, 99*(2), 353–395.

Byers, P., & Byers, D. H. (1972). Non-verbal communication in the education of children. In C. Cazden, V. John, & D. Hymes (Eds.), *Functions of language in the classroom.* New York: Teachers College Press.

Chestang, L. W. (1972). *Character development in a hostile environment* (Occasional Paper No. 3). Chicago: University of Chicago Press.

Children's Defense Fund. (1985). *Black and white children in America: Key facts.* Washington, DC: Children's Defense Fund.

Clark, K. B., & Clark, M. K. (1939). The development of consciousness of self and the emergence of racial identity in Negro children. *Journal of Social Psychology, 10,* 591–599.

Clark, K. B., & Clark, M. K. (1940). Skin color as a factor in racial identification of Negro preschool children. *Journal of Social Psychology, 11,* 159–169.

Clarke-Stewart, K. (1989). Infant day care: Maligned or malignant. *American Psychologist, 44,* 266–273.

Clarke-Stewart, K., & Fein, G. (1983). Early childhood programs. In P. Mussen (Ed.), *Handbook of child psychology* (Vol. 2). New York: Wiley.

Cooper, E., Pelton, S., & LeMay, M. (1988). Acquired immunodeficiency syndrome: A new population of children at risk. *The Pediatric Clinics of North America, 35,* 1365–1388.

Cross, T. L., Bazror, B. J., Denis, K. W., & Isaacs, M. (1989). *Toward a culturally competent system of care. A monograph on effective survival for minority children who are severely emotionally disturbed.* Washington, DC: CASSP Technical Assistance Center.

DeCharms, R. (1968). *Personal causation: The internal affective determinants of behavior.* New York: Academic Press.

Family Support Administration. (1989). *Characteristics and financial circumstances of AFDC recipients.* Washington, DC: U.S. Government Printing Office.

Farley, R., & Allen, W. R. (1987). *The colorline and quality of life in America.* New York: Russell Sage Foundation.

Fillmore, L. W., & Britsch, S. (1988, June). Early education for children from linguistic and cultural minority families. An unpublished paper prepared for the Early Education Task Force of the National Association of State Boards of Education.

Foote, N., & Cottrell, L. S. (1955). *Identity and interpersonal competence: A new direction in family research.* Chicago: University of Chicago Press.

Friedman, D. (1989, August). A more sophisticated employer response to child care. *Child care information exchange,* pp. 29–31.

Furstenberg, F., Brooks-Gunn, S., & Chase-Lansdale, L. (1989). Teenaged pregnancy and childbearing. *American psychology for the 1990's.* Washington, DC: National Academy Press.

Garbarino, J. (1982). *Children and families in the social environment.* New York: Aldine de Gruyter.

Garmezy, N. (1988). Stressors of childhood. In N. Garmezy & M. Rutter (Eds.), *Stress, coping, and development in children.* Baltimore: Johns Hopkins University Press.

Gary, L. E. (1981). Conclusion. In L. E. Gary (Ed.), *Black men* (pp. 277–292). Beverly Hills: Sage.

Goelman, H., & Pence, A. (1987). Effects of child care, family, and individual characteristics on children's language development: The Victoria day care research project. In D. Phillips (Ed.), *Quality in child care: What does the research tell us?* Research Monographs of the National Association for the Education in Young Children, 1.

Haskins, R. (1989). Beyond metaphor: The efficacy of early childhood education. *American Psychologist, 44,* 274–282.

Hayes, C. D., Palmer, J. L., & Zaslow, M. J. (1990) (Eds.). *Who cares for America's children?* Washington, DC: National Academy Press.

Hill, R. (1972). *The strengths of black families.* New York: Emerson Hall.

Irvine, J. J. (1989, January). *Black teachers and at-risk students: Present realities and future implications.* Paper presented to the 3rd Annual Conference on the Recruitment and Retention of Minority Students in Teacher Education, University of Kentucky, Lexington.

Irvine, J. J. (1990). *Black students and school failure: Policies, practices, and prescriptions.* Westport, CT: Greenwood.

James, A. (1981). The "multicultural" curriculum. In A. James & R. Jeffcoate (Eds.), *The school in the multicultural society* (pp. 19–28). London: Harper & Row.

Johnston, W. B. (1987). *Workforce 2000: Work and workers for the 21st century.* Indianapolis: Hudson Institute.

Kardiner, A., & Ovesy, L. (1951). *The mark of oppression: Exploration in the personality of the American Negro.* New York: Norton.

Lally, R., Mangione, P., & Honig, A. (1987). *The Syracuse University family development program: Long-range impact of an early intervention with low-income children and their families.* San Francisco: Far West Laboratory for Educational Research and Development.

Lazar, I., Darlington, R., Murray, H., Royce, J., & Snipper, A. (1982). Lasting effects of early education: A report from the consortium for longitudinal studies. *Monographs of the Society for Research in Child Development, 47* (2–3, Serial No. 195).

Lee, V. E., Brooks-Gunn, J., & Schwin, E. (1988). Does Head Start work? A 1-year follow-up comparison of disadvantaged children attending Head Start, no preschool, and other preschool programs. *Developmental Psychology, 24*, 210–222.

Levine, H. (1989). The education of at-risk students. *Educational Evaluation and Policy Analysis, 11*, 47–60.

Levine, R. (1977). Child rearing as cultural adaptation. In P. H. Leiderman, S. R. Tulkin, & A. Rosenfeld (Eds.), *Culture and infancy: Variations in the human experience*. New York: Academic Press.

McAdoo, H. (1973). *An assessment of racial attitudes and self-concepts in urban black children* (Report No. OCD-CD-282). Washington, DC: Office of Child Development.

McCartney, K., Scarr, S., Phillips, D., & Grajek, S. (1985). Day care as intervention: Comparisons of varying quality programs. *Journal of Applied Developmental Psychology, 6*, 247–260.

McLoyd, V. C. (1990). The impact of economic hardship on black families and children: Psychology distress, parenting, and socioemotional development. *Child Development, 61*, 311–346.

Ogbu, J. (1981). Origins of human competence: A cultural ecological perspective. *Child Development, 52*, 413–429.

Pawl, J. (Ed.). (1989). *Zero to Three, 9* (5).

Pettigrew, T. F. (1964). *A profile of the Negro American*. Princeton, NJ: Van Nostrand.

Phillip Morris Companies, Inc. (1989). *The Phillip Morris Companies, Inc. survey II: Child care*. New York: Author.

Phillips, D. (Ed.). (1987). *Quality in child care: What does the research tell us?* Research Monographs of the National Association for the Education of Young Children, 1.

Phillips, D., Scarr, S., & McCartney, K. (1987). Dimensions and effects of child care quality: The Bermuda study. In D. Phillips (Ed.), *Quality in child care: What does the research tell us?* Research Monographs of the National Association for the Education of Young Children, 1.

Presser, H. B. (1989). Can we make time for the children? The economy, work schedules, and child care. *Demography, 26*(4), 523–543.

Ramey, C., Bryant, D., & Suarez, T. (1985). Preschool compensatory education and the modificability of intelligence: A critical review. In D. Detterman (Ed.), *Current topics in human intelligence*. Norwood, NJ: Ablex.

Ramey, C., & Campbell, F. (1987). The Carolina Abcedarian Project: An educational experiment concerning human malleability. In J. J. Gallagher & C. T. Ramey (Eds.), *The malleability of children*. Baltimore, MD: Brooks.

Ramey, C., Farran, D., & Campbell, F. (1979). Predicting IQ from mother–infant interactions. *Child Development, 50*, 804–814.

Ramey, C., Yeates, K., & Short, E. (1984). The plasticity of intellectual development: Insights from preventive intervention. *Child Development, 55*, 1913–1925.

Robinson, B., Rowland, B., &. Coleman, M. (1986). *Latchkey kids*. Washington, DC: Lexington Books.

Rotheram, M. J., & Phinney, J. S. (1987). Introduction: Definitions and perspectives in the study of children's ethnic socialization. In J. S. Phinney & M. J. Rotheram (Eds.), *Children's ethnic socialization*. Newbury Park, CA: Sage.

Ruopp, R., Travers, J., Glantz, F., & Coelen, C. (1979). *Children as the center: Final report of the national day care study*. Cambridge, MA: Abt Associates.

Rutter, M. (1979). Maternal deprivation, 1972–1978: New findings, new concepts, new approaches. *Child Development, 50*, 283–305.

Rutter, M. (1981). *Maternal deprivation reassessed*. Harmondsworth, England: Penguin.

Rutter, M. (1988). Stress, coping, and development: Some issues and some questions. In N. Garmezy & M. Rutter (Eds.), *Stress, coping, and development in children*. Baltimore: Johns Hopkins University Press.

Sameroff, A., & Chandler, M. (1975). Reproductive risk and the continuum of caretaking casuality. In F. Horowitz (Ed.), *Review of child development research* (Vol. 4). Chicago: University of Chicago Press.

Semaj, L. T. (1985). Afrikanity, cognition, and extended self-identity. In M. B. Spencer, G. K.

Brookins, & W. R. Allen (Eds.), *Beginnings: Social and affective development of black children* (pp. 173–184). Hillsdale, NJ: Erlbaum.

Slaughter, D. T. (1983). Early intervention and its effects on maternal and child development. *Monographs of the Society for Research in Child Development, 48* (4, Serial No. 202).

Slaughter, D. T. (Ed.). (1988). *Black children in poverty: A developmental perspective.* New Directions for Child Development, *42.*

Slaughter, D. T., & McWorter, G. A. (1985). Social origins and early features and children. In M. B. Spencer, G. K. Brookins, & W. R. Allen (Eds.), *Beginnings: Social and affective development of black children* (pp. 5–18). Hillsdale, NJ: Erlbaum.

Spencer, M. B. (1970). The effects of systematic social (puppet) and token reinforcement on the modification of racial and color-concept attitudes in preschool-aged children. Unpublished master's thesis, University of Kansas, Lawrence.

Spencer, M. B. (1981, April). Final report: Personal-social adjustment of minority-group children (Report of #5-RO1-DHS-MH-31106). National Institute of Mental Health.

Spencer, M. B. (1982). Preschool children's social cognition and cultural cognition: A cognitive developmental interpretation of race dissonance findings. *Journal of Psychology, 112,* 275–286.

Spencer, M. B. (1983). Children's cultural values and parental child rearing strategies. *Developmental Review, 3,* 351–370.

Spencer, M. B. (1984). Black children's race awareness, racial attitudes and self-concept: A reinterpretation. *Journal of Child Psychology and Psychiatry, 25*(3), 433–441.

Spencer, M. B. (1985). Racial variation in achievement prediction: The school as a conduit for macrostructural cultural tension. In H. McAdoo & J. McAdoo (Eds.), *Black children.* Beverly Hills: Sage.

Spencer, M. B. (1987). Black children's ethnic identity formation: Risk and resilience of castelike minorities. In J. S. Phinney & M. J. Rotheram (Eds.), *Children's ethnic socialization.* Beverly Hills: Sage.

Spencer, M. B. (1988). Self-concept development. In D. T. Slaughter (Ed.), *Black children in poverty: A developmental perspective* (pp. 59–72). San Francisco: Jossey-Bass.

Spencer, M. B. (1989). Patterns of developmental transition for economically disadvantaged black male adolescents. Unpublished manuscript.

Spencer, M. B. (1990). Parental value transmission: Implications for black child development. In J. B. Stewart & H. Cheatham (Eds.), *Interdisciplinary perspectives on black families.* Atlanta: Transactions.

Spencer, M. B., Dobbs, B., & Swanson, D. P. (1988). Afro-American adolescents: Adaptational processes and socioeconomic diversity in behavioral outcomes. *Journal of Adolescence, 11,* 117–137.

Spencer, M. B., & Horowitz, F. D. (1973). Racial attitudes and color concept-attitude modification in black and Caucasian preschool children. *Developmental Psychology, 9,* 246–254.

Spencer, M. B., Kim, S., & Marshall, S. (1987). Double stratification and psychological risk: Adaptational processes and school experiences of black children. *Journal of Negro Education, 56*(1), 77–86.

Squibb, B. (1987). The dynamics of family day care: A review of the research. Prepared for the fellow program at the Bush Center in Child Development and Social Policy, Yale University, New Haven, CT.

Staples, R. (1978). Change and adaptations in the black family. In R. Staples (Ed.), *The black family: Essays and studies* (2nd ed.). Belmont, CA: Wordsworth.

Stipek, D., & McCroskey, J. (1989). Investing in children: Government and workplace policies for parents. *American Psychologist, 44,* 416–423.

U.S. Bureau of the Census. (1991). *Census and you: Monthly news, 27*(11), 14.

Washington, V. (1988). Historical and contemporary linkages between black child development and social policy. In D. T. Slaughter (Ed.), *Black children and poverty: A developmental perspective* (pp. 93–105). New Directions for Child Development, *42.*

Washington, V., & LaPoint, V. (1988). *Black children and American institutions: An ecological review and resource guide.* New York: Garland.

Washington, V., & Oyemade, U. J. (1987). *Project Head Start: Past, present, and future trends in the context of family needs*. New York: Garland.

Weikart, D. P. (1989). Quality preschool programs: A long-term social investment (Occasional paper, No. 5. Ford Foundation Project on Social Welfare and the American Future). New York: Ford Foundation.

White, B. (1989, September 23). Day-care program criticized. *The Atlanta Journal and Constitution*, p. B-2.

White, R. (1959). Motivation reconsidered: The concept of competence. *Psychology Review*, *66*, 297–333.

Wilson, W. (1987). *The truly disadvantaged: The inner city, the underclass, and public policy*. Chicago: University of Chicago Press.

Zigler, E., & Valentine, J. (Eds.). (1979). *Project Head Start: A legacy of the war on poverty*. New York: Free Press.

IV.   Health care

7   Health policy in the Family Support Act of 1988

Katherine S. Lobach

Health care services for poor children are often inadequate. In order for health services to be of high quality they must be accessible, available, appropriate, and acceptable. Accessibility is a basic and self-evident requirement. Access is usually assumed to imply financial access. However, considerations of time and distance are also access issues. Availability of services refers not only to the physical presence or absence of providers and facilities, but their willingness to serve the clientele in question, and sometimes even the clientele's awareness that the services exist. Appropriateness covers the gamut, from the provision of preventive care and management of health problems in accordance with accepted standards of practice to the organization and scope of services being offered. Acceptability acknowledges the perceptions and demands of the consumer that may encompass both the content and style of service delivery. Such matters as waiting times, bureaucratic requirements, and language and cultural compatibility could be mentioned here. If the four "As" are kept in mind, it becomes comparatively easy to determine whether a health policy issue has implications for quality of health care.

While these four components of quality can be broadly applied to all aspects of health care delivery in a variety of settings for people of all ages, our focus here is on children, and a few additional points need to be made in connection with this age group. The level of health services to children, as to others, can range from the simplicity of a band-aid and a kiss to the high technology of the neonatal intensive care unit, but inpatient services are a relatively small component (except financially) of the health care provided to and experienced by children (McManus, 1986) and will not be discussed in this chapter. Preventive care is or should be a rather large element of health services for children.

To many observers and participants in the childhood health care scene, however, the central quality issue is the appropriateness of the organization and scope of

The assistance of Sylvia Pirani was invaluable in the preparation of this chapter. Mildred A. Morehead, M.D. generously provided helpful information and suggestions as did Margaret McManus and Sara Rosenbaum. Staff at the American Academy of Pediatrics, including Sam Flint, Nancy Martin, Judith Cohen, and Beth Shapiro, have been an inexhaustible source of data and other material.

159

services to children. Services should be characterized by comprehensiveness, continuity, and coordination. These characteristics address the special needs and nature of children – the multifactorial nature of some of their health problems, the changes in the organism through time as a result of growth and development, and the dependency on older family members and other adults. When the three "Cs" are provided, there are improvements in some health outcomes (Schorr, 1988; Becker, Drachman, & Kirscht, 1974; Shadish, 1981).

Comprehensiveness in a program context refers to a broad scope of services. In a financing context it refers to benefits. Programmatically, as many services as possible should be at the same site and/or provided by the same individual. A comprehensive program might include nutrition, dental, social, and psychological services as well as medical ones; the primary care provider (doctor or nurse) would provide preventive, acute and chronic illness, inpatient, and follow-up care. These arrangements, of course, enhance coordination, as does continuity, but the latter two are desirable even when comprehensiveness is lacking. Continuity refers to the concept that every child should have a "medical home" – a continuing relationship with a primary provider who should either provide or coordinate all aspects of the child's care (Schiff, 1989).

Of course, the way in which services are organized will not in itself guarantee acceptable quality. A number of other factors play a role. Several are listed here because without them quality will be dubious or poor. They must be taken into account in any health policy initiative that claims to be concerned with quality. They include the following.

1. The qualifications, knowledge, skills, and attitudes of the health care professionals who provide services. At a minimum providers should have training and experience with children, and their practice should be in accordance with currently accepted standards.
2. Program administration that is responsive and intelligent, qualities that will usually produce efficient and effective services that may even be user-friendly.
3. Knowledgeable, discriminating, and vocal consumers. Educating poor families about the health care needs of their children and what services are appropriate for them, not to mention their rights as consumers, must be given high priority.
4. Adequate resources. Although economic issues are beyond the scope of this chapter, it must be stated here that there can be no satisfactory quality without adequate funding. Examples abound of ways in which the perceived need to save money has compromised quality in programs for poor children. Reductions in scope of services, caps on utilization, refusal by qualified providers to participate because of low fee schedules, and public health clinics operating with equipment as much as 30 to 40 years old are but a few that can be mentioned.
5. Monitoring services. It is unlikely that such services will be supported or maintained without monitoring. Monitoring of quality, especially when it has implications for cost containment efforts, is a widespread activity throughout the health care industry, but not particularly visible in the arena of services to poor children. Government agencies, provider-sponsored bodies, and consumer and advocacy groups may all be involved, but for the clientele we are concerned with, the government agencies that should be most involved are seldom a high-profile presence (Rosenbaum & Johnson, 1986).

Quality of services for poor children

Families enrolled in the Medicaid program have, by definition, obtained financial access to health care, and for them a major barrier to obtaining quality services has been overcome (Davis & Schoen, 1978). The situation of the many poor and near poor children who are not eligible for Medicaid is even more severe. In 1986, 50% of children in families below the federal poverty level were not covered (*Healthy Children*, 1988; Laudicina & Lipson, 1988). For children enrolled in the Medicaid program, is this access real or illusory? In terms of utilization, it is real. Poor children with Medicaid have almost as many medical visits as do middle-income children with private insurance, and these include visits for checkups and immunizations. Medicaid has changed the straight-line relationship between income and health care utilization to a biphasic curve (*Healthy Children*, 1988).

Has this improved access been paralleled by increased availability of services? The answer varies depending on regional and geographic characteristics (inner city versus rural), how states administer the program, and the local supply of providers. In general, according to the Office of Technology Assessment, children on Medicaid continue to be much more likely than middle-income children to use health clinics, hospital emergency rooms and outpatient departments (*Healthy Children*, 1988). Nevertheless, in many parts of the United States private-practicing pediatricians, in spite of low fees and significant administrative difficulties, have participated in Medicaid in large numbers. In 1983, 82% of a survey sample accepted Medicaid patients in some circumstances and 65% accepted them without limitation. By 1989 these percentages had fallen to 77% and 65% respectively.

The role of health maintenance organizations in providing services to Medicaid children remains to be elucidated. Some HMOs have contracted with states or localities to provide managed care to certain populations of Medicaid clients. The total number of children and the nature, completeness, and quality of services to them have not been reported. By the mid-1990s a number of states had received federal waivers allowing them to mandate enrollment of all Medicaid recipients into managed care. The states are rapidly proceeding to implement these mandates. Change is taking place so quickly that objective information about the effects of the mandates is not yet available, but given the increasing number of children involved, the need for reliable comprehensive data is even more pressing than it has been in the past.

Unique to inner cities (where there are high concentrations of Medicaid recipients) in states with relatively generous Medicaid benefits (New York, California, Illinois) are the storefront medical offices known colloquially as "Medicaid mills" (Morehead, personal communication). Little data are available on the volume of services they provide to children, but in the areas where they operate it is thought to be considerable. These offices are perhaps the only free market development in response to the Medicaid program.

The establishment and location of publicly supported programs, many of which provide a comprehensive range of services such as community health centers, maternal child health projects, and some local health department clinics, have taken place independent of the Medicaid program. But, because they target similar populations, where such services exist, they are available to and used by Medicaid recipients.

Availability requires that clients be aware of a service. What kind of outreach efforts do states extend to their Medicaid clients? The situation for children is best illustrated by the Early and Periodic Screening, Diagnosis, and Treatment (EPSDT) program, where outreach is a required component. Yet most states do no more than mention the program during AFDC eligibility interviews (Children's Defense Fund, 1988; American Academy of Pediatrics, Committee on Child Health Financing, 1987).

A description of the appropriateness of care provided by the different types of providers brings us to the heart of the matter of quality. Standards of practice in the various settings, including the provision of preventive care, along with comprehensiveness, continuity, and coordination are the critical criteria. In an early study assessing these features, Morehead compared community health centers, outpatient departments in teaching hospitals, Title V maternal and child health programs, health department clinics, and group practices (Morehead, Donaldson, & Scravelli, 1971). She rated the Title V MCH programs highest and the outpatient departments lowest. However, it would be risky to generalize about these categories of providers because in the intervening years many ambulatory care sites have reorganized to provide greater continuity and comprehensiveness while loss of funding and other administrative pressures have reduced the scope of services in other settings. Miller, Moos, Kotch, Brown, and Brainard (1981) surveyed a number of local health department clinics around the country and found many that were maintaining notably high standards.

For the Medicaid mills, however, the assessment has not changed. In reviewing the work of the Bronx Professional Standards Review Organization in connection with 60 such facilities in 1982 Morehead found that "Most pediatric care is episodic and related to acute illness. Screening procedures or monitoring of growth and development are minimal. . . . There have been problems with chronic disease, in part due to the failure of providers to obtain information on care they may be receiving elsewhere and in part due to lack of any follow-up system to assure ongoing contact with the children who do primarily use the facility" (Morehead, 1982, p. 130).

In the recent past, resources for evaluating pediatric ambulatory care providers of all types have been limited. Attention goes to inpatient and other more costly units where "quality" review goes hand-in-hand with cost containment efforts. Most knowledgeable observers feel there is room for improvement in quality of services to poor children in almost every setting, with the possible exception of those programs that are purposely designed and operated to be comprehensive and to be held to high standards.

An additional perspective on the question of quality of children's services in the Medicaid program as it now exists is provided by a brief look at the EPSDT program. Established as part of the original Medicaid program to ensure that children receive the preventive, screening, and follow-up services that are an essential part of their health care, the program has been beset by problems since its inception. Even after a major revision of the regulations in 1984, EPSDT continues to fall far short of meeting its potential. For example, in 1988 nationwide only 31% of eligible children received an initial and/or periodic screening. In the age groups 6–20 years, the proportion was 13.2%. Although the Health Care Financing Administration (HCFA) now encourages states to link children to continuing care providers, as of 1988 only 10% of eligible children were enrolled in continuing care (*Early and Periodic Screening, Diagnosis, and Treatment Program Participation Survey, Calendar Year 1988*).

Two components of the EPSDT program have an immediate bearing on quality of health care: the periodicity schedule for medical examinations and the establishment of provider standards or protocols for these examinations and their follow-up. In both cases there is wide variation in the way states deal with them. A Children's Defense Fund Survey in 1985 showed that only seven states used schedules that met or exceeded the American Academy of Pediatric's guidelines for child health supervision. The same survey found that only 40 states had established provider standards for use by EPSDT providers and "the level of quality and detail in protocols varied greatly" (Rosenbaum & Johnson, 1986).

Even when EPSDT standards have been promulgated, monitoring provider compliance (as opposed to auditing financial practices) appears to be given low priority by EPSDT administration. While occasionally one can find a well-organized and active monitoring unit such as that operated until recently by the New York City Department of Health, such units seem to be the exception rather than the rule. (The leadership of the New York City Department of Health group cannot identify counterparts of their unit anywhere else.)

In spite of its problems, no program has greater potential for ensuring needed and high-quality health services to low-income children than does EPSDT. A state that wanted to demonstrate a commitment to improved services for poor children would need to make a serious attempt to improve all aspects of its EPSDT program and find ways to maintain long-term Medicaid/EPSDT eligibility for children.

Effects of welfare reform on health services for children

Recent welfare reforms could have significant implications for the quality of health services provided to the children in these families. Specifically, the Family Support Act of 1988 provides for extension of Medicaid coverage for 12 months after a family leaves the AFDC program for employment, with the option for a state to charge premiums during the second 6 months or to purchase alternative plans. Also relevant are the child care provisions of the act, which require states not only to guarantee child care for participants (including a 12-month transition period after employment begins) but to ensure that health and safety standards are met in center-based care. Lastly, the JOBS component of the act, which provides education, training, and employment, has the potential to indirectly affect the quality of children's health services. Implications of each for children's health are considered.

Medicaid extension. The extension of Medicaid coverage for up to 1 year after beginning employment will certainly serve as an inducement for participants in the program and will eliminate gaps in coverage in cases where there is a waiting period for employer's coverage to take effect. It will also cushion the effects of any false starts the Family Support Act recipient makes in the job market. What are the implications for quality of providing this so-called transitional Medicaid? To the degree that continuity of coverage ensures continuity of care for as long as it lasts, the effect on quality should be positive. The Children's Medicaid Program, a demonstration in Suffolk County, New York, of Physician Reimbursement and Continuing Care under Medicaid, showed extremely high patient satisfaction rates when children were guaranteed eligibility and able to stay with the primary care physician of their choice (Davidson, Fleming, Hohlin, & Manheim, 1988). In the case of transitional Medicaid, that effect would depend on whether there had been continuity of services previously (as well as what other quality features had been present). Otherwise, the 1-year duration is really too short to allow for any meaningful assessment of continuity.

What *could* meaningfully be done during this transitional period to enhance the prospects for continuity would be to encourage and assist mothers to maintain links with their previous providers, when appropriate and feasible, or to help them find a more appropriate and acceptable source of care and to assist with transfer of records and other arrangements when there is to be a change of providers. (The Children's Defense Fund survey of EPSDT found that no states have formal mechanisms for transferring children losing Medicaid to other programs [Rosenbaum & Johnson, 1986]). To the extent possible the new provider should be one that offers comprehensive and continuing care.

A central question about transitional Medicaid is whether the states' financing arrangements for the second 6 months will enhance or diminish families' access to and utilization of appropriate services. In a consideration of quality issues, however, there seems to be no reason to distinguish between the effect of the arrangements during the last half of the transition period and what will be happening thereafter. If the family stays on Medicaid, their previous level and type of care will likely continue. If they are expected to accept (and perhaps pay for) their employer's coverage, the issues to be dealt with in the posttransitional Medicaid period will have to be confronted 6 months sooner. The main effects of this transitional period, then, will be to buy time for a family and those assisting it to make the best possible arrangements for care and to adjust to whatever changes ensue. If the time is not so used, the transitional period will have little value as far as quality of children's health services is concerned.

Transitional Medicaid implies that there will be transition to some other form of health insurance for these families as they enter the workforce. Will that in fact be the case? For a majority of families the answer is yes. In 1987, 75.2% of families with at least one employed adult had employment-related insurance (Short, Monheit, & Beauregard, 1988). Even when employment characteristics were subcategorized by employment status, type of industry, size of employing establishment, and hourly wage paid, over 50% of families were covered. (The one exception was agriculture, forestry, and fishing at 40.6%.) Not surprisingly, proportions were the lowest in the categories of employment likely to be entered by Family Support Act participants: only 62% of part-time workers, 53.4% of personal services workers, 56.7 % of those employed in firms with less than 10 workers, and 55.4% of those whose hourly wage was $3.50 or less had insurance through their employers.

Thus, a substantial minority of the newly employed individuals going off welfare will, barring major changes in national policy on health insurance, become uninsured when transitional Medicaid ends. But even when an employed parent *is* insured, the children may not be. An increasing number of firms do not offer coverage for dependents, or require the employee to pay for all or part of it. In 1988 employers fully paid for only 32% of dependent coverage. When coverage for dependents is an option to be paid for by families, many will of necessity forgo it. Overall from 1979 to 1988 the percent of privately insured children covered through another family member fell from 63% to 60% (Miller et al., 1981).

What about the nature of coverage provided to children who *are* insured? An examination of its restrictions and exclusions shows major implications for the quality of the child's care. Just two key elements of children's coverage – preventive care and services for chronic disease – will illustrate the point.

In no other population group except pregnant women is the direct value of preventive care (immunization, screening for health problems, anticipatory guidance, etc.) so well recognized and accepted for its cost-effectiveness and promotion of health as it is for children (Shadish, 1981). Failure to provide such care whether by the individual provider or the financing structure is incompatible with a satisfactory quality of care. Yet a recent report cites a survey of 2,000 companies that found that in 1987 only 41% covered voluntary physical examination for employees and even fewer provided preventive coverage for children (Chu & Trapnell, 1989). From the legislative standpoint, efforts to persuade state legislatures to require children's health insurance to include preventive coverage have been underway for the past 7 years. To date, just six states have mandated such coverage.

The private insurance situation for children with chronic disease (10% to 15% of all children) and disabilities is also problematic. At least 4% of noninstitutionalized U.S. children have limitation of activity due to disability, and in families with incomes below the poverty level (i.e., those who would be participating in the JOBS program), the proportion rises to 5.7%. And, not unexpectedly, the average yearly costs for health services for these children are almost three times the national average for all children. But data from the National Center for Health Statistics shows that for disabled children with private insurance coverage, 21.3% of charges are paid out-of-pocket, as compared to 2.7% when coverage is under public auspices. A recent estimate is that just 64% of employer-based insurance plans cover home health services for chronically ill children (Newacheck & McManus, 1988).

Another alternative could be sought for families in the group whose children's coverage and care will clearly suffer when they leave Medicaid: passage by state legislatures of the federal OBRA-87 amendments, which allow optional extension of Medicaid eligibility to pregnant women and children to age 5 with incomes up to 185% of the federal poverty level. This coverage would surely fill an important gap in that provided by many employers, and at the very least would ensure that younger children receive the preventive and other care they need. A statewide experiment with OBRA-87 could reveal the extent to which this particular gap in coverage could be eliminated.

Will those families that *are* able to maintain financial access to children's health care after Medicaid coverage ends find that care to be available and appropriate? If they continue to use the same sources of care that were available to them through Medicaid, the various concerns about quality described earlier will still apply. But now, with private coverage, they will presumably be able to obtain pediatric care in the mainstream, where at least some of the elements of quality such as continuity, coordination, adherence to accepted standards of practice, and some degree of amenity are more likely (although not inevitably) to be found. Families could make this change if there are such providers available in the communities where the families live, if they know where to find them, and if they perceive it worth the effort to change their previous patterns of utilization. The extent to which any of these conditions are met deserves further study. Information about the source, kind, and amount of care children in different localities obtained before and after their families went from Medicaid to private coverage would be helpful in the debate about whether financing of children's health services for low-income families should put greater or lesser emphasis on Medicaid improvements versus reform of private insurance. Given the availability and possibility of choosing among various providers, will mothers' arrangements differ according to whether information and advice were provided in the training and job assistance program they participated in?

Child care arrangements. That properly regulated and operated child care services can and do influence the quality of children's health services is well recognized and well documented. The best-known example is, of course, Head Start. By requiring or in some cases providing on-site services by nurses and other providers, Head Start programs reported in a 1982 survey that 84% of enrolled children completed medical screenings. Of the 25% who had conditions requiring follow-up, 93% received it. Ninety-three percent of children were reported to be up to date on immunizations. (Contrast this with the estimate by the Center for Disease Control that in some locations, including New York City, 40% to 50% of preschool children are not fully immunized.) Head Start children also usually receive necessary and appropriate nutrition and dental services (*A Review of Head Start Research since 1970*, 1983).

However, little is known about the provision of health care in child care programs other than Head Start. Standards are being developed. Will failure to enforce health standards leave children worse off than before or be merely a lost opportunity? Conversely, will overzealous enforcement of standards compromise the availability of otherwise acceptable child care?

Education and training. It is possible that in some states mothers will be given information and advice about health care matters as part of JOBS training in preparation for entering the workforce. Areas that require attention include the need for, reasons for, and content of preventive health care for children; the features that characterize health services of good quality and how to go about finding such services; evaluating employee benefit packages as part of a job search and what to consider in choosing among offerings of various health insurance options. (The American Academy of Pediatrics is preparing to issue a consumer booklet for parents that deals with the latter items.)

The effect of educating mothers about preventive care is particularly worth evaluating in light of the findings of Lurie et al. that even when care was completely free, only 59% of children age zero to 6 had received an immunization during the 3-year study period. (When cost sharing was a feature, the proportion was 49%.) Clearly, guaranteed access to care is not sufficient by itself to ensure children will get services.

A worthwhile demonstration program would develop curriculum material along the lines suggested and include it in training programs. It could then be evaluated on its own terms – changes in amount and kind of health care to children before and after training, given consistently accessible and available services throughout. More complex but more revealing would be a study of the relative influence of parent education versus child care requirements versus change in insurance coverage on the provision of specified health services to children.

Conclusion

Innovative and effective ways are needed to reach out and notify families with young children of expanded or extended medical eligibility levels and of available and appropriate service providers. Examples of settings where outreach is needed include hospital newborn nurseries, child care programs and welfare offices, as well as churches and other indigenous community organizations. These efforts should apply not only to the Family Support Act's transitional Medicaid but to the various medical expansion options and mandates called for in other recent health policy decisions at the federal level (Laudicina & Lipson, 1988).

Training programs for poor mothers need to include curriculum materials on children's health care needs, criteria for choosing providers, and information about health insurance benefits. Case management services might be initiated to assist mothers in identifying new and appropriate sources of care, using new and different systems of health care.

Monitoring systems need to be put in place. More information is needed about where Medicaid-covered children go for primary, ambulatory care in different localities and in the aggregate nationwide. What proportions use the various kinds of providers available in the public and private sectors and what patterns of use are found? Studies of the quality of care in the various settings used by poor children are also needed to update the material reported one to two decades ago. States and localities need to be surveyed to learn more about the existence and nature of efforts to monitor quality of health services to poor children. Attempts need to be made to assess the extent to which coverage for dependents through the health insurance of absent parents could fill the insurance gaps after Family Support Act families lose their Medicaid coverage.

Many families in which the mother leaves welfare and enters the workforce will ultimately lose financial access to a broad range of benefits. Perhaps the most hopeful health policy feature of current welfare reform is the concept of transitional Medicaid which, like a number of other recent congressional initiatives for women's and children's Medicaid coverage, establishes the precedent of separating Medicaid eligibility from AFDC eligibility. That is surely a step, but only a step, in the right direction. Whether continuing with these increments will ultimately allow us to reach the goal of universal financial access to health services for all children remains to be seen (Waxman, 1989), but there should be no doubt that by one route or another that is the goal we must reach.

REFERENCES

American Academy of Pediatrics, Committee on Child Health Financing. (1986). *Medicaid policy statement.*

American Academy of Pediatrics, Committee on Child Health Financing. (1987, September). *Medicaid's EPSDT program. A pediatrician's handbook for action.*

Becker M. H., Drachman R. A., & Kirscht, J. P. (1974). A field experiment to evaluate various outcomes of continuity of physician care. *American Journal of Public Health, 64,* 1062–1070.

Children's Defense Fund. (1988, March). *Facts about Medicaid's EPSDT program: Key strategies for improving EPSDT.*

Chu, R. C., & Trapnell, C. R. (1989, January). *Premiums for preventive pediatric care recommended by the American Academy of Pediatrics in employer health insurance programs.* Annandale, VA: Acturial Research Corporation.

Davidson, S., Fleming, G., Hohlin, M., & Manheim, L., et al. (1988, May). *Physician reimbursement* and continuing care under Medicaid. A demonstration. Children's Medicaid Program, American Academy of Pediatrics.

Davis, K., & Schoen, C. (1978). *Health and the war on poverty: A ten year appraisal.* Washington, DC: Brookings Institute.

Early and Periodic Screening, Diagnosis, and Treatment Program participation survey, calendar year 1988. Washington, DC: Health Care Financing Administration.

Healthy children: Investing in the future. (1988). Washington, DC: Office of Technology Assessment.

Laudicina, S. S., & Lipson, D. J. (1988, September). *Medicaid and poor children: State variations in eligibility and services coverage.* Alexandria, VA: National Association of Children's Hospitals and Related Institutions.

Lurie, N., Manning, W. G., Peterson, C., & Goldberg, G. A., et al. (1987). Preventive care: Do we practice what we preach? *American Journal of Public Health, 77,* 801–804.

McManus, M. A. (1986, February). *Medicaid services and delivery settings for maternal and child health.* Washington, DC: National Governors' Association Health Policy Studies.

McManus, M. A. (1989, Winter). *Dependent coverage eroding in private plans* (AAP Child Health Financing Report).

Miller, C. A., Moos, M. K., Kotch, J. B., Brown, M. L., & Brainard, M. D. (1981). Role of local health departments in the delivery of ambulatory care. *American Journal of Public Health, 71,* 15–29.

Morehead, M. A. (1982). Bronx Professional Standards Review Organization: Experience with ambulatory care review. *Bulletin of the New York Academy of Medicine, 58,* 127–132.

Morehead, M. A. Personal communication.

Morehead, M. A., Donaldson, R. S., & Scravelli, M. R. (1971). Comparison between OEO neighborhood health centers and other health care providers of ratings of the quality of health care. *American Journal of Public Health, 61,* 1294–1306.

Newacheck, P. W., & McManus, M. A. (1988). Financing health care for disabled children. *Pediatrics, 81,* 385–394.

Periodic survey of fellows. (1985; 1989). American Academy of Pediatrics.

A review of Head Start research since 1970. (1983). U.S. Department of Health and Human Services Office of Human Development Services.

Rosenbach, M. L. (1989). The impact of Medicaid on physician use by low-income children. *American Journal of Public Health, 79,* 1220–1226.

Rosenbaum, S., & Johnson, K. (1986). Providing health care for low-income children: Reconciling child health goals with child health financing realities. *The Milbank Quarterly, 64,* 442–478.

Schiff, D. A. (1989, September). *The medical home.* Paper presented at the United Hospital Fund Child Health Policy Retreat, Tuxedo, NY.

Schorr, L. B. (1988). *Within our reach: Breaking the cycle of disadvantage.* New York: Doubleday.

Shadish, W. (1981, April). *Effectiveness of preventive health care.* Washington, DC: Health Care Financing Administration Office of Research, Demonstrations, and Statistics.

Short, P. F., Monheit, A., & Beauregard, K. (1988, November). *Uninsured Americans. A 1987 profile.* National Center for Health Services Research and Health Care Technology Assessment. Paper presented at the annual meeting of the American Public Health Association, Boston.

Waxman, H. A. (1989). Kids and Medicaid: Progress but continuing problems. *American Journal of Public Health, 79,* 1217–1218.

8   Economic issues of health care

Barbara L. Wolfe

Among the large number of children in this country who are poor – nearly 15 million in 1993, according to U.S. Census Bureau figures – are many who have more health problems than their higher-income peers but receive more limited care. According to the National Center for Health Statistics (1991), approximately 40% of young children in families with incomes under $10,000 in 1990 were reported to be in excellent health, as compared to 63% of children in higher-income (over $35,000 annual income) families. Private health insurance covers much of the health care enjoyed by more affluent children, while most poor children either have no coverage or are publicly covered under Medicaid.

Relying on Medicaid to finance medical care for the poor has several problems: (1) not all poor families are eligible for it, and health care for those not covered is sometimes not received or is postponed; (2) quality of care received may be impaired by the inefficiencies that result from using different caregivers rather than a regular, non–emergency room provider; and (3) Medicaid may reduce the labor force participation of poor parents by providing an inducement to receive public assistance, and along with it Medicaid benefits, rather than work. Recent welfare reform, in particular the Family Support Act of 1988, attempts to redress the latter problem by extending, for a limited period of time, Medicaid coverage to families who lose eligibility because their earnings increase.

The effects of this change in Medicaid coverage can be studied by addressing several types of research question: How many children who would previously have gone without coverage will be covered under the Medicaid extension? Are they older or younger children (under or over age 9)? How does the extension influence utilization of medical care? As a consequence of the welfare reform, are women more likely to accept jobs that do not offer health care coverage? What is the

The research reported here was supported by a grant from the Foundation for Child Development, by a grant from the U.S. Department of Health and Human Services to the National Bureau of Economic Research, and by funds provided by the U.S. Department of Health and Human Services to the Institute for Research on Poverty. The research assistance of Juliana Pakes and Roseanne Woods is gratefully acknowledged.

potential for receiving private coverage when the Medicaid extension expires? What will be the response by those eligible if the state exercises its option to charge an income-conditioned premium during the second half of the period of extension? These questions are of general importance for policies that promote the transition from welfare to work.

This chapter anticipates some of the answers to these questions. It first describes the nature of Medicaid coverage and the current insurance coverage of the Aid to Families with Dependent Children (AFDC) population. It then considers the expected impact of the Family Support Act of 1988, discussing the link between insurance coverage and health. Alternative strategies for providing coverage to the AFDC population are presented as well.

Coverage of children under Medicaid

Medicaid is a joint federal–state public health insurance program that finances medical care for certain categories of people: low-income persons who are aged, blind, or disabled; members of families eligible to receive Aid to Families with Dependent Children (AFDC); and certain other low-income pregnant women and children. The majority (68%) of Medicaid recipients are on AFDC, and children make up nearly 45% of all Medicaid recipients. AFDC eligibility depends on state rules, which differ widely in income eligibility limits and in the nature and scope of Medicaid coverage. To be eligible, a family must have an income below 185% of a standard of need, determined by the state. Standards vary to a considerable degree: For example, in 1992 for a family of three in New Mexico the standard was $324 per month, but in Vermont it was $1,112 per month (Wolfe, 1992, p. 16). In addition, the family's income after work-related expenses must be less than the state's payment standard, or maximum benefit. As a result, more than a third of all children in families and more than one-half of all noninstitutionalized persons who are poor according to the Census Bureau definition are not covered by Medicaid. The situation of poor children deteriorated significantly between 1970 and 1987, while it has improved somewhat in the past few years.

Deterioration took place in both eligibility and depth of coverage through the mid-1980s. Medicaid coverage was 985 per 1,000 children in poverty in 1978, 737 in 1983, and 813 in 1985. In addition, restrictions enacted in 1981 and 1982 permitted states to extend cost sharing by recipients to nearly all services, reducing the value of coverage. Congress responded to these declines in coverage with legislation in 1984, 1986, and 1987 that required and enabled states to improve access to Medicaid for poor children and pregnant women: Eligibility was extended for 4 months to families who were on AFDC for at least 3 of the past 6 months and who left AFDC because of increased earnings or hours of work; pregnant women whose income and resources would make them eligible for AFDC if they had a child were required to be covered by Medicaid, as were children under 7 (under 5, after 1985) in two-parent families that met the earnings and resources tests. Since 1987 states may extend coverage and receive federal matching dollars for pregnant women and infants whose family incomes are below 185% of the poverty line and for children born after September 30, 1983, whose family incomes are below the federal poverty level. Since 1990 states are permitted to extend medical coverage to pregnant women, infants, and children under 6 with family incomes less than 133% of the poverty line. By July 1991 all pregnant women and children born after September 30, 1983, with incomes below the federal poverty line had to be covered. The coverage will eventually extend to children less than 19 living in a poor family. In addition, families that lost eligibility for AFDC via the 1981 removal of earnings disregards can retain Medicaid eligibility for 9 months.

Many states also have a program for the "medically needy," covering those who are in the categories eligible to receive welfare benefits but who have incomes before medical expenses that are somewhat above the state AFDC eligibility limit. To qualify, their incomes after deduction for medical expenses must be below the cutoff for welfare benefits.[1] About 12% of Medicaid payments for female family heads and their children are for the medically needy.

As a result of this structure of eligibility, 25% to 33%, or between 9.5 and 11 million, of poor families are without health insurance.[2] Among all children living in families below the poverty line, over 50% are covered by Medicaid, about 17% have private coverage, and the rest (about 30%) are uninsured.[3]

Medicaid has grown as a percentage of the total welfare benefit package, increasing the likelihood that persons are attracted onto AFDC to obtain its benefits,[4] and also that, once on AFDC, they have an incentive to remain there. An extensive literature on AFDC and food stamps finds strong evidence that these means-tested benefits reduce work effort (see Moffitt, 1988, for a review of this literature). There is far less evidence on Medicaid. One study (Blank, 1989) does not find a significant incentive effect, but a more recent investigation, which develops an index of the value of Medicaid for each family, finds strong evidence that Medicaid is an inducement to enter the welfare rolls (Moffitt & Wolfe, 1992). The effect is concentrated among those families whose members have health problems and is more an incentive to enter AFDC than to stay on it.

This latter study also suggests that coverage at the place of employment plays a larger role in influencing women's work–welfare choices than Medicaid. For example, if private coverage equivalent to Medicaid were extended to all single women who worked, the study predicts a decline in the AFDC caseload of over 20% and an increase of more than 15% in employment among these women. This argues for providing health insurance at the place of employment and for providing benefits that are similar to those of Medicaid.

Relationship of coverage to utilization of health care

Another drawback to present coverage under Medicaid concerns various aspects of utilization. Controlling for health status, persons with either private or public health insurance are more likely to use medical care than those not covered: Children in poor families that receive Medicaid have as many checkups and immunizations on average as middle-income children, but poor children not covered do not.[5] However, children with Medicaid do not receive care in the same locations as higher-income children with private insurance. Under Medicaid, care is more often received in health clinics, hospital emergency rooms, or outpatient clinics than in private doctors' offices. This pattern tends to reduce continuity of care, which in turn is believed to reduce the quality of care received.

Among children whose families go on and off Medicaid rolls, care tends to be received in hospitals, accentuating the problems of continuity and cost (U.S. General Accounting Office, 1987). Children covered by Medicaid rarely use private care, in part because of the low reimbursement rates paid by Medicaid in a number of states. This problem has grown more severe in recent years as Medicaid fees increased very little during the 1980s while private physicians' fees continued to rise.[6] A number of private physicians consequently will not provide care to those covered by Medicaid (Mitchell, 1991). A recent comparison across states provides evidence of greater use of care where Medicaid fees relative to private fees are higher (Wade, 1992). Since emergency room care is more expensive than the care given by private providers, present expenditures on Medicaid may exceed even those that would result from a modest increase in reimbursement rates.[7]

Utilization is important because it is connected to health status, although the link is difficult to establish because health is difficult to measure. Infant mortality rates provide one means to do so, but are a very limited measure of differences in health. In some cases, however, the link appears strong. A follow-up study of about 200 patients who lost eligibility for Medicaid in California showed a decline in health status, as measured by mortality and health problems, in comparison with a control group that maintained eligibility (Lurie, Ward, Shapero, & Brook, 1984). Results from the Health Insurance Study conducted by the Rand Corporation found only marginal effects from greater use of medical care, but the study compared groups with varying levels of insurance rather than those with full versus no coverage, which is more likely to be the circumstance of a family that loses Medicaid coverage.

Current coverage of the target population

In keeping with the goals of this volume the target population in this chapter consists of single mothers and their children. Approximately 12.9 million children live in such families, based on data collected in a 4-month period during winter and spring of 1984 in wave 3 of the Survey of Income and Program Participation (SIPP) (Moffitt & Wolfe, 1992). Of these children, 58.4% live in families with income below the poverty line, and another 23% live in families with incomes between one and two times the poverty line – the "nearly poor." About half of these children have fair or poor health, as reported by their mothers, and the other half are reported to have good or excellent health (68.9% versus 47.8% respectively).

Examination of the insurance coverage of these children indicated that 24.6%

(about a quarter of this population) had no insurance coverage, just over 40% had Medicaid coverage, and slightly more than a third (34%) had private coverage. Another 1.1% had both private and Medicaid coverage over the 4-month period. Two-thirds of children in poor families were covered by Medicaid, but less than 12% of those nearly poor had such coverage; more than a third in this group were uninsured. Over three-quarters of children living in families with incomes more than twice the poverty line (i.e., not in or near poverty) had private insurance coverage, yet nearly 20% of them had no health care coverage at all.

Children who were reported to have poor or fair health, as opposed to good or excellent health, were more likely to have Medicaid coverage, less likely to have private coverage, and about as likely to have no insurance as healthier children.[8] Children whose mothers were employed were less likely to have any form of health insurance coverage but more likely, if insured, to have private coverage than those whose mothers did not work.

Data from SIPP on employment-based health insurance in 1984 give some insight into the likelihood of private coverage. Using evidence from 1984 on employer-based coverage may, however, paint too positive a picture for 1989–90. Employer subsidization of family premiums for health insurance declined over the 1980s. For example, the U.S. Department of Labor (1987) reports that the percentage of medium-size and large firms that paid the full cost of family insurance coverage declined from 51% to 35% from 1981 to 1986.

The probability of being offered insurance is in part determined by the charac-teristics of the employer: Large firms are more likely to offer coverage than are small firms; the least likely are those with less than 25 employees. Coverage also differs by industry: Government and durable goods manufacturing are most likely to offer coverage; retail trade jobs, construction, and service jobs are those least likely. Because single mothers with low skills (those most at risk of being on welfare) are more likely to obtain jobs in retail sales or service jobs, not many will have the option of accepting or purchasing insurance at their place of employment.

The SIPP data (wave 3) give a fairly detailed picture of the possibilities of employment-based insurance for our population of interest. About 55% of the single mothers in this sample were in the workforce during 1984. Based on their employ-ment and earnings experience and controlling for individual characteristics such as age, education, health, and training, we concluded that if all single mothers who were below the poverty line worked, about 30% would have family coverage and another 5% individual coverage, so that about two-thirds would be without cover-age. Among women who are nearly poor, 43% could be expected to have family coverage if they were in the workforce and 9% would have individual coverage; nearly half would be without any coverage. Women with higher earnings are likely to do much better in terms of coverage: More than half will have family coverage and another 11% individual coverage. Yet even among this group, more than a third would be without coverage should they join the workforce (Moffitt & Wolfe, 1992).

The factors that increase a woman's probability of having insurance if employed include being older, having more education, being the head of the household, having good or excellent health, having a disabled child (which increases the value of insurance), receiving child support, working for one employer, working for the government, and working in manufacturing. Factors that decrease the probability of having insurance if employed include living in a state with higher per capita health expenditures and working in sales or personal services. Working single women with more children are less likely to have individual coverage, and perhaps family coverage as well (Moffitt & Wolfe, 1992).

Implications of welfare reform for health policy

The net result of the pattern just described is that the majority of single women with children would lack health insurance coverage if they were employed. The Medicaid extension provided by the Family Support Act of 1988, whose goal is to move single mothers from public assistance to self-support through work, is designed to address that problem by continuing Medicaid benefits for AFDC recipients who lose eligibility owing to an increase in earnings and assets. Coverage continues for 12 months; in the second half of this period, states have the option of charging an income-conditioned premium. The following sections explore the probable effect of the Medicaid extension, looking first at the importance of health insurance for medical care utilization and health.

The links among insurance, utilization, and health

Health status itself is of course a primary determinant of medical care utilization. A large part of medical care is for treatment of illness, but for those with children, a substantial portion is for well-baby and well-child care, including immunizations. Demand for health care is also affected by the factors that influence the demand for essentially all goods and services – the cost of care, including direct costs as well as time and transportation costs, and income. Where the demand for medical care is concerned, time is a significant component, so the location of facilities is important. Direct costs are the out of pocket costs paid by the consumer – the actual price charged, minus the amount paid by one's insurer.[9] In the case of full insurance coverage this direct price is, with rare exceptions, not charged to the customer. Insurance thus reduces the direct cost of care and increases the demand for care.

Determinants of utilization. For single women and their children, both Medicaid coverage and private coverage significantly increase utilization of outpatient care. For that population in SIPP, we estimated that utilization by those currently uninsured would rise from an average of 3.1 outpatient visits per year to 4.9 if covered by Medicaid or to 5.7 per year with private coverage. Nights hospitalized per year would be less affected, rising from 1.2 on average to 1.4 if covered by Medicaid and to 1.7 if covered by private insurance. For women currently receiving Medicaid, loss of coverage would mean that expected outpatient visits would decline from 5.7 to 2.2, and nights hospitalized from 1.8 to 1.5. We estimate that, on average, if children who are currently not insured were to be covered by Medicaid, their outpatient visits would rise from 9.4 to 10.6, and inpatient nights would remain at 0.1. If those currently covered by Medicaid were to lose coverage, the number of outpatient visits would decline from 10.5 to 9.4, and inpatient nights would decrease from 0.2 to 0.1 (Moffitt & Wolfe, 1992). These expected changes are consistent with other findings concerning the role of health insurance on utilization (see, e.g., Davis & Schoen, 1978; Lohr et al., 1986). The expectations are based on individual and family characteristics, including health status, age, race, education, mother's marital status, certain state characteristics, and insurance coverage.

Insurance plays an even more important role in prenatal care. For example, a study conducted in 1986 and 1987 found that women who were uninsured were more likely to go without sufficient prenatal care than were those who were insured (U.S. General Accounting Office, 1987). The uninsured women reported that the most significant barrier to adequate prenatal care was lack of money. Those covered by Medicaid were less likely to receive adequate care than those privately insured, and the most commonly reported barrier was lack of transportation.

Type of insurance also influences the site of care. In general, children covered by private insurance are more likely to use private offices for ambulatory care than are those who are covered by Medicaid or without coverage. For example, children in Rochester covered by Medicaid were more likely to use hospital-based outpatient care and health centers than private offices, whereas those covered by private insurance were more likely to use private offices and less likely to use hospitals and health centers, even after controlling for health status, income, distance to the nearest hospital, health center, or HMO, and the number of physicians relative to the population (van der Gaag & Wolfe, 1982).

Overall, then, there is clear evidence that insurance coverage is linked to utilization. Extending Medicaid by 12 months should increase utilization of care by both mothers and children for this period. The care is more likely to be received in clinics than private offices, but barriers in terms of location of facilities and hours of operation will also limit utilization.

Difficulties in measuring health. Linking health insurance and utilization of health care to health status is difficult, owing to the challenges in measuring health status. Infant mortality is often used but is a very gross measure. Other commonly collected data such as prevalence of chronic conditions, self-reported health status, and days ill or days missed from school are not comprehensive and may provide misleading information. Prevalence of chronic conditions is self-reported and may depend on having a diagnosis, which in turn depends on access to medical care.

Improved technology may also influence diagnosis, so that a time-series on prevalence of chronic conditions reflects not only health status but these other factors. Self-reported health depends in part on expectations, which may change over time, thus influencing such reports. For example, one person without any symptoms of chronic illness may report herself in only fair health, owing to a strained muscle that causes difficulty in raising an arm, whereas another person with arthritis may report herself in good health even though she has difficulty raising an arm. Days reported ill or days of school missed may also depend on access to care and on changing views of how childhood illness should be treated. Mother's labor force participation may also play a role: Mothers working face a direct opportunity cost when deciding whether or not to keep a child home from school. Changes in questionnaire design also influence reported patterns over time.

Infant mortality as a measure of health. Although it is difficult to measure child health in a comprehensive and accurate way, we can draw a general picture of children's health in response to insurance coverage and medical care utilization. First, there is substantial evidence that higher infant mortality rates and more babies of lower birth weight occur among low-income, unmarried, black, and adolescent women, and women without insurance. Low birth weight is itself a predictor of infant mortality and is also associated with high rates of chronic illnesses.

A recent report of the Office of Technology Assessment (U.S. Congress, 1988) summarizes results of studies linking prenatal care to birth outcomes. Most studies reviewed found a positive and significant relationship between use of early prenatal care and positive birth outcomes. A 1978 analysis that used somewhat more sophisticated techniques found that use of prenatal care was a significant and sizable factor in the reduction of neonatal mortality rates between 1964 and 1977, particularly for blacks (Corman, Joyce, & Grossman, 1987). The authors estimate that prenatal care accounted for a reduction of 0.4 deaths per 1,000 live births among whites and 1.9 deaths per 1,000 live births among blacks over this period. For a point of reference, infant mortality rates in 1977 were 8.7 for whites and 16.1 for blacks. More recent evidence suggests an important role for *enhanced* prenatal care, which includes nutrition counseling, education on substance abuse, and other forms of counseling (see studies cited in Wolfe, 1992). Other important factors include abortions, use of the WIC program (Supplemental Food Program for Women, Infants, and Children),[10] neonatal intensive care, and organized family planning. Because many of these factors also involve medical care, the real contribution of such care is much larger than that of prenatal care alone. An additional study, done at a more aggregate level, found that states with Medicaid programs that did not cover first-time pregnancies had higher neonatal mortality rates than states that did provide such coverage (Hadley, 1982). Availability of medical care, as measured by pediatricians per 1,000 live births, accounted for about 13% of the decrease between 1969 and 1978 in infant mortality (Hadley, 1982, p. 98).

Evidence from the Rand Health Insurance Study. Another source of information concerning the effect of medical care on health status is the Rand Health Insurance Study. This experiment was designed to assess the impact of cost sharing on the use of medical care and on health. Persons were enrolled for either 3 or 5 years, and comprehensive data on utilization and health status were collected. The results indicate that, if a family faced significant insurance cost sharing, utilization was reduced, particularly by low-income children. The only health effect detected among those of younger ages, however, was anemia among low-income children (Valdez, 1986). Among poor adults, reduction in medical care utilization resulted in greater incidence of high blood pressure and fewer corrections for near-sightedness, but not in other health problems. Because this was an experiment conducted over a limited time involving a limited number of enrollees, all of whom had quite comprehensive insurance coverage, health effects that occur over a long period or have a low incidence rate could not be detected.

Other evidence. There is other, although limited, evidence on the importance of the utilization of medical care for health. A study in Rochester, New York, found that several factors correlated with usage are associated with health, including permanent income, mother's labor force participation, race, and marital status (van der Gaag & Wolfe, 1982). The net result was that children in the lowest income group and children of divorced parents had the poorest health. Immunizations provide another piece of evidence. They have led to substantial declines in diseases once viewed as major killers or cripplers – measles, rubella, polio, diphtheria, and pertussis. Russell (1986) notes that just before the widespread introduction of the measles (rubeola) vaccine, about 500,000 cases, 400 deaths, and 1,300 instances of mental retardation or other permanent damage to the nervous system were reported annually from the disease, and 5,000 children developed other complications that led to hospitalization. After the governmental initiative to vaccinate the population, reported cases dropped dramatically – to 22,000 in 1968. However, a 90% immunization rate is needed to eradicate measles, and the percentage of children aged 1–4 years who receive vaccination has declined in recent years from a high of 65.9% in 1976 to 60.8% in 1985 (National Center for Health Statistics, 1993). Reported cases of measles have increased substantially (in 1989 and 1990); for other preventable illnesses, there is little increase.

Implications of the Family Support Act of 1988

This section explores the probable insurance coverage of the target AFDC population with and without the new Medicaid provision (extension up to 1 year after employment begins), as well as anticipated usage of medical care. The basis for this analysis is the estimate of utilization and probability of coverage using data from the 1984 Survey of Income Participation Program. The insurance coverage of the population of interest prior to the introduction of the Family Support Act of 1988 can be summarized briefly: Forty-one percent of AFDC children in single-mother households are covered by Medicaid, 34% by private coverage, and about 25% are uninsured. Of those below the poverty line, somewhat fewer are uninsured – 22%

Substantially more are covered by Medicaid – about 65%, or nearly two-thirds. Very few (12%) are covered by private insurance.

In order to get an estimate of the effect of the Family Support Act of 1988 on insurance coverage and medical care utilization, certain assumptions must be made. We start by assuming the worst case for insurance coverage in order to get an estimate of the maximum expected change due to the Medicaid extension. Assume that as a result of the Family Support Act, all women required to work under its provisions join the labor force and lose their Medicaid coverage. In this case, we project that only 25% of children of single mothers would have Medicaid coverage and the percentage of those uninsured would rise to 68%. The remaining children would be covered by private insurance. The children covered by Medicaid are primarily those in families with infants or those whose mother is disabled. If, instead, the Medicaid extension covers all children with family incomes under 200% of the poverty line, then we expect that nearly all (99%) children of single mothers currently covered would be covered by Medicaid or private coverage – only 0.6% would be uninsured for the period of the extension. The change in insurance coverage would have implications for utilization: For this population, losing Medicaid is expected to reduce physician visits among children by 7% and nights hospitalized by 34%. Under the 1-year extension, their utilization would be similar to current utilization.

We are not, however, able to project the health implications of these changes, except to suggest that children covered by Medicaid or private insurance are somewhat less likely to report poor or fair health. However, the Medicaid extension of the Family Support Act is at most for 1 year. After that period, many of the children of these working mothers are likely to be without health insurance coverage, given the current market for private insurance and current regulations concerning eligibility for Medicaid. This prompts consideration of alternatives to the Medicaid extension, or additions to it.

Alternative strategies for providing insurance to the target population

Two alternatives are to expand Medicaid to cover all single mothers and their children in families with incomes up to 200% of the poverty line, or to require that private coverage be provided to all employees (a major policy change). A third alternative could be a combination of the two, offering Medicaid coverage to those with incomes below twice the poverty line, perhaps on a sliding scale basis when incomes are 130% of the poverty line or greater, and requiring firms to offer private coverage or to pay a tax for the purchase of private plans by employees. Private coverage could be mandated to cover dependents. The effects of these three alternatives for all single women and children in our sample can be sketched as follows. (These estimates are based on the SIPP data and estimates reported in Moffitt & Wolfe, 1992.)

Extending Medicaid to all single-parent families below 200% of the poverty line would expand its coverage of all children of single mothers by 21.8 percentage points (about 50%), leaving less than 1% of such children uninsured. Visits to physicians are expected to increase by about 3.5%, and hospitalized nights would rise by a greater percentage – about 14%. Mandating private coverage for all employees is expected to increase the percentage of all children with private insurance coverage by 17.5 percentage points (by nearly 50%), while 8% would remain uninsured and the remainder would be covered by Medicaid. Physician visits would not increase under this simulation.

Under a combination of these two alternatives, we expect that nearly all children will have some form of health insurance coverage and that the increase in usage will be somewhat less than under the Medicaid coverage for all children in families with incomes less than 1.85 times the poverty line. The expected difference in utilization probably reflects greater out-of-pocket costs of private versus Medicaid coverage, and perhaps different patterns of use by type of provider. The major advantage of any of these alternatives is that they continue beyond 1 year, thus reducing the incentives to stop working and to seek care less often, and reducing the likelihood of receiving poorer quality care. Expanding private coverage also has the potential to improve the quality of care received. Unfortunately these programs are also more expensive than a 1-year extension of Medicaid.

Evaluating changes under the Family Support Act of 1988

We turn now to a discussion of issues related to assessing the effect of the Family Support Act of 1988 on children's health and health care utilization. It is hard to study the Family Support Act's impact on health itself, owing to the difficulty in measuring health and to the fact that many health problems develop over a longer period of time than the 12 months of the Medicaid extension. Furthermore, the Family Support Act does not mandate evaluation of the Medicaid extension by means of control groups. Thus, to study its impact, data would have to be collected on utilization, before implementation of the extension.

We can measure changes in two areas that are affected by the Family Support Act: health insurance coverage and health care utilization. The latter includes number of physician visits, number of days hospitalized, and location of care. These may be influenced through both the Medicaid extension and greater participation in the labor force by the mother, which might give her less free time during the usual hours of health care delivery and might also cause a shift to private insurance coverage.

Quasi-experimental design. To study the influence of the Family Support Act in these two areas, we need information resulting from differences in "treatment." Since the act is a nationwide program rather than an experiment in some states, it seems necessary to collect data on a before-and-after basis.

Women with children under age 3 years (or 1 year, at states' discretion) are not required to work. Hence, as an alternative to or in addition to before-and-after data collection, it might be possible to compare the health care utilization of children over 3 (born before September 30, 1983) in families with a child under 3 years (or an infant) and those without a young child (or an infant). In a sense, families with infants could play the role of a control group, though they may not be strictly comparable. This is not true of the other excluded group, women who themselves are ill or incapacitated or who are needed in the household because another member is ill. Because such illness may influence health care utilization of all family members, children in these families should not be used as a control group.

If there is any chance of picking up health effects, the sample will have to be both very large and targeted on children with particular illnesses – large, because otherwise change will not be detected and/or it will not be possible to determine if the change is due to the Family Support Act or other factors; and targeted, because it is most likely that any health effects would be among the children who are particularly at risk or who already have poorer health, since children with chronic illness or handicaps are more likely to be affected by changes in coverage than children in good health. These children could be selected on the basis of prior medical records. For example, children covered by Medicaid who had low birth weight and above-average expenditures at birth could be identified from Medicaid records. Through the use of an event/expenditure screen, children with lead poisoning could be identified by a questionnaire given to parents. Children at risk, such as those born addicted to drugs or of low birth weight, are a particularly interesting group that might be targeted for special study. A control group composed of similar children for whom there is no change in insurance and mother's participation in the labor force is needed to assess the effect of the Family Support Act. A control group could be based on observations prior to introduction of the Medicaid extension or on data on families exempted from the Family Support Act because of the presence of very young children.

Measuring change. The only change in children's health status found in the Rand Health Insurance study concerned anemia. Egbuona and Starfield (1982) report that lead poisoning, otitis media, and psychosocial and psychosomatic problems are particularly prevalent among poor children. These specific conditions are measurable, but would generally require a health examination that might be viewed as too expensive. We should therefore try to define factors for which information could be gained from questionnaires administered to the parent. A new questionnaire known as Medical Outcomes Study Short Form Health Profile (MOS) might be adapted for this purpose. School attendance data could also be collected, but this information is not likely to be helpful in measuring health, because it reflects access to medical care as well as parent's work time (or opportunity cost). For any of the targeted groups, specific measures of health status might be developed, depending on the nature of the group, in consultation with appropriate experts.

It is easier to measure changes in utilization. Recall on utilization is considered likely to be inaccurate if it covers too long a period. The standard periods used in the literature are 2 weeks, 1 month, and sometimes 1 year. Data could be collected on number of visits to a provider and nights hospitalized during any or all of these periods, although the shorter periods are likely to be more accurate. Questions could be included on type of provider used; delay in getting an appointment; transporta tion to provider; any copayment; treatment, such as whether a drug was prescribed; any follow-up suggested; time of appointment; and lab or radiology work. All of these will enable a more thorough analysis of actual utilization by type of provider than is possible by simply looking at number of visits.

It would also be important to collect data on type of insurance coverage: who is covered, who pays for coverage (for parent and for dependents), extent of coverage, and so forth. This information should be obtained for families who received AFDC-Medicaid before implementation of the act and then leave the rolls without taking advantage of the Medicaid extension as well as for those who initially are on Medicaid and then make use of the extension. A final area of study should concern the issue of whether families respond to the income-conditioned premium in the second 6 months. If families drop out of the program, do they have other coverage? Do they have incomes too high for eligibility? Are they low users or high users of medical care? These questions should of course be tied to analysis of utilization and health.

Indirect changes. Economists generally accept the proposition that employees pay some of any payroll tax, including health care premiums. This may not be the case, however, for low-wage workers, especially those working for minimum wage. An employer who hires a worker at the minimum wage and offers insurance coverage may well face a larger wage bill. (If an employer offers coverage to any employees, the offer must be made to new employees, sometimes with a waiting period.) However, if an employee has other coverage and turns down the offer of private coverage, the employer is hiring a less expensive worker. Thus, the extension could make former welfare recipients more attractive employees, at least for a limited period. These employees may well turn down private coverage if they can sign up for it later and it is less generous than Medicaid. The extension could therefore improve private employment opportunities among those eligible for it.

If a direct premium contribution is required, the employee who turns down the coverage temporarily increases her income, again making a job marginally more attractive. Thus, if the extension has any effect on employment, it should be positive. To determine these effects requires asking employers whether they offer coverage, who pays for the coverage, whether any employees reject the offer, whether there is a clause concerning preexisting conditions – and if so, what length of time is involved – and whether insurance can be initiated a year after employment. Similarly, persons covered by the extension should be asked about insurance coverage at their place or potential place of employment, whether or not they sign up for such coverage.

There may be a link between a mother's work effort and utilization of medical care as well as the health of her children. One, suggested above, is the limitation on time available to visit medical care providers. This link can be studied through utilization questions. A change in days of school missed may reflect medical care use and the parent's need to be at work rather than any change in health itself. This argues against using days of school missed as a variable. Another possible link is a change in use of day care, which might increase a child's exposure to germs and lead to short-run increases in acute illness and use of medical care. It is not clear that this is particularly important in evaluation of the extension, but research should be aware of this possibility.

In sum, a study of the impact of the Family Support Act of 1988 on children's health requires the use of control groups and measurement of health status of children particularly at risk (although there will be difficulties detecting changes among healthy children); it should be directed at changes in utilization – including changes in type of provider – and must take type of coverage into consideration. Indirect effects and some of the hidden possible distortions in measures of health should be evaluated. The Family Support Act of 1988 provides an opportunity to study a particular group of at-risk children, those born addicted to drugs, in terms of use of medical care and health, independent of the impact of the act on these children. Given the increasing number of such children, this possibility deserves serious consideration.

NOTES

1. Family income must fall below 133.3% of the maximum AFDC payment for a family of their size, and income net of medical expenditures must fall below the categorically needy standard. The period over which eligibility is calculated – the so-called spend-down period – varies from 1 to 12 months across the 39 states that have a medically needy program.

2. About 2% are covered by other public programs such as Medicare for the disabled. The near poor (between 100% and 125% of the poverty line) are also likely to be uninsured. As of 1987 about 27% were uninsured at a given point in time.

3. These estimates vary according to data source. According to *Health United States, 1991*, which uses the Health Interview Survey, as of 1989 11.4% of all children under 15 were covered by Medicaid, up from 10.4% in 1986, 9.8% in 1982, and 10.2% in 1980. The reported percentage with no insurance was also up – 15.9% compared to 15.8% in 1982 and 12.8% in 1980 (National Center for Health Statistics, 1988, Table 17; 1991, Table 133). However, according to estimates using the 1988 Current Population Survey, which asks additional questions concerning coverage of children, 16.3% of children under 15 are covered by Medicaid and 12.9% are uninsured (Moyer, 1989, Exhibit 1).

4. As of 1988 in-kind transfers accounted for over half of all means-tested programs. Medicaid accounted for roughly 70% of these transfers, or about 37% of the total package of benefits for the poor. A major "explanation" of this increased share is the decline in the real value of AFDC cash benefits.

This latter study also suggests that coverage at the place of employment plays a larger role in influencing women's work–welfare choices than Medicaid. For example, if private coverage equivalent to Medicaid were extended to all single women who worked, the study predicts a decline in the AFDC caseload of over 20%.

5. According to a 1980 national survey (National Medical Care Utilization and Expenditure Survey [NMCUES]), about 18% of children under 2 years of age without health insurance did not see a health provider in the previous year. A study in 1969, just 3 years after the introduction of Medicaid, found that among Medicaid recipients in good health, average annual visits to physicians were 4.09 compared to 2.69 among a similar group of low income persons who did not have coverage. Among those in average health, annual visits were 4.95 versus 3.36, and among those in poor health, 7.1 versus 5.12 (Davis & Reynolds, 1976, p. 404).

6. In a 1986 study (Holahan & Cohen, 1986, Table 21, pp. 63–64) the ratio of Medicaid to Medicare fee levels for specialists are reported by state for 1979 and 1984. In all but three states the ratio fell over this period. For New York State in 1984, the ratio was 0.23; for Wisconsin, 0.78.

7. Wade suggests that for children a modest increase in Medicaid provider fees may lead to increased medical office visits and other outpatient care but reduced inpatient and outpatient surgery. This suggests further offsetting savings.

8. The weighted percentages are 25.5, 48, and 26 for no insurance, Medicaid, and private insurance coverage, respectively, for the 50% of these children for whom poor or fair health was reported. Among the 50% of children who have good or excellent health, the respective percentages are 23.7, 32.7, and 42.2.

9. In fact, the price charged by a provider of medical care may not be the price received by the provider. Many insurers – in particular, public insurance – pay a fee schedule. The relevant direct price should be based on the amount received rather than the amount billed.

10. WIC is the Supplemental Food Program for Women, Infants, and Children, which provides food, nutrition, education and counseling, and health care to low-income pregnant and postpartum women, infants, and children. WIC's expenditures were about $1.5 billion in 1986 and have been increasing as a share of all U.S. public health spending. Funds are allocated to states by a formula that takes the percentage of eligible women and children served into account. As of 1988 about half of all eligible persons received services (Children's Defense Fund, 1989, pp. 78–79).

REFERENCES

Blank, R. (1989, Winter). The effect of medical need and Medicaid on AFDC participation. *Journal of Human Resources, 24*, 54–87.
Children's Defense Fund. (1989). *The health of America's children: Maternal and child health data book*. Washington, DC: Children's Defense Fund.
Corman, H., & Grossman, M. (1987). Birth outcome production function in the United States. *Journal of Human Resources, 22*, 339–360.
Corman, H., Joyce, T., & Grossman, M. (1987). *A cost-effectiveness analysis of strategies to reduce infant mortality.* National Bureau of Economic Research Working Paper #2346, August.
Davis, K., & Reynolds, R. (1976). The impact of Medicare and Medicaid on access to medical care. In R. Rossett (Ed.), *The role of health insurance in the health services sector.* Canton, MA: Neale Watson Academic Publications, for the National Bureau of Economic Research.
Davis, K., & Schoen, C. (1978). *Health and the war on poverty: A ten-year appraisal.* Washington, DC: Brookings Institution.
Egbuona, L., & Starfield, B. (1982). Child health and social status. *Pediatrics, 69*(5), 21.
Hadley, J. (1982). *More medical care, better health?* Washington, DC: Urban Institute Press.
Holahan, J., & Cohen, J. (1986). *Medicaid: The trade-off between cost containment and access to care.* Washington, DC: Urban Institute Press.
Lohr, K., Brook, R., Kamberg, C., Goldberg, G., Leibowitz, A., Keesey, J., Reboussin, D., & Newhouse, J. (1986). Use of medical care in the Rand Health Insurance Experiment: Diagnosis and service-specific analysis in a randomized controlled trial. *Medical Care, 24*(9, Pt. 2).

Lurie, N., Ward, N., Shapero, M., & Brook, R. (1984). Termination from Medi-Cal: Does it affect health? *New England Journal of Medicine, 311*, 480–484.

Mitchell, J. (1991). Physician participation in Medicaid revisited. *Medical Care, 29*, 645–653.

Moffitt, R. (1988). *Work and the U.S. welfare system: A review* (Special Report No. 46). Madison: Institute for Research on Poverty, University of Wisconsin

Moffitt, R., & Wolfe, B. (1992, November). The effect of the Medicaid program on welfare participation and labor supply. *Review of Economics and Statistics.*

Moyer, M. E. (1989, Summer). A revised look at the number of uninsured Americans. *Health Affairs,* 102–110.

National Center for Health Statistics. (1988, March). *Health United States, 1987* (DHHS Pub. No. [PHS] 88–1232, Public Health Service). Washington, DC: U.S. Government Printing Office.

National Center for Health Statistics. (1989, March). *Health United States, 1988* (DHHS Pub. No. [PHS] 89–1232, Public Health Service). Washington, DC: U.S. Government Printing Office.

National Center for Health Statistics. (1991). Current estimates from the National Health Interview Survey, 1990 (Series 10, No. 181). Hyattsville, MD: U.S. Department of Health and Human Services.

National Center for Health Statistics. (1993, March). *Health United States, 1992* (DHHS Pub. No. [PHS] 92–1232). Washington, DC: U.S. Government Printing Office.

Russell, L. (1986). *Is prevention better than cure?* Washington, DC: Brookings Institution.

Stewart, A., Hays, R., & Ware, J. (1988). The MOS short-form General Health Survey. *Medical Care, 26*, 724–735.

U.S. Congress, Office of Technology Assessment. (1988, February). *Healthy children: Investing in the future* (OTA Report No. H-345). Washington, DC.

U.S. Department of Labor, Bureau of Labor Statistics. (1987). *Employee benefits in medium and large firms, 1986* (Bulletin 2281). Washington, DC: U.S. Government Printing Office.

U.S. General Accounting Office. (1987, September). *Prenatal care: Medicaid recipients and uninsured women obtain insufficient care* (GAO Report No. HRD-87-137). Washington, DC.

U.S. General Accounting Office. (1989, February). *Health insurance: An overview of the working uninsured* (GAO Report No. HRD-89-45). Washington, DC.

U.S. House of Representatives, Committee on Ways and Means. (1989, March). *Background material and data on programs within the jurisdiction of the Committee on Ways and Means: The green book 1989.* Washington, DC: U.S. Government Printing Office.

U.S. House of Representatives, Committee on Ways and Means. (1992, May). *Background material and data on programs within the jurisdiction of the Committee on Ways and Means: The green book 1992.* Washington, DC: U.S. Government Printing Office.

Valdez, R. (1986, March). *The effects of cost-sharing on the health of children.* (Report No. R-3270-HHS). Santa Monica, CA: Rand Corporation.

Van der Gaag, J., & Wolfe, B. (1982). What influences children's health? *Children and youth services review, 4*, 77–109.

Wade, M. (1992). *Medicaid fee levels and Medicaid enrollees' access to care.* Paper presented at the 1992 Association for Public Policy and Management Meetings, Denver, CO.

Wolfe, B. (1994). Reform of health care for the nonelder poor. In S. Danziger, G. Sandefur, & D. Weinstein (Eds.), *Confronting poverty: Prescriptions for change.* Cambridge, MA: Harvard University Press.

V. Fathers

9   Dealing with dads: The changing roles of fathers

Frank F. Furstenberg, Jr.

One of the first lessons taught in sociology in the 1960s was that marriage was a universal or nearly universal institution. A cultural mechanism for regulating the potentially conflicting claims and obligations of parenthood, marriage simultaneously grants paternity rights to fathers and their families while ensuring social recognition and economic support for childbearers and their offspring. Marriage provides an added benefit for children by connecting them to a wider network of adults who have a stake in their long-term development (Malinowski, 1930; Davis, 1939).

This theory, purporting to explain the universality of marriage, became the subject of an intense debate in anthropology and sociology during the 1960s (Bell & Vogel, 1968; Coser, 1964). Evidence from cross-cultural investigations showed enormous variation in marriage forms, differing levels of commitment to the norm of legitimacy, and often minimal participation by biological or social fathers in the process of child rearing. More recently historical evidence indicates that the institution of marriage was not firmly in place until the end of the Middle Ages (Laslett, 1972; Goody, 1983; Gillis, 1985). The accumulation of contradictory data forced Goode (1960, 1971) to revise Malinowski's theory to take account of the high rates of cohabitation and nonmarital childbearing in many New World nations and among African-Americans. Goode argued that among lower status groups, where community standing and property rights are not at issue, the principle of legitimacy will be relaxed. The importance of regulating childbearing through marriage declines when women see limited benefit from marriage and when families have little honor to uphold. Speaking of the attenuation of the norm, Goode (1971, p. 478) concluded:

> No simple moral or technical solution exists for these problems. The mechanical process of marriage does not automatically create a family relationship, though it may confer the status of legitimacy on the child. Illegitimacy in the United States most often occurs precisely among those who are not deeply involved with one another emotionally and who have shared mainly a sexual experience. . . . Marriage would "give a name," but not a father, to the child. Fundamental changes in the social structure would be required to give full social rights to the illegitimate child, and these are not likely to take place in the next few generations.

189

Written nearly two decades ago, Goode's comments now seem prescient, though neither he nor any other sociologists anticipated the sweeping changes in the family that have taken place over the past quarter century. So extensive have these changes been that Malinowski's universal principle of legitimacy now seems to be seriously in doubt. In a number of societies, our own among them, marriage is an ineffective mechanism for regulating parenthood (Cherlin, 1989). The nuclear unit (biological parents and their offspring) – once regarded as the fundamental building block of our kinship system – is no longer the prevailing family form. And men – the weak link in the biological process of parenthood – have, in rising numbers, become unattached to their children.

Tracing the sources of the transformation in marriage patterns is not the main mission of this chapter, but some of the factors contributing to the changing role of men in the family are presented. In the initial section, the consequences of the declining significance of marriage for children's relations with the fathers and general well-being are discussed. Concern about the deteriorating situation of children has spawned a number of policy initiatives to strengthen the economic link between fathers and children. The second half of the chapter focuses on the implications of the Family Support Act of 1988 for fatherhood, looking at both the objectives of this far-reaching policy for fathers' role in the family and its prospects of success. How would we know if it were bringing about change in the behavior of males either in marriage or parenting patterns? While the examination of these questions inevitably touches on issues of child support, this topic is more directly addressed by McLanahan and Garfinkel in this volume. The emphasis here is rather on whether public policy can affect marital and family functioning. A few final, speculative comments about the future of fatherhood are presented in the concluding section.

Men in the family:
Where have all the fathers gone?

Family change is not peculiar to the latter half of the twentieth century. The form of the family has always been sensitive to economic conditions and ideological currents. Social historians have convincingly demonstrated to all but the truest of true believers that there was no stable, traditional family model against which to contrast our unstable contemporary family forms (Gordon, 1983; Hareven, 1978). Even disabused of any romantic images of family stability in times past, many recent trends in marriage and parenthood are unprecedented in both magnitude and scope. Their effect is heightened because they follow on the heels of a period (the 1950s and 1960s) when the nuclear family was nearly omnipresent (Cherlin, 1992).

The following section presents some demographic and social evidence to back up the claim that marriage is no longer effectively regulating parenthood and paternal responsibilities. First, recent trends in nonmarital childbearing will be reviewed, suggesting that the link between marriage and childbearing is weakening; many couples are not marrying before (or even after) they have children. Furthermore, fragmentary studies of the performance of never-married fathers show that most have a tenuous and often temporary relationship with their children. Second, trends in marital stability strongly suggest that divorce and remarriage are no longer anomalous events but intrinsic features of our kinship system. The growing pattern of conjugal succession blurs and confuses paternal responsibilities. This observation leads to a consideration of the consequences of the declining role of men in the family for children in the third part of this chapter. While not a thorough review of this complex issue, this section offers some comments on the uncertain state of our knowledge about this topic before addressing issues of public policy and fatherhood.

Nonmarital childbearing: The declining importance of marriage

Out-of-wedlock childbearing has been common in parts of the United States and Western Europe at various times (Laslett, 1972; Shorter, 1975; Vinovskis, 1981). Fluctuations in nonmarital childbearing can result from changes in the permissibility of sexual behavior, the availability of contraception and abortion, and the amount of control exercised by the community in forcing couples to marry in the event of pregnancy. Over the past several decades, the tolerance for nonmarital childbearing has increased in the United States as well as in many other Western nations (Davis, 1985; Popenoe, 1988). Responding to or merely reflecting these normative shifts, a growing number of couples are not marrying when a premarital pregnancy occurs (U.S. Bureau of the Census, 1992a). The risk of pregnancy for young single women rose from the late 1960s through the 1970s as premarital sex became acceptable and widespread. Even so, a decline in nonmarital childbearing might have been expected after abortion was legalized because single women who chose not to marry or give up their child for adoption had another acceptable alternative. It is therefore all the more surprising that the proportion of premarital pregnancies leading to marriage has diminished over the past quarter century. Some scholars have argued that this trend was precipitated by a wave of expert advice, counseling pregnant teenagers against precipitous unions (Vinovskis & Chase-Lansdale, 1987; Vinovskis, 1988). But the fact is that the decline of "shotgun" weddings began in the late 1950s, as marriage rates peaked, and occurred among all age groups, not just teenagers (Furstenberg, 1988a).

Since the 1940s, when vital statistics data first became available, the rate and ratio of nonmarital childbearing have risen steadily among teenagers. The pattern among older women is slightly more complex though it generally follows the upward trend (Furstenberg, 1991). An exception is nonmarital childbearing among mature women, which temporarily declined in the wake of the baby boom. This brief pause lasted for less than a decade, however. Beginning in the early 1970s rates started to rise again, first among women in their early 20s and then among older unmarried females (National Center for Health Statistics, 1993).

Contrary to popular impressions, nonmarital childbearing is not a teenage problem. Nor is it confined to women of color (Furstenberg, 1991). The most rapid increases in the past decade have occurred among mature women, while rate increases among younger teenagers have been relatively modest. Unmarried women in their 20s have similar rates of childbearing as 18- and 19-year-olds and are about twice as likely to bear a child out of wedlock as girls between the ages of 15 and 17. While black women are much more likely to bear children out-of-wedlock than are whites, the black–white differential has been steadily diminishing over the past half century. In 1950 blacks were more than 10 times as likely as whites to have a child out of wedlock; by 1970 the racial differential had declined to about 7:1; by 1980 it dropped to 5:1; in 1990 it had fallen to 3:1. In 1975 just 7% of white births were to single women compared to about half of the black births. By 1990 the fraction of out-of-wedlock white births had risen to 20% and for blacks, to 67%. Close to half of all births to white women and 90% of births to black women under the age of 20 occur to unmarried mothers (National Center for Health Statistics, 1993).

These striking changes suggest that marriage as a precondition for childbearing has all but disappeared among young blacks. And a majority of white women in their late teens and a substantial minority of those in their early 20s seem to be abandoning the longstanding pattern of marrying in the event of a pregnancy. Fewer white women, too, are marrying (presumably the fathers of their babies) in the immediate aftermath of childbirth (U.S. Bureau of the Census, 1989).

It is easier to describe this pattern than to explain it. Many believe that the declining economic position of males is strongly implicated in the decline of marriage and hence marital childbearing (Adams & Pittman, 1988; Sum & Pierce, 1988; Wilson, 1987; Cherlin, 1992). Certainly, the timing of the increases in nonmarital childbearing rates and ratios within the black community seem to fit this explanation. The most dramatic rise occurred in the late 1960s and early 1970s when rates of unemployment shot up among younger males. The long period of economic stagnation in the 1970s, which eroded the position of working-class, noncollege youth, probably affected the attractiveness of marriage for whites as well as blacks (Johnson, Sum, & Weill, 1988).

It is unlikely, however, that faltering economic conditions can entirely account for the declining significance of marriage. The change appears too rapid and too widespread to be the result of a single, albeit fairly lengthy period of economic stagnation. In any case, the economic downturn does not explain the changing patterns of marriage among older blacks and whites of all age groups in recent years (Bennett, Bloom, & Craig, 1989; Lichter, McLaughlin, Kephart, & Landry, 1992). More likely, these changes are linked to broader shifts in gender roles resulting from the economic independence of women (Cherlin, 1989; Huber & Spitze, 1988; Furstenberg, 1990). The rising rate of marital dissolution should also be credited as a source of the change in marriage attitudes (Thornton, 1989). High rates of conjugal instability reduce the perceived benefits of early marriage and probably increase the tolerance for nonmarital childbearing.

All of the above factors have figured in the changes in marriage patterns in the black community, accounting for a dramatic redefinition in the importance of marriage and its link to childbearing (Cherlin, 1992). In the mid-1960s, in a large sample of teenage childbearers in Baltimore, many young mothers felt compelled to marry in order to "give their child a name" (Furstenberg, 1976). A decade later, this standard had largely been abandoned. But even in the mid-1960s there was evidence of a deep ambivalence about the benefits of marriage for young mothers and their children. The teens' parents frequently urged them not to marry right away so that they could complete their schooling and gain a measure of economic self-sufficiency. Among the older generation, distrust of marriage was widespread, no doubt because of the high prevalence of marital instability within the black community (Moore, Simms, & Betsey, 1986).

Many parents expressed doubts that fathers could or would provide regular and steady support whether or not their daughters married. Evidence collected later in the Baltimore study seems to bear out these doubts. Half of the early marriages dissolved within 5 years; about three-fourths had ended by the 17-year follow-up. Formerly married fathers were not much more likely than never married fathers to provide economic support or to sustain close emotional ties to their children. And the women who entered unstable marriages fared less well economically because they frequently left school and were more likely to have additional children early in life (Furstenberg, Brooks Gunn, & Morgan, 1987a).

Twenty years later, when the offspring were studied as they entered early adulthood, it was plain that a transformation in marriage attitudes had taken place. Marriage, while still an ideal, was considered a foolish act early in life (Furstenberg, Levine, & Brooks-Gunn, 1990). Virtually none of the daughters who became pregnant in their teens elected to marry. As some of their parents had a generation before, the young mothers instead looked to their families for support. Along with welfare benefits, they saw their kin as providing a much more stable and predictable source of economic and emotional support than was offered by marriage (Furstenberg et al., 1990).

A corresponding decline in the involvement of unmarried fathers appears to have occurred, judging from the reports of the second-generation mothers in the Baltimore study. A small number of them attended prenatal classes with the mother and were assuming a major role in child care and support, but the majority could not be counted on for regular assistance. Half had either legal or informal child support agreements; however, not all of these fathers were contributing on a regular basis. Just about a third of the unmarried mothers received full and regular support from the fathers though another sixth could count on partial support on a fairly steady basis. About a third of the fathers had frequent contact with the child (once a week or more), a third saw the child less often (usually once or twice a month), and a third had not seen their child in the past year. Keeping in mind that parenthood is quite recent for these women, these figures do not auger well for the long-term support of their children (Furstenberg & Harris, 1993).

Data collected by the Census Bureau show that only a tiny minority of never-married fathers become regular providers (Select Committee on Children, Youth, and Families, 1989). And information from the National Survey of Children reveals a sharp decline in paternal involvement generally occurs soon after childbirth (Furstenberg & Harris, 1992). This behavioral evidence seems to undermine the observation of many service providers that young fathers often possess strong paternal commitments. A good deal has been written about how children give meaning to the impoverished lives of young men; and there is other evidence showing that many fathers want to be involved, participate in caretaking, and support their offspring at childbirth (Elster & Lamb, 1986).

In the Baltimore study the performance of the small number of males in their late teens and early 20s who acknowledged fathering a child was examined. These men do provide a more favorable picture of their paternal involvement than the one supplied by the teen mothers in our sample. Still, few had participated in prenatal services, the majority admitted that they provided no support or irregular support, and about two-fifths indicated that they saw their child less frequently than once a week on average. Unstructured interviews with young fathers uncovered a profound despair about the possibilities of fulfilling the duties of fatherhood (Furstenberg, Sherwood, & Sullivan, 1992). Most men wanted to do better for their children than their fathers had done for them, but their commitments were eroded by troubled relations with the baby's mother and her family, their precarious foothold in the job market, the temptations and pull of the street, and their own uncertain sense of how to balance immediate needs and parental obligations. Consider the testimony of one young father whom I interviewed in 1991 as he surveys his current and future plans for his child and the child's mother:

> **R**: Well he's 7 months old. But I love him a lot. I wish he was here with me but he's not. He will be with me one day, I'll see to that. I want him to know that I am his father. He needs me. I'll do all I can for him. I'm not saying my father wouldn't; he just didn't. I want my son to just be happy, more happy than I was.
> **I**: What about his mom? He's living with his mom now?
> **R**: Right, he's living with his mom and his grandmom.
> **I**: Sometimes guys I know have trouble with the girlfriend's mom.
> **R**: Okay, it's not all peaches and cream you know, she expects more from me than what I can do right now. But as time go on, of course, I'm gonna get better. Cause I am gonna try. If people see you trying, sometime they give you breaks.
> **I**: She expects more? More means more in what way?
> **R**: Financial. You know she says that. I do give what I can. But I have to live too. I have to keep my clothes clean. I have to, you know, take care of my utilities and all that other stuff, and my toiletries, and I have to have stuff like that. Nobody's gonna do it for me now that I am grown; she just have to understand that for now. Until one day maybe I can get a place of my own and take care of him best that I can. . . . I feel as though that I'm not really ready to live together with a female.

A growing body of evidence on relations between unmarried fathers and their children suggest that the results of the Baltimore study are not atypical. There is general agreement that the intentions of fathers far outstrip their ability to make good on their goal of becoming involved caretakers. Whether by design, desire, or default many fathers retreat – some almost immediately but most after their initial efforts end in frustration or their motivation flags (Sullivan, 1989; Ooms, 1981).

Parenting outside the home is difficult even when fathers have established strong bonds with their children and have reasonably trusting relations with the other parent. When neither of these conditions occurs, it is nearly impossible. Lacking material resources and the skills to manage a complex and delicate relationship with the child's mother and facing a suspicious and sometimes hostile set of maternal relatives, fathers frequently become disheartened and disaffected. Their efforts at maintaining ties with their offspring may seem large to them, but are likely to be regarded as inadequate by dispirited and overburdened former girlfriends. Rather quickly, the process of cooperative parenting can break down, to be replaced by mutual recriminations (Furstenberg et al., 1992).

It must be acknowledged that there are exceptions to this depressing scenario. Longitudinal data from both the Baltimore study and the National Survey of Children show that a minority of unmarried fathers do remain actively involved with their children. But the number dwindles over time. There is some reason to suspect that commitment to fathering requires both resources and a commitment to the role. Relatively little is known about the sources of paternal commitment (Marsiglio, 1988).

Marital disruption and remarriage

Prior to the past two decades, the incidence of nonmarital childbearing was low, especially for whites. Moreover, most unmarried parents quickly entered conjugal unions. Though the link between marriage and childbearing was nearly inviolable, by the middle of the twentieth century marriage had already become a less reliable mechanism for ensuring paternal involvement because of rising rates of divorce (Preston & McDonald, 1979; Weed, 1980). Today, close to half of all marriages end in divorce (Cherlin, 1992). Were marriages that are dissolved but are never legally terminated also included, the figure would rise even higher (Castro & Bumpass, 1989).

These trends represent a fundamental alteration in the institution of marriage. Americans, and to a growing extent Western Europeans, have moved from a permanent to a conditional matrimonial contract (Davis, 1985). Couples were once expected to remain together even if they did not retain strong affective ties; now they are much more likely to part if they are not emotionally gratified. Increasingly, marriage has become a discretionary arrangement (Furstenberg, 1982).

Seen from the perspective of children, this pattern of conjugal succession means that a shrinking number of children will spend their entire childhood living with both of their biological parents and a growing number will acquire stepparents before they reach adulthood. Because divorce and remarriage rates are continually changing, it is difficult to provide an exact estimate of the number of children who will encounter family instability. It is safe to say that about half of all children will witness a marital dissolution and close to 20% will spend some time living with a stepparent before they reach the age of 18 (Furstenberg, Nord, Peterson, & Zill, 1983; Bumpass & Sweet, 1989; U.S. Bureau of the Census, 1992b)

In the great majority of cases, the father becomes the nonresidential parent. Despite the growth of joint custody, close to 90% of children from divorced families initially are in the custody of their mothers (Rawlings, 1989). Over time, some of these children eventually live with their father on a part-time or full-time basis. But both census and survey data suggest that only a minority of children – a fourth at most – live with their fathers for any substantial amount of time after divorce (Sweet & Bumpass, 1987).

Two surveys conducted in the early 1980s reveal that most formerly married fathers living outside the home see their children infrequently or not at all (Furstenberg et al., 1983; Seltzer & Bianchi, 1988). Contact drops off sharply in the first 2 years after divorce. After several years, most fathers cease to see their children or see them only very occasionally. The majority of children living apart from their fathers never spend time in their father's home, talk to him by telephone infrequently, and rarely communicate by mail (Furstenberg & Nord, 1985; Teachman, 1992). It is hardly surprising that only a minority of children receive economic support or any kind of assistance from their fathers 3 or more years after the marriage breaks up (Ellwood, 1988; Garfinkel, 1992).

It is difficult to say whether these general patterns of low involvement by formerly married males have changed as divorce rates increased or as custody practices have altered to encourage greater paternal participation. Reliable data on father's involvement among nonresidential fathers are simply not available prior to this decade. One possibly revealing indicator is the persistently low level of child support assistance provided by fathers. Despite recent efforts by the federal government to strengthen collection procedures, child support remained at the same low level in 1985 as it was in 1978 (Select Committee on Children, Youth, and Families, 1989). Some encouraging trends in child support were evident in the more recent survey of child support payments conducted by the Census Bureau in 1988 (U.S. Bureau of the Census, 1990). Still, the increase in the level of child support in the more recent survey appears to be very modest. It is possible that aggregate data on child support may be concealing more encouraging trends in recent marriage cohorts. A better understanding of current trends requires more careful analysis of existing data sources on child support and fresh evidence on paternal contact (see Garfinkel & McLanahan, this volume).

Relatively little is known about men's motives for withdrawing from their children. Advocates of fathers' rights claim that men are locked out of the family. It is not clear from existing studies just how often mothers actually try to prevent visitation or thwart child-rearing efforts by former mates. Most existing data, based largely on surveys of women, suggest such attempts occur only infrequently. But residential mothers may have subtle ways of discouraging involvement even when they purport to encourage it. Nonetheless, the retreat of many divorced fathers seems to be based partly on the unwillingness or inability to pay child support, especially in the event of a remarriage by either former partner.

The behavior of the fathers who withdraw is consistent with the emergent pattern of conjugal succession. Just as marital obligations have become more discretionary, so, too, parenthood is viewed as voluntary (Furstenberg, 1990). As they move from one marriage to another, many men exhibit a pattern of child swapping – they relinquish their responsibilities for biological children in favor of children in their current household. Many men are inclined to regard marriage as a package deal. Their responsibilities to their children are linked to their marital bonds. When the conjugal bond is dissolved, the tenuous tie between father and child is broken. (For an extended discussion of the process of marital disengagement, see Furstenberg & Cherlin, 1991.) Malinowski's proposition that marriage is a mechanism for strengthening the weak biological link between fathers and children appears to apply only as long as a marriage survives.

While this pattern of child swapping describes a prevailing current in American society, a minority of nonresidential fathers retain strong and continuous ties with their biological children (Mott, 1993). The National Survey of Children, a longitudinal study of a nationally representative sample of children who were followed over a period of a dozen years from the mid-1970s onward, contains data on the changing relations of fathers who no longer lived with their children. The data set permits an examination of the reports of children about their relations with their nonresidential fathers in midadolescence and, then again, when the children were in their late teens and early 20s.

When the children were ages 11 to 16, slightly more than half of those whose parents had separated saw their father on at least an occasional basis. Just under two-fifths indicated that they were close to their father, and a third said that they would like to be like him when they grew up – about half the level reported by children in intact families. Five years later, when the youth were in late adolescence, these figures dropped even lower. Barely more than a third of the children were seeing the father regularly enough to report on the state of their relationship. Just one in four responded that they were close to him and would like to be like him when they grew up. Children in intact families were three times as likely to give positive evaluations of relations with their father (Furstenberg & Harris, 1992).

What are the sources of variation in relations between fathers and their children and the reasons for the high rate of emotional attrition? How much do preexisting relations between fathers and children set the pattern of postmarital relations as compared to events following the divorce? Existing data suggest that the maintenance of strong bonds between children and their fathers is not highly predicated on early relations; strong ties in early childhood are not always a necessary and certainly not a sufficient condition for close relations in late childhood and early adulthood. If men's relationships with their children are indeed often mediated by the relations among formerly married couples, then we must understand how the divorce process and its aftermath weaken the paternal bond.

A recent study by Maccoby and Mnookin (1992) examines a sample of California divorces, monitoring the management of postmarital parenting over time. They report much higher levels of paternal participation than were recorded in the National Survey of Children or even in the more recent study in the National Survey of Families and Households analyzed by Seltzer. In all likelihood, the preference for joint legal custody in California promotes and permits greater paternal participation. Their results do resemble the national surveys in one important respect: Substantial fluctuations occur in living arrangements and visitation patterns over time. These changes often seem to be governed by external factors such as work moves or new relationships, but they may also be associated with interpersonal bargaining related to child support and visitation.

To sum up, divorce often results in a withering of the paternal bond, though recently there may be a trend toward greater persistence in paternal contact (Seltzer, 1991; Maccoby & Mnookin, 1992). Still, it is too soon to tell whether recent changes in custody practices or child support regulations will alter the widespread practice of formerly married men relinquishing ties with their children. A small minority of nonresidential fathers do manage to maintain an active presence in the family, either because they are able to maintain collaborative relations with their former spouses or, more often, they negotiate a *modus vivendi* that usually involves each parent relating to their children with minimal consultation and minimal interference from the other (Furstenberg & Nord, 1985).

The consequences of paternal participation for children

It has been widely assumed that the maintenance of ties with fathers is good for children. That there are economic benefits for children when fathers remain involved is indisputable. The psychological results of continued contact are not so evident from the small amount of empirical data that has been collected. We know very little about the consequences of paternal participation for children's emotional and cognitive development in intact families. The effects of paternal involvement when fathers live apart from their children are even less well understood (Parke, 1989; Lamb, 1987).

The major source of evidence supporting the premise that a father's presence contributes to the emotional and intellectual well-being of his children comes from studies comparing children living in intact and nonintact families. While it is clear that children's adjustment is moderately higher in the aggregate when they grow up in intact families than in single-parent or stepfamily households, it is not so clear why (Garfinkel & McLanahan, 1986; Chase-Lansdale & Hetherington, 1990; Emery, 1988; Furstenberg & Cherlin, 1991). No consensus yet exists on how much or why marital disruption leads to poorer outcomes (Amato, 1993). To be sure, some part of the divorce effect can be traced directly to the economic disadvantage resulting from living in a single-parent family and the associated problems of downward mobility, residence in poorer neighborhoods, and limited educational opportunities. But most researchers have concluded that economic differences alone cannot account for the differences in children's school functioning and educational attainment, emotional health, behavioral problems, or differences in early adulthood, such as patterns of family formation and family stability (Dornbush, 1989; McLanahan, 1988; McLanahan & Sandefur, 1994).

How does the father's presence and involvement in the home, apart from his economic contribution, protect the child? Some suggestive studies indicate that the capacity of the mother to monitor her children's behavior effectively is reduced by the departure of the father from the home (Dornbush et al., 1985). Also, adolescent females seem to be more prone to early sexual behavior when they are not residing with their father, which has been interpreted as a result of weaker family controls. However, it must be said that the direct evidence that fathers play an important disciplinary or social control function in regulating children's behavior during adolescence is less than satisfactory. Gross comparisons between the family functioning of intact and nonintact families are an insufficient method of demonstrating the benefits of paternal involvement for children's development (Furstenberg & Teitler, 1991). Studies of the consequences of impaired paternal relationships in intact families come closer to showing how fathers may contribute to their children's adjustment. The tradition of research established by Patterson and his colleagues points to family malfunctioning when fathers are inconsistent, explosive, or highly irritable (Patterson, DeBaryshe, & Ramsey, 1989). Hetherington's (1987) astute observations of divorced families also shows how vicious cycles of punishment and behavioral problems are initiated in single-parent families, especially between mothers and their sons. Hetherington's data, however, do not demonstrate whether the continued involvement of fathers reduces or exacerbates this family dynamic.

Only a few large-scale studies have examined the impact of continued paternal involvement between nonresidential fathers and their children (Amato, 1993). Data from the National Survey of Children revealed a surprising result. There was no evidence that participation by fathers outside the home reduced the level of problems exhibited by children living in single-parent households (Furstenberg, Morgan, & Allison, 1987b). This result has been replicated using data from the Baltimore study, including both formerly married and never-married fathers (see also King, 1994). Children who reported frequent contact and emotional closeness with fathers outside the home did not do better on any of a number of measures of adjustment with one exception – they did have lower levels of depression (Harris & Furstenberg, 1990).

More recent analysis of the third wave of the National Survey of Children provided another opportunity to examine the impact of paternal participation. Again, closeness to father and regular contact were associated with lower levels of depression in late adolescence but were unrelated to school achievement, behavior problems, or early childbearing. Surprisingly, no strong evidence indicated that close-ness to fathers contributed to children's functioning in intact families though, of course, children from stable marriages generally experienced fewer problems than those whose parents had separated.

Where does this preliminary and admittedly insufficient evidence leave us? It leaves us thoroughly confused about the role of fathers in the family. Overall, fathers in the home improve children's chances of doing well in later life though the differences are much more modest than is commonly assumed (Amato & Keith, 1991; Furstenberg & Teitler, 1991). And to the extent that family structure matters at all, researchers have not done an adequate job of explaining why.

Participation of fathers outside the home may matter much less than is widely believed, though again, we do not know why. Data from observational studies or more complete survey information might demonstrate that children perform better in the long run when their fathers, living outside the home, maintain an active disci-plinary and supportive role. Evidence supporting this proposition is difficult to obtain because so few fathers living outside the home are intimately and actively involved in child rearing. For purposes of public policy, one might be tempted to conclude that the effect of fathers outside the home is trivial apart from the econom-ic support that they may contribute. The existing evidence, nonetheless, is too weak to draw so radical a conclusion. However, in the absence of strong supportive data, concluding that future policies designed to increase paternal involvement are likely to have a significant impact on the psychological well-being of children must, at least, be regarded as an undemonstrated assertion.

Fathers and public policy

This brings us to a consideration of the likely consequences of the Family Support Act of 1988 for fathers, and indirectly for their children. Following the lines of argument that have been advanced in this chapter, we want first to know how current welfare reform is affecting future marriage trends, that is, the formation and maintenance of stable unions. Will this legislation counteract the declining commit-ment to the norm of legitimacy or the prevailing pattern of conjugal succession, trends that have weakened the bond between fathers and their children? Second, how will current welfare reform efforts, such as the Family Support Act of 1988, shape or influence the behavior of fathers living apart from their children, specifi-cally the quantity and quality of fathering? Finally, if the levels or stability of unions or the patterns of parenting of nonresidential fathers are affected, how much more better off will children be as a result?

The impact of the Family Support Act of 1988 on marriage
and marital stability

The principal intent of the Family Support Act of 1988 is to increase the economic contribution of nonresidential fathers. As such, it recognizes the declining significance of marriage and attempts to compensate for what has become an increasingly impotent institution. The Family Support Act is designed to protect women and children from a collapsing system of marriage. It is primarily designed to replace rather than to restore marriage. As such, the legislation recognizes and thus unavoidably institutionalizes what has become largely a fait accompli.

It might be argued that the child support provisions of the Family Support Act that establish paternity, locate missing parents, and set guidelines for awards make nonmarital childbearing less appealing. If this is happening, marital childbearing could become relatively more attractive to men. While the latter proposition seems like a fairly remote possibility, it is entirely plausible that raising the economic costs of nonmarital childbearing to men may deter early and out-of-wedlock childbearing.

Recent trends on rates of nonmarital childbearing do not give much encouragement to those who believe that child support enforcement will deter early childbearing, but aggregate figures may conceal different effects among states such as Wisconsin and Michigan that have already adopted strict child support enforcement systems. The Family Support Act provides an opportunity to identify deterrent effects of child support enforcement by contrasting states that have more efficient implementation systems for paternity testing, location of missing parents, and collection of child support with those that have less efficient programs. A comparison of "strong" and "weak" state programs might demonstrate deterrent effects if differences among states were evident in the perceptions of men, not yet fathers, of the future costs of fatherhood and if unmarried fathers were more likely in the strong enforcement states to perceive more severe sanctions for unmet financial obligations to their children than in the weaker enforcement states. If rates of nonmarital childbearing drop more rapidly in the states with strong enforcement measures than the states with weak measures, a deterrent effect would be highly plausible.

Such a test is worth undertaking, but there is reason to be skeptical about the prospects of finding this result. Just as stronger child support enforcement discourages men from entering parenthood, the guarantee of financial support from nonresidential fathers makes nonmarital childbearing relatively more manageable for women. Most of the limited evidence on marital decision making among young and disadvantaged women suggests that only a small proportion see early marriage as a desirable choice when they become pregnant. The advantages of a precipitate marriage are likely to remain small, especially with the guarantee of child support by the nonresidential fathers. If anything, child support enforcement is likely to reinforce the increasingly popular view that single parenthood is a preferable alternative to hasty marriage. The Family Support Act could actually increase rates of nonmarital childbearing by increasing the proportion of pregnant women who elect to remain single.

In contrast to the child support provisions, the other components of current welfare reform, particularly the JOBS (Jobs, Opportunities, and Basic Skills) program, are primarily aimed at improving the economic prospects of welfare mothers. Up to five states are permitted to offer the JOBS program to noncustodial parents (fathers) in order to increase their potential contributions to child support. Clearly, however, the legislation is principally designed to make mothers more capable of providing for their offspring without providing parallel incentives for fathers. As such, it will do little to promote collective strategies between parents and perhaps might even work in the opposite direction – discouraging parents from forming separate households. It will be interesting to observe whether trends differ in the five states that direct job-training resources to fathers and those that cater exclusively to young mothers.

There is one provision of the Family Support Act of 1988 that explicitly intends to strengthen existing unions, referred to as AFDC-UP. Jobless fathers are permitted to live with their families without affecting eligibility for welfare payments. Higher earnings are allowed in the form of income disregards (job earnings permitted before AFDC is reduced). These stipulations could conceivably have some effect on union formation and stability though the magnitude of the disregards is quite modest, suggesting that their potential effect on union stability probably will be small if at all. A number of states have already instituted AFDC-UP, but little is known about the effect of this provision in maintaining family unions. Studying the impact of broadening this provision on union formation and stability would be worthwhile.

States are also permitted to require single mothers who are minors to live with their parents in order to receive benefits. This provision might encourage youthful parents seeking independence to enter marriage precipitously if they would qualify for AFDC-UP, but it is implausible to believe that this strategy will become common. Most teen mothers are not eager to marry and prefer instead to reside with their parents. Indeed, if anything, this requirement may discourage coupling because symbolically, and perhaps in actuality, the regulation reinforces the young mother's dependency upon her family.

Summing up, the overall effect of the Family Support Act on the occurrence of marriage and its stability is not likely to be large. If anything, it is likely to reinforce current trends away from early marriage and marital childbearing. Fathers are recognized from a policy standpoint more as potential economic contributors outside the home than important socializing agents inside the home. The Family Support Act protects against the absence of unions between parents more than it actively promotes unions or ensures their permanence. It must be said that stimulating family formation was not the principal intent of the legislation. But to the extent that children are best served by the presence of a father in the home, current welfare reform promises little in the way of assistance.

The impact of the Family Support Act of 1988 on fathering among noncustodial males

One of the main objectives of the Family Support Act of 1988 is to increase the child support provided by fathers living outside the home. Will these efforts to strengthen father's economic obligations lead to greater claims from males for a share of child rearing and greater acceptance from mothers for a more active paternal presence?

Men are more likely to retreat from the family when they are unable or unwilling to pay child support. And when they do not pay, mothers are more hostile to their participation in the family. It is entirely plausible that the provision of more regular support will lead to more regular visitation and greater involvement in child rearing (Seltzer, 1994). More involvement may then have the impact of reintegrating fathers into the family. These potential outcomes ought to be studied by looking at changing levels of paternal involvement over time and by comparing the participation of nonresidential fathers in states that are more or less effective in enforcing child support.

At the same time, we must be prepared to examine critically the benefits of paternal participation among fathers not living with their children. Unlike marriage, where couples presumably have a strong interest in coordinating their parenting roles, parenting apart can create competition between mothers and fathers and their respective extended kin. Thus, increasing economic obligations might expand conflict in some families while promoting greater cooperation in others.

The possibility of adverse side effects is perhaps greatest when fathers deny paternity, when they have been reluctant to pay child support, or when they have been denied access to their children. It will be especially important to consider the consequences of the Family Support Act on paternal participation and family functioning. Funding is allocated for special demonstration programs to increase access of noncustodial fathers to their children by encouraging judicial procedures when child visitation has been denied. The language of the legislation is vague, only calling for judicial experimentation. This possibly affords another opportunity to examine the impact of paternal involvement on family functioning, especially when such involvement may not be unwelcomed by the residential parent.

The impact of the Family Support Act of 1988 on relations between fathers and their children

The provisions of the Family Support Act aimed at increasing child support may significantly raise the standard of living of children of economically disadvantaged parents. If this were to happen, the social and psychological benefits to children would be enormous because poverty affects children's development and well-being in a variety of direct and indirect ways (see Garfinkel & McLanahan, this volume). Regarding the noneconomic effects of paternal participation on children, the research on how fathers, both inside and outside the home, affect the well-being of their children is not a good guide for evaluating the impact of the Family Support Act. To the extent that we can extrapolate from existing research, there is little reason to expect any dramatic effects on children.

It seems far more plausible that the child support enforcement provisions might increase paternal contact somewhat over time. The impact for children is likely to be relatively small, for the involvement of nonresidential fathers is not likely to rise enough to have strong positive effects on the well-being of children. Moreover, the participation of reluctant and sometimes recalcitrant fathers could diminish as often as promote family harmony.

Research opportunities

Much of the speculation in this chapter is based on a very slender pedestal of research. We need to consider and reconsider a number of unsettled questions involving fathers' roles and children's well-being.

1. Almost nothing is known about the practical dilemmas faced by prospective young parents making decisions about marriage and household formation. We know that they are increasingly reluctant to marry, but not why they are electing to remain single. How are their decisions influenced by the availability of resources? How do federal, state, and local policies enter into their choices about marriage and nonmarriage, if they do at all? We need to think more broadly about whether there should be a public interest in private decisions involving family formation.

A minor sort of experiment might be mounted to examine the effects of current welfare reform on the stability of family unions. Would the infusion of economic support help stabilize newly formed unions? Among the states that permit fathers to receive the JOBS program, is there any evidence that unmarried couples will elect to live together in marriages or informal unions? These questions address the link between precarious economic conditions and marriage patterns. While the legislation is unlikely to spawn powerful enough interventions to test the significance of the economic determinants of marriage, they may lead to bolder sorts of natural experiments.

2. Based on existing studies, there is some reason to believe that fathers' claims for participation in the family will escalate if they are providing child support. We do not know much about how paternal participation shapes relations between unmarried or formerly married parents. We need to assess how policies may influence alternative patterns of family functioning. Nonnuclear families are probably every bit as diverse, or perhaps even more so, as nuclear families. Exploring the circumstances that promote effective collaboration between parents living apart is important. Does a marriage, even one that does not survive, improve the chances of cooperation or does it have the reverse effect, creating a larger legacy of enmity and distrust? A comparison of the parenting experiences of never-married and formerly married parents would shed some light on the benefits or liabilities of promoting marriage as a matter of public policy.

3. We know little about the consequences of paternal involvement inside or outside the home for the well-being of children. We must confront our ignorance about this topic, for it raises the question of whether and how much children will benefit if their fathers become more active in child rearing. It can be assumed that a father's economic contribution will improve the child's well-being, but the psychological effects of paternal involvement are less clear. The evidence collected to date

simply is too weak to instruct policy makers. Rather than regarding paternal participation as either positive or negative for children's well-being, it would be most helpful to examine the conditions under which greater involvement by fathers increases or decreases a child's welfare. It is also essential to examine how these child support enforcement policies, in turn, may affect long-term family relations and the adjustment of children later in life. Carefully planned longitudinal studies on the development of children are required if we are to appreciate the full ramifications of fostering more active paternal participation.

Conclusion

Some readers might conclude that my appraisal of how the Family Support Act may affect the role of fathers is unsympathetic to the aims of the legislation, which was primarily designed to improve the status of poor women and their children. In emphasizing how this legislation could reinforce the prevailing pattern of single parenthood, I do not intend to suggest that it is poor public policy to insist that fathers contribute economic support or help mothers become more economically independent. But I insist that we should recognize that such efforts do little to promote the interdependence of fathers and mothers through formal and informal marriage. As such, legislation of this sort strengthens individualistic rather than collective tendencies in our kinship system and may reinforce the separate worlds of men and women.

In an earlier paper on the changing role of fathers, I traced the origin of two current and seemingly contradictory trends – the appearance of nurturant and involved fathers in family life and the retreat of formerly and never-married fathers from families – to a common source. The breakdown of the gender-specific division of labor set off both of these tendencies, which I termed the *good dads/bad dads complex* (Furstenberg, 1988b). I concluded that it is easier to figure out ways of reenforcing obligations of fathers outside the household than to craft policies that increase the involvement of fathers inside the home. This is partly because we do not know how to domesticate men once the vestigial privileges of patriarchy have been removed. Thus, our production of good dads is occurring at a much slower rate than our production of bad dads.

The concerns that I have expressed in this chapter are consistent with my earlier argument. Many of our policies that purport to support the "family" in fact give all too little consideration to involving men in ongoing domestic relationships with their children and their children's mothers. The situation is most acute among disadvantaged minorities, the target population of the Family Support Act. The legislation, I believe, is likely to widen the existing fault line that divides men and women by directing job-training and educational resources primarily toward young mothers while providing only limited services to their partners. We must be more creative in devising ways to increase the capacity of men to become good dads. This means giving equal attention and directing resources to residential fathers and men, living outside the home, who aspire to share parenting responsibilities but do not have the means to do so.

Of course, this is easier said than done. As one who has spent a professional lifetime studying both adolescent childbearing and marital dissolution, I am acutely aware that relations between young parents are fragile. It is unwise policy merely to promote marriage when parents lack the material and emotional resources to enter into stable relationships. Unquestionably, we ought to be discouraging with all the means available premature parenthood, which contributes disproportionately to our very high rates of nonmarital childbearing and marital instability. An important way of strengthening families is to postpone childbearing until both parents are able to meet its financial and emotional responsibilities. One potentially attractive feature of the new emphasis on child support enforcement is the possibility that raising the costs of fathering a child could deter premature parenthood.

At the same time, we must begin to think about other ways of making stable domestic partnership more attractive and more viable if such arrangements really best serve children's interests. It is beyond the scope of this chapter to develop a set of policies designed to promote union formation and stability. There is reason to be skeptical that any single policy is likely to have a powerful effect on family formation patterns. The declining significance of marriage is the product of a confluence of powerful social and economic trends and is not likely to be reversed by government policies. Still, it is worth thinking through what it might take to strengthen relationships between parents.

I suspect that this battle will have to be fought on two fronts. One direction might consider ways of enhancing the benefits of pooling resources between parents, thus restoring some of the economic incentives for coupling. Doing so without disadvantaging single parents is a problem, but our objective ought at least to be designing policies that do not make it economically unattractive for parents to live together. And we may want to tip the balance in the other direction so that incentives exist for establishing and maintaining unions.

The other policy front is even more complicated. It involves reducing the divergent cultural experiences associated with gender that make it difficult for men and women to live together. This problem may be especially acute among disadvantaged minorities, where children sometimes grow up having stable and attentive contact with fathers and father surrogates. I am convinced that gender distrust, which may itself have economic roots, complicates the process of stable coupling (Furstenberg et al., 1992).

These concerns go well beyond the important issues raised by the Family Support Act of 1988. Still, they have some relevance to the potential ripple effects of the legislation, which, if I am correct, may reinforce what Garfinkel and McLanahan have termed a "new American dilemma" (1986). We must think more broadly and more boldly about the advantages and disadvantages of alternative family arrangements. It has become almost an axiom of public policy that we can exercise little or no influence on our family futures. Is this true, or are we simply afraid of discussing the troubling value choices that are exposed by family change? A thorough evaluation of the Family Support Act will not yield a definitive answer to this question, but it may force us to reconsider the wisdom of our present policy of ideological stalemate and benign neglect.

REFERENCES

Adams, G., & Pittman, K. (1988). *Adolescent and young adult fathers: Problems and solutions.* Washington, DC: Children's Defense Fund.

Amato, P. R. (1993). Children's adjustment to divorce: Theories, hypotheses, and empirical support. *Journal of Marriage and the Family, 55*(1), 23–38.

Amato, P. R., & Keith, B. (1991). Parental divorce and adult well-being: A metanalysis. *Journal of Marriage and the Family, 53*(1), 43–58.

Bell, N. W., & Vogel, E. F. (Eds.). (1968). *A modern introduction to the family.* New York: Free Press.

Bennett, N., Bloom, D. E., & Craig, P. H. (1989). The divergence of black and white marriage patterns. *American Journal of Sociology, 95,* 692–712.

Bumpass, L. L., & Sweet, J. A. (1989). Children's experience in single-parent families: Implications of cohabitation and marital transitions. *Family Planning Perspectives, 21*(6), 256–260.

Castro, T., & Bumpass, L. (1989). Recent trends and differentials in marital disruption. *Demography, 26,* 37–51.

Chase-Lansdale, P. L., & Hetherington, M. (1990). The impact of divorce on life-span development: Short and long term effects. In P. Baltes, D. L. Featherman, & R. M. Lerner (Eds.), *Life-span behavior and development* (Vol. 10, pp. 105–150). Hillsdale, NJ: Erlbaum.

Cherlin, A. J. (1989). The weakening link between marriage and the care of children. *Family Planning Perspectives, 20*(6), 302–306.

Cherlin, A. J. (1992). *Marriage, divorce, remarriage* (rev. and expanded ed.). Cambridge, MA: Harvard University Press.

Coser, R. L. (Ed.) (1964). *The family: Its structure and functions.* New York: St. Martin's Press.

Davis, K. (1939). Illegitimacy and the social structure, *American Journal of Sociology, 45,* 215–233.

Davis, K. (1985). *Contemporary marriage: Comparative perspectives on a changing institution.* New York: Russell Sage Foundation.

Dornbush, S. M. (1989). The sociology of adolescence. *Annual Review of Sociology, 15,* 233–239.

Dornbush, S. M., Carlsmith, J. M., Bushwall, S. J., Ritter, R. L., & Leiderman, H., et al. (1985). Single parents, extended households, and the control of adolescents. *Child Development, 56,* 326–341.

Ellwood, D. T. (1988). *Poor support: Poverty in the American family.* New York: Basic Books.

Elster, A., & Lamb, M. E. (1986). *Adolescent fatherhood.* Hillsdale, NJ: Lawrence Erlbaum.

Emery, R. E. (1988). *Marriage, divorce, and children's adjustment.* Beverly Hills: Sage.

Furstenberg, F. F., Jr. (1976). *Unplanned parenthood: The social consequences of teenage childbearing.* New York: Free Press.

Furstenberg, F. F., Jr. (1982). Conjugal succession: Reentering marriage after divorce. In P. B. Baltes & O. G. Brim (Eds.), *Life-span development and behavior* (Vol. 4, pp. 107–146). New York: Academic Press.

Furstenberg, F. F., Jr. (1988a). Bringing back the shotgun wedding. *Public Interest, 90,* 121–127.

Furstenberg, F. F., Jr. (1988b). Good dads – bad dads: The two faces of fatherhood. In A. J. Cherlin (Ed.), *The changing American family and public policy* (pp. 193–218). Washington, DC: Urban Institute Press.

Furstenberg, F. F., Jr. (1990). Divorce and the American family. *Annual Review of Sociology, 16,* 379–403.

Furstenberg, F. F., Jr. (1991). As the pendulum swings: Teenage childbearing and social concern. *Family Relations, 40,* 127–138.

Furstenberg, F. F., Jr., Brooks-Gunn, J., & Morgan, S. P. (1987a). *Adolescent mothers in later life.* New York: Cambridge University Press.

Furstenberg, F. F., Jr., & Cherlin, A. J. (1991). *Divided families: What happens to children when their parents part.* Cambridge, MA: Harvard University Press.

Furstenberg, F. F., Jr., & Harris, K. M. (1992). The disappearing American father? Divorce and the waning significance of biological parenthood. In S. J. South & S. E. Tolnay (Eds.), *The changing American family* (pp. 197–223). Boulder, CO: Westview Press.

Furstenberg, F. F., Jr., & Harris, K. M. (1993). When fathers matter/why fathers matter: The impact of paternal involvement on the offspring of adolescent mothers. In R. Lerman & T. Ooms (Eds.), *Young unwed fathers* (pp. 117–138). Philadelphia: Temple University Press.

Furstenberg, F. F., Jr., Levine, J. A., & Brooks-Gunn, J. (1990). The children of teenage mothers: Patterns of early childbearing in two generations. *Family Planning Perspectives, 22*(2), 54–61.

Furstenberg, F. F, Jr., Morgan, S. P., & Allison, P. A. (1987b). Paternal participation and children's well-being after marital dissolution. *American Sociological Review, 52,* 695–701.

Furstenberg, F. F., Jr., & Nord, C. W. (1985). Parenting apart: Patterns of childbearing after disruption. *Journal of Marriage and the Family, 47*(4), 893–905.

Furstenberg, F. F., Jr., Nord, C. W., Peterson, J. L., & Zill, N. (1983). The life course of children of divorce: Marital disruption and parental conflict. *American Sociological Review, 48*(5), 656–668.

Furstenberg, F. F., Jr., Sherwood, K. E., & Sullivan, M. L. (1992, July). *Caring and paying: What fathers and mothers say about child support.* Report prepared for Manpower Demonstration Research Corporation on Parent's Fair Share Demonstration, New York.

Furstenberg, F. F., Jr., & Teitler, J. O. (1991, October). *Reconsidering the effects of marital disruption: What happens to children in early adulthood?* Paper presented at the European Population Conference, Paris.

Garfinkel, I. (1992). *Assuring child support: An extension of Social Security.* New York: Russell Sage Foundation.

Garfinkel, I., & McLanahan, S. (1986). *Single mothers and their children.* Washington, DC: Urban Institute Press.

Gillis, J. R. (1985). *For better, for worse: British marriages 1600 to the present.* New York: Oxford University Press.

Goode, W. J. (1960). A deviant case: Illegitimacy in the Caribbean. *American Sociological Review, 25*(1), 21–30.

Goode, W. J. (1971). Family disorganization. In R. K. Merton & R. Nisbet (Eds.), *Contemporary social problems* (3rd ed., pp. 467–544). New York: Harcourt Brace Jovanovich.

Goody, J. (1983). *The development of the family and marriage in Europe.* Cambridge: Cambridge University Press.

Gordon, M. (Ed.). (1983). *The American family in social-historical perspective.* New York: St. Martin's Press.

Hareven, T. (Ed.). (1978). *Transition: The family and the life course in historical perspective.* New York: Academic Press.

Harris, K. M., & Furstenberg, F. F., Jr. (1990, August). *Affective mobility: The course of parent-child relations in adolescence.* Paper presented at the annual meetings of the American Sociological Association, Washington, DC.

Hetherington, E. M. (1987). Family relations six years after divorce. In K. Pasley & M. Ihinger-Tallman (Eds.), *Remarriage and stepparenting today: Current research and theory* (pp. 185–205). New York: Guilford Press.

Huber, J., & Spitze, G. (1988). Trends in family sociology. In N. J. Smelser (Ed.), *Handbook of sociology* (pp. 425–448). Beverly Hills: Sage.

Johnson, C. M., Sum, A. M., & Weill, J. D. (1988). *Vanishing dreams: The growing economic plight of America's young families.* Washington, DC: Children's Defense Fund.

King, V. (1994). Nonresident father involvement and child well-being: Can dads make a difference? *Journal of Family Issues, 15*(1), 78–96.

Lamb, M. E. (Ed.). (1987). *The father's role: Applied perspectives.* New York: Wiley.

Laslett, P. (1972). Introduction: The history of the family. In P. Laslett & R. Wall (Eds.), *Household and family in past time.* Cambridge: At the University Press.

Lichter, D. T., McLaughlin, D. K., Kephart, G., & Landry, D. J. (1992). Race and retreat from marriage: A shortage of marriageable men? *American Sociological Review, 57*(6), 781–799.

Maccoby, E. E., & Mnookin, R. H. (1992). *Dividing the child: Social and legal dilemmas of custody.* Cambridge, MA: Harvard University Press.

Malinowski, B. (1930). Parenthood, the basis of social structure. In R. L. Coser (Ed.), *The family: Its structures & functions* (pp. 51–63). New York: St. Martin's Press.

Marsiglio, W. (1988). Commitment to social fatherhood: Predicting adolescent males' intentions to live with their child and partner. *Journal of Marriage and the Family, 50*(2), 427–441.

McLanahan, S. (1988). Family structure and dependency: Early transitions to female household headship. *Demography, 25,* 1–16.

McLanahan, S., & Sandefur, G. (1994). *Growing up with a single parent.* Cambridge, MA: Harvard University Press.

Moore, K. A., Simms, M. C., & Betsey, C. L. (1986). *Choice and circumstance.* New Brunswick, NJ: Transaction Books.

Mott, F. L. (1993). Absent fathers and child development: Emotional and cognitive effects at age five to nine. National Institute of Child Health and Human Development Grant HD 23160.

National Center for Health Statistics. (1993). *Monthly vital statistics report, 41* (No. 9, Suppl.). Hyattsville, MD: Public Health Service.

Ooms, T. (Ed.). (1981). *Teenage pregnancy in a family context: Implications for policy.* Philadelphia: Temple University Press.

Parke, R. D. (1989). In search of fathers: A narrative of an empirical journey. In I. E. Sigel & G. H. Brody (Eds.), *Family research: Volume I. Research on marriage and the family.* Hillsdale, NJ: Erlbaum.

Patterson, G. R., DeBaryshe, B. D., & Ramsey, E. (1989). A developmental perspective on antisocial behavior. *American Psychologist, 44*(2), 329–335.

Popenoe, D. (1988). *Disturbing the nest: Family change and decline in modern societies.* New York: Aldine de Gruyter.

Preston, S., & McDonald, J. (1979). The incidence of divorce within cohorts of American marriages contracted since the Civil War. *Demography, 16*(1), 1–26.

Rawlings, S. W. (1989). Single parents and their children. U.S. Bureau of the Census, Current Population Reports, *Studies in marriage and the family* (Series P-23, No. 162). Washington, DC: U.S. Government Printing Office.

Select Committee on Children, Youth, and Families. (1989). *U.S. children and their families: Current conditions and trends, 1989. A report.* Washington, DC: U.S. Government Printing Office.

Seltzer, J. A. (1991). Relationships between fathers and children who live apart. *Journal of Marriage and the Family, 53*(1), 79–101.

Seltzer, J. A. (1994). Consequences of marital dissolution for children. *Annual Review of Sociology, 20,* 235–266.

Seltzer, J. A., & Bianchi, S. M. (1988). Children's contact with absent parents. *Journal of Marriage and the Family, 50,* 663–677.

Shorter, E. (1975). *The making of the modern family.* New York: Basic Books.

Sullivan, M. (1989). Absent fathers in the inner city. *Annals,* American Academy of Political and Social Science, 501.

Sum, A., & Pierce, G. (1988, June). *An outline of potential themes/issues for the proposed report on the economic and social status of American families.* Report prepared for National Advisory Board on The Family Report Project, Washington, DC.

Sweet, J. A., & Bumpass, L. L. (1987). *American families and households.* New York: Russell Sage Foundation.

Teachman, J. D. (1992). Intergenerational resource transfers across disrupted households: Absent fathers' contributions to the well-being of their children. In E. J. South & S. F. Tolnay (Eds.), *The changing American family* (pp. 224–246). Boulder, CO: Westview Press.

Thornton, A. (1989). Changing attitudes towards family issues in the United States. *Journal of Marriage and the Family, 51*, 873–893.

U.S. Bureau of the Census. (1989). *Fertility of American women: June, 1988.* Current Population Reports (Series, P-20, No. 436). Washington, DC: U.S. Government Printing Office.

U.S. Bureau of the Census. (1990). *Child support and alimony: 1987.* Current Population Reports (Series, P-23, No. 167). Washington, DC: U.S. Government Printing Office.

U.S. Bureau of the Census. (1992a). *Households, families, and children: A 30-year perspective.* Current Population Reports (Series, P23–181). Washington, DC: U.S. Government Printing Office.

U.S. Bureau of the Census. (1992b). *Marriage, divorce, and remarriage in the 1990's.* Current Population Reports (Series P23–180). Washington, DC: U.S. Governement Printing Office.

Vinovskis, M. A. (1981). An "epidemic" of adolescent pregnancy? Some historical considerations. *Journal of Family History, 6*, 205–230.

Vinovskis, M. A. (1988). *An "epidemic" of adolescent pregnancy? Some historical and policy considerations.* New York: Oxford University Press.

Vinovskis, M. A., & Chase-Lansdale, P. L. (1987). Should we discourage teenage marriage? *Public Interest, 87*, 23–37.

Weed, J. A. (1980). *National estimates of marriage dissolution and survivorships: United States.* Vital and Health Statistics: Series 3, Analytic Statistics, No. 19 (DHHS Publication No. [PHS] 81–1043). Hyattsville, MD: National Center for Health Statistics.

Wilson, W. J. (1987). *The truly disadvantaged: The inner city, the underclass, and public policy.* Chicago: University of Chicago Press.

10 The effects of child support reform on child well-being

Irwin Garfinkel and Sara McLanahan

In 1988 about 25% of all children in the United States were potentially eligible for child support, in that they had a parent living apart from the family. According to recent estimates, over half of all children born during the past decade will be eligible at some point before reaching the age of 18 (Bumpass, 1984). A key feature of the Family Support Act of 1988 is a set of provisions for child support reform. These provisions are aimed at rationalizing the current child support system by increasing the proportion of eligible children who have awards, by developing guidelines for determining the size of the awards, and by strengthening procedures for collecting the money owed. These changes in child support have implications for over half of all children in this country. In contrast, the work provisions in the Family Support Act are relevant only for families who receive welfare. In 1987 only 11.4% of all children below age 18 received welfare (U.S. House of Representatives, Committee on Ways and Means, 1989).

The child support provisions are part of a broad trend that began during the mid-1970s and has strong bipartisan support, whereas attitudes toward requiring welfare mothers to work have shifted many times in the history of public assistance and are highly controversial at this time (see Chase-Lansdale & Vinovskis, this volume). We believe that the increasing number of married mothers working outside the home lends considerable force to the new set of work provisions. Yet there continues to be widespread resistance from both the left and right to requiring welfare mothers to work (McLanahan & Booth, 1989). Finally, whereas the work provisions allow for considerable local discretion in implementing work requirements, child support reform appears to be moving toward more universal principles. While one cannot be sure that this pattern will continue, the progress thus far has been impressive.

This chapter examines the potential impact of child support reform on the long-

Portions of this chapter are reprinted by permission of Kluwer Academic Publishers (Garfinkel, I., & McLanahan, S. [1990]. The effects of the child support provisions of the Family Support Act of 1988. *Population Research and Policy Review, 9*, 205–234).

term social and economic well-being of children. The new provisions are expected to lead to increases in child support payments which, in turn, should reduce the poverty and economic insecurity of children who live apart from a parent. The first question is, How big will the increases in child support payments be?

Increased child support payments in turn are likely to lead to increased contact between nonresident parents and their children. We hypothesize that on average the increased contact will lead to further increases in child well-being. Thus, two additional questions are: Will increased child support payments increase contact between the nonresident parent and the child? Will increased contact lead to further increases in child well-being?

Increased contact between the nonresident parent and child will also lead to greater contact between the two parents, which may provoke conflict. This leads to the final critical question for evaluating the effects of the child support provisions of the 1988 Family Support Act: Will greater contact between resident and nonresident parents provoke conflict and thereby reduce child well-being?

The outcomes we have chosen to focus on in this chapter are not by any means exhaustive. Other consequences of child support reform of interest to policy makers are the effects on the labor supply, remarriage, and welfare dependence of both residential and nonresidential parents. Each of these also could affect child well-being. Each is worthy of investigation. Elsewhere, we have described how these outcomes must be studied in a comprehensive evaluation of child support reforms (Garfinkel et al., 1988). Because other effects of child support reform hinge upon changes in payments, any evaluation must begin with the effects on payments. Our rationale for focusing on changes in visitation and custody rather than changes in labor supply, remarriage, or welfare dependence is that we think the former are likely to be ignored in evaluations unless their potential effects are highlighted.

Four issues are considered in this chapter. First, the child support system in the United States and changes in the system are briefly reviewed. Second, research is reviewed on children from disrupted families, including children living with divorced and separated parents as well as children born out of wedlock. Most of these children are eligible for child support, and the changes in child support provisions are expected to directly affect their economic status. It is important, therefore, to know something about the long-term prospects for these children and the extent to which their overall well-being is determined by economic factors. Third, the potential impact of the new child support provisions on child well-being is analyzed. Different mechanisms for increasing child support payments are examined as well as their potential effect on income. In addition to examining the direct effect of increased payments on family income, we discuss how the provisions are expected to alter father–child relationships and parental relationships. Specific research issues for evaluating child support reform, including key variables that should be measured and potential sources of data, are considered in the final section.

The child support system in the United States

The past 15 years have been characterized by the enactment of increasingly strong legislation to enforce the payment of child support. During this time – long in the lives of those who have witnessed it, but short in terms of twentieth-century American history – the child support system has taken giant strides away from a system best characterized by judicial discretion toward the bureaucratic regularity characteristic of our social insurance and personal income tax systems.

Prior to 1975 child support was nearly exclusively a state and local matter. State laws established the duty of nonresident parents to pay child support but left all the details up to local courts (Krause, 1981; Chambers, 1979; Cassetty, 1978). Judges had the authority to decide whether any child support should be paid and, if so, how much. They also had full authority over what to do if the nonresident parent failed to pay. Jail was the ultimate punishment for failure to pay.

Critics of the old system claimed that it condoned and therefore fostered parental irresponsibility, that it was rife with inequity, and that it contributed to poverty and welfare dependence (Sawhill, 1983; Garfinkel & Melli, 1982; Cassetty, 1978). The earliest reliable national estimates indicated that in 1974 only about one of every four nonresident fathers paid child support at all. In 1979 the U.S. Census Bureau began gathering data on child support every other year. The first Census study indicated that slightly more than one in three nonresident parents paid some child support (U.S. Bureau of the Census, 1981). Either way, this was a dismal record. The details of the study revealed weaknesses at every step in the child support process. Only six of 10 children potentially eligible for child support had child support awards. (Only one of 10 children born out of wedlock had legal entitlement to support.) Among children with legal awards, about half received the full amount to which they were entitled, and over a quarter received nothing. Few argued with the judgment that the system condoned parental irresponsibility. Other studies documented alleged inequities. Child support awards for children and parents in similar economic circumstances varied widely (White & Stone, 1976; Yee, 1979). Whereas most nonresident fathers paid no child support and suffered no consequences, thousands were sent to jail (Chambers, 1979). And poor nonresident fathers who were legally obligated to pay child support were required to pay a substantially higher proportion of their incomes than middle- and especially upper-income nonresident fathers (Cassetty, 1978). Finally, nearly half of single mothers and their children were poor and dependent on welfare (Garfinkel & McLanahan, 1986).

The critics suggested many specific reforms. The common element of virtually all of these suggestions was to replace judicial discretion with bureaucratic regularity. This tendency is most clearly articulated in the proposal to add to our menu of Social Security programs a new Child Support Assurance System (CSAS) (Wisconsin Department of Health and Social Services, 1979; Garfinkel & Melli, 1982). Under CSAS, nonresident parents are required to share their income with their nonresident children. More specifically, nonresident parents are required to pay a fixed proportion of their annual income as determined by simple legislative guidelines; the amount owed is withheld from wages and other sources of income, just as income and payroll taxes are withheld from wages; and the government guarantees a minimum level of child support to the child and custodial parent just as social insurance guarantees a minimum pension to all eligible recipients. It is remarkable how far the country has moved in the past 5 years toward implementation of the guidelines and withholding components of CSAS. There is no stronger evidence of the steady movement away from judicial discretion to bureaucratic regularity.

Federal interest in child support reform grew as the caseload of the Aid to Families with Dependent Children (AFDC) program grew, and shifted from orphans to children with living absent parents. Although the first federal legislation to enforce child support was enacted in 1950, and although additional bills were passed in 1965 and 1967, the establishment of the Office of Child Support Enforcement in 1975 was a particularly significant piece of legislation. The new law required all states to establish State Offices of Child Support Enforcement, and it provided federal reimbursement for about three-quarters of each state's enforcement costs. That is to say, the 1975 act created the public bureaucracy to enforce the private child support obligation.

The 1975 legislation provided federal matching funds for child support enforcement services for children who were not on welfare as well as for AFDC recipients, and it required states to provide services to nonrecipients upon request. Yet federal funding for nonrecipients was made available to the states only through 1976. After a series of temporary extensions, in 1980 Congress permanently extended federal support for child support services to all children potentially eligible for private child support, irrespective of income and AFDC status.

The Child Support Enforcement Amendments of 1984 moved the nation modestly toward two of the three key components of a new child support assurance system by requiring states to adopt numeric child support guidelines that courts could use to determine child support obligations, and by requiring them to withhold child support obligations from wages and other income of nonresident parents who become 1 month delinquent in their payments of child support. The 1984 bill also took an extremely cautious step in the direction of assuring a minimum child support benefit by directing the Secretary of the Department of Health and Human Services (DHHS) to grant the state of Wisconsin a waiver that would allow it to use federal AFDC monies to help fund an assured child support benefit.[1] Finally, the 1984 bill contained two minor provisions relating to paternity establishment: one permitting paternity to be established up until the child's 18th birthday, and the other encouraging states to develop expedited processes for establishing paternity, that is, administrative or bureaucratic procedures. With respect to routine income withholding, the 1988 legislation requires withholding of the child support obligation from the outset for all IV-D cases as of 1990 and for all child support cases as of 1994. As mentioned earlier, the previous legislation (1984) had required withholding only in cases of delinquency.

The Family Support Act also strengthens paternity requirements. It requires states to either establish paternity in at least half of the out-of-wedlock cases on AFDC or increase the proportion of such cases in which they establish paternity by 3 percentage points each year; to obtain the Social Security numbers of both parents in conjunction with the issuance of birth certificates; and to require all parties in a contested paternity case to take a genetic test upon the request of any party, with the federal government paying 90% of the cost of the test.

In addition to these major provisions, the Family Support Act contains some other notable changes. Whereas the 1984 Child Support Act urged states to expedite procedures for establishing paternity, the 1988 legislation further exhorts them to simplify paternity establishment by setting up a civil process for voluntarily acknowledging paternity and a civil procedure for determining paternity in contested cases. Further, whereas the 1984 statute urged states to develop demonstrations of more efficient techniques to enforce child support when the father was in a different state, the 1988 statute makes it more financially attractive for states to undertake such demonstrations and also establishes a federal advisory council to make recommendations for future legislation on interstate child support enforcement.

Finally, in 1988 Congress enacted a waiver for New York State to use federal funds that would otherwise have been devoted to AFDC to help fund a restricted version of an assured child support benefit. Whereas Wisconsin failed to take advantage of its 1984 waiver, New York State implemented its child assistance program in seven counties in late 1989 and early 1990. Unfortunately, whereas the assured child support benefit as originally conceived was to be available to families from all income classes, just like Social Security, eligibility for the Child Assurance Program (CAP) is limited to families with incomes low enough to qualify for welfare.

Interest in and support for further strengthening the child support system continue to grow, suggesting the possibility that the nation will adopt a full-fledged national child support assurance system. (The addition of child support assurance to our menu of Social Security programs is discussed in Garfinkel's new book, *Assuring Child Support: An Extension of Social Security* [1992].) The National Commission on Children – a bipartisan commission appointed by President Reagan and Congress and chaired by Senator John D. Rockefeller IV – endorsed the proposal for a government guarantee of a minimum child support benefit and called for federally subsidized state pilot programs (National Commission on Children, 1991). In 1992 the Commission on Interstate Child Support Enforcement rejected the idea of federalizing child support enforcement, but made a number of recommendations for strengthening intra- as well as interstate child support enforcement and also endorsed state piloting of an assured child support benefit (U.S. Commission on Interstate Child Support Enforcement, 1992). Congress enacted legislation in 1992 to prohibit individuals from crossing state lines to avoid paying child support. Senator Dodd has proposed legislation to fund state pilot programs of an assured child support benefit. And, in 1992, Congressmen Downey and Hyde floated a proposal to establish a full-fledged national child support assurance system.

This brief historical review makes it very clear that the recent child support reforms do not represent a sharp break with the immediate past, but rather intensify a 15-year trend. The implication for the evaluation of these child support reforms is profound. Because the child support enforcement system has been changing slowly, we expect that the effects also will take place gradually over time, and that the effects of any particular change will be much smaller than the effects of the overall change. The first implies that the effects should be measured over 5- and 10-year periods. The second implies that an evaluation of the effects of strengthening the child support system should seek to measure the overall change as opposed to the change in any one component.

Research on children in disrupted families

Whether child support reform will improve the well-being of children depends upon whether children who live apart from a parent are in fact worse off than other children, and, if so, whether lack of child support is a cause of their disadvantage. Interestingly, academic as well as public perceptions of how family disruption affects children have undergone several revisions during the past three decades. In the 1950s and most of the 1960s the prevailing view was that divorce and out-of-wedlock births were harmful to children, in part because family instability was indicative of parental pathology that was transferred from generation to generation, and in part because the absence of a male role model was viewed as detrimental to children's psychosexual development. Family income or living conditions associated with income were not studied as possible factors accounting for harmful effects of single parenthood. Much of the research at this time was based on highly selective samples, such as children being treated for psychological disorders or those who were wards of the criminal justice system. Thus, it is not surprising that personal failure rather than structural factors or family income appeared to account for the disadvantages associated with growing up in a single-parent family.[2]

This perception began to change in the early 1970s, as evidenced by Herzog and Sudia's lengthy review (1973) of the research on children in "fatherless families." The authors challenged earlier interpretations of the relationship between family structure and children's well-being and showed that existing studies of mother-only families contained serious methodological flaws. In particular, they argued that many of the differences between one- and two-parent families could be explained by differences in race and socioeconomic status as opposed to differences in family culture or individual traits.

The Herzog and Sudia review offered a new perspective on single motherhood that, together with a changed political climate in which black families and non-married mothers of all races were viewed more positively, stimulated new studies focusing on the "strengths" of mother-only families, that is, the ways in which single mothers coped successfully with poverty and stress. Despite Herzog and Sudia's assertion that the absence of a father *did* have some negative consequences for children, their methodological critique was taken by many as evidence that differences between one- and two-parent families were minimal or due entirely to differences in social class.

More recently the academic community has moved away from the rather simplistic pathological and idealizing perspectives that prevailed during the 1970s, and a number of researchers have begun to reexamine the consequences of divorce and single parenthood with a more critical eye. Unlike earlier work, many of the recent studies are based on large, nationally representative surveys, some of which have longitudinal designs. Moreover, in addition to examining the immediate effects of divorce on children, which was characteristic of earlier studies, the more recent work has followed children through adolescence and into young adulthood. Thus, we now know something about both the immediate and long-term consequences of family disruption.

The new research indicates that children who grow up in mother-only and stepparent families are disadvantaged not only during childhood but during adolescence and young adulthood as well. Moreover, the negative consequences associated with family structure extend across a wide range of outcomes, many of which are directly associated with long-term economic insecurity and dependence. We know, for example, that children from single and stepparent families are more likely to drop out of high school and less likely to attend college than children from intact families (McLanahan, 1985; Sandefur, McLanahan, & Wojtkiewicz, 1992; Krein & Beller, 1988; McLanahan & Sandefur, 1994). Not surprisingly, these children have lower earnings in adulthood and are more likely to experience unemployment and poverty than other children (Corcoran, Gordon, Laren, & Solon, 1987; Hill, Augustyniak, & Ponza, 1987; McLanahan & Sandefur, 1994).

They are also disadvantaged with respect to the formation of their own families (McLanahan & Bumpass, 1988a; Abrahamson, Morrison, & Waite, 1988; Hogan & Kitigawa, 1985; Bumpass & McLanahan, 1989; McLanahan & Sandefur, 1994). Children from single- and stepparent families are more likely to marry and have babies while in their teens, and they are more likely to give birth out of wedlock than children from two-parent families. Those who marry are more likely to divorce. Consequently, daughters who grow up in such families are at greater risk of becoming single mothers themselves and of having to rely on welfare for their economic support than daughters who grow up with both natural parents (McLanahan, 1988). Finally, offspring from mother-only families are more likely to commit delinquent acts and to use drugs than offspring from two-parent families (Matsueda & Heimer, 1987).

In addition to demonstrating a negative association between single parenthood and children's attainment, several conclusions can be drawn from the literature on the intergenerational consequences of family disruption. First, the effects of living in a single-parent or stepparent family appear to be constant across a variety of racial and ethnic groups. Recent studies have shown that family disruption is associated with lower attainment among whites, blacks, Mexican-Americans, Puerto Ricans, Cubans, and Native Americans, although the effects are somewhat more negative for whites (Sandefur et al., 1992; McLanahan & Bumpass, 1988b). Second, children living with single fathers do not appear to be very different from children living with single mothers. Most important, perhaps, remarriage does not reduce many of the disadvantages associated with family breakup, even though stepfamilies have more income than single-parent families. Whether this is due to a lack of commitment on the part of the stepparent or to a rejection of the parent on the part of the child is not clear. But the evidence that remarriage itself is not a solution to the problems associated with family disruption has important policy implications.

What are the central mechanisms underlying the relationship between family instability and children's lower attainment, and, more important, which of these mechanisms are potentially affected by child support reform? At present two major hypotheses are relevant.[3] The first of these hypotheses attributes lower attainment to economic deprivation. According to this view, family disruption reduces the economic resources available to children, and, in particular, children's access to the resources of the nonresident parent. This, in turn, affects the characteristics of offspring as well as their future opportunities. Economic deprivation may lead a child to assume an adult role early by curtailing his or her education in order to contribute time and money to the household. Daughters with limited opportunities may see marriage and parenthood as a means of escaping hardship and establishing an adult identity.

The empirical evidence lends considerable support to the economic deprivation hypothesis. We know, for example, that mother-only families have much higher poverty rates than two-parent families and much lower median family incomes (Garfinkel & McLanahan, 1986). In 1985 the poverty rates were 46% and 9.3% for the two family types, and median incomes were $13,660 and $31,100 (U.S. Bureau of the Census, 1987). We also know that family disruption causes a decline in family resources. Estimates of the income loss for women during the first year after divorce range from 30% to 70% of predivorce income (Duncan & Hoffman, 1985; Weitzman, 1985). For children born to never-married mothers, the income loss is more difficult to measure, because many of these mothers were living in poor families to begin with. However, it is reasonable to assume that the average expected income of children born to unwed mothers would have been higher had their parents married and remained together (Bane, 1986). Finally, we know that income is the single most important factor in accounting for differences in the attainment of children in one-parent and two-parent homes. Differences in family income account for between 25% and 50% of the differential risk of dropping out of high school and for about 25% of the differential risk of premarital birth (McLanahan & Sandefur, 1994).

The second hypothesis for the lower attainment of children from one-parent and stepparent families stresses the importance of the socialization process. According to this view, family disruption (or nonmarriage) affects parent–child relationships by undermining parental control and interfering with the transmission of parental values and expectations. A number of factors are involved in this process. First, in a one-parent family, a smaller quantity of parental time is available to children. The father's time is reduced because he does not live in the household, and the mother's time may also be reduced because she has the dual roles of parent and breadwinner. Second, the quality of parent–child relationships is different in single-parent families. This occurs for several reasons. First, parents under stress are known to be less consistent and reasonable in their demands (Hetherington, Cox, & Cox, 1978). Second, single parents have less power over their children, either because the child can play one parent off against the other, or because the mother has less support. Finally, conflict or hostility between the parents undermines children's perceptions of their parents, and may negatively affect the internalization of parental values (Chase-Lansdale & Hetherington, 1990).

The empirical evidence is consistent with the socialization hypothesis, although the effects of socialization on child well-being are weaker than the effects of family income. With respect to the quantity of time invested in children, recent estimates suggest that between 35% and 50% of children who live only with their mothers do not see their fathers at all and less than 20% see their fathers at least 1 day per week (Seltzer & Bianchi, 1988; Furstenberg, Nord, Peterson, & Zill, 1983). Similarly, analyses of time-use data indicate that single mothers spend less time with their children, primarily because they are more likely to work outside the home (Douthitt, 1990). Not surprisingly, single parents are less likely to supervise their children's social activities and to monitor their school work (Astone & McLanahan, 1991; McLanahan & Sandefur, 1994). Mother–child relationships may be less hierarchical in mother-only families than in two-parent families, and single mothers may be more likely to use authoritarian or controlling parenting styles (Nock, 1988; Weiss, 1978). Finally, ongoing conflict between the parents is harmful for children's post-divorce adjustment (Rutter, 1971; Emery, 1982; Rutter & Quinton, 1977; Emery & O'Leary, 1984). Altogether these findings lend substantial support to the notion that single mothers have less power and less influence on their children than parents in two-parent families.

Studies that confine themselves to the impact of divorce have found considerable evidence that children in single-parent families are exposed to somewhat different parenting practices than children whose parents remain married. However, these differences may not be due entirely to the divorce itself (see Cherlin et al., 1991). Furthermore, even if we knew for certain that divorce caused changes in parental behavior, it is not clear that the latter are critical in determining children's long-term well-being. While theory (and most small studies) indicates that having a good relationship with the nonresident father is an important predictor of children's postdivorce adjustment (Chase-Lansdale & Hetherington, 1990; Wallerstein & Kelly, 1980), at least one large-scale study has raised serious questions about this assumption. Furstenberg and his colleagues found that neither the quantity of father–child contact nor the quality of the father–child relationship was related to children's school achievement or psychological adjustment (Furstenberg, Morgan, & Allison, 1987). As these authors note, none of the fathers in their sample met all of the criteria for "high parental involvement," which may explain why contact with the father had little effect on the children. The importance of the father–child relationship after divorce is an important issue for future research.

The potential impact of child support reform

In discussing the potential consequences of child support reform for child well-being, three intermediate outcomes are considered: (1) increases in child support payments, (2) increases in father–child contact, and (3) increases in parental contact and possible conflict. Increases in payments is by far the most important factor, because the association between family income and children's long-term economic well-being has been clearly established. Increases in father–child contact are believed to have benefits for child well-being, although the current evidence is mixed. Finally, increases in parental contact may lead to greater parental conflict, which could reduce children's well-being and offset some of the gains from increases in payments and father–child contact, although no current research directly addresses this issue.

Increases in payments

The Family Support Act of 1988 solidifies a consistent 15-year trend that substantially strengthens several key components of the old child support system that was woefully inadequate. Thus, it is reasonable to expect a large increase in both child support payments and the incomes of children potentially eligible for child support. However, some argue that legislation will not really change anything. If nonresident fathers cannot afford to pay any more child support than they currently pay, it is hard to see how reforms will lead to substantial increases in payments (Schorr, 1966). The evidence on ability to pay suggests otherwise. Oellerich, Garfinkel, and Robins (1991) compared actual child support payments in 1983 ($6.8 billion) to an estimate of maximum potential payments ($28.0 to $32.4 billion) under a perfect child support regime in which all eligible children had awards; all awards were established and updated according to either the Colorado or Wisconsin child support guidelines; and payments were equal to awards.[4] The gap between current payments and maximum payments was quite large – $21.2 to $25.6 billion. In short, nonresident fathers can afford to pay substantially more child support than they currently pay, which means that the potential for increases in child support enforcement dollars is quite large.

Whether the current child support provision will actually succeed in increasing child support payments by a substantial amount is difficult to predict because very little research bears directly on the question. For the most part, we must rely upon informed inferences. The likely effects on payments of the three main thrusts of the act are examined: increasing paternity establishment, mandating guidelines, and mandating routine income withholding. Then potential magnitudes of the various reforms are compared, showing how the various reforms reinforce one another.

Increasing paternity establishment

In response to incentives and prodding from the federal government, states are doing much better in establishing paternity than they did only a decade ago. The proportion of paternities established to out-of-wedlock births doubled between 1975 and 1985 – from 14% to 28% (Nichols-Casebolt & Garfinkel, 1991). A doubling of any rate within a single decade is a big change.

On the one hand, the trend suggests that the Family Support Act of 1988 is likely to lead to substantial improvements in the establishment of paternity and therefore in the proportion of cases with child support awards. On the other hand, not all married mothers want a child support award. Of those without awards, 42% indicate they would prefer not to have an award. Another 50% say they have no award because the fathers of their children cannot be located (U.S. Bureau of the Census, 1989). These data suggest that unless new incentives are created for mothers to establish paternity and unless the process begins earlier, there will not be much improvement in the proportion of cases in which paternity is established.

An assured child support benefit would create an incentive for unwed mothers to establish paternity. How strong the effects of such an incentive would be is not known at this time. The state of Wisconsin has not yet begun its assured benefit pilot program. Although New York State has started piloting an assured benefit, it is too early for results. Moreover, the New York benefit is limited to children who live in families with sufficiently low income to be eligible for welfare. Therefore, it is unlikely to serve as an incentive for mothers not on welfare. Early establishment of paternity would also increase the number of children with child support awards since the proportion of unwed mothers who continue to have a relationship with the father of their child declines over time. At this point, no research has been done on the efficacy of earlier establishment of paternity.

Because the prognosis for improvement in the establishment of paternity hinges on efforts to begin earlier and to ensure the cooperation of the mother, and because we have no data on the likelihood and effects of these changes, it is difficult to predict how big any effects will be. About all that seems certain at this point is that some improvement will occur. The rate of improvement will probably be slow for some time to come and will depend ultimately upon whether legislation continues to change the system from one of judicial discretion to one of bureaucratic regularity.

The likely effects of guidelines on child support payments

The effects of the numerical guidelines for establishing and maintaining adequate levels of child support are less ambiguous than the paternity provisions and should lead to substantial increases in child support payments. As mentioned earlier, all but a few states have adopted numerical guidelines similar to those of Wisconsin or Colorado. If these guidelines had been used to determine all current awards, and if all awards had been kept up to date, child support payments in 1985 would have totaled between $19.6 billion and $16.7 billion respectively, rather than the current $9.7 billion (Oellerich et al., 1991). Because courts are permitted to depart from the guidelines if the outcome is deemed to be unfair to any of the parties, it is possible that this loophole will be used to undermine the intent of the law. Equally important, there may be a great deal of slippage in updating child support awards. The new federal law requires states to update awards every 3 years. Updating every third year rather than annually is expected to reduce average award levels by about 5%.[5] A more serious concern is that, as yet, the updating applies only to IV-D cases – that is, cases that are part of the state child support enforcement system. Whether this provision will be extended to all child support cases depends upon future legislation. Perhaps the most serious concern is that the courts will find the updating so burdensome and costly that they will refuse to comply. In the past, laws made it very difficult to revise child support awards in order to avoid overburdening the courts (Krause, 1981). How burdensome and costly it will be to update child support awards will depend in large measure upon the complexity of the numerical guidelines and the extent to which the updating procedures can be handled administratively. Under the best of circumstances some administrative costs will be associated with updating. At this point, we have no way of knowing whether these costs will be sufficient in many jurisdictions to deter the effort.

Skeptics might also note that the average real value of child support awards has decreased between 1978 and 1985 by 25% (Robins, 1992). In the 1979 Current Population Survey (CPS) child support survey, the average child support award was for $2,003. In 1985 it was $2,495.[6] Adjusting for inflation, the average award in 1985 was worth only $1,744.

An understanding of the causes of this decline, however, leads us to believe that child support will provide more protection for children in the future (Robins, 1992; Garfinkel, Oellerich, & Robins, 1991; Graham & Beller, 1988). First, a good deal of the decline in real payments was due to the failure to update. Second, the most important factor in accounting for the decline was the increase in resident parent's earnings. Because many courts consider the income of both resident and nonresident parents in establishing child support and because the ratio of women's to men's earnings has increased during the past 20 years, awards have declined. Finally, the composition of those eligible for child support awards has changed over time so that paternity cases make up a larger proportion of the total.

In short, the average real value of child support awards has decreased in the past decade because awards have not been updated, because the ratio of women's to men's earnings has increased, and because nonresident parents with less ability to pay have been brought into the system. The guidelines in Family Support Act of 1988 address the first two problems. As noted above, updating is required for all IV-D cases. Moreover, the standards being used to determine child support obligations will increase awards even in families where the resident parent has substantial earnings. The Wisconsin standard ignores the earnings of the resident parent, and the Colorado standard, which takes account of the resident parent's income, increases obligations by $7 billion. The third factor – a shift in the composition of children with awards – is a sign of progress rather than a problem. To the extent that the country succeeds in increasing the proportion of children with child support awards, the average size of an award will continue to decrease. This is because the ability to pay is clearly lower among nonresident parents currently not required to pay than it is among those with child support obligations.

On balance then, there is good reason to believe that the new child support standards and updating of awards required by the 1988 Family Support Act will substantially increase the average level of child support awards. But previous differences between laws on the books and laws in practice suggest that the implementation of the 1988 legislation should be monitored carefully.

Evidence of routine income withholding on child support payments

Wisconsin began piloting routine income withholding in 1984 in 10 counties. An evaluation of the experience in these 10 pilot counties and 10 matched comparison counties suggests that routine withholding increased child support payments by between 11% and 30% (Garfinkel & Klawitter, 1990). The lower-bound estimate[7] suggests that routine income withholding would increase national child support payments by $0.7 billion while the upper-bound estimate suggests that the increase would be equal to $2.0 billion.[8] Although even the upper-bound estimate is only a fraction of the gap between actual and potential payments, neither of the two figures is trivial in absolute terms. It is important to note that the increase in child support payments resulting from routine income withholding also has taken place slowly over time. States had until 1990 to implement withholding for IV-D cases and until 1994 to implement withholding for all child support cases.

The relative and cumulative effects of paternity, guidelines, and withholding

Total child support payments depend upon three elements: (1) the proportion of children potentially eligible for support who actually have child support awards; (2)

the size of the child support awards; and (3) the proportion of awards that are actually paid. Paternity establishment affects the first element, guidelines the second, and routine withholding the third. In order to achieve substantial gains in child support payments, all three elements must be improved. Estimates indicate that increasing the proportion paid to 100% of the amount owed without increasing either the proportion with awards or the size of awards would increase payments by only $2.9 billion. Increasing the proportion with awards to 100% without increasing either the size or the proportion paid would increase child support by 150% or $4.4 billion. Increasing the size of awards to those prescribed in the Wisconsin percentage-of-income standard without increasing either of the other two components would increase payments by $6.5 billion (Oellerich et al., 1991).

These estimates are useful for putting the different components of reform in proper perspective. For example, the reform that has gotten the most media attention is routine income withholding. Yet, by itself, increasing the payment rate has the least potential for increasing child support payments.

Even more important, the estimates indicate the need to improve all parts of the system at once. If child support awards were established in all cases, if the amount of awards was based on reasonable standards (and updated), and if all that was owed was paid, child support payments in the United States would increase by $25.6 billion. This is nearly twice the sum of the improvements gained by perfecting each element by itself. Here is a case where the whole is greater than the sum of the parts. An improvement in any element makes an improvement in any other element more efficacious.

Increases in father–child contact

In addition to having a direct effect on children's economic well-being, child support reform is also expected to increase the amount of time fathers spend with their children. As noted in the previous section, one of the explanations of the lower socioeconomic attainment of children from single-parent and stepparent families, compared to children in two-parent families, is that the father–child relationship is much weaker.

There are several reasons for expecting that changes in the child support system will lead to changes in father–child relations. First, paying child support may increase the amount of satisfaction a father experiences from spending time with his children and therefore increase his desire for visitation (Seltzer & Schaeffer, 1989). Given the importance of the breadwinner role in defining a "good father," it is likely that fathers who pay support feel better about themselves and better about their children than fathers who avoid paying support. Those who pay nothing or who pay irregularly are likely to avoid contact with their children, if only because such contact reminds them of their failure to perform their social duty.[9] Second, child support reform will also increase fathers' incentive to spend time with their children. According to Weiss and Willis (1985), one reason nonresident parents resist paying support is that they have no control over how their money is spent. If this is so, increases in payments should increase visitation between children and nonresident fathers if only so the fathers can monitor the mothers' expenditures.

Furthermore, as child support becomes more universal and awards become substantially higher, fathers' visitation rights will be strengthened. Obligations are normally linked to rights. One of the principal claims of fathers' rights organizations today is that nonpayment of child support is a response to a mother's refusal to let the father spend time with the child (Furstenberg et al., 1983). Some legislation has already been passed to strengthen fathers' access rights (e.g., Michigan now jails mothers who refuse access as well as fathers who refuse to pay child support) and there is likely to be more.

In addition to increasing the amount of visitation time, child support reform may affect both residential and legal custody arrangements. By securing joint residential custody, fathers can legitimately reduce their child support obligations. By securing sole residential custody, they eliminate it entirely and are entitled to child support from the mothers of their children. To the extent that child support reform increases child support payments, therefore, the incentive for fathers to obtain joint and sole residential custody will increase. Increases in either joint or sole residential custody of fathers will increase the time they spend with their children and presumably decrease the time that mothers spend with the children.

Child support reform should also increase the proportion of fathers who request and obtain joint legal custody. This should occur for reasons similar to those outlined above. First, the redistribution of parental financial responsibility from mothers to fathers implies a similar redistribution of legal custodial rights. Whereas for the past century mothers have had the stronger claim on custodial rights, fathers' rights have been increasing during the past two decades. While child support reform is not responsible for the shift in fathers' rights, it is compatible with such a shift and will most likely strengthen the current trend. Second, as mentioned earlier, increasing payments will increase fathers' motivation to monitor the expenditure of child support dollars, and joint legal custody is one way of increasing fathers' decision-making power vis-à-vis the mother. We should note that some people believe that fathers will use joint legal custody not only as a means of controlling expenditures but as a way of reducing the amount of their child support obligation. If this is true, joint legal custody may have a negative feedback effect on child support awards and payments.

What can the empirical literature tell us about the relationships among child support, visitation, and custody? And what are the implications for child support reform? To answer the first question, numerous studies have found that paying child support and visitation are complementary activities, that is, fathers who pay child support are more likely to spend time with their children (Seltzer & Schaeffer, 1989; Furstenberg et al., 1983; Seltzer, Schaeffer, & Charng, 1989; Chambers, 1979). This relationship persists even after controlling for differences in socioeconomic characteristics such as parental income, education, length of marriage, and number of children, and it appears to grow stronger over time. With respect to legal custodial arrangements, Seltzer has found that custody has no effect on the average size of payments once social class is taken into account (Seltzer, 1989). Fathers with joint legal custody pay more support than fathers without custody because the former have more resources than the latter. In sum, Seltzer's research indicates that fathers are *not* using legal custody as a way of avoiding support, at least not those fathers who currently have joint custody (Seltzer & Schaeffer, 1989).[10]

No existing research demonstrates cause-and-effect relationships among payments, visitation, and custody. Chambers suggests that fathers who pay support and visit their children regularly may simply have a stronger commitment to their family than fathers who fail to provide either economic or emotional support. Whether child support reform can increase such a commitment remains to be seen.

Parental contact and the potential for conflict

The arguments presented thus far emphasize the potential positive effects of child support reform. Increases in payments are expected to improve the economic status and security of mother-only families, which in turn should improve children's socioeconomic achievement. In addition, increases in payments, and anticipated increases in payments, are expected to strengthen father–child relations by increasing the amount of time fathers spend with their children and by increasing fathers' decision-making roles in child rearing.

Not everyone views child support reform in such a positive light. Some critics argue that increasing the amount of awards and strengthening collection will lead to greater parental conflict which, in turn, will reduce children's well-being. According to this view, divorced (or never-married) parents will not be able to carry out their coparenting activities without expressing the conflicts and hostilities that led them to separate in the first place. If this is true, joint custody and increases in father–mother contact may undermine the positive gains obtained from greater economic security and increased father–child contact.

There are several reasons for expecting contact between parents to increase. First, visitation and joint residential custody require parents to coordinate schedules and make arrangements for the father to pick up and return the children. Similarly, joint legal custody requires parents to discuss major decisions regarding their child's education as well as social activities. Thus, increases in father–child contact imply increases in parent–parent contact which, if the parental relationship is negative to begin with, may reduce child well-being.

Does increased parental contact lead to increased conflict? The best evidence to date on this topic comes from a longitudinal studies by Maccoby and Mnookin, who have been following 1,000 families who divorced during 1984 and 1985 (Maccoby & Mnookin, 1990). Based on their analysis of a subgroup of families in which father–child contact was high (an average of at least 4 hours per week), they reached the following conclusions: (1) about 33% of parents who have a good deal of contact with one another also have high levels of conflict; (2) postdivorce conflict is strongly associated with initial level of parental conflict; and (3) custodial arrangements (sole-mother, joint custody, and dual residence) are *not* related to levels of conflict.

Conflict in joint custody and dual residence families is just as high as but no higher than conflict in sole-mother custody families. On the other hand, by increasing the incentive for fathers to obtain joint or sole residential custody of their children, the child support reforms are likely to increase custody disputes.

While parental conflict is indeed an undesirable outcome, there are reasons for expecting the new child support reform to reduce conflict overall. To the extent that the current system encourages parental irresponsibility and to the extent that judicial discretion results in a considerable amount of horizontal inequity, the system itself may be said to increase uncertainty and parental conflict. Nearly all fathers know someone in similar economic circumstances who is paying less support and nearly all mothers know someone with the same needs and assets who is receiving more support. To the extent that the current system itself contributes to parental conflict, recent reforms may actually reduce hostilities. Thus, while greater parent–parent contact increases the potential for conflict, and while more custody conflicts are likely to arise, the shift toward a more rationalized child support system should reduce conflict.

Evaluating child support reform

We present a model that recapitulates what we view as the key variables that should be measured when evaluating child support provisions. Although many of these variables could be taken from either official records or survey data, we argue that the best strategy is to build upon existing surveys by selectively supplementing these data with both additional questions and some official record collection. Because we believe that the full impact of child support reform will occur over a number of years, it is essential that the data used to evaluate reform also extend over a period of time. This would mean using both longitudinal surveys and repeated cross-sectional surveys. Ideally, we would like to have baseline data on payments and other child support behavior from at least the early 1980s which could then be compared with payments and behavior through the 1990s.

The model

Figure 10.1 presents a picture of our model for evaluating child support reform. Changes in child support laws – the box at the extreme left-hand side of the picture – start the whole process. The changes increase the proportion of potential children with awards, the average level of awards, and the proportion of awards that are paid. The total increase in child support payments is much larger than the independent effects of each of the components.

Increases in child support payments affect child well-being. In Figure 10.1, child well-being is at the extreme right-hand side of the picture. The effects of child support payments on child well-being follow two routes. One is direct. Increased payments lead to increases in children's income. The second route is indirect and operates through the effect of increased payments on changes in nonresident and

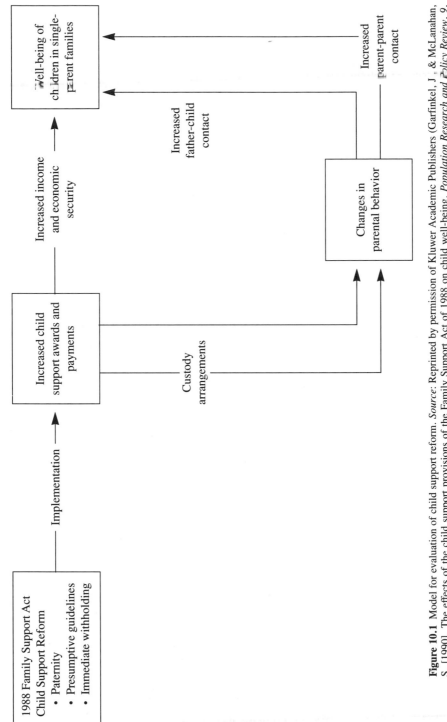

Figure 10.1 Model for evaluation of child support reform. *Source*: Reprinted by permission of Kluwer Academic Publishers (Garfinkel, J., & McLanahan, S. [1990]. The effects of the child support provisions of the Family Support Act of 1988 on child well-being. *Population Research and Policy Review, 9*, 205–234).

resident parent behavior. For example, we hypothesize that nonresident parents will spend more time with their children as a result of paying more child support. On average, this should improve child well-being.[11] On the other hand, increases in the time nonresident parents spend with their children should increase contact between the parents (former spouses) which, assuming that parental conflict is high, could be harmful to child well-being. To the extent that legislative guidelines and more routine income withholding reduce conflict between the parents, increases in contact should have no negative consequences for children. Finally, child support reform also affects residential and legal custodial arrangements which, in turn, alter parent behavior and parent–child relationships.

Variables and potential data sources

The key variables in our model are: receipt of an award (whether a child with a nonresident parent has an award); legal and physical custody agreements; amount of the original award and whether payments are automatically withheld from earnings; level and stability of payments; amount of contact between the nonresident parent and the child and the quality of the parent–child relationship; amount of contact between the resident and nonresident parents and the quality of the parent–parent relationship; and indicators of child well-being. The latter include measures of school achievement (e.g., grades, attendance, cognitive test scores) and measures of social and psychological adjustment.

The three major data sets

The strategy we recommend for evaluating the effects of the child support provisions of the Family Support Act of 1988 is to utilize existing nationally representative data sets and to selectively supplement these data collection efforts. The following discussion focuses on three data sets: the Child Support Supplements to the March CPS (CSS-CPS), the National Survey of Families and Households (NSFH), and the National Longitudinal Survey of Youth, Child Survey (NLSY-Child). Each of these data sets has unique advantages; while none of them is perfect, together they will enable us to identify changes in key variables and relationships among the variables in our evaluation model. Upon reflection, other data sets may be even better suited for some parts of the evaluation.

The Current Population Survey (CPS). The March CPS is a nationally representative sample of 50,000 households that gathers information on income and demographics. Beginning in 1979 and continuing biannually since 1982, the March CPS has been used to identify a sample of mothers with children potentially eligible for child support. These mothers are reinterviewed about their child support status in April of the same year, and the two files are merged. The Child Support Supplement includes questions about whether the mother was initially awarded child support. If the answer is no, she is asked to explain why; if the answer is yes, she is asked about the amount of payments due in the previous year and the amount actually paid. In addition, questions about child support services received are included.

The major advantages of the CPS-CSS are its large sample size, its long baseline data series of cross-sections, and its detailed information on awards and payments. The CPS is a random sample of 50,000 households, including 3,500 mothers in the child support supplements. The CPS-CSS was first conducted in 1979 and has been conducted every other year since 1982. Garfinkel and Robins have recently begun using the CPS-CSS to evaluate the effects of the 1984 Child Support Act.

A major weakness of the CPS-CSS data is their limitation to children who live apart from their fathers. Eventually this design will vitiate its usefulness for evaluating the effects of child support reforms on child support payments. To the extent that one of the consequences of the child support reforms is that the number of children living with their fathers and apart from their mothers increases, the CPS-CSS sample will become increasingly unrepresentative of children potentially eligible for child support. For this reason, we recommend that the CPS-CSS sample be extended to include children who live apart from their mothers.

Another limitation in the CPS-CSS is the lack of data on visitation or other forms of contact between the nonresident parent and the child and how this affects the child's well-being. The only information on child well-being is school enrollment (available for children currently living in the household). This can be used to determine whether child support payments are related to finishing high school. For the CPS-CSS to regularly include questions on visitation, contact, and child well-being would increase the length of the interview and thereby increase costs and perhaps decrease quality by increasing refusals and noncompletions. Moreover, the NSFH and NLSY-Child contain such data. If the sample sizes of the NSFH or NLSY prove to be too small, however, it may make sense to collect such data in the CSS every third or fifth time.

The National Longitudinal Survey of Youth (NLSY). The NLSY is a survey of approximately 13,000 young men and women who have been interviewed annually since 1979. The sample consists of a national sample of civilian and military respondents between the ages of 14 and 21, with overrepresentation of poor whites, blacks, and Hispanics. The panel contains extensive information on respondents' school, employment, and family formation behavior as well as information on annual household income and sources of income (earnings, public and private transfers). For respondents who become parents, the survey asks about child care utilization and parental time with children. For respondents who become single parents, either because of divorce or out-of-wedlock birth, the survey asks about child support payments and visitation between the child and nonresidential father.

In 1986 and 1988 the children of NLSY female respondents were given an extensive set of tests designed to measure their cognitive, socioemotional, and physiological development (Chase-Lansdale, Mott, Brooks-Gunn, & Phillips, 1991). The child measures vary according to the age of the child, which ranges from 1 month to 12 years. The child sample consists of nearly 5,000 children, including about 2,400 whites, 1,600 blacks, and 900 Hispanics. When combined with the information on parents in the NLSY panel, the child assessment data provide an excellent means of examining the relationship between family environment and child well-being. Analyses of the NLSY-child data are currently under way. If extended to child support issues, such analysis will provide baseline data for subsequent evaluations of child support reform (Chase-Lansdale, Michael, & Desai, 1991; Brooks-Gunn & Baydar, 1991).

The major advantages of the NLSY data are the high quality of the child well-being measures, the longitudinal design, and the large sample of children. As currently structured, the NLSY survey can be used to evaluate several components of the child support model outlined above. Specifically, the annual information on child support, alimony, and visitation can be used to estimate changes in the level of payments; effects of child support payments on child well-being; and effects of payments on father–child contact and child well-being. The fact that children are followed over time allows us to examine the effects of changes in child support payments on changes in child well-being.

The major limitations of the NLSY data are the lack of representations of children; the absence of information on children living with their fathers; and the difficulty in linking child support and paternity to specific children in the family. Because the child sample is limited to children born to mothers who were between 14 and 21 in 1979, it is not representative of all children – for example, all children over 8 years old in the 1986 supplement were born to teenage mothers since none of the mothers are over 28. This limitation is self-correcting to some extent: As the NLSY women grow older, the child sample will become increasingly representative. However, children in the upper age ranges will continue to overrepresent those born to teenage mothers.

The second limitation in the NLSY-Child data arises from the fact that all of the children in the survey are living with their natural mothers. Thus, we cannot examine the effects of child support on the well-being of children who live apart from their mothers. Moreover, it means that the information on payments and father–child contact is based on the mothers' reports. While at first glance these would appear to be serious problems, recent analyses comparing mothers' and fathers' responses to questions about child support indicate that the mother's report is consistent with information on income tax records. Moreover, even though we cannot examine the well-being of children living with their fathers, we can determine where the child lives and therefore whether child support reform alters residential custody. Because we have complete fertility histories on all of the NLSY women, we can identify cases in which children no longer live with their mothers.

We recommend several additions to the current NLSY questionnaire that would increase its usefulness for evaluating child support reform. First, adding a question on the regularity of payments would enhance our ability to evaluate the impact of stability of payments along with the level of payments on child well-being. Ideally, we would like to obtain retrospective information on the stability of payments dating back to the time of the original award. Second, obtaining mothers' reports of the quality of father–child relations and the level of parental conflict would be useful in helping assess the net effect of payments on child well-being.

The National Survey of Families and Households (NSFH). The NSFH is a representative sample of approximately 13,000 households in the United States in 1987, including an oversample of single-parent families, black families, and recently married couples. The survey contains detailed information on family relationships, including parent–child relationships and parent–parent relationships. For children with a nonresidential parent, the survey asks about legal agreements regarding child support and physical custody, the level and stability of current child support payments, the quantity and quality of time spent with nonresidential parents, and the level of agreement or conflict between parents. Child well-being is based on parents' responses to questions concerning school achievement as well as psychological and social adjustment. Several NICHD projects are currently using the NSFH data to examine the relationships among child support payments, custodial arrangements, visitation, parent–child relations, parent–parent relations, and child well-being. A follow-up survey of NSFH respondents was planned in 1992 and includes about 500 children whose parents divorced between 1987 and 1992.

The NSFH survey has three major advantages over other data sets. First, no other survey contains such extensive information on the financial aspects of child support, including level and stability of formal payments, informal contributions, and property settlements; and custodial arrangements, including legal custody, residential custody, and visitation. Second, no other survey contains such detailed information on the quality of parent–child relationships and parent–parent relationships. Finally, no other survey collects information on children living apart from their mothers and no other survey collects fathers' reports as well as mothers' reports on all aspects of parental behavior and child well-being.

The major limitation of the NSFH is sample size. The 1987 survey contains information on approximately 1,500 children who were eligible for child support. Estimates indicate that the follow-up survey will yield approximately 500 additional children whose parents divorced between 1987 and 1992. This makes it difficult to examine race differences in child support patterns and it also limits our ability to examine atypical family arrangements, such as children of divorced families who live with their fathers. In addition to supporting the planned follow-up of the NSFH survey, we recommend two changes or additions: that retrospective information be collected on the original amount of child support awards for respondents who divorced or had an out-of-wedlock birth between 1987 and 1992, and that child well-being information be supplemented with data from children's school records.

The three surveys discussed above are by no means the only possible databases for evaluating child support reform. Given our interests in children's well-being, however, they seem the most likely candidates at the present time. Other longitudinal data sets that should be considered in light of possible extensions and modifications are the Panel Study of Income Dynamics (PSID), the NLS Class of 1972 survey, and the High School and Beyond.

Conclusion

With funding from the Ford Foundation and the Foundation for Child Development, we have begun to pursue the research agenda laid out in this chapter. To establish a baseline for the late 1980s against which the experience in the 1990s can be compared, we organized a conference on child support and child well-being and published the papers as chapters in a monograph (Garfinkel, McLanahan, & Robins, 1994). Four chapters examined the extent to which child support reforms were being implemented and the effects of the reforms on child support payments. The papers found significant differences across jurisdictions in implementation and collection effectiveness. Two chapters investigated the effects of alternative forms of an assured child support benefit, including New York State's CAP program. Both the costs and benefits of CAP were small. Not surprisingly, both the benefits and costs of a non–income tested assured benefit were found to be significantly larger. Finally, four chapters, utilizing four different data sets, analyzed the effects of child support payments on child well-being. All four papers found a strong positive relationship between payments and well-being. Taken as a whole, these papers suggest the potential fruitfulness of further research on child support and child well-being.

NOTES

1. In effect, Wisconsin was to be given a block grant to run both a child support assurance stem and the AFDC system at the same cost to the federal government as the old AFDC system alone. Extra costs or savings were solely to be borne by, or to be of benefit to, the state.

2. The literature described in this section of the chapter includes studies of children from divorced families, children born to never-married mothers, and children living in single-parent families. For more detailed discussion of the research in this area, see McLanahan and Sandefur (1994).

3. For a more complete discussion of the mechanisms linking family disruption to children's achievement, see McLanahan and Sandefur (1994).

4. All but a handful of states now have guidelines similar to those of Colorado or Wisconsin (National Center for State Courts, 1989). For a comparison of the two, see Garfinkel and Melli (1990) and Garfinkel (1992).

5. This assumes that earnings of nonresident parents increase by 5% per year and that in any given year one-third of the orders are up to date, one-third are 1 year behind, and one-third are 2 years behind.

6. Note that in each survey all women with children under the age of 21 who are potentially eligible for child support are interviewed. Thus, in each survey the child support awards had been made between 1 and 20 years earlier.

7. The lower and upper bounds are calculated in two different fashions. To obtain the 11%, the increases in child support payments in the control counties were subtracted from the increases in child support payments in the pilot counties. The increases in each case are calculated by subtracting collections in the 3 years (1981–83) before the pilot counties implemented routine income withholding from child support collections in the 3 years (1984–86) after implementation. For two reasons this estimate is a lower bound. First, the pilot counties utilized immediate withholding of child support obligations in only about 80% of the cases in which it was feasible. Second, the control counties turned out to be imperfect controls in that they utilized immediate income withholding in an increasingly large percentage of cases. Although the pilot counties utilized immediate withholding more than twice as often as the control counties in the first 2 years after the pilots began, by the third year the difference between the control counties and pilot counties in utilization rates was only 12 percentage points. Thus, the difference between pilot and control county increases in child support collections is almost certainly an underestimate of what the impact on national child support collections will be of full implementation of immediate withholding.

To obtain the 30%, child support collections of those without immediate income-withholding orders were subtracted from child support collections of those with immediate income-withholding orders. Although this upper bound was calculated with the aid of statistical techniques designed to control for other differences between those who are and are not subject to immediate income withholding, it is clear that the controls are imperfect. For example, if the nonresident parent has no income, it is impossible to utilize income withholding. In 20% of the court records used in the evaluation, there was no information on the income of the nonresident parent. Thus, it was not possible to perfectly control for this possible difference between those with and those without income assignments. Obviously, those with no income will pay less child support than those with income. To the extent that the absence of income can only be imperfectly controlled for, the difference between child support collections of those who are and are not subject to immediate income withholding will be an overestimate of the effect of routine income withholding on national child support collections.

8. The figures are obtained by multiplying total child support collections in 1983 of $6.8 billion times 0.11 and 0.30 respectively.

9. There is at least one reason for expecting that increases in payments could reduce father–child contact. Assuming that fathers have a constant level of commitment with respect to their children, and assuming that time and money are substitutes for one another, it is possible that increasing payments will reduce the amount of time fathers spend with their children.

10. Seltzer and Schaeffer (1989) find that while the average level of support in joint-custody families is similar to that in sole-custody families, the relationship between fathers' income and payments is stronger in joint-custody families than in mother-custody families. This suggests that in joint-custody families, payments are more closely related to fathers' circumstances. This has two implications for child well-being. First, in low-income families, it means that payments may be slightly lower, although reductions in money contributions are offset by increases in time contributions. Second, it may increase fathers' perceptions of fairness, which may affect father–child relations as well as father–mother relations.

11. As noted above, increased contact between nonresident fathers and children may not always have beneficial effects. Specifically, in cases where the father is abusive, increased contact would make children worse off than before. On balance, however, we believe that more contact with the father is desirable and that children will be better off overall if fathers play a more active role in rearing their children.

REFERENCES

Abrahamson, A., Morrison, D., & Waite, L. (1988). *Beyond stereotypes: Who becomes a single mother*. Santa Monica, CA: Rand Corporation.

Astone, N. M., & McLanahan, S. S. (1991 June). Family structure, parental practices, school completion. *American Sociological Review, 56*, 309–320.

Bane, M. J. (1986). Household composition and poverty. In S. H. Danziger & D. H. Weinberg (Eds.), *Fighting poverty: What works and what doesn't*. Cambridge, MA: Harvard University Press.

Brooks-Gunn, J. B., & Baydar, N. (1991). *The relationship between child support payments, parent–child contact, and child well-being*. Paper presented at the Conference on Child Support and Child Well-Being, Arlie House, VA.

Bumpass, L. (1984). Children and marital disruption: A replication and update. *Demography, 21*, 71–82.

Bumpass, L., & McLanahan, S. S. (1989). Unmarried motherhood: Recent trends, composition, and black–white differences. *Demography, 26*, 279–286.

Cassetty, J. (1978). *Child support & public policy: Securing support from absent fathers*. Lexington, MA: D. C. Heath.

Chambers, D. (1979). *Making fathers pay: The enforcement of child support*. Chicago: University of Chicago Press.

Chase-Lansdale, P., & Hetherington, E. M. (1990). The impact of divorce on life-span development: Short- and long-term effects. In P. B. Baltes, D. C. Featherman, & R. M. Lerner (Eds.), *Life-span development and behavior* (Vol. 10, pp. 107–157). Hillsdale, NJ: Erlbaum.

Chase-Lansdale, P. L., Michael, R., & Desai, S. (1991). Maternal employment during infancy: An analysis of children of the National Longitudinal Survey of Youth (NLSY). In J. Lerner and N. L. Galambos (Eds.), *Employed mothers and their children*. New York: Garland.

Chase-Lansdale, P. L., Mott, F., Brooks-Gunn, J., & Phillips, D. A. (1991). The Children of the NLSY: A unique research opportunity. *Developmental Psychology, 27*, 918–931.

Cherlin, A. J., Furstenberg, F. F., Jr., Chase-Lansdale, P. L., Kiernan, K. E., Robins, P. K., Morrison, D. R., & Teitler, J. O. (1991). Longitudinal studies of effects of divorce on children in Great Britain and the United States. *Science, 252*, 1386–1389.

Corcoran, M., Gordon, R., Laren, D., & Solon, G. (1987). The association between men's economic status and their family and community origins. *Journal of Human Resources, 28*(4), 575–601.

Douthitt, R. A. (1990). *A comparison of time spent with children by mothers in single- versus two-parent households*. Madison: Department of Consumer Science, University of Wisconsin.

Duncan, G. J., & Hoffman, S. D. (1985). A reconsideration of the economic consequences of martial disruption. *Demography, 22*, 485–498.

Emery, R. E. (1982). Inter-parental conflict and the children of discord and divorce. *Psychological Bulletin, 92*, 310–330.

Emery, R. E., & O'Leary, K. D. (1984). Marital discord and child behavior problems in a non-clinic sample. *Journal of Abnormal Child Psychology, 12*, 411–420.

Furstenberg, F. F., Morgan, S. P., & Allison, P. D. (1987). Paternal participation and children's well-being after marital dissolution. *American Sociological Review, 52*, 695–701.

Furstenberg, F. F., Nord, C. W., Peterson, J. L., & Zill, N. (1983). The life course of children of divorce: Martial disruption and parental contact. *American Sociological Review, 48*, 656–668.

Garfinkel, I. (1992) *Assuring child support: An extension of Social Security*. New York: Russell Sage Foundation.

Garfinkel, I., et al. (1988). *Evaluation design for the Wisconsin child support assurance demonstration*. Madison: Institute for Research on Poverty, University of Wisconsin.

Garfinkel, I., & Klawitter, M. (1990). The effects of routine income withholding on child support collections. *Journal of Policy Analysis and Management, 9*, 155–177.

Garfinkel, I., & McLanahan, S. S. (1986). *Single mothers and their children: A new American dilemma*. Washington, DC: Urban Institute Press.

Garfinkel, I., McLanahan, S. S., & Robins, P. K. (1994). *Child support and child well-being*. Washington, DC: Urban Institute Press.

Garfinkel, I., & Melli, M. (1982). *Child support: Weaknesses of the old and features of a proposed new system* (Special Report 32A). Madison: Institute for Research on Poverty, University of Wisconsin.

Garfinkel, I., & Melli, M. (1990) The use of normative standards in family law decisions. Developing mathematical standards for child support. *Family Law Quarterly, 24*(2), 157–178.

Garfinkel, I., & Oellerich, D. (1989). Non-custodial fathers' ability to pay child support. *Demography, 26*, 219–233.

Garfinkel, I., Oellerich, D. T., & Robins, P. K. (1991). Child support guidelines: Will they make a difference? *Journal of Family Issues, 12*(4), 404–429.

Graham, J. W., & Beller, A. H. (1988). Child support payments: Evidence from repeated cross sections. *American Economic Review, Papers and Proceedings, 78*, 81–85.

Herzog, E., & Sudia, C. E. (1973). Children in fatherless families. In B. Caldwell & H. N. Ricciuti (Eds.), *Review of child development research* (Vol. 3). Chicago: University of Chicago Press.

Hetherington, E. M., Cox, M., & Cox, R. (1978). The aftermath of divorce. In J. H. Stevens, Jr., & M. Matthews (Eds.), *Mother-child father-child relations*. Washington, DC: National Association for the Education of Young Children.

Hill, M. S., Augustyniak, S., & Ponza, M. (1987). *Effects of parental divorce on children's attainments: An empirical comparison of five hypotheses*. Photocopy. Ann Arbor: Survey Research Center, Institute for Social Research, University of Michigan.

Hogan, D. P., & Kitigawa, E. M. (1985). The impact of social status, family structure and neighborhood in the fertility of black adolescents. *American Journal of Sociology, 90*, 825–855.

Kidder, R. L. (1986). Legal impact: Does law make any difference? In *Connecting law and society*. Englewood Cliffs, NJ: Prentice-Hall.

Knox, V., & Bane, M. J. (1991). *Effects of child support payments throughout childhood on adult attainment*. Paper presented at the Conference on Child Support and Child Well-Being, Arlie House, VA.

Krause, H. O. (1981). *Child support in America: The legal perspective*. Charlottesville, VA: Michie.

Krein, S. F., & Beller, A. H. (1988). Educational attainment of children from single-parent families: Differences by exposure, gender, and race. *Demography, 25*, 221–224.

Maccoby, E. E., & Mnookin, R. H. (1990). Co-parenting in the second year after divorce. *Journal of Marriage and the Family, 52*, 141–155.

Matsueda, R. L., & Heimer, K. (1987). Race, family structure and delinquency: A test of differential association and social control theories. *American Sociological Review, 52*, 826–840.

McLanahan, S. S. (1985). The reproduction of poverty. *American Journal of Sociology, 91*, 873–901.

McLanahan, S. S. (1988). Family structure and dependency: Early transitions to female household headship. *Demography, 25*, 1–16.

McLanahan, S. S., Astone, N. M., & Marks, N. (1991). The role of mother-only families in reproducing poverty. In A. Huston (Ed.), *Children and poverty* (pp. 51–78). New York: Cambridge University Press.

McLanahan, S. S., & Booth, K. (1989). Mother-only families: Problems, prospects, and politics. *Journal of Marriage and the Family, 51*, 557–580.

McLanahan, S. S., & Bumpass, L. (1988a). Intergenerational consequences of marital disruption. *American Journal of Sociology, 94*, 130–152.

McLanahan, S. S., & Bumpass, L. (1988b). Comment: A note on the effect of family structure of school enrollment. In G. Sandefur & M. Tienda (Eds.), *Divided opportunities: Minorities, poverty, and social policy*. New York: Plenum.

McLanahan, S. S., & Sandefur, G. (1994). *Growing up with a single parent: What hurts, what helps*. Cambridge, MA: Harvard University Press.

National Center for State Courts, Washington Project Office. (1989). *Child support guidelines summaries*. Arlington, VA.

National Commission on Children. (1991). *Beyond rhetoric: A new American agenda for children and families*. Final report of the National Commission on Children. Washington, DC.

Nichols-Casebolt, A., & Garfinkel, I. (1991). Trends in paternity adjudications and child support awards. *Social Science Quarterly*, *72*, 83–97.

Nock, S. (1988). The family and hierarchy. *Journal of Marriage and the Family*, *50*, 957–966.

Oellerich, D. T. (1990). The income distributional impacts of private child support transfers in the United States. In J. K. Brunner & H. G. Petersen (Eds.) *Simulation models in tax and transfer policy* (pp. 399–421). Frankfurt/New York: Campur Verlag.

Oellerich, D. T., Garfinkel, I., & Robins, P. K. (1991). Private child support: Current and potential impacts. *Journal of Sociology and Social Welfare*, *18*, 3–23.

Pearson, J., Thoennes, N., & Tjaden, P. (1989). Legislating adequacy: The impact of child support guidelines. *Law and Society Review*, *23*, 569–590.

Robins, P. K. (1992). Why did child support award amounts decline from 1975 to 1985? *Journal of Human Resources*, *27*, 362–379.

Rutter, M. L. (1971). Parent-child separation: Psychological effects on children. *Journal of Child Psychology and Psychiatry*, *12*, 233–260.

Rutter, M., & Quinton, D. (1977). Psychiatric disorder: Ecological factors and concepts in causation. In H. McGurk (Ed.), *Ecological factors in human development*. Amsterdam: North Holland.

Sandefur, G. D., McLanahan, S., & Wojtkiewicz, R. A. (1992). The effects of parental marital status during adolescence on high school graduation. *Social Forces*, *71*(1), 103–122.

Sawhill, I. V. (1983). Developing normative standards for child support payments. In J. Cassetty (Ed.), *The parental child support obligation*. Lexington, MA: D. C. Heath.

Schaeffer, N. C., Seltzer, J. A., & Klawitter, M. (1991). Estimating nonresponse and response bias: Resident and nonresident parents' reports about child support. *Sociological Methods and Research*, *20*, 30–59.

Schorr, A. (1966). The family cycle and income development. *Social Security Bulletin*, *29*, 14–25.

Seltzer, J. (1989). Legal and physical custody arrangements in recent divorces. *Social Science Quarterly*, *21*, 250–266.

Seltzer, J. A., & Bianchi, S. M. (1988). Children's contact with absent parent. *Journal of Marriage and the Family*, *50*, 663–678.

Seltzer, J., & Schaeffer, N. C. (1989). *Another day, another dollar: Effects of legal custody on paying child support and visiting children*. Paper presented at the American Sociological Association meeting, San Fransisco, CA.

Seltzer, J., Schaeffer, N. C., & Charng, H. (1989). Family ties after divorce: The relationship between visiting and paying child support. *Journal of Marriage and Family*, *51*, 1013–1031.

U.S. Bureau of the Census. (1981). Current Population Report ([CPR], Series P-23, No. 112). *Child support and alimony: 1978*. Washington, DC: U.S. Government Printing Office.

U.S. Bureau of the Census. (1986). Current Population Reports ([CPR], Series P-23, No. 148). *Child support and alimony: 1983*. Washington, DC: U.S. Government Printing Office.

U.S. Bureau of the Census. (1987). *Statistical abstract of the United States: 1988*. Washington, DC: U.S. Government Printing Office.

U.S. Bureau of the Census. (1989). Current Population Reports ([CPR], Series P-23, No. 154). *Child support and alimony: 1985*. Washington, DC: U.S. Government Printing Office.

U.S. Commission on Interstate Child Support. (1992). *Supporting our children: A blueprint for reform*. Washington, DC: U.S. Government Printing Office.

U.S. House of Representatives, Committee on Ways and Means. (1989). *Background material and data on programs within the jurisdiction of the Committee on Ways and Means* (1989 ed.). Washington, DC: U.S. Government Printing Office.

Wallerstein, J. S., & Kelly, J. B. (1980). *Surviving the breakup: How children and parents cope with divorce*. New York: Basic Books.

Weiss, R. (1978). Growing up a little faster: The experience of growing up in a single-parent household. *Journal of Social Issues*, *35*, 97–111.

Weiss, Y., & Willis, R. (1985). Children as collective goods and divorce settlement. *Journal of Labor Economics*, *3*, 268–292.

Weitzman, L. (1985). *The divorce revolutions*. New York: Free Press.

White, K. R., & Stone, R. T. (1976). A study of alimony and child support rulings with some recommendations. *Family Law Quarterly, 10,* 83.

Williams, R. (1991). *Implementation of the child support provisions of the Family Support Act: Child support guidelines, updating of awards, and routine income withholding.* Paper presented at the Conference on Child Support and Child Well-Being, Arlie House, VA.

Wisconsin Department of Health and Social Services. (1979). *Wisconsin welfare study 1978: Report and recommendations of the welfare reform study advisory committee.* Madison, WI.

Yee, L. M. (1979). What really happens in child support cases: An empirical study of the establishment and enforcement of child support awards in the Denver district court. *Denver Law Quarterly, 57,* 21.

VI. Future policy and research directions

11   Losing ground or moving ahead? Welfare reform and children

Ron Haskins

Introduction

It was a telling moment. The Human Resources Subcommittee of the powerful Committee on Ways and Means was about to approve what a liberal witness correctly predicted would be the high-water mark of welfare reform. After 2 years of hearings, immense background research by the Congressional Research Service and the Congressional Budget Office, endless drafts of bills, and repeated negotiations between the administration and Capitol Hill Democrats and Republicans, on April 9, 1987, the subcommittee passed, on a straight party-line vote following rancorous debate, a bill that provided many new welfare benefits but contained no strong work requirements. Before the final subcommittee vote, it was time for politicians to wax eloquent. Harold Ford, the black Democrat chairman of the subcommittee, gave a moving speech about poverty, the importance of the subcommittee bill, and his own childhood. He reminisced about the trials his family had faced, about how hard his father had worked, and about the importance of schooling. Above all, he emphasized the importance of welfare benefits in supporting the development of poor children. In fact, he argued that his greatest desire was to establish a minimum national benefit in the Aid to Families with Dependent Children program, but that budget pressures prevented him from doing so in the bill the subcommittee was about to approve.

It was a passionate, personal speech, typical of the kind good politicians can cook up at a moment's notice. When he finished, the audience, composed primarily of children's advocates who strongly supported the subcommittee bill, applauded – a respectful, supportive applause.

Hank Brown, the senior Republican on the subcommittee and the unquestioned leader of Republican welfare reform in the House, looked pensively over at Ford, seated perhaps 2 feet from Brown on the dais facing the audience. Brown, who had been reared in modest circumstances by a single mother and had worked his way through college and law school, graciously complimented the chairman on his effective leadership of the subcommittee and his victory over the outnumbered

Republican forces. Amidst laughter on all sides, he told Chairman Ford he was sorry to hear that Republicans had been "easy to work with" on the welfare bill. Brown then paused for a very long time and looked out over the people packed into Room B-318 of the Rayburn House Office Building, most of whom would strongly disagree with what he was about to say. As usual, he started gently: "We have just done the worst possible thing we could do to America's poor families. We have passed a bill that will make them even more dependent on welfare and even less dependent on their own efforts. I'm going to do everything I can to kill this bill."

It is a commonplace observation that politics, especially the politics of welfare reform, is complex. Even so, it is surprising how much understanding can be achieved by keeping elementary facts squarely in view.

Congressmen Harold Ford and Hank Brown represent the fundamental point of disagreement in America's longstanding debate on welfare and even, more generally, of all government programs intended to help the unfortunate. Virtually all Americans agree that the old and disabled should receive public benefits, as in fact they do. Spearheaded by Social Security, Medicare, and Supplemental Security Income, the nation's programs for the elderly and disabled have been spectacularly successful in reducing poverty. If in-kind benefits are counted, the poverty rate among the elderly has plummeted to around 6% (U.S. Bureau of the Census, 1992a, p. 100).

But public benefits for the able-bodied is another matter. Many Americans believe that people who can should work. Other Americans believe society has a responsibility to give things – money, food, housing, health care – to those who can but do not work, especially if they are single parents. As was inevitable from the start, Congress compromised on this fundamental issue when it passed the Family Support Act of 1988 some 18 months, and 1,000 political deals, after the evocative Ford–Brown debate. The final bill contained numerous benefit expansions – of the welfare program for two-parent families, of Medicaid coverage, of child support enforcement services, of day care, and of education and training – but many of these benefits could also be used by welfare families to prepare for, find, begin, and sustain work. Moreover, the Job Opportunities and Basic Skills (JOBS) Training program established by the bill required states, for the first time, to involve a specific percentage of their welfare caseloads in job preparation activities; by 1995 at least 20% of the nonexempt AFDC caseload (10% of the entire caseload) had to participate in education, training, or employment activities.

Within 4 years after implementation of the Family Support Act, somewhat contradictory information about its impacts began to appear (Friedlander, Riccio, & Freedman, 1993; Hagen & Lurie, 1992; see also the summer 1992 issue of *Public Welfare*). By 1993 welfare reform was once again a surprisingly hot topic in state capitals and in Washington. President Clinton's repeated emphasis on "ending welfare as we know it" since taking office and his appointment of David Ellwood and Mary Jo Bane of Harvard as assistant secretaries in the Department of Health and Human Services implied that the president intended to deliver on his campaign promise. For its part, as early as 1993 Congress was poised to undertake major welfare reform legislation, as shown by the introduction of several major reform bills, one of which was sponsored by over 160 Republicans in the U.S. House of Representatives.

It is in the context of implementation of the Family Support Act of 1988, sharp disagreement about whether welfare reform is aimed at more welfare or more work, dramatic expansion of the welfare rolls, and serious proposals for yet another round of welfare reform that the editors of this volume have wisely decided to adopt a somewhat unique perspective on welfare reform. In a word, the unique perspective is that of children. Don't get me wrong. I know politicians love children and talk about them often. Congressional debate on the Family Support Act did not suffer from a shortage of references to helping children. But in truth, the actual policy decisions made in congressional passage of the act betrayed only slight calculation of impacts on children, and much of the current reform talk ignores children or, at most, involves mere platitudes about the impacts of reform on children – in part because nobody knows much about the impact of either welfare or welfare reform on children.

But this serious deficiency in social science knowledge seems to be changing. Thanks in large part to the activities of the Department of Health and Human Services, developmental psychologists, economists, and a few foundations, there is a nascent and, one hopes, growing movement to determine what impact the Family Support Act is having on children. Within a few years, we should have empirical information from experimental studies of whether and how the Family Support Act has influenced children's behavior and development.

There is, of course, every reason to worry about the future of children on welfare. At the most obvious level, these children are members of families that have serious financial problems. In 1990 the average cash income from AFDC payments and earnings for the 4 million families on AFDC was around $5,100 per year (Committee on Ways and Means, 1992, pp. 675–677), less than 5% lived in a house owned by their parents, and only 17% had any countable assets. Financial and asset destitution at a given moment is only part of the story; a very large percentage of the families on welfare are dependent on public benefits for many years. Of the 4.8 million families enrolled in AFDC in June 1992, about 3 million have been or will be on welfare in 8 or more years (extrapolated from Bane & Ellwood, 1983). Senator Moynihan has succinctly captured the long-term material condition of children dependent on AFDC: "They are paupers – not a pretty word; but not a pretty condition either."

Data from the University of Michigan's Panel Study of Income Dynamics show that around 22% of all children and 72% of black children born between 1967 and 1969 were on welfare at some time before their 19th birthday (Duncan, Laren, & Yeung, 1991). More interesting, however, is the number of children on welfare for extended periods during their childhood. Direct measures are not available, but with a certain bravery in extrapolation, we can generate an estimate. According to the

Duncan et al. study (see their Table 1), about 8% of all children and 42.4% of black children spent 7 years or more on welfare. If we assume that these same percentages applied in 1992, we can calculate that about 5.3 million children live in families that will be on welfare for 7 or more years. Of these children, 4 4 million or more than 80% are black (U.S. Bureau of the Census, 1992b, pp. 4–5).

In addition to being at risk for poor development because of poverty and welfare, AFDC children are also at a disadvantage because, to use the delicate language of Zill and his colleagues, parent–child interactions in "some welfare families may not foster optimal child development" (this volume). Scholars and advocates tend to dance around this issue, despite the fact that the logic of preschool intervention programs has always been that the learning experiences of a good program will promote the development of poor children more than staying at home with their own parents.

There is an extensive literature on differences in parenting practices of middle-income and low-income parents. This literature shows both that there are several dimensions of parent–child relations – warmth, avoidance of physical punishment, setting expectations and maintaining discipline, use of language – that differentiate the behavior of middle- and low-income parents and that these dimensions are correlated with measures of children's development. Nearly all of the studies show that the parenting practices adopted by middle-income parents are associated with better child outcomes (see Haskins, 1986). This conclusion is supported by time-use studies, conducted primarily by economists, which show that middle-income parents spend more time with their children and that time spent with children is correlated with advanced development (Leibowitz, 1974).

So here is the problem defined in this volume. We are concerned, not just with adults dependent on welfare, but with how public policy can help their children. At any given moment, the nation has at least 5.5 million children in the midst of long welfare spells who are at great risk of growing up badly. These children have three substantial obstacles to overcome, all of which are associated with poor developmental outcomes: the poverty of their families (Huston, 1991; Hill & O'Neill, 1992), the single-parent (and often never-married) composition of their families (Garfinkel & McLanahan, 1986), and the demographic characteristics (Jencks, 1972, 1979) and child-rearing practices (Haskins, 1986) of their parents.

There is little disagreement that children on welfare are more likely than other American children to have problems as children and as adults. But thinking about what public policy should aim to achieve with these children is not nearly as clear. Perhaps the most frequently encountered goal is that we should try to create conditions to help children reach their full potential. Years of exposure to rousing chapters, journal articles, and political speeches about helping children reach their full potential have led me to a certain skepticism about the wisdom of this goal. First, I have never understood how we would know when children have reached their full potential. Second, much of the empirical literature about intervention to stimulate development attempts simply to document that a given intervention has produced a significant increase in some desirable trait such as IQ or school achievement. Third, I doubt that reaching full potential is the goal the American taxpayer has in mind. Finally, as I hope to show, years of experience with intervention programs should leave us with a certain humility about what is possible.

For all these reasons, I want to posit a simpler, more understandable, and more measurable goal. The major objective for children's programs should be to help them arrive at late adolescence or early adulthood with the ability to achieve financial independence. Reflecting on this goal suggests an interesting perspective on the purpose of public spending for children. Most American children arrive at adolescence or young adulthood ready to occupy a productive place in our society. They are prepared to achieve independence by some combination of what might be called the routine socializing forces of American society: family, church, community organizations, peer group, and the educational system. This group of young Americans is not a focus of federal social policy. But there is another group, perhaps 10% of each age cohort, which arrives at early adulthood unprepared to achieve financial independence by legitimate means. Their characteristics are all too familiar: disproportionately black and Hispanic, from low-income and welfare-dependent families, delinquent, school dropout, pregnant or parenting before marriage, little or no work experience, out of the labor force, and so forth. These are the children we want to help.

There are now, and have been for at least three decades, three general approaches to helping these youngsters achieve independence:

- public cash and in-kind assistance to help poor and low-income families provide a good child-rearing environment for their children (the *welfare strategy*)
- intervention programs that attempt to stimulate the health or development of children judged, primarily on the basis of family demographic characteristics, to be at risk for poor development (the *intervention strategy*)
- employment and training programs that help young parents, especially single mothers, achieve financial independence through work (the *work strategy*)

My purpose in this chapter is to examine evidence on the impact of each of these approaches on children's development and, more specifically, their readiness to achieve financial independence as young adults.

Growing toward self-sufficiency

The welfare strategy

Through a process of accretion, the federal government has created a set of some 330 programs that provide low-income citizens with cash, housing, food, health care, and social services worth at least $250 billion in 1993. Claims that federal spending on these programs declined over the past decade are wrong. Table 11.1 shows constant dollar spending in 1980 and 1991 on the largest individual programs or combinations of programs designed to help children and families. Over the period,

Table 11.1. *Federal spending on major programs for children and families, 1980 and 1991*

Program	Year		Change	
	1980	1991	In $	In %
Foster care and adoption	$ 465	$ 2,269	$ 1,804	388.0
Earned income tax credit	3,263	8,806	5,543	169.9
Medicaid	23,716	52,533	28,817	121.5
Subsidized housing	7,696	13,554	5,858	76.1
Dependent care tax credit	1,571	2,650	1,079	68.7
Head Start	1,208	1,952	744	61.6
Supplemental Security Income	10,894	15,926	5,032	46.2
Food stamps	15,492	18,684	3,192	20.6
Selected health programs	15,653	18,650	2,997	19.1
Aid to Families with Dependent Children	12,418	13,520	1,102	8.9
Social services	10,690	11,526	836	7.8
Child nutrition	8,010	8,362	352	4.4
Education	25,584	25,106	−478	−1.9
Unemployment compensation	30,673	27,084	−3,589	−11.7
Training and employment	18,073	5,388	−12,685	−70.2
Totals	$185,406	$226,010	$ 40,604	21.9

Sources: Falk, Rimkunas, & Martin, 1992, pp. 59, 85, 107, 135; Committee on Ways and Means, 1992, pp. 847, 1025, 1019, 1696.
Note: Figures in millions of constant 1991 dollars.

there was a small decrease in federal education expenditures, a more substantial decrease in unemployment compensation (caused primarily by changes in state laws and by a lower unemployment rate in 1991 than 1980), and very substantial decreases in training and employment programs (recommended by President Reagan and approved by Congress, primarily because evaluations showed the programs to be ineffective and because they were subject to graft at the local level). Despite these reductions, the 12 other program areas grew by more than $57 billion in constant dollars, bringing average growth in all 15 program areas to nearly 22%.

Table 11.2 shows changes in constant-dollar spending on safety net programs between 1979 and 1991. Although there is no widely accepted definition of the safety net, I simply selected the major programs that provide cash, food, health care, and housing to poor and low-income families. Spending on families with children in safety net programs increased even more rapidly than spending on the programs summarized in Table 11.1. The average increase across the five programs between 1979 and 1991 was 54% (although the per capita value of AFDC declined by nearly 15%). Nor was this increase due simply to an increase in the number of poor people; spending per person in poverty (before federal taxes and benefits) increased from $2,803 in 1981 to $3,796 in 1991, an increase of around 35%.

The point of this blizzard of numbers is that the federal government has never spent more money on poor and low-income families than it now does. In order to

Table 11.2. *Changes in federal and state spending on safety net programs between 1979 and 1991*

Program	Year					Percent change	
	1979	1981	1989	1990	1991	1979–91	1981–91
AFDC	$22.5	$22.5	$22.0	$22.9	$24.0	6.7	6.7
Food stamps	8.8	12.8	12.0	13.4	15.9	80.7	24.2
Child nutrition	7.7	7.4	7.6	7.9	8.3	7.8	12.2
Medicaid	13.5	14.2	19.4	23.2	29.8	120.7	109.9
Housing*a*	4.2	5.6	8.8	9.1	9.3	121.4	66.1
Total	56.7	62.5	69.8	76.5	87.3	54.0	39.7
Persons in poverty*b*	17.6	22.3	20.7	22.2	23.0	30.7	3.1
Spending per person in poverty	$3,222	$2,803	$3,372	$3,446	$3,796	17.8	35.4

Sources: Poverty data from Census Bureau; spending data from Congressional Budget Office or Congressional Research Service.
Note: Figures in billions of constant 1991 dollars. Figures include spending on families with children only.
*a*Excludes spending for housing aid administered by the Farmers Home Administration. Because there are no housing expenditure data specifically on households with children, estimates by the Congressional Budget Office involved a series of calculations based on simplifying assumptions.
*b*Millions of persons living in married-couple families with children and in female-householder families with children; poverty definition is before transfers from government means-tested programs but after state and federal taxes (Census Bureau definition #11); see U S Bureau of the Census, 1992a, pp. 109, 111.

obtain the most general possible picture of the impact of federal and state taxes and spending on the income of American families, Republican members of the Ways and Means Committee asked the Census Bureau to conduct special analyses of income data from the Current Population Reports (see U.S. Bureau of the Census, 1992a, for analyses of this sort). In particular, we divided families into five groups of equal size (called quintiles) and then determined the net amount of taxes paid by families and government benefits received by families. To obtain an idea of whether the net amount of government taxes and spending had changed in the past decade, the Census Bureau used the earliest (1979) and most recent (1991) year for which it had the type of data required for this analysis.

The results are portrayed in Figure 11.1. As shown by the dark bar graphs, the net effect of taxes and spending on families was highly progressive in 1979. The average family in the bottom quintile enjoyed net benefits of $9,546 while the average family in the top quintile paid net taxes of $19,862; the middle three quintiles fell between these extremes in progressive fashion. By 1991 the impact of government taxing and spending had become even more progressive. Every quintile except the top was better off in 1991 than in 1979 – the bottom two quintiles because their net benefits had increased, the third and fourth quintiles because their net taxes had decreased. The magnitude of increased benefits was substantial for the

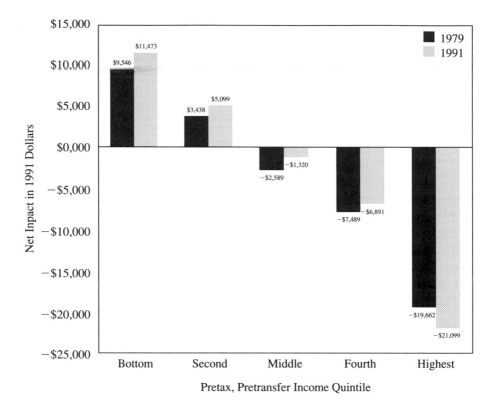

Figure 11.1 Changes in net government benefits and taxes for households between 1979 and 1991 by income quintile.

bottom two quintiles. Families in the bottom quintile enjoyed net benefits of $11,473 in 1991, nearly $2,000 or 20% higher than in 1979. Even more impressive, families in the second quintile had a 50% increase in net benefits. By contrast, families in the top quintile paid $1,237 or 6% more in net taxes than in 1979.

These facts about federal taxes and spending serve as a useful starting point for an analysis of poverty spending. It should be reassuring to those advocating for children to know that Congress and recent administrations have been responsive to the needs of children, and that the federal government is taking money away from upper-income families and giving it to lower-income families.

But the question before us is whether these benefits promote the development and adult success of children from poor and low-income families. There is ample evidence that absence of money is detrimental to children's development and their prospects upon reaching adulthood. There is a huge literature, for example, on the impacts of family socioeconomic status on children's educational achievement and adult employment (Coleman, 1966; Jencks, 1972, 1979). There is also a growing literature on the short- and long-term impacts of growing up in poverty on children's futures. Reviews of the evidence by Huston (1991) and others show, in many cases unequivocally, that poor children suffer from a series of conditions and outcomes that may not provide adequate support for subsequent development: inferior prenatal care; more maternal health problems; more infectious diseases and hospitalization during childhood; a higher incidence of illegitimate births and single-parent families; neighborhoods characterized by crime, violence, and a high incidence of single-parent families; families with no workers; families living on welfare; schools that are inferior by many standards; and a host of other conditions that wealthier parents spend lots of time and money trying to avoid.

Many of the circumstances to which poor children are consigned by fate are correlated with poor outcomes. There are, of course, children who succeed despite these constraints (Werner & Smith, 1982), but on average these children have a lot to overcome. If our yardstick is economic independence as adults, it is not surprising that many fail.

But the abundant evidence that poverty is associated with impeded development provides at best indirect evidence that the welfare strategy will improve children's outcomes. Despite the fact that the federal government has conducted major welfare programs since at least 1935, there is surprisingly little direct evidence about the impact of these benefits on children. Most Americans agree that, regardless of the empirical evidence, it is obligatory for government to ensure a basic level of existence to children, the disabled, and the elderly – citizens, in short, who are not expected to work. But to justify these benefits or additional benefits on the grounds that children's development will be enhanced requires evidence. This is a role developmentalists, as well as other scholars, are now trying to fill.

If scholars are to bring quality evidence to bear on this issue, and thereby elevate debate and improve policy, the best way to produce the evidence is through well-designed experiments. Children from poor families should be assigned randomly to experimental and control groups; the experimental group should receive additional benefits – more (or better) food, health care, housing, cash, and so forth. Then the children should be followed to determine whether there are long-term impacts.

Fortunately, some evidence of this type is already available. Beginning in the late 1960s the federal government conducted four income maintenance experiments in which several thousand families in seven states were provided with a guaranteed income (sometimes called a "negative income tax"). Various combinations of guarantee levels, in many cases equivalent to over $19,000 in 1991 dollars, and tax rates on earned income, generally between 30% and 80%, were tested, primarily to determine the impact of welfare income on work effort. All the experiments also gathered at least some information on the impact of guaranteed income on the health or education of participating families and their children (for an overview, see Munnell, 1987).

Although these data are not extensive, they do provide some support for the generalization that increased family income can have beneficial effects on children.

Most of the evidence is succinctly reviewed by Hanushek (1987; see also Mallar & Maynard, 1981), who argues that the experiments provided moderately strong evidence that a guaranteed income increased years of schooling by adolescents but weak evidence of impacts on school achievement. Even so, Hanushek concludes that increased schooling and high school graduation "by youth may be one of the positive sidelights of a negative income tax" (p. 117). Similarly, the experiment conducted in Gary, Indiana, produced evidence of reduced fertility among mothers (Wollin, 1978) and increased birth weight of babies born to families receiving the guaranteed income (Kehrer & Wollin, 1979); the experiment in North Carolina produced evidence of better nutrition among children in experimental families (O'Connor & Madden, 1979; Salkind & Haskins, 1982). As with the evidence on schooling, these results were not consistent across sites or treatment groups.

Taken together, the studies from the income maintenance experiments, although far from definitive, do support the conclusion that higher levels of welfare income can produce positive effects on children. On the other hand, there is no information on whether these effects last for even a year after the financial supplements end.

There are many arguments for supporting increased funding of welfare programs on behalf of children, but it is not possible to argue, based on the evidence currently available, that the welfare strategy will have much impact on children's development or the probability they will be financially independent as adults. But the correlational evidence suggests that such an effect is plausible, and the small amount of experimental evidence does nothing to undermine this suggestion. It is now incumbent on developmentalists and other social scientists who want to strengthen the argument for the welfare strategy to initiate new experiments. In the meantime, the case for increased welfare must rest primarily on value arguments.

The intervention strategy

If evidence on the welfare strategy is skimpy, the evidence on interventions designed to promote early development is moderate to abundant. Given the Brooks-Gunn chapter on intervention programs in this volume, I will touch only lightly on these studies, especially those of early intervention programs. I divide the literature on programs aimed at promoting development into three categories: infant programs, early childhood programs, and adolescent and young adult programs.

Intervention with expectant mothers and infants. The interventions designed to promote healthy births and adequate development in the first year of life are diverse and fascinating. Although there are now many such programs and perhaps a few dozen careful evaluations, three reports convey the outcomes that can be reasonably expected.

One of the more remarkable intervention programs of recent years is addressed to reducing low birth weight and promoting the early development of infants from low-income families. As reported in a series of publications by Olds and his colleagues (e.g., Olds, Henderson, Tatelbaum, & Chamberlin, 1988), the intervention was a prenatal and postpartum home visitation program for poor women having their first baby. Over 80% of the 400 mothers who participated were either under age 19, unmarried, or of low socioeconomic status. Mothers were randomly assigned to one of four groups: two control conditions, a home visitation during pregnancy, or a home visitation during pregnancy and up to age 2. Nurse visitors tried to form what Olds calls a "therapeutic alliance" with the mothers by focusing on the mothers' strengths while carrying out three activities: (1) education on the effects of smoking, drinking, and drug use; (2) guidance on enhancing social support by relatives and friends; and (3) assistance in obtaining locally available health and human services.

Several outcomes are notable. During pregnancy, the entire group of nurse-visited mothers improved their diets and reduced the number of cigarettes smoked more than women who were not visited. Two groups of nurse-visited women – those below the age of 17 and those who smoked when they joined the study – gave birth to heavier babies and had longer gestation periods than women who were not visited.

After birth, poor, unmarried, teen mothers who were nurse-visited had 75% fewer verified cases of child abuse than other mothers. Further, the poor and unmarried mothers who received nurse visits worked 82% more during the 46 months after birth than control mothers, they punished and restricted their infants less in the home, and they had 43% fewer subsequent pregnancies. An analysis of the costs and benefits of the program (Olds, Henderson, & Phelps, n.d.) showed that for poor women in the sample, about 90% of the $3,400 cost of the program was recovered in the 4 years after birth through increased taxes, reduced welfare expenditures, reduced Medicaid expenditures, and reduced expenditures for abuse and neglect services. There are few parallels to these impressive results in the literature on social intervention programs.

A second large-scale study illustrating what can be accomplished with infant programs was designed to promote the development of low birth weight, premature infants (Infant Health and Development Program, 1990). This project provided comprehensive intervention consisting of three parts: home visits weekly for the first year of life and biweekly for years 2 and 3, full-time care in a child development center when children were 2- and 3-year-olds, and bimonthly parent group meetings to provide parents with information on child rearing, health, and safety as well as social support. The home visits and center program followed a curriculum of several hundred activities designed to promote the physical and intellectual growth of children in the first 3 years of life (Sparling & Lewis, 1979).

The 985 infants who participated in eight geographically diverse projects were subdivided into heavier preterm infants (those between 2001 g and 2500 g) and lighter infants (those below 2001 g). Parents at the eight sites, over half of whom were black and over half of whom had less than a high school education, brought their infant to a clinic for assessments several times between birth and 36 months of age. Assessments consisted of parent reports of behavioral competence, parent reports of several measures of health status, and tests of intellectual development.

Infants who received the intervention had higher IQs at 36 months, with the heavier intervention group receiving almost average IQs (mean = 98) and the lighter group averaging 91 as compared with an average score of about 85 for controls. Infants in the intervention groups were also reported by their mothers to have fewer behavioral problems. Finally, mothers of the lighter experimental infants reported fewer illnesses, although on five other measures of growth and health status experimental and control infants did not differ.

This study is the largest multisite, randomized study of infant intervention ever attempted, and it produced impacts on IQ scores of nearly one standard deviation (15 IQ points) in the heavier group of premature infants by age 3. Moreover, looking behind the mean IQ scores, we find that in the group of infants with birth weights between 2001 g and 2500 g, only 5% of the intervention group but 18% of the control group had IQs below 70, a seriously low IQ level with substantial clinical significance. Unfortunately, a follow-up study conducted when the children had reached age 5 found that the group differences had narrowed (Brooks-Gunn et al., 1994).

A third set of evidence on infant interventions is summarized by a recent study of the Special Supplemental Food Program for Women, Infants, and Children (WIC) conducted by the U.S. General Accounting Office (1992). The popular WIC program provides low-income pregnant women, infants, and children with nutrition supplements, nutrition education, and health referrals; in 1990 about 4.5 million women, infants, and children participated.

The GAO study estimates that, during the first year of life, WIC produces $2.89 in savings for every $1 invested – and even greater savings thereafter. Savings are realized through reduced expenditures for initial hospitalizations, outpatient services, and rehospitalizations – all of which are in turn due to the decreased incidence of low birth weight and very low birth weight infants. Savings after the first year of life are based on reductions in expenditures on disability programs and special education.

Although the GAO study is thorough and innovative, the assumptions and methods underlying the study bear careful examination. To produce their estimates of WIC impacts on low birth weight, GAO averaged data from 17 studies (see their Table II.1, p. 55). Only one study (Metcoff, 1985), however, used random assignment and that study found no impacts of WIC on the incidence of low birth weight babies. Given the widespread sentiment among researchers that quasi-experimental designs yield questionable results, the basic data in the GAO analysis are somewhat suspect.

Further, as pointed out by the Department of Agriculture's critique of the analysis (see Appendix VI of the GAO report), GAO overestimated the size of the WIC-eligible population used to generate the estimates of cost savings. In addition, the weighing method used to combine the 17 studies relied heavily on a 1990 study (U.S. Department of Agriculture, 1990) that focused on very-low-income women. Because very-low-income women are more likely to have low birth weight infants than other women, generalizing from this group to the entire WIC-eligible population produces an overestimate of savings. Finally, GAO overlooked the possibility that, ironically enough, WIC could increase some medical costs if babies that ordinarily would have died are saved but then require high rates of medical and educational services.

As these three studies imply, evaluations of infant intervention programs show that well-designed and carefully delivered education, nutrition, and behavior modification services, especially smoking reduction, can improve birth outcomes and that center-based and home-visitor infant programs can produce at least short-term impacts on intellectual development. Moreover, the WIC studies suggest that large-scale programs, and not just hot-house, university-affiliated programs, can produce good effects. Nonetheless, there is no evidence on whether the effects of these interventions last into the elementary school years, let alone into young adulthood. Label them hopeful.

Intervention with preschool children. Arguably, there is more solid research information about the effects of preschool education than any other type of intervention program. This research shows that both high-quality, small-scale research projects and typical Head Start programs can produce short-term impacts of 5 to 10 IQ points as well as similar impacts on school achievement. More impressive still, the high-quality, small-scale research projects can produce long-term impacts on grade retention and placement in special education (Darlington, Royce, Snipper, Murray, & Lazar, 1980; Haskins, 1989; Lazar, Darlington, Murray, Royce, & Snipper, 1982). There is some evidence that these programs reduce delinquency and crime (Zigler, Taussig, & Black, 1992), and inconsistent evidence of impacts on welfare use (Haskins, 1989). These findings are especially important because most of the studies on which they are based meet the highest standards of good research, including random assignment and longitudinal designs.

Unfortunately, there is inconsistent evidence of impacts on employment, the variable of greatest interest for our purposes in this chapter. Four preschool projects participating in the Consortium for Longitudinal Studies obtained evidence on employment when the children had reached ages 19 to 22; three of the four found no significant impacts (Royce, Darlington, & Murray, 1983). By contrast, the Perry Preschool Project produced several impacts on employment and earnings when children had reached age 19 (Berrueta-Clement, Schweinhart, Barnett, Epstein, & Weikart, 1985). These results lead to the conclusion that it is possible but difficult to produce impacts on employment with high-quality, small-scale preschool programs. There is no evidence that typical preschool programs can produce impacts on employment.

As impressive as the findings from preschool programs are, the greatest weakness in this literature is that virtually all of the studies of long-term effects involved high-quality, small-scale programs. If preschool intervention is to help the millions of children of welfare-dependent families prepare for financial independence, it must be demonstrated that the hopeful results achieved by small projects like those in the Consortium for Longitudinal Studies and the Abecedarian project (Campbell & Ramey, 1992; Ramey & Campbell, 1991) can be achieved on a broad scale throughout the country by programs employing typical facilities and teachers. Head Start, of course, is such a broad-scale program, but despite the sometimes extravagant claims for its effectiveness, research simply does not show that Head Start produces long-term gains in IQ, school achievement, special class placement, grade retention, welfare use, crime and delinquency, or employment (Haskins, 1989; McKey et al., 1985; White, 1985–86).

Intervention with adolescents and young adults. For several decades, conventional wisdom has held that the early years are especially important for human development. Some theories even held that there were "critical periods" during which certain abilities or behaviors had to develop; if they did not, they would never develop adequately (White, 1975). This theory supported the idea that early childhood education was crucial if the poor development of kids from low-income families were to be avoided. Hence, the critical period and early experience jargon entered the public and even the political vocabulary and was used to support government funding for infant and preschool programs.

As early as 1976, however, Clarke and Clarke assembled impressive evidence showing that the critical importance of early experience to human development was, as they put it, a "myth." Though some developmentalists and educators still hold the view that early experience is somehow more crucial than later experience, there seems to be a growing consensus that experience at every stage of development is important, and that gains during early periods can be lost if children are returned to difficult environments while deprivation during infancy and early childhood can be ameliorated by later experience (Brim & Kagan, 1980).

Regardless of one's views on early experience, few would be willing to simply write off adolescents from poor families who demonstrate poor development and school achievement. Even more to the point, many of the interventions used with struggling adolescents are juxtaposed in time with the outcome I have argued is most fundamental: financial independence. For millions of teenagers, graduation from high school at age 18 marks the beginning of the time when they are expected to achieve independence; for those who have babies at an earlier age and for those who drop out of school before age 18, the need to achieve independence occurs even earlier. There is a certain logic to the claim that the moment when teens begin to realize they must provide for themselves is precisely the moment when they would be most receptive to intervention, especially if the intervention can be tied to the promise of success in the job market.

And, in fact, a growing number of programs are trying to help disadvantaged adolescents move into the productive economy. At least two multicity and carefully evaluated programs have aimed at increasing school achievement and postsecondary education of disadvantaged teens. The STEP program conducted by Public/Private Ventures (Walker & Vilella-Velez, 1992) in five cities provided 14- and 15-year-olds with a half day job, instruction in reading and math, and classes on practical issues such as sex, drugs, and careers during the summer. About 75% of the adolescents who started the program came back for a second summer. Although initial impacts on both reading and math were encouraging, a follow-up conducted 3 years later showed no differences in school completion, college attendance, pregnancy, or employment.

A similar project conducted by the Manpower Demonstration Research Corporation obtained only somewhat more encouraging results (Cave & Quint, 1990). Over 1,200 adolescents who had completed their junior year and planned to go to college participated in workshops during the summer and during their senior year. Workshops included preparing for college entrance exams, obtaining financial aid, and planning careers. Students were also supposed to be provided with an adult mentor who would serve as a role model and help them study and prepare for college, but only about 65% of the students actually received the mentoring. Even so, interviews 1 year after high school completion showed that college attendance was increased by around 10% for the experimental group (53% versus 48% for controls).

Though important, programs designed to promote college attendance by teens are probably not as critical to welfare reform as programs for poor teen mothers. In 1990, the most recent year for which statistics are available, there were almost 533,000 births to teens, up about 61,000 or 13% in just 3 years. Over 360,000 of the births were to unmarried mothers (Moore, Snyder, & Halla, 1993).

It would be difficult to overemphasize the role of these births in accounting for poverty, welfare use, and inner-city problems in general. A recent study by the Congressional Research Service (Gabe, 1992) suggested that between 50% and 70% of the spectacular rise in welfare caseloads between 1989 and 1992 was due to the increase in births to unmarried mothers. Similarly, the inability of the 1980s economic boom to remove more families from poverty is accounted for in large part by the increase in out-of-wedlock births. The mathematics of this development is simple enough. The poverty rate for families headed by never-married mothers is nearly 60% (Gabe, 1993); that for married-couple families is about 8% (U.S. Bureau of the Census, 1992b, p. 6). As the number of married-couple families held steady throughout the 1980s at around 26 million, the number of female-headed families increased by nearly 20% to 7.7 million. Because the divorce rate was nearly constant throughout the 1980s, the increase in female-headed families was caused exclusively by the increase in unmarried births. Given these demographic shifts, even though the poverty rate within both married-couple and female-headed families declined, the overall child poverty rate declined little because of the increasing proportion of households headed by unwed mothers with their exceptionally high poverty rates.

If demography is destiny, it is no surprise that perhaps the most serious consequence of these demographic shifts is increased welfare dependency. "Love and
marriage go together like a horse and carriage," according to the old song; the
updated version is that illegitimate birth and welfare go together. At the time of the
birth, only about 13% of unmarried adolescent mothers are on welfare. But within 1
year, the percentage jumps to 50; within 5 years, to 77. Among blacks, 84% are on
welfare within 5 years (Congressional Budget Office, 1990). These striking numbers have been translated into annual costs to taxpayers by the Center for Population
Options (1992). The center estimates that in 1990 taxpayers spent $25 billion for
just AFDC, Medicaid, and food stamp benefits for families started by teen mothers.

Clearly, a major cause of the nation's problem with welfare dependency is out-of-
wedlock births to teens. If successful programs for teen mothers could be developed, the battle against welfare dependency would take a great leap forward. But
the evidence on such programs is only mildly encouraging.

An early experimental program, called Project Redirection, was conducted by
MDRC beginning in 1980. Over 800 pregnant teens or teen mothers were recruited
through social welfare agencies in four cities. The intervention consisted of peer
group sessions, mentoring by a big sister, a $30 monthly stipend, and brokered
services. As compared with similar teens in other cities, a 5-year follow-up revealed
no impacts on high school graduation, employment, earnings, welfare receipt, or
subsequent pregnancies. On the other hand, mothers who received the intervention
had fewer subsequent abortions and better scores on a measure of the home environment they provided for their children; further, their children had higher verbal skills
and better social behavior. Unfortunately, these mothers also had more births than
comparison mothers.

Two recent projects with teen mothers enjoyed greater success. LEAP is a controversial program in Ohio that requires all teen mothers on welfare to attend high
school or an equivalent program and to maintain good attendance (Bloom, Fellerath, Long, & Wood, 1993). Mothers who do not attend suffer a $62 reduction in
their welfare check; mothers who enroll in high school receive an AFDC bonus
payment of $62 and an extra $62 in their paycheck each month if they stay in school
and attend regularly. In addition, money is provided for child care and transportation
and many counties provide case management to the young mothers. MDRC is
conducting a sophisticated evaluation of the program involving random assignment
of around 7,000 teens in seven counties to experimental and control groups.

Eighteen months after program entry, of girls who were in school when the
experiment began, those in the experimental group were about 20% more likely to
meet the attendance requirement (61% versus 51%). Even more impressive, of
mothers who had quit school, about 40% more of the experimental than control
adolescents had returned to school (47% versus 33%).

A similar program, called the Teen Parent Demo, was conducted by Mathematica
Policy Research in Chicago, Camden, and Newark (Maynard, Hershey, Rangarajan, & Snipper, 1992). Unmarried AFDC applicants under age 21 were randomly

assigned to an experimental or control group in all three sites. Experimental mothers were required to attend school and to participate in program activities. These activities included workshops on motivation, home management, parenting skills, family planning, drug use, child support, and employment. Parents also had the option of attending adult education or GED courses. But the heart of the intervention was case management. Social workers who served as case managers helped participants select education and training options, pressured or encouraged mothers to stick to their plans, counseled the mothers through family crises, sought out cases of non-compliance, and used sanctions when mothers refused to comply with program requirements. The major sanction was a reduction in the mother's AFDC grant by between $50 and $100 per month. More than 60% of the mothers were threatened with sanctions and over one-third of them actually received a sanction. Thus, as in the LEAP program in Ohio, sanctions were a central part of the intervention. Day care and transportation subsidies were also available to mothers, although about 80% preferred to use day care provided by relatives.

Preliminary results from the Teen Parent Demo are even more impressive than those from LEAP. Indeed, the Teen Parent Demo appears to have hit the welfare reform trifecta: more school attendance, more employment, and less welfare use by experimentals. These results are especially impressive because they were achieved with the demographic group – teen mothers – most likely to become dependent on welfare.

Materials from the Teen Parent Demo should be required reading for everyone interested in helping young mothers on welfare. During legislative consideration of welfare reform over the past decade, child advocates and many researchers have fought strongly against sanctions. Their major argument is that sanctions, especially financial sanctions, simply hurt children without motivating parents. Yet the social scientists who conducted the Teen Parent Demo argue explicitly that the program would have been ineffective without sanctions. The case managers, almost all of whom opposed sanctions when the project began, "felt strongly that their ability to reach teenage parents and help them work out their problems was greatly facilitated by [sanctions]" (Maynard et al., 1992, p. 24). The researchers' explanation for the Demo's impressive results is the combination of toughness and helpfulness provided by case managers, backed up by their ability to impose serious consequences on mothers who refused to meet requirements.

Overview of intervention programs. Peter Rossi (1987), one of the nation's leading authorities on evaluation, proposes what he calls the iron law of evaluation: "The expected value of any net impact assessment of any large scale social program is zero" (p. 4). Perhaps so, but the evaluations reviewed above provide at least partial exceptions. The point captured so succinctly, if brutally, by Rossi's iron law is that the past three decades of huge expenditures on social programs and their evaluation show that in fact it is extremely difficult to design social programs that produce impacts. All the more reason, then, to take note of some of the intervention studies reviewed above. In my view, the Consortium for Longitudinal Studies (1983), the Olds program in New York, the LEAP program in Ohio, and the Teen Parent Demo show that Rossi's law may permit some exceptions.

If we take the Consortium for Longitudinal Studies' evaluation as the apogee of what preschool programs have achieved, we cannot fail to be impressed by the fact that all the programs were small-scale, intense programs conducted by specialized staff. If Head Start, with its lack of evidence for long-term effects or good benefit–cost figures, represents what happens when small-scale preschool programs go national, we should note the fact that both LEAP and the Teen Parent Demo programs were not only large-scale but were conducted within the context of the regular AFDC program and were delivered by regular welfare workers who had received only modest training. Further, the education was provided by ordinary public schools.

Equanimity requires us to avoid concluding either that the intervention strategy is bankrupt or that it produces great successes and big savings of public dollars. Evaluations of preschool programs show that long-term impacts are possible; evaluations of adolescent programs show that large-scale interventions conducted under real-world circumstances by regular welfare workers can produce short-term impacts, including impacts on employment. There is room here for moderate optimism. Policy makers should continue to fund preschool programs and find additional funds to expand adolescent programs and to continue quality evaluations. However, the available evidence provides little support for the view that intervention programs will substantially increase economic independence among young welfare mothers.

The work strategy

In recent testimony before the Senate Committee on Finance, Wayne Bryant, the black former leader of the New Jersey State Assembly, argued that it was impossible to conduct a welfare system based on the principles of nonwork and nonmarriage and then expect its participants to join the rest of American society as workers and members of two-parent households. We teach people on welfare to "live by different rules," he claimed.

Although almost everyone agrees that inducing AFDC parents to work is desirable, there are huge differences in how people would go about it. The most straightforward way to ensure that welfare mothers join the mainstream economy is to end their cash welfare benefits (Kaus, 1992; Murray, 1984). This single action would force a revolution in their daily lives. Equally important, over a period of years it would change the thinking of adolescent females who get pregnant and then rely primarily on welfare benefits to establish their own household. It would also bring increased financial difficulty – some would say disaster – to many female-headed families.

Rather than abruptly ending welfare, some analysts argue that Congress should time-limit AFDC by establishing a limit on the number of years a family could receive unrestricted cash benefits. President Clinton, for example, has said that able-bodied welfare mothers should work after 2 years of education and training. Similarly, House Republicans have introduced legislation that would turn AFDC into a 2-tier system (Shaw, Johnson, & Grandy, 1992). In the first tier, parents would have 2 years to participate in education, training, work experience, or job search activities to help them prepare for work. After 2 years, parents still on AFDC would be required to work 35 hours a week in exchange for their AFDC, food stamp, and Medicaid benefits. In the median state, this package of benefits was worth about $12,000 in 1994.

Nor is the concept of time-limited AFDC attractive solely to conservatives. A 1986 welfare reform task force appointed by Governor Mario Cuomo, a 1989 commission report sponsored by the Ford Foundation, Harvard poverty scholar David Ellwood's heralded 1988 book *Poor Support*, and the recent bipartisan National Commission on Children (1991) all recommended time limitations on AFDC. Mickey Kaus, in his controversial book *The End of Equality* (1992), goes even further by recommending that all welfare benefits – AFDC, food stamps, housing, Medicaid – be entirely replaced by government jobs. Only those who work would receive any public benefits. That groups and individuals representing a broad spectrum of political views support the concept of time limiting or even abolishing AFDC indicates that the idea must be taken seriously.

Authors of mandatory work and welfare limitation proposals are concerned primarily about the deleterious effects of welfare on adults, especially on work incentive. Given our concern with the impact of welfare reform on children, we can broaden the list of issues that Congress must address in its consideration of time-limited AFDC:

- reduced income, especially if mothers work at very-low-wage jobs or are frequently unemployed, could lead to the type of deleterious effects on children's health and development discussed above
- increased labor force work by mothers means more nonmaternal child care; whether child care harms or helps children is a matter for serious debate
- increased labor, accompanied by responsibility for child care, transportation, shopping, routine household maintenance, and so forth, brings a tremendous amount of pressure or, as psychologists prefer, "stress," on young mothers; such stress could interfere with the mother's parenting ability
- increased labor imposes a certain regimen on family life; planning, clocks, bedtimes, and schedules assume great importance; these in turn could bring consistency and planning to many otherwise chaotic households
- the increased self-reliance achieved by substituting earned income for welfare could have positive effects on the mother's self-esteem and, in turn, on the children's perceptions of their mother; these effects could directly affect the mother's satisfaction with her life and improve family relations
- being reared in a household oriented to labor force participation could influence children's development and their future expectations through social modeling.

The evidence on most of these effects is moderate to nonexistent and does not lead to clear predictions about the impact of mandatory work on children. Consider stress. The chapter by Wilson, Ellwood, and Brooks-Gunn in this volume comes to the conclusion that not much is known about whether work by welfare mothers would induce stress and if so, whether the additional stress would have an impact on their children. Although the measurement of stress appears to be somewhat suspect, perhaps because the concept itself lacks conceptual clarity, there is some evidence that stressed parents behave differently toward their children. Zelkowitz (1982), for example, reports that poor mothers under stress were inconsistent in their use of punishment and Longfellow, Zelkowitz, and Saunders (1982) report that stressed or depressed mothers are more likely to be unresponsive, inattentive, and even hostile toward their children. If work increases stress on mothers, if mothers are unable to respond constructively to this stress, if the stress has negative impacts on the mothers' behavior toward their children, and if such behavior influences their children's development, then increased stress would be an argument against the work strategy. None of the links in this causal chain, however, are well established.

Wilson, Ellwood, and Brooks-Gunn also review evidence about the impact of work on welfare mothers' self-esteem. They summarize the research in this area as "ambiguous and unstable." Perhaps the best evidence on several psychological variables (sense of control, self-esteem, and so forth) comes from the Panel Study of Income Dynamics. After more than a decade of following the economic success of 5,000 American families, Panel Study researchers concluded that "there is virtually no consistent evidence that motivational and psychological characteristics measured in the study affect subsequent achievement, either within or across generations" (Corcoran, Duncan, & Gurin, 1985).

More research information is available on the impacts of preschool programs and child care. A number of researchers (Clarke-Stewart, 1992; Hayes, Palmer, & Zaslow, 1990; Zaslow, Moore, & Zill, 1992) have argued that low-income families are forced to use cheap and inferior child care. Some studies have produced evidence that children in poor-quality care exhibit poor development up to 3 years later. I have argued elsewhere, however, that there is little reliable information on the quality of care used by welfare mothers, on the claim that quality has major impacts on development, or on the argument that it is day care quality itself that produces the small effects reported to date (Haskins, 1992).

Moreover, recent research on the probability sample of mothers and children in the National Longitudinal Survey indicates that the proportion of time mothers spend working during the preschool years has no significant impact on their children's IQ scores (Hill & O'Neill, 1992). Although the authors present no information about the types of child care used by participating mothers, if child care had had an adverse impact on children, their IQ scores should have been affected. Other factors, including being firstborn, number of siblings, mother's IQ and schooling, and welfare use all had significant impacts on IQ. As Hill and O'Neill conclude:

"Evidently women who work extensively have provided reasonable substitutes for child care" (p. 18).

Of course, Hill and O'Neill's no-effect finding on a cross-section of families may not generalize to low-income families. Previous research with small samples found that low-income, black mothers working full-time had children with higher IQ scores (Woods, 1972), that children from poor families with working mothers had higher achievement test scores than children from families whose mothers did not work (Rieber & Womack, 1968), and that black children with single mothers had higher test scores if their mothers worked (Milne, Myers, Rosenthal, & Ginsburg, 1986).

These findings are strengthened by a recent study based on low-income mothers participating in the same National Longitudinal Survey (NLS) used by Hill and O'Neill. Vandell and Ramanan (1992) selected the oldest children in the NLS whose mothers met their criteria for low income. Of the resulting sample of 189 second-graders, 46% were black, 41% lived in poverty, 48% had single mothers, 80% had been born to adolescent mothers, and on average their mothers had less than a high school education. Vandell and Ramanan found that in this low-income sample, second-graders whose mothers had worked when the children were young attained significantly higher math and reading scores than children whose mothers had not worked. Mothers reported no differences in problem behaviors between the groups.

The implication of this study, based on a large sample, is that children from low-income families who have extensive day care during the preschool years will be as well behaved at home as those who have less day care and will actually have better school achievement in the early elementary years. Again, we do not know much about the child care these children received, but the logic of probability samples is that they received the same types of care as other poor and low-income preschool children with working mothers. Researchers who have been sounding alarms about deficient day care and long-term impacts on poor and low-income children (e.g., Hayes et al., 1990) should respond to this small but growing body of research. Even so, the questions of whether low-income families use low-quality day care and whether such care has long-term impacts on children's development must be considered unresolved.

It might appear at first glance that findings like those of Vandell and Ramanan could be used to support the argument that poor and low-income children will do better if their mothers go to work. But this argument is tenuous – and for the same reason that caution is required when interpreting much of the intervention research discussed previously: Without random assignment, selection bias is always an issue. In the case at hand, low-income mothers who work may be different in other ways from low-income mothers who do not work; these other ways can confound observed correlations or group difference and must prevent us from concluding that work itself accounts for the findings.

Much to their credit, Vandell and Ramanan investigated these selection factors in the NLS sample. They found that low-income mothers with high IQ scores and more education, mothers less likely to be in poverty, and mothers with higher scores on a measure of the home environment were more likely to work. This evidence supports the existence of selection factors in naturally occurring samples of low-income mothers who work. Hence, the studies showing that their children do better cannot necessarily be generalized to make the claim that requiring welfare mothers to work will lead to better outcomes for their children. Perhaps the most that can be claimed is that these studies are suggestive; they certainly do not support the claim that requiring welfare mothers to work will harm children.

Moving ahead

Congress is once again headed toward a battle on welfare reform. Many members of Congress, Clinton administration officials, and child advocates continue to favor the welfare strategy. Indeed, the *welfare coalition*, as we might call this influential group of policy makers and advocates, played a major role in convincing President Clinton to insert a host of welfare expansions in his 1994 budget bill. These expansions included food stamps, childhood immunizations, a food program for pregnant women and infants, public education, community development, public housing, child welfare, and home energy assistance. The 5-year cost of all these expansions would have been about $110 billion. Only a few of these initiatives were enacted, and even then only after being substantially streamlined.

Though the welfare strategy may be popular in Washington (and on college campuses), noncontingent benefits are not very popular among the American people. Polls repeatedly indicate that although Americans want to help the poor, they also think people on welfare should work. In a recent Yankelovich poll, for example, 87% of Americans favored a proposal to "require all able-bodied people on welfare, including women with small children, to work or learn a job skill." Even in Washington, perceptions about the work strategy appear to have moved a little further in the direction of former Congressman, now Senator, Hank Brown.

At least two new elements contributed to this shift. First, building on the state-level welfare reform movement of the 1980s, the fiscal pressure on state budgets prompted by the 1990 recession and the fabulous growth of Medicaid in recent years have stimulated bold reform proposals from Republican and Democrat governors alike. These proposals, quickly dubbed the "New Paternalism," focused on demanding more responsible behavior from welfare families. In addition to mandatory work, they included sanctions on parents for failure to have babies immunized or make their children attend school, reduction or elimination of additional benefits for additional babies, and creation of financial incentives for marriage and work. About 30 states have requested waivers from current law to implement New Paternalism reforms. Approved by both the Bush and Clinton administrations, these reforms are now being implemented. The upshot has been to add the prestige and authority of the nation's governors to the demand for tough welfare reform.

The second factor accounting for increased interest in the work strategy is the election of a Democrat president who campaigned on putting a 2-year limit on AFDC benefits. Both during the campaign and his first several months in office, President Clinton frequently repeated his intention to "end welfare as we know it" by providing 2 years of education and training and then requiring work.

Most Democrats on Capitol Hill, deeply committed to supporting the first Democrat to win the presidency in 12 years, are at least paying lip service to the concepts of time-limited AFDC and mandatory work. But not all Democrat lips are paying the same service. As recently as 1988, during debate on the Family Support Act, Democrats could accuse those who supported mandatory work of making welfare families "sing for their supper." Even more recently, Harold Ford, chairman of the welfare subcommittee of the Ways and Means Committee, told the *New York Times* (DeParle, 1993) that he would not even permit hearings on mandatory work. There are, in short, many Democrats for whom mandatory work is anathema.

Given the Democrats' control of the committees with jurisdiction over welfare legislation, until Clinton's election it would have been virtually impossible to pass reform bills that required work. But if the president is committed to changing welfare as we know it, and if he can bring key congressional Democrats along with him, things could get interesting on Capitol Hill. In that case, some of the most fascinating disputes in the coming welfare debate will be among Democrats.

President Clinton's support for the work strategy is especially important because many of Washington's advocacy groups are, to be circumspect, unimpressed with the idea of ending people's welfare benefits unless they work. After decades of struggle to increase the funding of safety net programs and to protect the fundamental concept of poor citizens having an "entitlement" to basic welfare benefits, the Children's Defense Fund, the Child Welfare League of America, the Center for Law and Social Policy, the Center for Budget and Policy Priorities, and other influential liberal groups can be expected to fight any attempt to make welfare benefits contingent on work. Many of these groups had grave concerns about the Family Support Act, especially the mandatory participation standards included in the act. Thus, they can be expected to fight even harder against a direct attack on the entitlement concept.

Like Mark Twain, I hesitate to make predictions, especially when they involve the future. Lots of experience with surviving foolish predictions, however, causes me to guess that in the looming debate on welfare reform, Democrats will try to focus attention on what might be called the purchase price for mandatory work. During the campaign, candidate Clinton repeatedly stated that able-bodied parents on welfare must work after 2 years. During the transition period and the first years of the Clinton presidency, however, it has become clear that the president's top advisors are setting several conditions on the administration's support for mandatory work. Generally, they fall under the rubric of "making work pay."

The most important of these conditions is expansion of the Earned Income Tax Credit (EITC). Under current law, low-income workers with children can receive cash income supplements through the tax code. In 1994 qualified workers earning less than about $24,000 were eligible for cash supplements of as much as $2,500 as well as an additional $500 to purchase health insurance. The scope of the current program is vast – 13.7 million families receive cash and tax relief worth $12 billion (Committee on Ways and Means, 1992, p. 1019).

President Clinton sent to Congress, as part of his 1994 budget, a dramatic expansion of the EITC, which was enacted by Congress near the end of the 1993 session, despite its $21 billion price tag. Under his proposal, by 1996 the upper-income eligibility limit will be raised from $24,000 to $28,500 and the maximum cash credit from $2,500 to $3,500. The Joint Committee on Taxation estimates that by 1996 nearly 19 million families will receive the credit at a cost of a little more than $25 billion per year.

A second precondition for administration support of mandatory work is universal health coverage. Under current law, families leaving welfare because of work are entitled to 1 year of Medicaid coverage. In addition, since 1986 Congress and Republican presidents have frequently expanded Medicaid coverage of poor and low-income families. Federal law now requires states to provide Medicaid to pregnant women and children under age 6 with incomes up to 133% of the poverty level (in 1993 the poverty level for a family of 4 was about $14,500). States are also required to phase in coverage of children in families with incomes below 100% of the poverty level; by 2002 all children under age 19 in families below the poverty level will be entitled to Medicaid. Finally, states have the option of providing Medicaid to pregnant women and infants under age 1 in families between 133% and 185% of the poverty level; nearly half the states have taken advantage of this option to cover additional women and children.

Despite these expansions, there appears to be strong support among advocates and Democrats in Congress and the administration for some sort of long-term health care guarantee for families leaving welfare. Thus, the welfare reform debate will include serious conflict about whether Medicaid should be expanded further before families can be required to work. In all likelihood, the administration will propose something like expanding the transition Medicaid entitlement from its present 1 year to 2, 3, or even 4 years. Republicans will then try to hold the expansion to the current 1 year.

Another of the administration's major preconditions for mandatory work is reform of the nation's child support enforcement program. Like welfare itself, the child support enforcement program seems to be in a condition of almost permanent reform. In addition to minor changes enacted on virtually an annual basis, major reform bills were passed in 1984 and 1988. The most important reforms have been to require that states use guidelines in establishing child support awards and wage withholding in all child support cases. In addition, several incentives and penalties have been established to encourage paternity establishment, a crucial issue because about a quarter of the children on welfare have mystery fathers.

The nation already has a vast and expensive Child Support Enforcement program with 230 federal and 42,000 state officials and elaborate computer facilities at the federal and state levels. Further, all states have tightened their laws several times in recent years to promote child support enforcement, and all states have procedures by which paternities are established, with blood tests playing an increasingly important role. By 1993 states and the federal government were spending about $2.2 billion conducting the Child Support Enforcement program (Office of Child Support Enforcement, 1993, p. 49).

Child support is potentially a key ingredient of the work strategy. Not only does it provide single mothers and children with another source of income; it does so in a way that maintains work incentive. If a mother on welfare has children whose father makes child support payments, she receives an additional $50 in her monthly welfare check. If the father pays more than $50 per month, the remainder is kept by the state and federal governments as an offset to welfare payments. However, when the mother leaves welfare, all the child support money goes with her, regardless of her earnings. Note the crucial difference between child support money and any form of welfare, including the EITC. As earnings increase, welfare income declines; by contrast, as earnings increase, child support remains constant or, in the case of mothers leaving AFDC, actually increases. Given the strong work disincentives of welfare benefits, which in some income ranges suffer from an implicit tax rate of 100%, the importance of child support to the work strategy cannot be overemphasized.

But here's the problem: Only 12% of fathers whose children are on AFDC pay child support; even for this 12%, the average monthly payment is only around $200. Nor is the cause of this poor payment record the father's low income; several studies of fathers with children on AFDC show that their average income is around $15,000 per year (Shaw et al., 1992, p. 26).

For those trying to create a rational, effective welfare-to-work system, child support income is tantalizing. It maintains work incentive, saves taxpayer money, keeps child financial support within the family, and encourages responsible behavior by young men and women. But despite nearly two decades of intense federal and state effort, the Child Support Enforcement program still collects very little money from AFDC fathers. Congress is awash in proposals for improving the enforcement program: establish a national registry of child support orders, expand the efforts to establish paternity, use the Internal Revenue Service to collect child support, federalize the entire system, and so forth.

Within the next years, Congress will enact some of these reforms. The Clinton administration included a series of major child support reforms as part of its welfare reform package. But whether these reforms will succeed in boosting child support payments by fathers whose children are on AFDC is another question. If current performance were doubled, 75% of AFDC fathers would still pay nothing. More to the point, 75% of the mothers leaving AFDC for work would still not be able to count on cash assistance from the children's father.

For this reason, noted scholars such as Irwin Garfinkel (Garfinkel & McLanahan,

1986) and David Ellwood (1988) have proposed that a new federal entitlement program be created to guarantee a minimal child support payment. They argue that an assured child support benefit would represent society's guarantee that children in single-parent families would have at least some income. If states failed to collect child support, or if states did not collect an amount at least equal to the assured benefit (perhaps $3,000 per year), government would make up the difference from general revenue.

Most conservatives are strongly opposed to an assured benefit. They do not see it as an income supplement or as society's commitment to children in single-parent families. Rather, they see the assured benefit as merely another form of welfare, as a new entitlement program at a time when government already provides too many entitlements, and as a reward for getting a divorce or having a child out of wedlock. To the extent that ending welfare as we know it is held hostage to creating a child support assurance program, most Republicans can be expected to fight the bill. On the other hand, the administration may propose a compromise in which several states would conduct demonstrations on child support assurance. A number of key Republicans have already declared their support for the demonstration proposal.

In addition to an expanded EITC, guaranteed health coverage, and improved child support or an assured benefit, the Clinton administration has also supported an expansion of the minimum wage and more money for and perhaps federal oversight of day care as the price of time-limited AFDC and mandatory work. The battle lines on most of these issues are already quite clear. For the most part, Democrats want more protections and more spending, Republicans want less of both. Republicans can also be expected to point out that when candidate Clinton promised to reform welfare, he did not make it clear that adults on welfare had to have more protections against market risks than other working Americans.

For Democrats, these several issues of making work pay are paramount in the welfare debate. Republicans, though interested in the making work pay issues, will focus most of their attention on other issues. One of the most important is whether mothers will actually be required to work. Conservative Democrats and most Republicans believe the antidote to welfare is work. Previous programs, including those authorized under the Family Support Act of 1988, merely required participation. This requirement can be satisfied by attending school, going to training classes, or simply attending courses in parenting skills. These activities are fine for some initial period, perhaps 2 years, but at some point parents must be required to work for 30 or more hours per week.

There has been a great deal of talk in Washington and in the media about huge public jobs programs costing $30 billion or more. But jobs for welfare mothers who do not find their own can be established at a much lower price. Republicans have already proposed that states expand the Community Work Experience Programs (CWEP) most of them are already conducting. Parents would be working for their welfare benefits, including AFDC, food stamps, and Medicaid, a package of benefits worth around $12,000 in the median state ($3,000 more than a full-time minimum wage job). Thus, the cost of the work program could be limited to the administrative expenses of arranging the jobs, providing supervision, arranging transportation, and so forth. The Congressional Budget Office estimates these costs at $1,700 per person per year If a million mothers were in CWEP jobs, the total administrative cost would be about $1.7 billion exclusive of day care.

Another major issue for Republicans will be whether there are serious sanctions for mothers who refuse to work. Under current law, welfare departments are prohibited from doing more than reducing the AFDC grant by about one-third. Many analysts, and a majority of Republicans, believe this sanction to be too little. Once the debate begins, there will be substantial support for a permanent end to the cash AFDC benefit for the family of mothers who refuse to work, although these families would be allowed to keep their Medicaid and food stamp benefits. Without question, this issue will occasion bitter debate because it strikes directly at the concept of entitlement. Democrats and advocates will mount a ferocious attack on ending welfare for people who refuse to work.

Finally, there will, as always, be serious differences between Republicans and Democrats on cost and financing. The reforms sponsored by the Clinton administration and passed by Congress in 1993 have already increased spending by $6 or $7 billion per year on the EITC and perhaps $1 billion per year on immunizations. In addition, to pay for education, training, and work programs, and for expanded Medicaid coverage, another $3 billion or so per year would be required. This brings the total cost of Democratic welfare reform to around $11 billion per year, more than half of which has already been enacted. Republicans, by contrast, have introduced reform legislation that would cost about $2 billion per year. However, Republicans are also intent on funding the new spending by cuts in other means-tested programs, an approach that most Democrats reject. Finally, there is growing support among Republicans to reduce the federal budget deficit by, among other actions, enacting deep reductions in the growth of spending on several welfare programs including AFDC, day care, Supplemental Security Income, child nutrition, food stamps, and Medicaid.

So the battle lines are already drawn, and each side is polishing its weapons for the impending clashes. As always happens in big congressional debates, many claims and counterclaims will be based on opinion, innuendo, and partial or misleading interpretations of demographic data and scientific studies. But members of Congress might be forgiven these excesses in view of the paucity of evidence supporting any of the major reform strategies. Even more to the point, although claims of promoting child welfare will be tossed about by all sides during the debate, there is embarrassingly little good evidence about the impact of the welfare, intervention, and work strategies on children's long-term prospects. Worse, unless this round of reform is accompanied by more and better studies of impacts on children, Congress will continue its endless reform of the nation's welfare laws with only the slightest idea of whether their actions will contribute to the development of children capable of supporting themselves and their families as adults.

REFERENCES

Bane, M. J., & Ellwood, D. (1983). *The dynamics of dependence: The routes to self-sufficiency* (Report to the U.S. Department of Health and Human Services) Cambridge, MA Urban Systems Research and Engineering.

Berrueta-Clement, J. R., Schweinhart, L. J., Barnett, W. S., Epstein, A. S., & Weikart, D. P. (1985). *Changed lives: The effects of the Perry Preschool Program on youths through age 19*. Ypsilanti, MI: High/Scope.

Bloom, D., Fellerath, V., Long, D., & Wood, R. G. (1993). *LEAP: Interim findings on a welfare initiative to improve school attendance among teenage parents*. New York: Manpower Demonstration Research Corporation.

Brim, O. G., Jr., & Kagan, J. (Eds.). (1980). *Constancy and change in human development*. Cambridge, MA: Harvard University Press.

Brooks-Gunn, J., McCarton, C. M., Casey, P. H., McCormick, M. C., Bauer, C. R., Bernbaum, J. C., Tyson, J., Swanson, M., Bennett, F. C., Scott, D. T., Tonascia, J., & Meinert, C. L. (1994). Early intervention in low-birth-weight premature infants: Results through 5 years from the Infant Health and Development program. *Journal of the American Medical Association, 272*(16), 1257–1262.

Campbell, F. A., & Ramey, C. T. (1992). *Intellectual and educational outcomes in poverty adolescents with and without educational intervention in infancy, preschool and the primary grades*. Unpublished manuscript. Chapel Hill, NC: Frank Porter Graham Child Development Center, University of North Carolina.

Cave, G., & Quint, J. (1990). *Career beginnings impact evaluation: Findings from a program to disadvantaged high school students*. New York: Manpower Demonstration Research Corporation.

Center for Population Options. (1992). *Teenage pregnancy and too-early child bearing* (5th ed.). Washington, DC: Author.

Clarke, A. M., & Clarke, A. D. B. (1976). *Early experience: Myth and evidence*. New York: Free Press.

Clarke-Stewart, A. (1992). Consequences of child care for children's development. In A. Booth (Ed.), *Child care in the 1990s: Trends and consequences*. Hillsdale, NJ: Erlbaum.

Coleman, J. S. (1966). *Equality of educational opportunity*. Washington, DC: U.S. Department of Health, Education, and Welfare.

Committee on Ways and Means. (1992). *1992 green book: Background material and data on programs within the jurisdiction of the Committee on Ways and Means* (WMCP: 102–44). Washington, DC: U.S. Government Printing Office.

Congressional Budget Office. (1990). *Sources of support for adolescent mothers*. Washington, DC: Author.

Consortium for Longitudinal Studies. (1983). *As the twig is bent: Lasting effects of preschool programs*. Hillsdale, NJ: Erlbaum.

Corcoran, M., Duncan, G., & Gurin, P. (1985). Myth and reality: The causes and persistence of poverty. *Journal of Policy Analysis and Management, 4*, 516–536.

Cuomo Task Force on Poverty and Welfare. (1986). *A new social contract: Rethinking the nature and purpose of public assistance*. Albany, NY: Author.

Darlington, R. B., Royce, J. M., Snipper, A. S., Murray, H. W., & Lazar, I. (1980). Preschool programs and later school competence of children from low-income families. *Science, 208*, 202–204.

DeParle, J. (1993, June 21). Clinton aides see problem with vow to limit welfare. *New York Times*, p. A1.

Duncan, G. J., Laren, D., & Yeung, W. J. (1991). *How dependent are America's children on welfare? Recent findings from the PSID*. Unpublished manuscript, Survey Research Center, University of Michigan.

Ellwood, D. T. (1988). *Poor support: Poverty in the American family*. New York: Basic Books.

Falk, G., Rimkunas, R., & Martin, B. (1992). *1993 budget perspectives: Federal spending for the social welfare programs* (92–244 EPW). Washington, DC: Congressional Research Service

Ford Foundation. (1989) *The common good. Social welfare and the American future*. New York: Author.

Friedlander, D., Riccio, J., & Freedman, S. (1993). *GAIN: Two-year impacts in six counties*. New York: Manpower Demonstration Research Corporation.

Gabe, T. (1992). *Demographic trends affecting Aid to Families with Dependent Children (AFDC) caseload growth (93-7 EPW)*. Washington, DC: Congressional Research Service, 1992.

Gabe, T. (1993). Personal communication on out-of-wedlock births.

Garfinkel, I., & McLanahan, S. S. (1986). *Single mothers and their children: A new American dilemma*. Washington, DC: Urban Institute.

Hagen, J. D., & Lurie, J. L. (1992). *Implementing JOBS: Initial state choices*. Albany, NY: Nelson A. Rockefeller College of Public Affairs and Policy, State University of New York.

Hanushek, E. A. (1987). Non-labor-supply responses to the income maintenance experiments. In A. H. Munnell (Ed.), *Lessons from the income maintenance experiments*. Washington, DC: Brookings Institute.

Haskins, R. (1986). Social and cultural factors in risk assessment and mild mental retardation. In D. C. Farran & J. D. McKinney (Eds.), *Risk in intellectual and psychosocial development*. New York: Academic Press.

Haskins, R. (1989). Beyond metaphor: The efficacy of early childhood education. *American Psychologist, 44*, 274–282.

Haskins, R. (1992). Is anything more important than day care quality? In A. Booth (Ed.), *Child care in the 1990s: Trends and consequences*. Hillsdale, NJ: Erlbaum.

Hayes, S., Palmer, J. L., & Zaslow, M. (Eds.). (1990). *Who cares for America's children? Child care policy for the 1990s*. Washington, DC: National Academy Press.

Hill, M. A., & O'Neill, J. (1992). *The transmission of cognitive achievement across three generations*. Unpublished manuscript, Center for Business and Government, Baruch College, City University of New York.

Huston, A. C. (1991). Antecedents, consequences, and possible solutions for poverty among children. In A. C. Huston (Ed.), *Children in poverty: Child development and public policy*. New York: Cambridge University Press.

Infant Health and Development Program. (1990). Enhancing the outcomes of low-birth-weight, premature infants: A multisite, randomized trial. *Journal of the American Medical Association, 263*, 3035–3042.

Jencks, C. (1972). *Inequality: A reassessment of the effect of family and schooling in America*. New York: Basic Books.

Jencks, C. (1979). *Who gets ahead? The determinants of economic success in America*. New York: Basic Books.

Kaus, M. (1992). *The end of equality*. New York: Basic Books.

Kehrer, B., & Wollin, C. (1979). Impact of income maintenance experiments on low-birth weight: Evidence from the Gary Experiment. *Journal of Human Resources, 4*, 434–462.

Lazar, I., Darlington, R., Murray, H., Royce, J., & Snipper, A. (1982). Lasting effects of early education: A report from the Consortium for Longitudinal Studies. *Monographs of the Society for Research in Child Development, 47* (2–3, Serial No. 195).

Leibowitz, A. (1974). Education and home production. *American Economic Review, 64*, 243–250.

Longfellow, C., Zelkowitz, P., & Saunders, P. (1982). The quality of mother–child relationships. In D. Belle (Ed.), *Lives in stress: Women and depression*. Beverly Hills: Sage.

Mallar, C. D., & Maynard, R. A. (1981). The effects of income maintenance on school performance and educational attainment. In A. Khan & E. Sirageldin (Eds.), *Research in human capital and development* (Vol. 2). Greenwich, CT: JAI Press.

Maynard, R. A., Hershey, A., Rangarajan, A., & Snipper, R. (1992, October). *The wisdom of mandatory programs for welfare-dependent teenage mothers*. Paper presented at the annual meeting of the Association for Public Policy Analysis and Management, Denver, CO.

McKey, R. H., Condelli, L., Ganson, H., Barrett, B. J., McConkey, C., & Plantz, M. C. (1985). *The impact of Head Start on children, families, and communities* (DHHS Publication No. OHDS 85–31193). Washington, DC: U.S. Government Printing Office.

Metcoff, J. (1985). Effect of food supplementation (WIC) during pregnancy on birthweight. *American Journal of Clinical Nutrition, 41*, 933–947.

Milne, A. M., Myers, D. E., Rosenthal, A. S., & Ginsburg, A. (1986). Single parents, working mothers, and the educational achievement of school children. *Sociology of Education*, *59*, 125–139.

Moore, K. A., Snyder, N. O., & Halla, C. (1993). *Facts at a glance*. Washington, DC: Child Trends.

Munnell, A. H. (Ed.). (1987). *Lessons from the income maintenance experiments*. Washington, DC: Brookings Institute.

Murray, C. (1984). *Losing ground: American social policy, 1950–1980*. New York: Basic Books.

National Commission on Children. (1991). *Beyond rhetoric: A new American agenda for children and families*. Washington, DC: Author.

O'Connor, J. R., & Madden, J. P. (1979). The negative income tax and the quality of dietary intake. *Journal of Human Resources*, *4*, 507–517.

Office of Child Support Enforcement. (1993). *Sixteenth annual report to Congress* (DHHS Publication No. [ACF]93–33001). Washington, DC: U.S. Department of Health and Human Services.

Olds, D. L., Henderson, C. R., Tatelbaum, R., & Chamberlin, R. (1988). Improving the life-course development of socially disadvantaged mothers: A randomized trial of nurse home visitation. *American Journal of Public Health*, *78*, 1436–1445.

Olds, D. L., Henderson, C., & Phelps, C. (n.d.). *Impact of prenatal and postpartum nurse home visitation on government revenues and expenditures*. Unpublished manuscript, Department of Human Development and Family Studies, Cornell University.

Ramey, C. T., & Campbell, F. A. (1991). Poverty, early childhood education, and academic competence: The Abecedarian experience. In A. C. Huston (Ed.), *Children in poverty: Child development and public policy*. New York: Cambridge University Press.

Rieber, M., & Womack, M. (1968). The intelligence of preschool children as related to ethnic and demographic variables. *Exceptional Children*, *34*, 609–614.

Rossi, P. H. (1987). The iron law of evaluation and other metallic rules. *Research in Social Problems and Public Policy*, *4*, 3–20.

Royce, J. M., Darlington, R. B., & Murray, H. W. (1983). Pooled analyses: Findings across studies. In Consortium for Longitudinal Studies (Ed.), *As the twig is bent: Lasting effects of preschool programs* (pp. 411–459). Hillsdale, NJ: Erlbaum.

Salkind, N. J., & Haskins, R. (1982). Negative income tax: The impact on children and low-income families. *Journal of Family Issues*, *3*, 165–180.

Shaw, E. C., Johnson, N., & Grandy, F. (1992). *Moving ahead: How America can reduce poverty through work*. Washington, DC: Republican Staff Document, Committee on Ways and Means.

Sparling, J., & Lewis, I. (1979). *Learning games for the first three years: Guide to parent/child play*. New York: Walker.

U.S. Bureau of the Census. (1992a). Measuring the effect of benefits and taxes on income and poverty: 1979–1991. *Current Population Reports* (Series P-60, No. 182-RD). Washington, DC: U.S. Government Printing Office.

U.S. Bureau of the Census. (1992b). Poverty in the United States: 1991. *Current Population Reports* (Series P-60, No. 181). Washington, DC: U.S. Government Printing Office.

U.S. Department of Agriculture. (1990). *The savings in Medicaid costs for newborns and their mothers from prenatal participation in the WIC program* (Vol. 1). Washington, DC: Author.

U.S. General Accounting Office. (1992). *Early intervention: Federal investments like WIC can produce savings* (GAO/HRD-92-18). Washington, DC: Author.

Vandell, D. L., & Ramanan, J. (1992). Effects of early and recent maternal employment on children from low-income families. *Child Development*, *63*, 938–949.

Walker, G., & Vilella-Velez, F. (1992). *Anatomy of a demonstration*. Philadelphia: Public/Private Ventures.

Werner, E., & Smith, R. (1982). *Vulnerable but invincible: A study of resilient children*. New York: McGraw-Hill.

White, B. L. (1975). *The first three years of life*. Englewood Cliffs, NJ: Prentice-Hall.

White, K. R. (1985–86). Efficacy of early intervention. *Journal of Special Education*, *41*, 401–416.

Wollin, C. M. (1978). *Fertility of unmarried females in the Gary Income Maintenance Experiment*. Princeton, NJ: Mathematica Policy Research.

Woods, M. B. (1972). The unsupervised child of the working mother. *Development Psychology, 6,* 14–25.

Zaslow, M., Moore, K., & Zill, N. (1992). *Implications of the JOBS program for children.* Unpublished manuscript. Washington, DC: Child Trends.

Zelkowitz, P. (1982). Parenting philosophics and practices. In D. Belle (Ed.), *Lives in stress: Women and depression.* Beverly Hills: Sage.

Zigler, E., Taussig, C., & Black, K. (1992). Early childhood intervention: A promising preventative for juvenile delinquency. *American Psychologist, 47,* 997–1006.

12   National surveys as data resources for public policy research on poor children

Nicholas Zill

The eventual impact of welfare reform, such as the Family Support Act of 1988, depends greatly on the vigor and imagination with which regulations are implemented by the states. A resource that would aid both implementation and evaluation is accurate, up-to-date information on the characteristics of the welfare population of each state and of the nation as a whole. Data on the characteristics of current welfare recipients would be useful in helping state officials understand the needs and capabilities of dependent families. In order to plan services and get a sense of the kinds of occupations at which AFDC parents can realistically be expected to work, it would be helpful if state agencies had profiles of their dependent populations that included assessments of physical health and disability, functional literacy, work motivation, psychiatric impairment, and drug and alcohol use, as well as measures of educational attainment, vocational training, and work experience. Such information would make it possible to estimate the numbers of parents who would be eligible for immediate employment and the numbers who would require basic education, vocational training, or rehabilitation. Ideally, one would also like to know how many recipients need relatively limited services and how many require extensive rehabilitation and support if they are to have any hope of becoming self-sufficient.

Data on the development and well-being of AFDC children, the quality of the home environments AFDC parents provide for their children, and the calibre of substitute care available to them would help in assessing the potential harmfulness to young children of "workfare" and "learnfare" requirements such as those in the Family Support Act (see Zill, Moore, Smith, Stief, & Coiro, this volume). Such data would also help show the need for providing adequate child care and parent education.

These estimates would provide Congress, federal monitoring agencies, and child and family advocates with benchmarks against which the performance of the states could be judged. For example, the success of a work-oriented reform would be assessed quite differently if only 10% of AFDC recipients were found to be disabled

272

or of low ability than if 40% were found to be impaired in these ways. Moreover, the data would serve as reference points for determining what changes had occurred in the size, composition, behavior, and well-being of the dependent population when samples of AFDC recipients are examined in the future.

One might think that detailed data on the characteristics of welfare recipients would be readily available from the administrative records of state welfare agencies. Unfortunately, this is generally not the case. A good deal of data on AFDC recipients can be obtained from statistical surveys conducted by the federal government. However, the pertinent data are spread across various programs that differ in size, sampling procedure, and coverage. The data have not been tabulated and assembled in ways that would make them most useful for the planning and evaluation of changes in AFDC legislation.

This chapter summarizes the kinds of data about the AFDC population that are available from existing and planned surveys of families and children. It describes the current and potential uses to which these data are being and might be put in planning and monitoring public policy changes such as the Family Support Act of 1988. The chapter notes gaps in existing knowledge and recommends actions that would increase the utility of survey-based data for informing social policies affecting impoverished families.

National surveys as data resources: Relevance to AFDC families

Nearly all household surveys provide some coverage of the welfare population. But in order to determine the usefulness of a given survey as a source of information on AFDC parents or children, one must ask the following questions: Is the coverage of the AFDC population adequate? Are there questions in the survey that permit identification of families that receive AFDC? Is the sample large enough, or have low-income or minority families been oversampled, so as to furnish enough AFDC cases for meaningful analysis of this subpopulation?

Surveys that make use of the telephone or mailed questionnaires will tend to underrepresent welfare families. These families are less likely to have telephones and more likely to move frequently without leaving forwarding information than non-AFDC families. Adults in welfare families tend to have relatively low education levels, making it harder for them to deal with self-administered questionnaires. Surveys also tend to suffer from underidentification of AFDC recipients because those who have been on welfare for only short periods of time are less likely to report receipt of assistance. Of course, it is the long-term recipients who are of greatest policy interest.

In the not-too-distant past, many surveys lacked questions about the receipt of AFDC, making it impossible to identify welfare families in their samples. This was true even of some federal health and education surveys, where one might assume that questions on sources of income would routinely be included. This problem has been remedied in recent years, largely through the efforts of the Office of the Assistant Secretary for Planning and Evaluation (ASPE) in the U.S. Department of Health and Human Services.

The proportion of the population receiving AFDC payments during a given year is relatively small, about 10% of all families and 16% of all children (U.S. Bureau of the Census, 1992a, Table 7). Thus, the absolute number of AFDC recipients in a national survey sample will be small unless the sample is sizable or has been drawn so as to include an oversample of minority, low-income, or welfare families.

Making use of existing surveys

Despite the difficulties just described, there are a number of national surveys available that can help illuminate the welfare reform process. These data sets include the National Integrated Quality Control System (NIQCS), the Current Population Survey (CPS), the Survey of Income and Program Participation (SIPP), the National Longitudinal Survey of Youth (NLSY) and its Child Supplement, the National Health Interview Survey (NHIS) and its Child Health Supplement, and the National Household Education Survey (NHES). Before examining the information these data sets contain, let us consider how they might be used.

First, survey data can be used to estimate the number and types of families that will be eligible for or affected by various provisions of government programs, in particular AFDC. Second, existing data can be used to get a better understanding of the characteristics of AFDC parents and children. Better understanding may lead to more realistic and effective programs for meeting the needs and changing the behavior of AFDC recipients. Third, the surveys provide measures that could be employed in longitudinal studies of the implementation and effects of the welfare reform on AFDC participants in specific areas. Using parallel measures would allow comparisons to be made between local samples and nationally representative ones. Fourth, the surveys furnish potential baseline data for future assessments of the results of welfare reforms, after relevant laws and regulations have been in effect for a number of years.

The last application involves nationwide or state-level comparisons between what AFDC parents and children were like in the early 1990s, when the Family Support Act and other reforms were just going into effect, and what comparable populations are like in the late 1990s and beyond, after the new policies have had a chance to show results. In order to make such appraisals, the survey questionnaires or modules will have to be replicated in the future, with the relevant measures repeated closely enough to allow meaningful comparisons to be made between the present and future situations of AFDC children. In addition, it is desirable to be able to distinguish families that participated in employment training programs such as JOBS from those that did not, and to know how vigorously and in what manner training programs were implemented in different sampling areas.

Evaluations of program effects based on survey data are, of course, no substitute for social experiments using random assignment of AFDC recipients to program or control conditions. The Manpower Demonstration Research Corporation has been conducting a study under contract to the Department of Health and Human Services to do such an evaluation of the JOBS program (see Smith, this volume). Random assignment is not possible for all facets of welfare reform, however. Survey-based studies can also be valuable in giving a measure of the overall impact of particular programs on the size, well-being, and behavior of the dependent population, which the JOBS evaluation study will not provide. Modern statistical techniques permit estimates of the role of selection factors in shaping observed results (see Berk, 1983; Wainer, 1986).

Available data on AFDC parents and children

Existing surveys collect a wide range of information on AFDC parents and children. Available data include basic demographic characteristics, such as age, sex, and ethnic background; employment-related attributes of the parents; current child care arrangements and presence of household members who could potentially provide care; and amounts of child support received from absent parents. Existing data even speak to the quality of the home environments in which AFDC children are being reared, the extent to which AFDC fathers are involved in their children's lives, and the development and well being of the children themselves. Although all of this information is potentially available, much of it has not been tabulated in ways that could be helpful to planners and evaluators (see Zill et al., this volume).

The following section reviews the available data by topical area, illustrating the uses to which the data may be put, and describing some of the gaps in our knowledge of AFDC families.

Demographic characteristics of AFDC parents and children

Data on the basic demographic characteristics of AFDC parents and children in each state and in the United States as a whole are available from the National Integrated Quality Control System (NIQCS). The NIQCS is based on an annual random sample of some 67,000 recipient households drawn from the welfare case records of each state, with state samples varying in size from 300 to 2,700 cases (Family Support Administration, 1989). Information obtained includes the age, sex, race, and Hispanic origin of each adult and child in the household; the reason for the child's eligibility for AFDC; the length of time on assistance; the receipt of other assistance, such as food stamps, rent subsidies, and child support, the employment status of each adult in the household, including whether employed full-time or part-time; registration in work programs, and if exempt from these programs, the principal reason for being exempt; amounts of family income by source; income disregards; and countable assets.

For example, the NIQCS data permit estimates to be made for each state of the

numbers of persons who are eligible for the JOBS program of the Family Support
Act of 1988, under both the mandatory requirement that parents with children aged
3 years and above participate, and the optional provision that parents with children
aged 1 year and above participate. Estimates of this sort were made by Zill and Stief
(1989a) with NIQCS data for fiscal year 1987. They show that extending eligibility
from women with children aged 6 years and above to women with children aged 3
years and above increases the number eligible for work programs from 1,044,000 to
1,756,000, and increases the proportion of eligible adult female AFDC recipients
from 32% to 54%. Extending eligibility further to women with children aged 1 year
and above expands the pool of eligibles to 2,561,000 women, or 79%.

Estimates can also be made of the numbers of persons who fall into groups that
are given high priority by the Family Support Act, such as young parents and
parents who are about to become ineligible for AFDC because their youngest child
will turn 18. When Zill and Stief (1989b) cross-tabulated the ages of AFDC mothers
against the ages of their youngest children, they found that relatively few young
mothers had children aged 3 years and over. Of some 802,000 AFDC mothers under
age 24, only 168,000, or 21%, had children 3 and over. Coupled with high attrition
rates from work-related programs, these data suggest that states may have to include
young mothers with children aged 1–2 in their programs in order to get sufficient
numbers of this high-priority group.

Limitations of the NIQCS. The NIQCS data have serious gaps. Information on
parent educational attainment is virtually useless because of extensive missing data.
Furthermore, in states that do not now have the AFDC-Unemployed Parent program, the NIQCS tells nothing about the characteristics of two-parent families that
are eligible for the program under the Family Support Act.

Using CPS and SIPP data. In order to fill these gaps, it is possible to make use of
data from the March Supplement to the Current Population Survey (CPS) and the
personal history module of the Survey of Income and Program Participation (SIPP).
Both the CPS and the SIPP contain data on the educational attainment of AFDC
parents and the characteristics of two-parent families that have become eligible for
assistance under the mandated AFDC-UP program. The SIPP also contains information on characteristics of families that leave the AFDC rolls (U.S. Bureau of the
Census, 1991a).

The CPS and SIPP samples do not allow for state-level statistics the way the
NIQCS does, although by combining data from 2 or 3 years of surveys, state-level
estimates for the 10 to 12 largest states can be made using CPS data. The CPS is
known to undercount the number of AFDC recipients because of underreporting by
those who are on the welfare rolls for only short periods of time. The CPS or SIPP
data can be used to make estimates of needed parameters (such as the proportion of
young AFDC mothers who have not completed high school or have no work experi-

ence), and these parameters can be used in conjunction with the state-specific NIQCS data to make projections for individual states.

Employment-related characteristics of AFDC parents

National survey data on employment-related characteristics of AFDC parents are available in the National Longitudinal Survey of the Labor Market Experience of Youth (NLSY), the National Health Interview Survey (NHIS), the Survey of Income and Program Participation (SIPP), the Current Population Survey (CPS), and the Panel Study of Income Dynamics (PSID). Limited employment information is available in the NIQCS, mainly current employment status and eligibility or exemption from work programs, along with the reason for exemption. Information on functional literacy levels is available in the National Adult Literacy Survey, conducted for the U.S. Department of Education (Educational Testing Service, 1990), and in a related study of low-income job seekers for the U.S. Department of Labor (Kirsch, Jungeblut, & Campbell, 1992). Again, these data can be used to help inform and guide the implementation of the JOBS program, but little of this sort of use has been made of the survey data.

The following kinds of employment-relevant information are contained in the surveys listed above: (1) educational attainment (with the exception of the NIQCS, surveys listed above contain data on the parents' educational attainment; the NIQCS has so much missing data on this variable as to make the information of no value); (2) current labor force status; (3) labor force history (available in the NLSY, SIPP, PSID, and, to a more limited extent, in the CPS); (4) general intellectual aptitude and specific skills (only the NLSY and NALS have test scores; the NLSY scores are for the Armed Services Vocational Aptitude Battery, consisting of both a general, IQ-type score [the AFQT] and a series of specific, job-relevant aptitude scores; the NALS scores are on three functional literacy scales: prose literacy, document literacy, and quantitative literacy); (5) vocational training (information on the receipt of such training is present in the NLSY, SIPP, and PSID); and (6) health status and disability (the best source of health information is the NHIS, but data on health-related limitations are also available from the SIPP, NLSY, and PSID, and to a much more limited extent from the CPS).

The kinds of data listed above can be used to provide guidance on what kinds of employment-related services are needed by what numbers of AFDC parents. Specifically, given some working assumptions about job requirements, estimates can be made of: (1) the proportion of AFDC parents who seem ready for gainful employment; (2) the proportion who require vocational instruction or on-the-job training; (3) the proportion who need and seem capable of benefiting from academic instruction at the high school level; (4) the proportion who have such low levels of functional literacy that they qualify for unskilled occupations only or require jobs that are structured so as to take their limitations into account; and (5) the proportion who, because of a chronic illness or handicapping condition, are unable to work, can work only at certain kinds of jobs, or must get rehabilitative training before they can be employed.

The data contained in three of these surveys are summarized in Tables 12.1 and 12.2.

Table 12.1. *Sample characteristics and survey content with respect to AFDC Parents of National Longitudinal Survey of Youth, Current Population Survey, and National Health Interview Survey on Child Health*

	NLSY	CPS	NHIS-CHS
Sample characteristics		March	January–December
Year(s) of survey	1979–87	1988	1988
Total sample size	5,369 women (in 1987)	59,000 HH	17,110 parents
Number of current AFDC parents in sample[a]	597	1,628	1,752
Blacks oversampled	Yes	No	No
Hispanics oversampled	Yes	Yes	No
Poor whites oversampled	Yes	No	No
Age range of parents in sample	22–30	15–64+	15–64+
	(in 1987)	(in 1988)	(in 1988)
Content			
Ability test	ASVAB	No	No
Education	Yes	Yes	Yes
Family income	Yes	Yes	Yes
Current employment status	Yes	Yes	Yes
Hours worked	Yes	Yes	Yes
Occupation	Yes	Yes	Yes
Earnings	Yes	Yes	No
Work history	Yes	Yes	No
Vocational training	Yes	Yes	No
Health status	Limited	No	Extensive
Work disability	Yes	Yes	Yes
Chronic illness	No	No	Yes
Drug abuse history	Limited	No	No
Alcohol abuse	Yes	No	Yes, but in different module
Welfare history	Yes	No	No
Marital status	Yes	Yes	Yes
Marital history	Yes	No	Yes
Fertility history	Yes	No	Yes
Migration history	Yes	No	No
Household composition	Yes	Yes	Yes, detailed
Work-related attitudes	Yes	No	No
Child care arrangements	Limited	No	Yes

Note: All numbers are unweighted.
[a]Self-identification of AFDC recipients in surveys tends to produce an undercount when compared with administrative records. The recipients missed appear to be predominantly those who received welfare for relatively short periods of time.

Table 12.2. *Design characteristics of child supplement to National Longitudinal Survey of Youth,*
Current Population Survey, and National Health Interview Survey on Child Health

	NLSY	CPS	NHIS-CHS
		March	January–December
Year(s) of survey	1986, 1987	1988	1988
Total sample size (in 1986)	5,226 children[a]	43,030 under 18	17,110 children
Number of AFDC children in sample[a]	1,316	4,553	1,752
Blacks oversampled	Yes	No	No
Hispanics oversampled	Yes	No	No
Poor whites oversampled	Yes	No	No
Age range of children in sample	0–13 (in 1986)	0–17 (in 1988)	0–17 (in 1988)

Notes: The NLSY is predominantly a sample of younger children and the children of early childbearers. The CPS and NHIS-CHS are probability samples of all U.S. children in target age range. Self-identification of AFDC recipients in surveys tends to produce an undercount when compared with administrative records. The recipients missed appear to be predominantly those who received welfare for relatively short periods of time.
[a]Data actually collected on 4,971 children.

Needed data. There are several topical areas on which better employment-related data are needed. These include the parent's history of alcoholism or drug dependence; presence of depression or other psychologically incapacitating conditions; presence of criminal record that could be a barrier to employment; proficiency in English, in cases where English is not the parent's primary language; and an assessment of the parent's attitudes about working and participating in job-search or job-training activities.

Information on drug and alcohol use and abuse is available in the NLSY files, but it has not been collected regularly. Moreover, there is evidence of systematic underreporting of drug use by some groups (Mensch & Kandel, 1988). There are comparatively few questions in the NLSY on work related attitudes, and those were asked only in early waves of the study, casting doubts on their relevance to adult employment patterns. Data on alcoholism are available from another supplement to the NHIS that was given in 1988, but only for a portion of the AFDC parents. Older data from the National Health and Nutrition Examination Survey and the National Survey of Children indicate high levels of depression among never-married mothers in welfare and other low-income families. Given the apparent importance of maternal attitudes and depression as moderators of possible effects of maternal employment on children, adding such measures to future data collection efforts should be given high priority. Data on drug and alcohol abuse would permit estimates of the proportion of JOBS participants who may require treatment for substance dependency in addition to basic education or vocational training.

Development and well-being of AFDC children

Data on the development and well-being of AFDC children may be found in a few national surveys. In the past decade, several survey projects have sought to bridge the gap between the macroworld of economics and social policy and the microworld of family interaction patterns and developmental psychology (see Smeeding, this volume). These studies have taken large probability samples of the population and gathered information about both the economic and social situations of families and the development and well-being of children or youth within those families, using individual families and children as basic units of measurement and analysis.

Two studies are notable because they include information on young children, are longitudinal, and make use of innovative data collection methods. They are the Child Supplement to the National Longitudinal Survey of the Labor Market Experience of Youth (NLSY) and the National Survey of Children (NSC). Other sources of data on young people from AFDC families are the Child Health Supplements to the National Health Interview Surveys (NHIS), the National Education Longitudinal Surveys (NELS), the National Household Education Survey (NHES), and the National Survey of Families and Households (NSFH). In the future, useful data should be available from two studies that are now in the field: the third cycle of the National Health and Nutrition Examination Survey (NHANES) and the National Maternal and Infant Health Survey (NMIHS). Descriptions of all of these studies are available in *Researching the Family: A Guide to Survey and Statistical Data on U.S. Families* (Zill & Daly, 1993).

Although some of these surveys emphasize a particular domain, such as academic achievement in the NHES and NELS and physical health in the NHIS, they all take a broad view of youth development, collecting data on young people's social development, problem behavior, and emotional well-being, as well as on their health and achievement. Most of the studies do not rely solely on traditional parent-interview methods, but also make use of achievement tests, school records and teacher reports, interviewer observations, or interviews with the young people themselves. Specific data items that are available in two of the surveys, the NLSY and the NHIS, are shown in Table 12.3. (See Chase-Lansdale, Mott, Brooks-Gunn, & Phillips [1991] for further information on child data and potential uses of the Children of the NLSY.)

Quality of the home environments that AFDC parents provide

It would also be useful to have information on the kinds of home environments AFDC parents provide their children, and to be able to compare the quality of home care with the quality of the substitute care available now and in the future.

Data of this sort are available in the Children of the NLSY. The NLSY made use of an abbreviated version of the HOME scale developed by Baker and Mott in consultation with the original scale developers, Bettye Caldwell and Robert Bradley

Table 12.3. *Survey content with respect to AFDC children of Child Supplement to National Longitudinal Survey of Youth and National Health Interview Survey on Child Health*

	NLSY	NHIS-CHS
Conditions at birth		
Late or no prenatal care	Yes	Yes
Mother smoked, drank during pregnancy	Yes	Yes (smoked only)
Low birth weight	Yes	Yes
Physical health and safety		
General health status	No	Yes (scale)
Frequency of illness in past year	Yes	Yes
Accidents, injuries in past year	Yes	Yes
Handicapping conditions		
Health limitation	Yes	Yes
Chronic physical illness or impairment	Yes	Yes
Delay in growth or develoment	No	Yes
Learning disability	Yes	Yes
Chronic emotional condition	Yes	Yes
Intellectual stimulation		
HOME scale	Yes	No
Enrolled in nursery school or kindergarten	Yes	Yes
Attended Head Start	No	Yes
Cognitive development and school performance		
Vocabulary test score	Yes	No
Grade placement	Yes	Yes
Grade repetition	No	Yes
Standing in class	No	Yes
School discipline problem	No	Yes
Emotional well-being		
Behavior Problems Index	Yes	Yes
Temperament scales	Yes	No
Needed/got psychological help in past year	Yes	Yes
Medical care		
Reg source of medical care	Yes	Yes
Last time saw doctor	Yes	Yes
Last time saw dentist	Yes	Yes
Covered by Medicaid/private health insurance	Yes	Yes

(1989). The scale assesses the intellectual stimulation, supervision, and emotional support the child receives at home. Summary scores are derived from parent responses to structured questions and interviewer ratings recorded after observing the parent and child in interaction during the survey procedures. The shortened scale showed reasonable reliability and validity coefficients, although the emotional support portion of the scale was less internally consistent than the intellectual stimulation portion (Baker & Mott, 1989).

Information on quality of home environments is also available in the 1988 Child Health Supplement and the 1993 National Household Education Survey. The NHIS measures have to do with health-related aspects of the home, such as whether the mother obtained timely prenatal care or smoked during pregnancy, whether any adults in the household are currently smokers, whether the child wears seat belts while riding in the family car, or whether the child is put to bed at a regular and reasonable hour. The NHES measures deal with family learning activities, such as reading or telling stories to young children, involving them in chores, and taking them on outings. Both the indicators of a healthful home environment and the indicators of an intellectually stimulating home show substantial differences by parent education and family income, favoring children from more educated and affluent families.

Health status, medical care, and health insurance coverage

Most of the surveys mentioned earlier as sources of data on the development and well-being of AFDC children contain information on the health status of these children. The 1988 Child Health Supplement to the NHIS is also a rich source of data on the medical care received by AFDC children. The survey has questions on whether the child has a regular source of routine care, a regular source of care for treatment of injuries and illnesses, the types of facility providing this care, and items tapping the quality of the care provided. For example, the mother is asked whether there is someone familiar with the child's history with whom she can consult by telephone. Questions are also asked about the last time the child received a health checkup and dental care, and the frequency of doctor visits and hospitalizations during the past year.

The CHS contains data on whether the child is covered by Medicaid or by private health insurance. It does not contain data on specific health-related expenditures, however. These sorts of data are being collected in the National Medical Expenditure Survey that is conducted periodically by the National Center for Health Services Research (NCHSR). The expenditure survey also collects more complete and accurate data on the extent of insurance coverage, obtaining this information through supplementary surveys of employers and insurance providers.

Problems with health status measures. It should be noted that survey measures of children's health status that depend on recall or recognition of medical terminology may produce spurious results when groups that differ in education or income level are compared. Respondents with more education or exposure to high-quality care tend to be more "productive" survey respondents in the sense of knowing what is meant by specific diagnostic terms and remembering episodes of disability. Such differences in survey responding may make it appear that children of more advantaged respondents have more health problems than those of less advantaged respondents.

For example, there is evidence in several health surveys of more underreporting of illness and disability days by black than by nonminority respondents. By contrast, when parents are asked to rate their children's health status from "excellent" to "poor," black parents report their children to be in poorer health then do nonminority parents.

It should also be noted that most respondents cannot report accurately on the extent of coverage their health insurance provides. Accurate data on coverage requires contacting employers or insurance providers, which is a costly proposition.

Child care provisions and possibilities

Until recently, the primary sources of data on the child care arrangements of U.S. families with young children were occasional supplements to the Current Population Survey (CPS) and a child care module in the Survey of Income and Program Participation (SIPP) (U.S. Bureau of the Census, 1990; O'Connell & Bloom, 1987). These surveys have provided much useful data on the kinds of child care used by different groups of parents and on changes over time in use of specific forms of care (U.S. House of Representatives Select Committee on Children, Youth, and Families, 1989, Tables 38–40). In addition, national data on enrollment in nursery school and kindergarten were available from the October Education Supplement to the CPS (Tables 57–58).

However, these surveys have significant deficiencies, namely, a failure to treat preschool and child care arrangements in a coordinated fashion, lack of data on the care used by mothers who are not employed, and little or no information on the characteristics of the care situations, the options available to the families, or the factors they considered in choosing a specific type of care. These deficiencies are at least partly remedied by data that will soon be available from the 1988 Child Health Supplement to the National Health Interview Survey, the National Child Care Consumer Survey, and the National Household Education Survey.

The 1988 Child Health Supplement (Adams & Hardy, 1989, pp. 225–227) collected data in an integrated fashion on the educational and care arrangements for children under 6, including those whose mothers were currently unemployed or not in the labor force. Information was also gathered about the quality of the care provided in the child's main care arrangement, as indexed by the number of children who were cared for together, the adult:child ratio, and the early childhood training of the main caregiver. However, these characteristics could only be assessed to the extent that they were known to the parent respondent.

The Child Health Supplement has the advantages of being an in-person rather than a telephone survey, with a large sample and a high completion rate, containing a rich body of accompanying information on family characteristics, including receipt of AFDC and the child's health and development. The survey did not collect information on the care options available to the family, though, nor did it ask about factors parents considered in making their care decisions. This sort of information is being gathered in one of the other new surveys, the National Child Care Consumer Survey.

Both the *National Child Care Consumer Survey*, 1990 (Hofferth, Brayfield, Deich, & Holcomb, 1991; Brayfield, Deich, & Hofferth, 1993) and the National Household Education Survey (West, Germino Hausken, & Collins, 1993) contain data on the use of child care, early education, and before- and after-school programs by families with preschool and primary-school children. The studies attempt to understand the factors underlying parents' choice of particular child care and educational arrangements. They also provide descriptive information about characteristics of care arrangements and educational programs that are thought to relate to the quality of the care or instruction. In the 1993 edition of the NHES, information has also been collected about the development and well-being of the children themselves. Both surveys used random-digit-dialing and telephone interviewing of parents. Low-income and minority families are therefore underrepresented, because these families are less likely to have telephones. The surveys apply population weights to their data in an effort to adjust for this underrepresentation.

The Child Care Consumer Survey is linked to a provider study that gathered data about unregulated family day care and care by relatives and friends of the family. The study is also linked to the Profile of Child Care Settings Study (Kisker, Hofferth, Phillips, & Farquhar, 1991), a telephone survey of child care centers, early education and preschool programs, and regulated family day care providers that will be carried out in the same 120 sampling areas as the consumer survey. The principal objective of the provider survey is to obtain in-depth descriptive information on the current structures and programs of formal, extrafamilial care for young children, and to assess the quality of these programs in terms of existing standards. Also making use of the same sampling frame is a similar telephone survey of 1,300 providers of before- and after-school care for school-age children.

Other national survey programs that have collected information on nonmaternal child care arrangements within the past 5 years are the National Longitudinal Survey of the Labor Market Experience of Youth (NLSY); the National Survey of Family Growth (NSFG, Cycle IV, conducted in 1988); the National Survey of Families and Households (NSFH, conducted in 1987); the Panel Study of Income Dynamics (PSID); and the National Educational Longitudinal Survey (NELS 1972 Cohort, followed up at 5 points through 1986).

Needed data on child care. The studies listed above should help illuminate the use of child care by poor families as well as how AFDC participation patterns and employment requirements play a role in child care usage. There are several areas where more comprehensive data about child care supply and demand would be helpful for planning and evaluation, but where the right kinds of data are difficult to come by. First, and most daunting, is good data on the supply and costs of different kinds of care in each of the states and for the United States as a whole. Although the linked National Child Care Consumer Survey and Profile of Child Care Settings Study will give us a better picture of supply and costs on the national level, it does not have sufficient sample size to make state-level estimates for even the largest states.

A second area of difficulty is estimating the kinds of informal care that might be available to AFDC families. The NIQCS and most national surveys tell us about the presence and employment status of other adult household members, but they are generally uninformative about relatives or friends who live close by, but not in the same household. The Child Care Consumer Survey and the National Survey of Families and Households can give some assistance here, but it would be desirable to have data on friends and relatives who are potential care providers based on a larger sample of AFDC families.

A third problem area is that parents, particularly low-education parents, are not particularly good informants about those characteristics of child care or early education programs that are thought to relate to the quality of the care or instruction. This means that in order to get valid data on the quality of care poor children receive, it will be necessary to take the relatively expensive step of interviewing providers or even observing care situations directly. At least we may get instruments for carrying out such assessments from studies such as the Profiles of Care Settings Study and a forthcoming observational study of the preschool education and care received by a sample of disadvantaged 4-year-olds (Love, 1992).

Finally, in order to understand the potential effects on children of mothers' work fare requirements such as JOBS participation, the quality of the care provided by the mother and the quality of substitute care should be assessed by common or comparable measures. This would enable us to say whether children are getting better or worse care as a result of having their mothers participate in employment training programs. Some comparisons are relatively straightforward, such as when we compare the mother's educational attainment and ability test scores with those of a regular babysitter. But applying a common metric to individual mother care and the group care provided in day care centers or nursery schools is a more challenging proposition.

Child support and father involvement in AFDC families

The primary sources of survey data on receipt of child support have been a periodic supplement to the Current Population Survey sponsored by the Office of Child Support Enforcement (U.S. Bureau of the Census, 1991b) and a module of the Survey of Income and Program Participation. The 1990 CPS supplement showed, for example, that 37% of all women in the United States with children from an absent father received support payments from the father in 1989 (U.S. Bureau of the Census, 1991b, p. 5). The mean amount received by those who received any support was $2,995 per year. Women were less likely to receive support if, like many AFDC recipients, they had less than a high school education, were black or Hispanic, or had never been married to the father (U.S. House of Representatives Select Committee on Children, Youth, and Families, 1989, Tables 51–53).

Limited state and national data on child support among AFDC families are also available in the NIQCS. This database shows whether the AFDC family received a $50 pass-through of child support payments collected by the state. In FY 1987 only 4% of the AFDC caseload nationwide received such payments (Family Support Administration, 1989).

As these survey mechanisms are repeated at regular intervals, they will give some indication as to whether the continuing policy initiatives to strengthen child support enforcement have resulted in more mothers and children receiving support and in higher payment levels. However, there are technical problems. For example, to arrive at its published child support estimates, the Census Bureau has made adjustments in the amounts of child support that women in the CPS report. These adjustments have been questioned (Meyer, 1992).

There are changes in survey questions and tabulation procedures underway that will make the CPS Child Support data more useful. A continuous need is for better data on the earnings, employment, and employability of absent fathers. Constructing an adequate sample of absent fathers is not easy, because many stop seeing their children after a few years of separation (Furstenberg, Nord, Peterson, & Zill, 1983). Single mothers may not know the whereabouts of their former mates. Also, when men are interviewed cold, without the researcher having prior knowledge of their mating histories, some simply do not report previous marriages or children with whom they do not live (Cherlin, Griffith, & McCarthy, 1983).

Probably the best studies are those that follow both mother and father after a marital breakup or the birth of a child outside marriage. This is obviously a lengthy and expensive process.

Studies of absent parents that take advantage of existing longitudinal studies, such as the Panel Study of Income Dynamics or the NLSY, have been done (Duncan & Hoffman, 1985; Duncan & Rodgers, 1987; Hill, 1985). However, the samples involved are relatively small. The Survey of Income and Program Participation (SIPP) is a logical vehicle for developing periodic samples of absent parents (Bianchi & McArthur, 1991). There are analytic problems causes by differential attrition of absent fathers in the SIPP panels, however (Bianchi, 1992). The relatively short intervals over which families were followed in SIPP also reduced the usefulness of these data, but this problem is being corrected. The Department of Health and Human Services had planned to do a Survey of Absent Parents (SOAP), but funding was not forthcoming after an instrument had been developed and a pretest carried out (Sonenstein, 1989).

Fathers' involvement in child rearing. Survey data on the participation of AFDC fathers in the care and rearing of their children, be they present or absent from the household, are extremely limited. Mott (1990) has used NLSY data to examine the dynamics of the father's presence or absence during a child's first few years of life. Recent SIPP and CPS child support supplements contain very limited data on contact by absent fathers (U.S. Bureau of the Census, 1991b), but these have not yet been adequately analyzed. The HOME scale in the NLSY contains items on the child's contact with the father or a father substitute. The NHIS contains data on amount of contact absent fathers maintain with their children, but these data may be flawed due to an error in the questionnaire's skip instructions. Data on fathers' participation in family activities are also available from the National Survey of Families and Households (NSFH) and the National Household Education Survey (NHES).

What is probably the most extensive body of survey data on the involvement of both absent and resident fathers in their children's lives, as well as on conflict between fathers and mothers and on the quality of the child's relationship with each parent, was obtained in the National Survey of Children (Furstenberg & Nord, 1985). However, these data are dated for use in conjunction with current policy decisions, since the children involved were teenagers in the early 1980s. Up-to-date replication is badly needed.

Need for periodic surveys of absent parents. The need to develop a viable mechanism for periodic surveys of absent parents should be given high priority in the research agenda. For example, the Family Support Act's requirement that the Social Security numbers of both parents be recorded at the birth of a child may facilitate the process of identifying and locating absent parents, as well as providing a link to administrative data files on earnings and other characteristics, and to surveys such as the CPS and NHIS, which ask for the Social Security numbers of respondents. Needless to say, Social Security numbers are not much help with regard to an absent parent's earnings in the underground economy or employment in the criminal labor force. Periodic surveys should also inquire about the father's involvement, if any, in the lives of the children with whom he does not live, as well as those with whom he does live. The surveys should also collect data about current marital situation and employment.

Actions to increase the utility of survey-based data

There are a number of steps that could be taken to increase the usefulness of survey-based data in planning for, implementing, and evaluating policies related to poor children, especially those on AFDC. Six recommended actions are presented below, along with brief rationales.

1. Make better use of existing data. Several current efforts to analyze existing relevant data have been described in this chapter. Similar projects should be initiated that make use of other data sets that have not yet been exploited or the same data sets for different purposes. Care should be taken, however, to not make too much of conclusions that are based on analysis of small subgroups within the survey samples. Survey measurement is generally more noisy than laboratory-based measures, and substantial numbers of cases are needed to be confident about the generalizability of observed results. There is no substitute for replication with independent samples.

2. Put items that identify AFDC families in ongoing surveys. Where they are not already present, items that identify AFDC families should be added to national surveys that are large enough to have a goodly number of such families and that have content relevant to child and family well-being. Two examples of good steps in this direction are the addition of AFDC and other income and employment items to the National Health Interview Survey and the recurring NIDA household survey on drug abuse.

3. Plan now for replication of key surveys and piggyback modules. It is not too early to begin planning and assembling funding for the replication in the late 1990s of surveys that provide important data on the AFDC population. An example would be another round of the Child Health Supplement to the National Health Interview Survey. Also, planning should get underway for relevant modules that could be added to major longitudinal projects that may be repeated in the 1990s. Examples here are the Department of Education's planned Early Childhood Longitudinal Study and the Bureau of Labor Statistics' planned new youth cohort of the NLSY.

4. Develop contextual variables on the implementation of training programs in different states and on the participant status of AFDC recipients. Efforts should be supported to code variations on the ways in which training programs and other interventions are being implemented in different states and in the largest cities and metropolitan counties. These coded variables could later be merged with survey-based data sets to permit analysis of the effects of differences in FSA implementation on the well-being and behavior of AFDC families.

Similarly, a project should be mounted to find standardized ways of ascertaining and coding the participant status of individual AFDC recipients in training programs. It seems unlikely that the recipients themselves will know the details of their participation, so some sort of standard welfare agency coding scheme may be needed.

5. Explore the possibility of enlarging the CPS or SIPP samples in the mid-1990s. Discussions should be initiated with the Census Bureau and federal and private funding agencies about bolstering the samples for the Current Population Survey or Survey of Income and Program Participation during the 1990s so as to provide larger samples of AFDC families and state-level data from the CPS, at least for the larger states. Obviously, larger samples would be useful for a number of other social policy purposes as well. An expansion and extension of the SIPP is already planned for 1996.

6. Explore the possibility of strengthening and expanding the data collected in the AFDC Quality Control System. The NIQCS is an important source of state-level data on the welfare population. However, as described above, the system now has important gaps, namely poor data on educational attainment, and a lack of information in other areas. Discussions should be initiated with the Department of Health and Human Services about the possibilities for strengthening this important data source.

These six suggestions would go a long way toward strengthening our capabilities for monitoring and analyzing the children in our nation's welfare system. Although some of the recommendations would be quite costly, others could be carried out with minimal expense. Even the inexpensive steps would result in significant increases in our understanding of how changes in social policies affect the lives of poor children.

REFERENCES

Adams, P. F., & Hardy, A. M. (1989). Current estimates from the National Health Interview Survey: United States, 1988. *Vital Health Statistics, 10*(173).

Baker, P. C., & Mott, F. L. (1989, June). *NLSY child handbook, 1989*. Columbus: Center for Human Resource Research, Ohio State University.

Berk, R. A. (1983). An introduction to sample selection bias in sociological data. *American Sociological Review, 48*(3), 386–398.

Bianchi, S. (1992). *The situation of children, mothers, and fathers after divorce*. Paper presented at the annual meeting of the American Statistical Association, Atlanta, GA.

Bianchi, S., & McArthur, E. (1991). Family disruption and economic hardship: The short-run picture for children. *Current Population Reports* (Series P-70, No. 23). Washington, DC: U.S. Government Printing Office.

Brayfield, A. A., Deich, S. G., & Hofferth, S. L. (1993). *Caring for children in low-income families: A substudy of the National Child Care Survey, 1990* (Report No. 93-2). Washington, DC: Urban Institute.

Chase-Lansdale, P. L., Mott, F. L., Brooks-Gunn, J., & Phillips, D. A. (1991). Children of the National Longitudinal Survey of Youth: A unique research opportunity. *Developmental Psychology, 27*(6), 918–931.

Cherlin, A., Griffith, J., & McCarthy, J. (1983). A note on maritally-disrupted men's reports of child support in the June 1980 Current Population Survey. *Demography, 20*, 385–389.

Duncan, G. J., & Hoffman, S. D. (1985). A reconsideration of the economic consequences of marital dissolution. *Demography, 22*, 485–497.

Duncan, G. J., & Rodgers, W. (1987). Single-parent families: Are their economic problems transitory or persistent? *Family Planning Perspectives, 19*, 171–178.

Educational Testing Service. (1990). *National Adult Literacy Survey*. Princeton, NJ: Author.

Family Support Administration. (1989). *Characteristics and financial circumstances of AFDC recipients, FY 1987*. Washington, DC: U.S. Government Printing Office.

Furstenberg, F. F., Jr., & Nord, C. W. (1985, November). Parenting apart: Patterns of childrearing after marital dissolution. *Journal of Marriage and the Family, 47*, 893–904.

Furstenberg, F. F., Jr., Nord, C. W., Peterson, J. L., & Zill, N. (1983). The life course of children of divorce: Marital disruption and parental contact. *American Sociological Review, 48*, 656–668.

Hill, M. S. (1985, March). *Child support: What absent fathers do and could provide*. Paper presented at the annual meeting of the Population Association of America.

Hofferth, S. L., Brayfield, A., Deich, S., & Holcomb, P. (1991). *The National Child Care Survey, 1990*. Washington, DC: Urban Institute Press.

Kirsch, I. S., Jungeblut, A., & Campbell, A. (1992). *Beyond the school doors: The literacy needs of job seekers served by the U.S. Department of Labor*. Princeton, NJ: Educational Testing Service.

Kisker, E. E., Hofferth, S. C., Phillips, D. A., & Farquhar, E. (1991). *A profile of job care settings: Early education and care in 1990*. Washington, DC: U.S. Government Printing Office.

Love, J. (1992). Personal communication to the author.

Manpower Demonstration Research Corporation. (1989, August). *JOBS evaluation technical proposal* (Chapters 1–2), (RFP-26–89 HHS OS). New York: Author.

Mensch, B. S., & Kandel, D. B. (1988). Underreporting of substance use in a national longitudinal youth cohort. *Public Opinion Quarterly, 58*, 100–124.

Meyer, D. R. (1992, June). *Data adjustments in the Child Support Supplement of the Current Population Survey*. Washington, DC: Office of Income Security Policy, Office of the Assistant Secretary for Planning and Evaluation, U.S. Department of Health and Human Services.

Mott, F. (1990). When is a father really gone? Paternal-child contact in father-absent homes. *Demography, 27*(4), 499–517.

O'Connell, M., & Bloom, D. E. (1987). Juggling jobs and babies: America's child care challenge. *Population Trends and Public Policy*. Washington, DC: Population Reference Bureau.

Sonenstein, F. (1989). Personal communication to author.

U.S. Bureau of the Census. (1990). Who's minding the kids? Child care arrangements: Winter, 1986–87. *Current Population Reports* (Series P-70, No. 20). Washington, DC: U.S. Government Printing Office.

U.S. Bureau of the Census. (1991a). Transitions in income and poverty status: 1987–88. *Current Population Reports* (Series P-70, No. 24). Washington, DC: U.S. Government Printing Office.

U.S. Bureau of the Census. (1991b). Child support and alimony: 1989. *Current Population Reports* (Series P-60, No. 173). Washington, DC: U.S. Government Printing Office.

U.S. Bureau of the Census. (1992a). Poverty in the United States: 1991. *Current Population Reports* (Series P-60, No. 181). Washington, DC: U.S. Government Printing Office.

U.S. Bureau of the Census. (1992b). Marital status and living arrangements: March 1992. *Current Population Reports* (Series P-20, No. 468). Washington, DC: U.S. Government Printing Office.

U.S. House of Representatives, Select Committee on Children, Youth, and Families. (1989). *U.S. children and their families: Current conditions and recent trends, 1989* (4th ed.). Prepared by Child Trends. Washington, DC: U.S. Government Printing Office.

Wainer, H. (Ed.). (1986). *Drawing inferences from self-selected samples*. New York: Springer-Verlag.

West, J., Germino Hausken, E., & Collins, M. (1993). *Profile of preschool children's child care and early education program participation* (Statistical Analysis Report No. 93–133). Washington, DC: Office of Educational Research and Improvement, U.S. Department of Education.

Zill, N., & Daly, M. (1993). *Researching the family: A guide to survey and statistical data on U.S. families*. Washington, DC: Child Trends.

Zill, N., & Stief, T. (1989a). [Memo to Barbara Blum, October 3, 1989]. Preliminary estimates of number of women in each state eligible for JOBS.

Zill, N., & Stief, T. (1989b). [Memo to Barbara Dyer, November 20, 1989]. Preliminary estimates of number of women in each state eligible for JOBS; age of mother by age of child.

13 An interdisciplinary model and data requirements for studying poor children

Timothy M. Smeeding

The purpose of this chapter is both proscriptive and descriptive. Foremost, its larger and broader proscriptive objectives are to provide the framework for an interdisciplinary model for studying the well-being of poor children. The model is driven by public policies and social programs that affect disadvantaged children and their families. On a more limited level, the chapter tries to build a bridge between the research questions that surround the impact of current policies for poor children and the data resources needed to address the effects of these policies. It also discusses the emergence of some research projects, data sources, and interdisciplinary collaborations that are beginning to add meat to the bones of the model outlined here.

The underlying premise is that to study the impacts of public policy on children, data on children per se are primarily what is needed. Lacking a household panel data project focused entirely on children, we turn to secondary resources and opportunities for client or family-based data to inform researchers about poor children's participation in child care, preschool, and related support service activities. To the extent that these sources are panel data, they might also be broadened in future data collection efforts to focus on children more directly and explicitly. Little, if anything, is said about the aggregate state-level data concerning the impact of current policy initiatives in terms of numbers of child care slots and Head Start slots available per state and the number of eligible children who actually receive such services. These aggregate data opportunities, however, are critical to an understanding of the effects of national initiatives on poor children at the local and state levels, where programs are eventually implemented and services are delivered.

The author would like to thank the National Academy of Sciences Panel on Child Development, the Working Group on Communities and Neighborhoods, Family Processes, and Individual Development of the Social Science Research Council, and Lindsay Chase-Lansdale, Barbara Starfield, Jeanne Brooks-Gunn, and Nicholas Zill for comments. The author holds all parties to this interpretation harmless, except himself.

*The ideal research design: A marriage of macrosocial and
microbehavioral science perspectives*

Economists, sociologists, and most public policy analysts measure children's well-being indirectly, by focusing on the well-being of their parents. That is, they use measurable socioeconomic variables that are really inputs into children's well-being: household consumption, income, wealth, and capital goods (e.g., computers, television and video equipment, own room for each child). Social standing or lack thereof (poverty, underclass) is also measured largely by parents' characteristics until children reach the age of majority, labor force participation, or criminal institutionalization, whichever comes first. Beyond birth weight, and in a few cases Apgar scores or other measures of neonatal health such as length of hospital stay, children largely disappear as *individual* social, economic, and statistical entities as far as state record keeping and social science household survey practice are concerned. The result is that children are largely invisible in most large-scale (macro-oriented) household surveys beyond parentally provided evidence on their age and sex. Our "macro" databases, while quite large and representative of major ethnic, racial, and demographic groups, simply do not deal well with children as individual entities.

To study the well-being of children from this "macro" data starting point, analysts must make rather strong assumptions (e.g., equal sharing of resources within the household, because intrahousehold sharing of goods, money, time, and space is still largely a black box). Recent efforts by Lazear and Michael (1988) and Gronau (1991), while a beginning, have made only some headway in this area. Jenkins (1991) offers a critical review of this research as it affects poverty measurement. But rarely do economists even try to combine resources such as income, wealth, and/or time as substitutable or complimentary inputs into the child's well-being (Haveman, Wolfe, Finnie, & Wolff, 1988), mainly because economists by and large do not directly measure children's well-being independent of that of their parents. The "income" approach to topics such as generational equity is fraught with pitfalls and difficulties, because most "children" are neither wage earners nor direct income recipients (Palmer, Smeeding, & Jencks, 1988).

Sociologists and epidemiologists contribute other types of measures of social status via social indicators of levels of living, but these are also mainly family- or household-based and are not representative of children per se (Mayer & Jencks, 1989). While social indicators of need offer some promise of negatively measuring well-being by considering such things as lack of sufficient resources for basic needs (e.g., food, medical care, clothing, heat, etc.) among families with children, they still do not directly measure the impact of resource insufficiency on children per se.

Developmental psychologists, educators, anthropologists, and pediatricians come at children's well-being from the other or "micro" end of the spectrum. That is, they employ direct measures of children's well-being: cognitive, social, intellectual, educational, or other developmental outcome measures for psychologists, educators, and anthropologists; and physical and mental health status for pediatricians (Brooks-Gunn, 1989). The measures are usually for a small subset of children drawn from a local sample or institution. Some researchers (e.g., Brooks-Gunn & Furstenberg, 1986; Gross, Brooks-Gunn, & Spiker, in press; Starfield, 1988) are just beginning to combine the psychological, psychosocial, and physical domains of well-being in an individual child-based database, albeit for a limited subset of children. But even in these broader microstudies, macrolevel variables such as family characteristics and environmental variables are rarely measured (Wilson, Ellwood, & Brooks-Gunn, this volume).

Another complicating factor in traditional microdevelopment studies is the fact that they are based on children who are by and large white and middle class and thus little affected by dysfunctional contextual variables such as those found in welfare-dependent families. While progress is being made to move beyond these groups, as Brooks-Gunn (this volume) and Spencer, Blumenthal, and Richards (this volume) warn, theoretical and empirical research on child well-being based on primarily middle-class white children may need to be reconceptualized if applied to underclass, ethnic, and racial minority children. Even in cases where the children studied vary by background and/or health status, the economic, social, environmental, and other contextual measures on which the "macro" disciplines focus are often measured inadequately in "micro" studies. New projects, such as the Social Science Research Council's "Multidisciplinary Cluster Approach to the Study of Critical Processes in the Lives of Poor Children and Adolescents" will hopefully shed light on these differences within a few years (O'Connor, 1991).

Very recently researchers have tried to marry the two perspectives. These efforts are to be encouraged (see also Duncan, 1991). To measure the impact of adult-focused programs like child support, welfare reform, or welfare-to-work programs on children's well-being, or to find out why some children succeed while others do not, some appreciation if not an outright marriage of these two perspectives is in order. Important public policy questions, such as the indirect effect of family-based money income subsidies on children, rest on this linkage. Unless policy makers have evidence that higher child allowances or child care subsidies actually benefit children, and not just their parents, such programs will be underfunded and not politically supported.

Toward an interdisciplinary model of child well-being

One way to begin such a marriage is to specify a model of child well-being that includes both macro and micro elements and that might be operationalized by adding measures or markers of child development to existing macro–household panel study databases. Such a model, including both the macrolevel contextual variables that economists, demographers, and sociologists use and the microlevel child outcome measures that developmental psychologists, educators, anthropologists, and pediatricians employ is outlined here in skeletal form. At the very least, such a model should provide a common ground for the various disciplinary perspectives to gain some appreciation of the interests, measures, and research questions used by other disciplines. Several of the other authors in this volume (e.g., Wilson et al.; Furstenberg) had something like the model we propose in mind as they wrote their chapters. The model sketched here is not complete, but is intended to be suggestive of the types of conditions, processes, and life events that shape children's lives and therefore their well-being. In short, it is an attempt at the big picture.

Figure 13.1 represents the skeletal model. Exogenous (to the child) contextual variables create an environment that represents the constraints and/or opportunities facing children and their families at a particular point in time. Presumably public policy influences children's well-being by affecting one or more of these family characteristics (income support, jobs), neighborhood environment (crime, drugs, danger and their concentration in slums or underclass neighborhoods), community social services (ameliorative activities by public, nonprofit, church, neighborhood, or other institutions), and/or social context (degree of racism, discrimination, segregation, and integration in the local neighborhood and its institutions).

These contextual variables set the stage and feed into the various parent and family processes and community and life processes in which the child operates. Family processes include family functioning, parenting behavior, expectations, aspirations (for self and for child), and sharing of resources and other behaviors that affect children within the household. Community processes include the time path (duration and quality of experience) of children as they pass through community and life processes in the act of growing up: medical care at birth and beyond, day care (outside the home), preschool (child development-oriented child care), school, adolescence, and community activities (sports, clubs, gangs, church). Public policies such as the child support reform and welfare-to-work programs will affect both family processes and community processes and in so doing impact children's lives. For instance, if an initiative like the Family Support Act of 1988 fosters better linkages between family and community processes and better linkages among the elements within these boxes (e.g., medical care and child care and schooling in community processes), it may positively affect child health outcomes.

These three sets of forces – context, family processes, and community processes – affect developmental outcomes (the dependent variable) measured in several domains: genetic endowment, functional health and disorder, self-image and comfort, resilience or vulnerability (opposite ends of a developmental spectrum according to Spencer, Blumenthal, & Richards, this volume), academic functioning or cognitive achievement, and socioemotional functioning. These outcomes may be combined to provide an index of life chances (or some idea of predictors for adult success) or may be studied individually.

The final element of the model is a set of life events or milestones for both parents and children. These events may be anticipated or unanticipated by the parent or child. What sets them apart is the lasting impact they have on the other variables in the model. That is, these events and milestones affect some or all of the three other

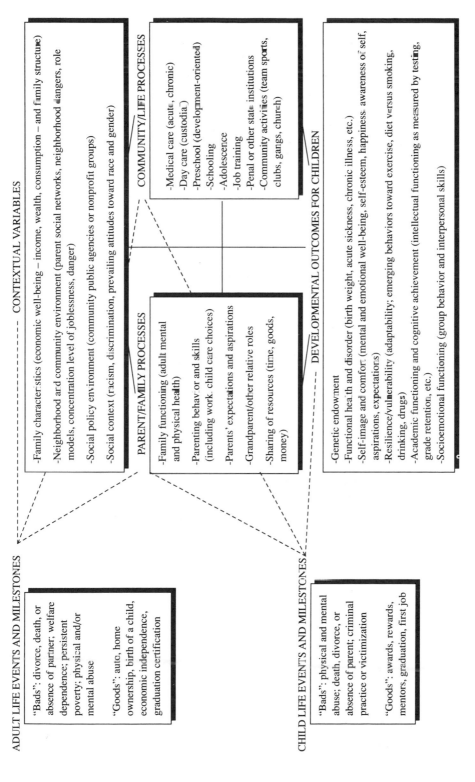

Figure 13.1 A skeletal macro–micro model of child well-being.

CONTEXTUAL VARIABLES

ADULT LIFE EVENTS AND MILESTONES

"Bads": divorce, death, or absence of partner; welfare dependence; persistent poverty; physical and/or mental abuse

"Goods": auto, home ownership, birth of a child, economic independence, graduation certification

CHILD LIFE EVENTS AND MILESTONES

"Bads": physical and mental abuse; death, divorce, or absence of parent; criminal practice or victimization

"Goods": awards, rewards, mentors, graduation, first job

Family characteristics (economic well-being – income, wealth, consumption – and family structure)

Neighborhood and community environment (parent social networks, neighborhood dangers, role models, concentration level of joblessness, danger)

Social policy environment (community public agencies or nonprofit groups)

Social context (racism, discrimination, prevailing attitudes toward race and gender)

COMMUNITY/LIFE PROCESSES

- Medical care (acute, chronic)
- Day care (custodial)
- Preschool (development-oriented)
- Schooling
- Adolescence
- Job training
- Penal or other state institutions
- Community activities (team sports, clubs, gangs, church)

PARENT/FAMILY PROCESSES

- Family functioning (adult mental and physical health)
- Parenting behavior and skills (including work, child care choices)
- Parents' expectations and aspirations
- Grandparent/other relative roles
- Sharing of resources (time, goods, money)

DEVELOPMENTAL OUTCOMES FOR CHILDREN

- Genetic endowment
- Functional health and disorder (birth weight, acute sickness, chronic illness, etc.)
- Self-image and comfort (mental and emotional well-being, self-esteem, happiness, awareness of self, aspirations, expectations)
- Resilience/vulnerability (adaptability; emerging behaviors toward exercise, diet versus smoking, drinking, drugs)
- Academic functioning and cognitive achievement (intellectual functioning as measured by testing, grade retention, etc.)
- Socioemotional functioning (group behavior and interpersonal skills)

clusters of determining variables (contextual, parent, and community processes), which in turn affect child development. These markers can be generally classified as negative events (death of a parent, divorce, family welfare dependence, persistent family poverty, physical or mental abuse) or, less often for lower-class families and children, positive events (first real mentor, first job, various awards and rewards). Presumably public policy attempts to ameliorate the negative and promote the positive, although both effects might follow from a particular action. For instance, the Family Support Act's state option to require that teenage parents live with their parents to receive AFDC, or to complete school, may have both positive and negative effects on child development (Chase-Lansdale, Brooks-Gunn, & Paikoff, 1991).

Data implications

What kinds of data would be needed to implement this skeletal model? As should be implicit from the discussion, the data would have to be longitudinal panel data such that it follows a representative sample of children over time, collecting data on the child as he or she passes through various processes and institutions (as suggested by the case management approach to affecting positive child developmental outcomes through public policy). The paths through which various events or policy changes move are complex, as are the outcomes and their measurement. Hence not only would data on the child outcomes be collected, but also information from the three process clusters. Presumably this ideal database would allow for the measurement of qualitative processes (parenting quality, day care quality) as well as quantitative ones (length of time in a particular state, such as poverty, child care, poor neighborhood, or welfare).

Not all such data need to be aggregated into a single database. Data collected in different times and places but studying the same outcomes allow for comparative studies across locations (neighborhoods, states, nations) to promote metanalytic research on their outcomes. Studies and databases might be further disaggregated by age groups (preschool, elementary school, middle school, high school). For instance, such a project might follow the form of the Social Science Research Council's new study of Multigenerational Family Processes, which combines data from a relatively small (150) sample of multigenerational black families in Harrisburg, a small sample (135) of African-American adolescent mothers in Baltimore, a large sample (900) of low birth weight, preterm infants in eight cities, and an even larger (2,300) subsample of adolescents from the Panel Study of Income Dynamics (O'Connor, 1991).

The types of databases we have in mind would also allow us to estimate differential effects of various types and quality of child care (Spencer, Blumenthal, & Richards, this volume). It would allow us an opportunity to estimate the direct effects of child care from the effects of higher income, increased parental initiative, good self-worth, and increased home resources (Cherlin, this volume). The impact of coordinated medical care in early childhood on later developmental outcomes could be assessed (Lobach, this volume), as could child support enforcement and payments on child well-being (Garfinkel & McLanahan, this volume). It would also allow us to separate the effects of various public policy initiatives that might have similar impacts on families and children. For instance, the Job Training Partnership Act, Family Support Act, refundable dependent care tax credits, or an expanded earned income tax credit are all liable to enhance children's well-being.

Conclusions

Some data with many of these characteristics are currently available or just beginning to be collected (Smith, this volume; Zill, this volume). Researchers have begun or are just beginning to link macrocontextual variables with micro-child outcome perspectives using some of these determining variables. For instance, Furstenberg, Brooks-Gunn, and Morgan (1987), using a sample of young Baltimore mothers, found that persistent low income and welfare dependence do contribute negatively to child development outcomes (Brooks-Gunn, this volume). Researchers at the University of Michigan led by Duncan have constructed neighborhood macrocontextual variables for the Panel Study of Income Dynamics (PSID) based on the 1980 Census. Using the PSID data to measure outcomes for adolescents and the Infant Health and Development Program (IHDP) data to focus on outcomes in early childhood, Brooks-Gunn, Duncan, Klebanov and Sealand (1993) have been able to begin to unpack the independent effects of neighborhood characteristics on the socioeconomic development of children. Proposals to add a battery of children's developmental outcomes to the PSID are also under review. The Children of the NLSY already offers a unique opportunity for the integration of "macro" and "micro" perspectives (Chase-Lansdale, Mott, Brooks-Gunn, & Phillips, 1991). More of this type of data collection will allow us to move beyond our disciplinary purviews into a more integrated world of policy relevant research on and for children.

REFERENCES

Brooks-Gunn, J. (1989, June). Mapping developmental trajectories. A report to the Social Science Research Council Committee on the Underclass.
Brooks-Gunn, J., Duncan, G., Klebanov, P., & and Sealand, N. (1993). Do neighborhoods influence child and adolescent development? *American Journal of Sociology, 99*(2), 353–395.
Brooks-Gunn, J., & Furstenberg, F. (1986). The children of adolescent mothers: Physical, academic and psychological outcomes. *Developmental Review, 6*, 224–251.
Chase-Lansdale, P., Brooks-Gunn, J., & Paikoff, R. (1991). Research and programs for adolescent mothers: Missing links and future promises. *Family Relations, 40*, 396–404.
Chase-Lansdale, P., Mott, F., Brooks-Gunn, J., & Phillips, D. (1991). Children of the National Longitudinal Survey of Youth: A unique research opportunity. *Developmental Psychology, 27*, 918–931.
Duncan, G. (1991) Made in heaven : Secondary data analysis and interdisciplinary collaborators. *Developmental Psychology, 27*, 949–951.

Furstenberg, F. F., Jr., Brooks-Gunn, J., & Morgan, S. P. (1987). *Adolescent mothers in later life.* New York: Cambridge University Press.

Gronau, R. (1991). The intrafamily allocation of goods: How to separate the adult from the child. *Journal of Labor Economics*, *9*, 207–235.

Gross, R., Brooks-Gunn, J., & Spiker, D, (in press). Efficiency of educational interventions for low birth weight infants: The infant Health and Development Program. In S. Friedman & M. Sigman (Eds.), *The psychological development of low birth weight children: Advances in applied developmental psychology.* Norwood, NJ: Ablex.

Haveman, R., Wolfe, B., Finnie, R., & Wolff, E. (1988). Disparities in well-being among U.S. children over two decades: 1962–83. Reprinted from J. Palmer, T. Smeeding, & B. Torrey (Eds.), *The vulnerable.* Washington, DC: Urban Institute Press.

Jenkins, S. (1991). Poverty measurement and within-household distribution: Agenda for action. *Journal of Social Policy*, *20*(4), 457–483.

Lazear, E., & Michael, R. (1988). *Allocation of income within the household.* Chicago and London: University of Chicago Press.

Mayer, S., & Jencks, C. (1989). Poverty and the distribution of material hardship. *Journal of Human Resources*, *24*, 88–114.

O'Connor, A. (1991, July). Neighborhood and family influences on the development of poor urban children. New York: Social Science Research Council.

Palmer, J., Smeeding, T., & Jencks, C. (1988). The uses and limits of income comparisons. In J. Palmer, T. Smeeding, & B. Torrey (Eds.), *The vulnerable.* Washington, DC: Urban Institute Press.

Starfield, B. (1988, March). *Child health status profile.* Baltimore: Johns Hopkins University Press.

14 Two-generation programs: A new intervention strategy and directions for future research

Sheila Smith

A set of new program models that target welfare-dependent women with young children may someday yield valuable lessons about how to break an intergenerational cycle of poverty and disadvantage. These models, while different in several respects, are all testing a potentially powerful intervention strategy: They help families attain economic self-sufficiency through education and job training while also providing other services, such as parenting education and high-quality child care, which support children's healthy development. As two-generation interventions these programs show promise of addressing both immediate and long-term impediments to healthy development and educational success for poor children. In the short term, these interventions can help ameliorate the negative effects of poverty with high-quality early childhood programs and preventive health care. Over time, the improvements in parents' education, employment, and income status sought by these programs may help sustain children's early developmental gains beyond the limited duration of benefits commonly found in early childhood interventions (Farran, 1990).

In the future, new knowledge that emerges from experience with these intervention models may influence the design of the mainstream self-sufficiency programs, called JOBS (Jobs, Opportunities, and Basic Skills), which has been implemented under the Family Support Act of 1988. At present, vigorous efforts to address the developmental and health needs of at-risk children whose parents participate in JOBS are evident in only a small proportion of programs (Smith, Blank, & Collins, 1992). Models that can demonstrate an effective strategy for enhancing both the employability of parents and outcomes for children related to their future self-sufficiency could help transform the JOBS program into a two-generation intervention.

This chapter provides an introduction to four new initiatives that employ a two-generation strategy and related research efforts to study program effects on parent employment and child development outcomes. One of the initiatives links the JOBS

This chapter is an update of a paper that appeared in the spring 1991 *Social Policy Report* 5(1), Society for Research in Child Development.

program to developmental early childhood services, specifically the Head Start program. Three other program models were developed independent of the Family Support Act of 1988. These are the Comprehensive Child Development Program, New Chance, and Even Start.

The discussion begins with an overview of the Family Support Act of 1988 and a description of the efforts that coordinate JOBS with early childhood services. Next, the three other program models and related research efforts are described. The four models are then examined from two perspectives. First, differences between the new models and previous interventions for welfare-dependent families highlight the potential of two-generation programs to exert a stronger, more sustained influence on children's development. Second, differences among the four two-generation models in the scope and structure of their services are examined. Following a discussion of gaps in our current knowledge about the benefits of different program models and service components, the chapter concludes with recommendations for conducting research on the effectiveness of interventions that incorporate a two-generation strategy.

The Family Support Act of 1988 and two-generation programs linked to JOBS

After a long period of debate and eventual compromise, major reform of the nation's welfare system commenced with the passage of the Family Support Act (FSA) in 1988 (Chase-Lansdale & Vinovskis, this volume; Reischauer, 1989; Institute for Research on Poverty, 1988; American Public Welfare Association, 1988). The two goals embodied in this legislation were: (1) to foster economic self-sufficiency of families through education and job training for heads of welfare-dependent families, mostly single mothers; and (2) to increase the economic support that noncustodial parents, mostly fathers, provide to families. The centerpiece of the Family Support Act is the Jobs Opportunities and Basic Skills (JOBS) program, which provides education, skills training, and other job readiness services to parents. During their participation in JOBS program activities, parents are guaranteed assistance with child care. Parents continue to receive child care assistance, on a sliding fee scale, for a period of 12 months from the time they lose welfare benefits as a result of employment earnings. During this 12-month period of "transitional benefits," JOBS also provides an extension of Medicaid benefits.

By targeting specific groups of parents, the Family Support Act encourages states to serve those most at risk of long-term welfare dependency. Federal funding provides incentives for states to serve four target groups: (1) parents under age 24 without a high school education; (2) parents with little or no work experience; (3) parents who have received assistance for more than 36 months in the previous 5 years; and (4) parents heading families in which the youngest child is within 2 years of becoming ineligible for assistance. Parents whose children are under age 3 are exempted, but states also have the option to require participation of parents with children as young as age 1. In addition, states can require that parents under age 20 who have not completed high school or a GED participate in JOBS educational activities, regardless of the age of their child. Recognizing the enormous task of implementing the JOBS program at the state and local levels, the federal legislation sets yearly participation rates that begin at 7% for FY 1990 and rise to 20% in FY 1995 (see also Chase-Lansdale & Vinovskis, this volume.)

The other major piece of the Family Support Act is a set of provisions that will strengthen governmental efforts to collect child support from noncustodial parents. These provisions include requirements that states institute automatic wage withholding to collect child support; follow guidelines, set in 1984, for determining the size of support awards; and increase efforts to establish paternity (Roberts, 1989). It should be noted that several of the child support provisions apply to all noncustodial parents and not exclusively to noncustodial parents of children receiving AFDC.

All states have established JOBS programs in compliance with the inauguration deadline of October 1990. However, there is considerable diversity in states' progress toward full implementation of JOBS and in the structure and content of JOBS services. While several states, such as Massachusetts, New Jersey, Michigan, and California, had launched their own welfare-to-work programs before passage of the Family Support Act, other states had little prior experience with such programs. Observers of the early implementation of the Family Support Act have been especially interested in the degree to which programs emphasize job training and the remediation of educational deficits (Figueroa & Silvanik, 1989). States have been encouraged to develop these services in JOBS, partly as a result of research showing only modest employment and income gains among participants in older, state-sponsored welfare-to-work programs (Gueron & Pauly, 1991; Porter, 1990). These programs typically provided low-cost job readiness services such as job search assistance and workfare rather than more intensive education and training. Early analyses of state JOBS programs suggest that several states are emphasizing education and vocational training in their services to adult participants, but the strength of this trend is still unclear (American Public Welfare Association, 1990; Greenberg, 1990).

Although the sponsors of the Family Support Act viewed the JOBS program as an important vehicle for improving the life chances of poor children, the federal legislation provides few mandates to address children's health and developmental needs. Instead, certain program provisions and new funding provided by the legislation give states opportunities to design JOBS programs that are responsive to children (Smith, Blank, & Bond, 1990). As a starting point, programs may use the initial assessment of the participant's readiness for employment, a required component of JOBS, to identify family and child needs. Another opportunity arises from the option states have to use and receive partial reimbursement for case management. If caseloads are small enough to permit attention to individual family circumstances, case managers could help families obtain a variety of needed services that might enhance parents' employability and children's well-being. One example of an

innovative effort to respond to children whose parents' participate in JOBS is the
practice, prescribed in Minnesota's state JOBS plan, of enrolling children in the
Early and Periodic Screening, Diagnosis, and Treatment (EPSDT) program.
EPSDT provides regular health and developmental assessments and interventions
for identified problems. Another example is found in Baltimore's JOBS program,
which contracts with a child care resource and referral program to help parents
choose the best child care arrangement from available options (Smith et al., 1992).

Head Start and JOBS

A new model that could transform the JOBS program into a two-generation intervention is one that links JOBS to the Head Start program. This linkage is being
encouraged by the Administration for Children and Families (ACF), which oversees
Head Start program development, and the Family Support Administration, the federal agency responsible for JOBS (Administration for Children and Families, 1991).
Approximately 50% of Head Start parents are AFDC recipients and potential JOBS
participants. Two central goals of the Head Start/JOBS collaboration are: (1) to
provide extended-day child care to Head Start children whose parents work or
whose training schedules necessitate such care; and (2) to provide comprehensive
case management that will address family needs, the child's development, and the
mother's successful progress toward employment. In addition, the initiative will
foster linkages that enable Head Start programs to serve as JOBS training sites for
participants interested in the field of early childhood education and child care as
well as in other occupations represented in Head Start staff, such as nutritionists and
social service coordinators.

The Administration for Children and Families (ACF) and the Family Support
Administration are using several methods to promote Head Start/JOBS collaborations. These include federal guidance on policy issues involved in collaboration and
the use of multiple funding streams, technical assistance to individual programs,
and the dissemination of best-practice models of local Head Start/JOBS coordination. Another stimulus for this model is the Head Start Family Service Center
Demonstration Projects. Since 1990 ACF has funded 41 local projects designed to
demonstrate the capacity of Head Start agencies to develop linkages with other
services to address serious problems experienced by many of today's Head Start
families (Children's Defense Fund, 1992). The projects, implemented as 3-year
demonstrations, focus on the goals of reducing substance abuse among Head Start
adult family members, improving the literacy skills of adult family members, and
increasing the employability of Head Start parents. Individual agencies are charged
with conducting evaluations of their efforts, and ACF plans to conduct a national
evaluation beginning in the second year of the demonstration. A related ACF initiative, the Head Start State Collaboration Projects, has provided grants to 22 states to
promote statewide partnerships between Head Start and other service systems that
will lead to more effective, comprehensive supports for low-income families with

young children One priority of this program is to foster partnerships between Head Start and welfare-to-work programs, including JOBS, which will increase training and job readiness opportunities for Head Start parents (Head Start Bureau, 1992).

Conditions for these collaborations are especially favorable (Head Start Bureau, 1992). Head Start, which served about 30% of eligible children in 1990, is expanding as a result of its reauthorization in the 101st Congress (Children's Defense Fund, 1991). This legislation authorizes increases in Head Start funding to permit all eligible 3- and 4-year old children to participate by 1994 (National Commission on Children, 1991). The expansion of Head Start, combined with federal-level guidance supporting collaborations with JOBS, may provide a strong impetus for the further development and implementation of this two-generation model.

Two-generation models developed apart from JOBS

Three other two-generation models represent relatively new efforts to integrate multiple supports for families, including services to help parents move from welfare dependence to employment and services focused on child development. These models are operating as multisite demonstrations with major process and impact evaluations that will investigate the kinds of services that families receive and the effects of participation on a variety of parent and child outcomes. Final results of the studies will be reported between 1994 and 1996, although interim findings may also be disseminated.

The Comprehensive Child Development Program (CCDP)

Created by legislation passed in 1988, the Comprehensive Child Development Program (CCDP) is operating in 24 sites around the country (Head Start Bureau, 1991). Programs recruit poor families with children under age 1 and pregnant women. Families receive CCDP services for 5 years. The Administration for Children and Families oversees the program and its evaluation, which is being conducted by two research firms: Abt Associates is responsible for the evaluation of program effects on children and their parents while CSR, Inc. is conducting an extensive study of the program's implementation and provision of services.

CCDP sites use case management to ensure that families receive coordinated services that respond to their individual needs. A diverse group of providers, including public schools, universities, community-based social service agencies, and health centers, is implementing the CCDP model. These agencies provide some services directly and link families to other available services in order to provide the full complement of supports participants need. The core services for children are health screening, immunization, treatment and referral; child care and developmental early childhood programs; and nutrition services. Parents and other family members receive prenatal care, parenting education, referral to education and employment training and assistance with housing, income support, and other needed services.

The evaluation of CCDP will compare families enrolled in CCDP sites with non-intervention families on a host of measures related to the program's goals of improving family functioning, child health and development, parenting skills, and family self-sufficiency (Abt Associates, 1990a; Smith, 1990). Twenty-four sites will be included in the study. Each site will recruit 360 families and randomly assign them to intervention, control, and intervention replacement groups. The evaluation will also examine the relationship of implementation and family participation variables to outcomes. Through integrated analyses of data from the process and impact evaluations, the evaluators hope to: (1) determine the feasibility of implementing the CCDP model; (2) assess the impact of the program, examining program effects across projects as well as differences among individual sites; and (3) identify effective practices in the delivery of comprehensive services to low-income families.

New Chance

Another comprehensive two-generation model is New Chance, a 16-site research demonstration designed and managed by the Manpower Demonstration Research Corporation (MDRC) and funded by private foundations and the Department of Labor (Quint, Fink, & Rowser, 1991). New Chance targets a particularly disadvantaged subset of the AFDC population – young mothers aged 16–22 who are high school dropouts. Unlike the Comprehensive Child Development Program, the New Chance model is highly structured and most services are delivered on site during the first 5 to 8 months of the program. These features provide a relatively intensive experience for parents who participate in scheduled activities for an average of 30 hours a week and remain in the program for up to 18 months. The program's components include basic adult education and GED preparation, job training, life skills instruction, parenting education, family planning and other health services, child care (on-site at several programs), and pediatric care. Like CCDP, the program uses case management to support families' participation in the program. Schools and community-based social service organizations that have experience delivering services to teen parents are implementing the New Chance model.

Across the 16 demonstration sites, MDRC is randomly assigning approximately 2,200 families to the treatment or control groups (Manpower Development Research Corporation, 1990). The study will assess multiple outcomes, including the parents' education and employment status, repeat pregnancies, and children's health and development. The researchers will also investigate the different sites' implementation of the model, relate implementation strategies to successful outcomes, and conduct benefit–cost analyses. Although the main focus of the study is an experimental comparison of outcomes between the treatment and control groups, the researchers also plan analyses to investigate important mediators of outcomes, such as fertility control, educational gains, and parents' psychological functioning. In addition, an observational substudy will assess key dimensions of parenting and the parent–child relationship that might be affected by the family's participation in

New Chance. The target children in the study are about 18 months old at the time of entry into New Chance, and families will be followed for at least 3 years.

Even Start

The Even Start program was created by legislation passed in 1988 and is adminis-tered at the federal level by the Department of Education (Abt Associates, 1991). Currently operating in 240 sites, Even Start serves low-income families with chil-dren aged 1 to 7. The program provides three types of services: (1) adult basic education (including GED preparation and literacy training); (2) early childhood education; and (3) parent–child activities designed to encourage interactions that support healthy child development. Local school districts are the recipients of program funds. While some programs directly provide the three components, others coordinate services for families through collaborations with existing programs in the community. Programs are also required to provide home visits. The amount of time families spend in program activities varies across sites, from about 2 hours to more than 20 hours per week.

The evaluation of Even Start, being conducted by Abt Associates with a sub-contract to Research Corporation, includes the collection of limited process and outcome data from all funded programs and participants (Abt Associates, 1990b). In addition, an in-depth study of the program's implementation and impact in 10 sites is planned. The in-depth study will include a variety of program types that serve children ages 3 to 4. Outcome measures will assess child development, parent–child interactions, and employment-related domains for parents, such as attendance in adult education programs and functional literacy. In most sites, families will be randomly assigned to program and control groups. Children in all sites will be followed through school entry and possibly beyond.

Comparing newer two-generation models with older interventions

Program models that combine the goals of family self-sufficiency and healthy child development represent a marked departure from most previous interventions with welfare-dependent families. In the past, adult-centered programs that provided edu-cation and employment services to welfare recipients traditionally paid little atten-tion to the needs of children and to the participant's role as a parent. At the same time, child-centered interventions for low-income families typically offered child development, parent education, and family support services, but little assistance in helping families move out of poverty.

There is some evidence that each of these approaches, by itself, is limited in its power to improve developmental outcomes among low-income children. First, de-spite evidence that high-quality early childhood programs can reduce poor outcomes for at-risk children, including adolescent pregnancy and school failure, the capacity of child-centered interventions to improve the life chances of disadvantaged children seems limited. Program benefits, most often reflected in measures of cognitive development, have usually been found to wash out within a few years of the intervention (see Brooks-Gunn, this volume; Farran, 1990). In the few studies that have demonstrated long-term social and educational benefits, a disturbingly high proportion of intervention participants nonetheless experience poor outcomes. For example, results of the Perry Preschool Project indicate that 33% of program participants failed to complete high school, 31% had been arrested for criminal acts, and 18% were receiving public assistance at age 19 (Weikart, 1989). These findings do not point to the failure of this early intervention program to demonstrate significant benefits for participants. Instead, the findings suggest the need for interventions that place even greater emphasis on eliminating long-term impediments to healthy development, particularly family poverty.

Because studies of adult education and employment training programs have rarely included assessments of children, little direct evidence of their effects on child development is available (Brooks-Gunn, this volume). A growing body of research does demonstrate modest gains in family income resulting from relatively low-cost employment readiness programs (Friedlander & Gueron, 1990). At present, it is unknown whether these gains increase over time and produce positive changes in parenting, the home environment, and other influences on children's development. In effect, we do not know whether significant benefits automatically accrue to children when parents' economic status improves.

Recent analyses by Zill, however, suggest that on a range of indicators, children in low-income families with working parents appear to be as disadvantaged as children in welfare-dependent families. Using several national data sets, including the National Longitudinal Survey of Labor Market Experience of Youth and the National Health Interview Survey on Child Health, Zill compared working poor families and families receiving AFDC (Zill et al., this volume). The groups were roughly similar on indicators of the quality of the home environment and children's academic achievement. For example, 66% of AFDC families and 65% of poor, non-AFDC families were rated as having a nonsupportive home environment compared to 32% of nonpoor families. Comparing groups on indicators of school success, Zill et al. report that poor children, whether they are in AFDC or non-AFDC families, are about twice as likely to repeat a grade in school as children in nonpoor families. Percentages of children who had repeated a grade by ages 12 to 17 were 36% for AFDC families, 32% for poor, non-AFDC families, and 17% for nonpoor families. At the very least, these analyses suggest that adult-oriented programs that move families from welfare dependence into the ranks of the working poor may do little to reduce children's risks of developmental harm and educational failure.

It is important to recognize that findings suggesting the limited potency of single-focus interventions aimed at either child development or adult employment needs, do *not* constitute evidence that an integration of these approaches will necessarily lead to more positive outcomes for children. Compared with previous interventions, however, two-generation programs may have greater potential for reducing a multiplicity of known risk factors in the lives of disadvantaged children. To the extent that two-generation interventions lead to increases in family income, many risk factors associated with economic distress might be reduced (McLoyd, 1990). Although significant changes in family income are likely to take some time to achieve, more rapid change might occur in parental characteristics that are strongly implicated in parents' capacity to respond to their children's needs. Although we do not know the specific pathways by which two-generation programs may exert short- and long-term influences on children's development, certain processes might be set in motion by a parent's experience of success and new opportunities in a welfare-to-work program. For example, this experience could lead to improvements in the parent's mental health, particularly reduced depression and psychological distress. In turn, parents might also gain a stronger sense of self-efficacy and interest in planning for the future. Considerable evidence now links the psychological well-being of the parent to parenting behavior and children's development (McLoyd, 1990).

In addition to these changes in parenting that might sustain long-term support for healthy child development, early childhood services, especially high-quality child care and preschool programs, could reduce declines in cognitive functioning commonly found among low-income children and confer gains in social and emotional development that are critical to later school success (Bryant & Ramey, 1987). It is the *combination* of these short-term and sustained supports for healthy development that could produce exceptionally strong, long-lasting benefits for children. Two-generation programs that explicitly relate the parent's new educational and employment opportunities to the child's developmental needs and the role of parenting may provide an especially strong stimulus for family change processes that benefit children.

One pioneer two-generation program, Project Redirection, provides some basis for cautious optimism (Polit, Quint, & Riccio, 1988). In Project Redirection, disadvantaged teen mothers received a variety of services for themselves and their infants, including education and employment, family planning, life management, parent education, child health care, and case management services. The findings of the 5-year follow-up assessments showed significant benefits for Project Redirection parents and children compared to control families that received less intensive services. Project Redirection children were more likely to have been enrolled in Head Start programs, and demonstrated both higher vocabulary test scores and lower behavior problem scores (Polit, 1989). Project Redirection families received more positive scores on the HOME scale, which assesses aspects of parenting and the home environment that support the child's cognitive and emotional development. In addition, fewer Project Redirection parents were receiving welfare, and the earnings of these parents were significantly higher than those of control group parents. However, the finding that less than half (47%) of Project Redirection participants had completed high school or earned their GED raises concerns about the long-term impact of this program. The New Chance demonstration, described earlier, was designed with the aim of improving certain features of the Project Redirection model, including the quality and intensity of educational services for parents and the provision of high-quality child care.

Differences among the two-generation models

The four two-generation models described in this chapter differ from each other in several respects. Here we highlight potentially important differences in programs' scope, structure, and duration that may affect their impact on families, cost, and potential for expansion.

Perhaps the most obvious feature differentiating the models is their degree of comprehensiveness. The models that place the most emphasis on comprehensive, coordinated services are the Comprehensive Child Development Program (CCDP), the Head Start/JOBS collaboration, and New Chance. Each of these models uses case management to promote parents' progress toward economic self-sufficiency and to support the use of child health and development services. The Even Start program also provides support services such as child care and counseling, but only a subset of projects use case management; it does, however, encourage strong integration of its adult education and child development services through its parent–child component.

The models also vary in the degree of structure in their delivery of services. In the first phase of the New Chance program, lasting from 5 to 8 months, and in some Even Start programs, parents and children follow a regular daily pattern of activities intended to be fairly uniform for all participants. The other models appear less structured. For example, in the Head Start/JOBS model, parents may be participating in different kinds of JOBS activities, which may in turn, affect their involvement in Head Start-related family and child development components. Similarly, in the CCDP, services at any point during families' involvement in the program are individually tailored to the needs of participants. CCDP services, such as child care, may change as particular family needs are met and different goals established.

While highly structured programs may ensure a greater degree of program intensity, they might also fail to provide sufficiently individualized services for families. Moreover, programs that rigidly adhere to a "one size fits all" approach to service delivery run the risk of high program attrition or the neglect of family problems that impede successful participation in the intervention. It is also possible that with certain case management practices, both highly structured and more flexibly organized programs could achieve levels of program intensity and individualization that produce significant benefits. For example, targeted case management and supplementary services for families experiencing multiple problems could help participants maintain their involvement in highly structured programs. Similarly, case management in a less structured program might emphasize a "required" level of participation in core activities such as education and job training for parents and a high-quality early childhood program for children.

The duration of families' participation in the intervention program may vary both across and within the models. For example, the duration of program participation may be determined mainly by the age of the child upon enrollment into the program (Even Start) or by a more fixed intervention period (New Chance). In a model with a relatively short intervention period, it is possible that families will be linked to services that will continue beyond their involvement in the formal program. Only one program, the Comprehensive Child Development Program, restricts enrollment to families with infants and provides services through the child's entry into school. Of course, in CCDP, as in the other models, the actual duration of families' participation will depend on the programs' ability to engage and maintain families in program activities and services. Thus, a program's scope, structure, intensity, and duration are all likely to be interrelated in their effects on the program's operation and on families' participation and outcomes.

Can we predict differences in program efficacy?

Variations in the two-generation program models are considered here mainly to highlight the heterogeneity of the four models under discussion, especially along dimensions that bear potential relationships to program impact, cost, and replicability. While this chapter is intended to illuminate the two-generation intervention strategy shared by these models, it also emphasizes the importance of recognizing the marked differences in how this new strategy is currently being implemented. Because the models combine employment readiness and child development services in new ways, there may be trade-offs in some of the program variations. At this juncture, serious gaps in our knowledge base preclude predictions about which models are likely to offer the greatest benefits in different domains and for different kinds of families. In addition to our current lack of knowledge about how various services will influence family change processes in concert, there is still much to be learned about the efficacy of key component services in both the employment readiness and child development domains.

At present, little is known about the relative efficacy of different kinds of education and training for the parents targeted by JOBS. A recently completed study by Mathematica Policy Research suggests that for minority parents with limited education, a program that integrates basic remedial education with on-the-job vocational training might be more effective than programs that sequence these components (Burghardt & Gordon, 1990). Additional comparative studies are needed to investigate the merits of the integrated work–training model. In general, since relatively high-cost basic education and skills training have rarely been used in welfare-to-work experiments, we do not know much about their impact, although some evidence suggests that greater investments in preemployment services lead to higher earnings, especially for the most disadvantaged participants (Friedlander & Gueron, 1990; Houseman, Sherman, & Greenberg, 1989). It is notable that most discussions of the benefits of higher-cost job readiness services are limited to a consideration of employment and income gains. This restricted focus might underestimate the cost-effectiveness of human capital welfare-to-work models by neglecting savings associated with increased benefits to children's development.

Our limited knowledge of effective component services extends to child development services (Brooks Gunn, this volume). Past studies of early childhood interventions have not fully identified the essential components and characteristics of the child-centered services needed to achieve optimal outcomes for children. Although some intervention researchers have speculated about the importance of parent education and joint parent–child activities, it is not clear how critical these services are to achieving desired child development outcomes and how they should be designed (Powell, 1989). Ironically, some early childhood models that provided the most attention to the parent–child relationship are now viewed as posing obstacles to parents' progress toward educational attainment and self-sufficiency (Halpern, 1990). One of the special challenges in the development of effective two-generation programs may be the integration of effective supports for a healthy parent–child relationship and home environment with services that prepare the parent for employment. While this goal is complicated by parental time constraints and limitations of program resources in two-generation interventions, it may prove integral to achieving desirable levels of long-term program benefits.

With respect to child care, a key component of two-generation models, much is already known about indices of quality that are related to child development outcomes, especially in center-based settings. Nevertheless, many questions remain about the characteristics of high-quality care in family day care and informal settings, the relative contributions of different quality dimensions, the consequences of care in the first year of life, and the effects of experiencing multiple forms of care at one stage of development or frequent shifts in child care arrangements over time (Cherlin, this volume; Hayes, Palmer, & Zaslow, 1990). Many of these questions could be addressed in studies of two-generation programs in ways that would enrich both child development theory and the knowledge base needed to design effective interventions.

Recommendations for evaluating two-generation programs

While two-generation interventions employ a new and potentially powerful approach to assisting low-income families and improving the life chances of disadvantaged children, these programs may be considerably more costly than circumscribed child development or adult employment programs. At the same time, a potent intervention that produces large, long-term economic gains for families as well as social and educational gains for children could be highly cost-effective compared with other interventions. The possible value of these programs, in human and economic terms, and the costliness of implementing them on a significant scale, argue for rigorous evaluations of their effectiveness. Because the models described here are being evaluated in separate efforts, and target similar, but nonidentical, populations, comparisons of program impact across studies will be difficult. Nevertheless, findings from this first wave of program development, research on program implementation, and impact evaluations will yield a wealth of new knowledge that should be integrated and applied to ongoing efforts to study two-generation models. In addition, a major study of the JOBS program, funded by the Department of Health and Human Services (HHS) and being implemented by MDRC, will include an investigation of the impact of JOBS on children. This research, the "Child and Family Impacts Study," will be conducted by Child Trends in three of the 10 sites of the overall JOBS evaluation (Moore, 1990). Following are recommendations for building on these current studies in future evaluations of two-generation interventions.

1. A network of studies should be developed to compare the benefits of different types of two-generation programs for different subgroups of families. Families within even relatively restricted categories, such as those headed by teen parents, are known to be quite heterogeneous (Polit et al., 1988). Our current lack of knowledge about how such program features as the structure of service provision and the intensity of families' involvement in different service components affect a program's capacity to meet families' needs suggests the critical need for an integrated set of studies that systematically vary program characteristics and investigate differential impacts on subgroups. Forthcoming analyses from current two-generation studies may be useful in identifying important subgroups to target in future studies Smith (1995). For example, these analyses may reveal whether characteristics of parental functioning such as maternal depression or academic level are more important than maternal age or family composition in predicting program participation and impacts on children. In addition, analyses of differential program effects across the current models may offer clues about how certain program features affect participation and program impact. These clues could inform the design of studies that directly compare the most promising program models.

2. An interdisciplinary group of scholars should collaborate in the design and implementation of planned variation studies. The effectiveness of two-generation programs is likely to depend on several features of both the adult education and employment activities and the child development services. Moreover, program implementation variables, individual and family change processes, and outcomes of interest in two-generation studies range across the disciplines of child development, adult education and employment training, and the economics of service delivery. Ongoing research should assemble teams that include expertise in these domains. Although project advisory groups and ad hoc consultations may be extremely helpful, the complexity of two-generation research probably requires an intensive and long-term commitment from an interdisciplinary team of investigators. To achieve the highest quality research, this team should work together from the inception of the research through data analyses and the interpretation of research findings.

3. Future research should emphasize the careful assessment of the quality of component services. The quality of services, such as adult education, child care, and parenting education, is likely to be as important as overall program intensity

and comprehensiveness. In future comparative studies it will be necessary to hold the quality of some components constant across models and vary the quality and cost of other components. Designing component services in accordance with sound criteria for quality and assessing the quality achieved in program implementation should be priorities of future studies that compare program models. For several types of services and supports, such as adult education and case management, the development of quality standards will require the application of professional consensus in the absence of strong research evidence.

4. A federal interagency effort could provide the needed policy guidance, scientific standards, and resources to stimulate planned variation studies of two-generation programs. Expertise and interests relevant to the design and study of two-generation models range across several federal departments and agencies. Currently, the Department of Health and Human Services and the Department of Education are involved in several two-generation initiatives, including four of the models discussed here. If resources and interests could be coordinated among agencies, the support needed for ongoing research on two-generation studies would be strengthened. A federal interagency committee could assemble a team of investigators to formulate questions, identify and in some cases develop needed measures, and design and implement studies. In addition to maximizing the resources needed to answer highly complex questions that range across agencies' interests, such a collaboration would help bridge the concerns of researchers and policy makers.

REFERENCES

Abt Associates. (1990a, June). *Project summary of CCDP impact evaluation*. Paper prepared for the 2-generation research network meeting sponsored by the Foundation for Child Development, Washington, DC.

Abt Associates. (1990b, June). *Project summary of Even Start evaluation*. Paper prepared for the 2-generation research network meeting sponsored by the Foundation for Child Development, Washington, DC.

Abt Associates. (1991). *National evaluation of the Even Start Family Literacy Program: First year report*. Cambridge: Abt Associates.

Administration for Children and Families. (1991). Information Memorandum, Subject: Collaboration between JOBS and Head Start. Log No. ACF-IM-91-23.

American Public Welfare Association. (1988). *Welfare reform legislation enacted by the 100th Congress* (W-Memo #12–14). Washington, DC.

American Public Welfare Association (1990). *Early state experiences and policy issues in the implementation of the JOBS program: Briefing paper for human service administrators*. Washington, DC.

Bryant, D., & Ramey, C. (1987). An analysis of the effectiveness of early intervention programs for environmentally at-risk children. In M. Guralnick & F. Bennett (Eds.), *The effectiveness of early intervention for at-risk and handicapped children*. London: Academic Press.

Burghardt, J., & Gordon, A. (1990). *The minority female single parent demonstration. More jobs and higher pay: How an integrated program compares with traditional programs*. New York: Rockefeller Foundation.

Children's Defense Fund. (1991). *The state of America's children: 1991*. Washington, DC: Children's Defense Fund.

Children's Defense Fund. (1992, May). *CDR Reports* (p. 4). Washington, DC: Children's Defense Fund.

Farran, D. C. (1990). Effects of intervention with disadvantaged and disabled children. In S. J. Meisels & J. P. Shonkoff (Eds.), *Handbook of early childhood intervention*. Cambridge: Cambridge University Press.

Figueroa, J. R., & Silvanik, R. A. (1989). *The provision of education and other services in state welfare-to-work programs*. Washington, DC: National Governors' Association.

Friedlander, D., & Gueron, J. (1990, April). *Are high-cost services more effective than low-cost services? Evidence from experimental evaluations of welfare-to-work programs*. Paper prepared for a conference on evaluation design for welfare and training programs, Arlie, VA.

Greenberg, M. (1990). *What's happening in JOBS: A review of initial state data*. Washington, DC: Center for Law and Social Policy.

Gueron, J. M., & Pauly, E. (1991). *From welfare to work*. New York: Russell Sage Foundation.

Halpern, R. (1990). Community-based early intervention. In S. J. Meisels & J. P. Shonkoff (Eds.), *Handbook of early childhood intervention*. Cambridge: Cambridge University Press.

Hayes, C. D., Palmer, J. L., & Zaslow, M. J. (Eds.). (1990). *Who cares for America's children? Child care policy for the 1990s*. Washington, DC: National Academy Press.

Head Start Bureau. (1991). *Comprehensive Child Development Program – a national demonstration: First annual report*. Washington, DC: CSR.

Head Start Bureau. (1992). *National Head Start Bulletin # 40* (pp. 5–7). Washington, DC: Head Start Bureau.

Houseman, A., Sherman, A., & Greenberg, M. (1989). *Welfare reform and education: Learning from experience*. Washington, DC: Center for Law and Social Policy.

Institute for Research on Poverty. (1988). Welfare reform and poverty [Special Issue]. *Focus*. Madison: University of Wisconsin.

Manpower Development Research Corporation. (1990, June). *Project summary of New Chance*. Paper prepared for the 2-generation research network meeting sponsored by the Foundation for Child Development, Washington, DC.

Mathematica Policy Research. (1992). *Project summary for the expanded child care options demonstration*.

McLoyd, V. C. (1990). The impact of economic hardship on black families and children: Psychological distress, parenting, and socioemotional development. *Child Development, 61*, 311–346.

Moore, K. A. (1990, June). *Project summary of the Child and Family Impact Study*. Paper prepared for the Two-generation research network meeting sponsored by the Foundation for Child Development, Washington, DC.

National Commission on Children. (1991). *Beyond rhetoric: A new American agenda for children and families*. Washington, DC: National Commission on Children.

Polit, D. F. (1989). Effects of a comprehensive program for teenage parents: Five years after Project Redirection. *Family Planing Perspectives, 21*(4), 164–169.

Polit, D. F., & O'Hara, J. J. (1989). Support services. In P. H. Cottingham & D. T. Ellwood (Eds.), *Welfare policy for the 1990s*. Cambridge, MA: Harvard University Press.

Polit, D. F., Quint, J. C., & Riccio, J. A. (1988). *The challenge of serving teenage mothers: Lessons from project redirection*. New York: Manpower Demonstration Research Corporation.

Porter, K. (1990). *Making JOBS work: What the research says about effective employment programs for AFDC recipients*. Washington, DC: Center on Budget and Policy Priorities.

Powell, D. R. (1989). Families and early childhood programs. In *Research monographs of the National Association for the Education of Young Children, 3*. Washington, DC: National Association for the Education of Young Children.

Quint, J. C., Fink, B. L., & Rowser, S. L. (1991). *New Chance: Implementing a comprehensive program for disadvantaged young mothers and their children*. New York: Manpower Demonstration Research Corporation.

Reischauer, R. D. (1989). The welfare reform legislation: Directions for the future. In P. H. Cottingham & D. T. Ellwood (Eds.), *Welfare policy for the 1990s*. Cambridge, MA: Harvard University Press.

Roberts, P. (1989). *Turning promises into realities: A guide to implementing the child support provisions of the Family Support Act of 1988*. Washington, DC: Center for Law and Social Policy.

Select Committee on Children and Families. (1990). *Federal programs affecting children and their families*. Washington, DC: U.S. Government Printing Office.

Smith, A. (1990, June). *Project summary of CCDP process evaluation*. Paper prepared for the two-generation research network meeting sponsored by the Foundation for Child Development, Washington, DC.

Smith, S. (1995). *Two-generation programs for families in poverty: A new intervention strategy*. Norwood, NJ: Ablex Publishing Corp.

Smith, S., Blank, S., & Bond, J. T. (1990). *One program, two generations: A report of the forum on children and the Family Support Act*. New York: Foundation for Child Development.

Smith, S., Blank, S., & Collins, R. (1992). *Pathways to self-sufficiency for two generations: Designing welfare-to-work programs that benefit children and strengthen families*. New York: Foundation for Child Development.

Weikart, D. P. (1989). *Quality preschool programs: A long-term social investment*. (Occasional paper No. 5, Ford Foundation Project on Social Welfare and the American Future). New York: Ford Foundation.

Index